RELIGION AND GLOBAL ORDER

RELIGION AND GLOBAL ORDER

Edited by Roland Robertson and William R. Garrett

A New ERA Book

PARAGON HOUSE PUBLISHERS
New York

Published in the United States by

International Religious Foundation
481 8th Avenue
New York, New York 10001

Distributed by Paragon House Publishers
90 Fifth Avenue
New York, New York 10011

Copyright © 1991 by International Religious Foundation

All rights reserved. Except for use in reviews, no part of this book may be reproduced, stored in a retrieval system, or transmitted in any form or by any means, electronic, mechanical or otherwise, without the prior written consent of the publisher.

A New Ecumenical Research Association Book

Library of Congress Cataloging-in-Publication Data

Religion and global order / edited by Roland Robertson and William R. Garrett.
   297 p.   cm.
   Includes bibliographical references and index.
   ISBN 0-89226-090-4. — ISBN 0-89226-091-2 (pbk.)
   1. Religion.   I. Robertson, Roland.   II. Garrett, William R.
BL50.R42636   1991
291—dc20   90-44569
                                                                            CIP

To my mother,
> Molly Robertson,
> With thanks

To my parents,
> Floreaca and Raymond Garrett,

Who trained up a son in the way he should go,
    and he went that way—well mostly

Contents

    Religion and Globalization: An Introduction   ix
    William R. Garrett and Roland Robertson

1. Globalization and Religion: Themes and Prospects   1
   John H. Simpson

2. Old Testament Universalism: Prophetic Seeds on Particularistic Soil   19
   Theodore E. Long

3. Two Aspects of the Development of Universalism in Christianity: The First to the Fourth Centuries   35
   James F. Strange

4. The Reformation, Individualism, and the Quest for Global Order   47
   William R. Garrett

5. The Conquest of the Americas: The Spanish Search for Global Order   65
   James M. Muldoon

6. The Goddess and the Guru: Two Models of Universal Order in Tamil India   87
   Glenn E. Yocum

7. The Holy Ghost and the Ordering of the World   119
   Stanley Johannesen

8. Consumer Culture, Postmodernism, and Global Disorder   133
   Mike Featherstone

9. Politics and Culture in Islamic Globalism   161
   Bryan S. Turner

CONTENTS

10. Globalization versus Religious Nativism:
    Japan's Soka Gakkai in the World Arena 183
    Anson Shupe

11. The Whole World in His Hand?: Ways and Means of
    Establishing a Unificationist Theocracy 201
    Eileen V. Barker

12. The Globalization of American Televangelism 221
    Jeffrey K. Hadden

13. Radical Democratization and Radical Monotheism:
    Mannheim and Niebuhr on Global Order 245
    Lonnie D. Kliever

14. Religion, Law, and Global Order 263
    Frank J. Lechner

15. Globalization, Modernization, and Postmodernization:
    The Ambiguous Position of Religion 281
    Roland Robertson

    Contributors 293

    List of Tables 295

    Index 297

RELIGION AND GLOBALIZATION
AN INTRODUCTION
William R. Garrett and Roland Robertson

The Problem of Origins and the Idea of World History

EVERY HISTORICAL ERA CAN BE APPREHENDED in proportion to its own distinguishing structural features, its unique ideational perspectives, and, certainly not least, in terms of those peculiar socio-cultural legacies which it has effectively managed to bequeath to generations yet to come. Social scientific inquiries are animated not only by a concern for devising analytic schemata for understanding the resultant patterns of previous ages, but also with creating the requisite generalizations for anticipating the emergent order toward which we are presently tending. Accordingly, the salient presupposition informing this introductory essay is that we are at present ineluctably poised on the brink of, and in some ways already participating in, a new age of global change (Moore 1979: 19).

The processes of globalization entail more than simply the maturation of modern thought-forms and structures, however. The present circumstance presupposes, or so we shall argue, that the world is rapidly coming to be apprehended as "one place," that is as a totality wherein discrete selves, nation-states, and even civilizational traditions have their respective niches, each interconnected by complex, reticular relationships of belligerence and beneficence, competition and compromise, discordance and detente. Yet, whatever the mode of linkage among the sub-sets, the crucial fact remains that each unit is couched within the frame of the whole so that, willy nilly, action must be referenced against the coordinates of "the world," and not simply against limited geopolitical segments such as Europe, the Pacific Rim, North America, Africa, and so forth.

The contemporary global circumstance is clearly predicated on preceding stages of socio-cultural development. When that development commenced so as to produce the current trend toward global order remains, however, a matter of considerable theoretical debate. One long view can be derived from the paradigm constructed by Talcott Parsons (1966; 1971a; 1971b), for example, which traced the emergent, evolutionary trajectory of modernized, Western societies from the "seed bed" cultures of the ancient Hebrews and Greco-Romans. Rosenstock-Huessy's ([1938] 1969; 1966) perspicacious analysis of Western historical experience would chart the start of the modern world and, by extension, contemporary developments, from the revolution in canon law effected from the eleventh to the thirteenth centuries. The master German sociologist Max Weber ([1904–1905] 1958) credited the Calvinist wing of the Reformation with the crucial motive influence responsible for stimulating the break with medieval patterns in law, economy, politics, and the arts, and hence with ushering in the modern world and its possible postmodern developments. Weber's friend and colleague at Heidelberg, Ernst Troeltsch (1931; 1958), meanwhile, viewed the Enlightenment as a more appropriate dating of the onset of modern thought forms whose influence might now be regarded as the foundational base from which globalism derives today. More recently and from a decidedly more secular frame of reference, Fernand Braudel (1982) and Immanuel Wallerstein (1974; 1979; 1980; 1989) would cite the emergence of capitalism in the sixteenth century as the take-off point for the present world-system.

And these alternatives, whether taken singly or in concert, do not represent the only historical options. One could cogently contend that the emergence of nation-states in the context of contention with the papacy during the period from 1450 to 1500 represents a sort of coming-of-age of nationalism in Europe, and therefore marks the beginnings of modern societal groupings. Or again, one could—with different presuppositions—contend that the emergence of popular nationalism and the rise of ethnicity as a focal point of identity in the early nineteenth century constitutes a better benchmark for the take-off of global tendencies.

Although the dating of those forces responsible for the emergence of contemporary global patterns is not an insignificant or irrelevant issue, we are not *primarily* concerned with the question of origins in this introductory essay or in the contributions collected in this volume. Nor, by the same token, are we fundamentally concerned with resolving the question of the periodization of historical experience through the construction of some grand scheme of immanent development. Rather, the historically and cross-culturally grounded essays included herein are more narrowly confined to the effort of discerning those threshold tendencies, themes, and tensions pressing toward the creation of recrudescent social structures. Thus, while historical and cross-cultural studies may provide little in the way of direct insight connected intrinsically to the emergence of a global system in our own time (in part, because it constitutes such a qualitative leap into new cultural-structural patterns), research of this sort certainly can provide clues as to how various themes and issues of a similar nature have articulated with political, economic, ethnic, class, and ideational structures in former social contexts.

This point needs to be introduced at the outset so that readers will have a clearer grasp of what sort of enterprise is being undertaken in the pages that follow. For it almost goes without saying that we are participating in a venture which is certainly exploratory—although we believe it is, at the same time, neither simplistic nor timid in its intellectual formulations. Indeed, to a degree quite unanticipated both by the conference organizers and the participants, similar themes resurfaced in papers investigating quite disparate cultural, historical, religious, and societal issues pertaining to the question of global order.

We would be remiss were we not to mention that in addition to the strong tendency to argue that the origins of the globalized world are to be found almost exclusively in distinctly Western developments—that the world has been made by and only from the West—there has existed for a long time a tradition of philosophical reflection which is almost exclusively German in its main thrust. With Kant in the background and with Hegel as its main source, the philosophy of universal history has tended to construct the history of the world around the theme of the superiority or "absoluteness" of certain Western philosophical or theological structures of thought.

Globalization: A Religious or Secular Phenomenon?

The processes of globalization and the emergent order of the postmodern world are currently in the early stages of identification, thematization, and explication. Already, however, one of the more pressing questions related to these dynamics has to do, at least in the present context, with the issue of the degree to which processes and patterns of globalization are to be understood as primarily secular or whether, on the other hand, they have a distinctly religious flavor. The whole matter can be stated in explicit and axiomatic terms by means of the following two questions: Is the globalization process a manifest or latent consequence of palpably religious ideas and/or movements? Or, by contrast, is the contemporary global circumstance largely the outcome of secular forces of economic, political, technological, or cultural moment whose connection with religious influences is either non-existent or, at most, tenuous?

In this connection, consider two very different points of view pertaining to recent times:

> Telephones penetrate and thus profane all places.... Never before the age of the wireless and airplane did the heavens seem so close or accessible.... The omnipresence and penetrating capacity of wireless waves rivaled miraculous action and reversed the direction of divine intervention. Planes invaded the kingdom of heaven, and their exhaust fumes profaned the realm of the spirit. Upwards was still the direction of growth and life, but in this period (1880–1920) it lost much of its sacred aspect (Kern 1983: 316–317).

In contrast, Arend Van Leeuwen argued in his greatest work a quarter of a century ago, *Christianity In World History*, that the sociohistorical forces of technology, urbanization, democracy, and human rights, as worldly effects of spiritual forces in secular garb, bear with them deep implications for social transformation. They would shatter all the particular autocracies of hierarchy and traditionalism in Asia and Africa, as they had begun to do in the West. That would open the horizon to evangelization and spur the development of a global community. His views were severely criticized at the time; they may well be in need of modification still. But he may not have been entirely misguided. The most remarkable thing about the international embrace of technology is that modern humanity has agreed with Christianity that we have a right, indeed a duty, to change the world—a notion many cultures do not swallow easily (Stackhouse 1989: 469).

How one formulates a response to these basic questions and the differing points of view represented in the two positions above will hinge, to a very large degree, on how one reads the intimate relationship of religious features and themes to such constituent elements of the contemporary social order as cultural symbols, ideologies, society, the state, political parties, and patterns of political legitimation; with components of the economic institution such as business enterprises, labor unions, cooperatives, professional organizations, welfare systems, as well as the framing of attitudes toward work; with groups promoting cultural identity such as national bodies politic, ethnic communities, class strata, vested interest groups, voluntary associations, and the media; with socializing collectivities such as the family, neighborhood, reference groups, peer groups, and the like. Clearly, the increasing differentiation and pluralization of contemporary societies renders the articulation of religion with these diverse components of the social order ever more complex and, from an interpretive point of view, problematic.

Historically, of course, and especially in the Occident, religion has been prominently articulated with the affairs of state, cultural identity, economic processes, and family/socialization dynamics. But has this historical connection endured into the present age? Are the theorists of secularization, despite all the nuanced qualifications to their sundry proposals, now being proved essentially correct that the era of puissant religious forces has come to an end—perhaps during the waning days of the modern age—and that globalization processes are intractably predicated on fully secular presuppositions? And, if this should be the case, does this mean that religious ideas and movements are likely to be ever more systematically exorcised from the global order of the postmodern age?

There are indicators from some quarters, certainly, that postmodern culture is more areligious than modern culture—which inherited from the central figures of the enlightenment tradition some starkly antireligious sentiments (Gay 1967; 1969). Indeed, many of the classical theorists who laid the foundations for the discipline of sociology were altogether convinced that religion had reached the pinnacle of its influence in the early modern period and could no longer be regarded as a formative institution for giving definition to late-modern patterns of development. The participation of major religious communities during the last decade in the world's trouble spots—for example, Northern Ireland, the Middle East, Latin America, and so forth—can even be dismissed as a last ditch effort by fundamentalists of one stripe or another to forestall the inevitable eclipse of religious hegemony in a world already well on the way toward deep structural secularization.

Other interpreters, largely in tune with the major themes of the radical secularizationists, concur that the macro level functions of religion have been sharply attenuated, but that religion still persists at the micro level where it provides selves with a complex of meanings and symbols sufficient to orient their lives in a world confounded by complexity and change. Thus, religion is not to be regarded so much as dead, according to this account; it is simply to be relegated to the privatized interstices of contemporary existence where it may well have found an enduring function to perform for those atomistic individuals who comprise the mass societies of postmodern nation-states.

Still other analysts would contend that it was the Enlightenment project itself which was misguided and that there is ample empirical evidence to suggest an interpretation which regards widespread disaffection with religion largely an intellectual bias of Northern European culture and its tributaries. Elsewhere, modernity and religious decline have not been coterminous phenomena. Furthermore, the lapse of religious commitment in the genuinely secularized sections of Europe may well be more properly construed as a function of the manner whereby religion was institutionalized, politically aligned, and class-related rather than as a harbinger of the inevitable dynamics this institution would experience in other societal contexts during the postmodern age. Adherents of this point of view, therefore, would regard religious persistence leading into the processes of globalization as "normal" and the secularization experience of European culture as deviant and thus requiring explanation as a limited socio-cultural sphere.

This very brief excursion into the debate over secularization—which neither seeks to survey the full range of intricacies and complexities of that controversy nor resolve the critical issues bound up in it—does serve to bring into focus a salient feature of the globalization conundrum. That is to say, how one views the matter of secularization has important implications for the subsequent assessment of globalization— and, *vice versa*, how one depicts the bases and dynamics of globalization exerts enormous influence on how secularization as a sociocultural trend is likely to be explained and/or evaluated.

We would hasten to add, however, that the relationship between the analysis of secularization and globalization is not in practice one of absolute symmetry. Analysts can, and more relevantly, do delve deeply into the real or imagined manifestations of secularization without being necessarily drawn into a consideration of global processes. In fact, at least until very recently, the opposite does not appear to be the case. Theories of what we here call globalization must define, willy nilly, the role of cultural factors in establishing the parameters of that order by which the world is apprehended as "one place." Particular theorists of globalization—who deny any significant role to cultural forces generally—inevitably take their stand with that cortege of radical proponents of secularization who claim that religious influence has entered a period of sharp denouement in the postmodern world (for example, Braudel and Wallerstein). Globalization theorists, still convinced of the consequence of cultural factors in providing definition to the emergent international order, may or may not be adamant secularizationists.

INTRODUCTION

The argument can be advanced, for example, that global order is predicated on normative rubrics, but rubrics without a vital connection to any religious tradition. Or, global theorists can embrace a mediating position which regards the basic patterns of universal order as a product of purely secular forces which, nonetheless, affords niches wherein religious groups or sentiments may find some degree of security (see, for example, Martin 1978) or at least serve as a barometer for some emergent patterns of globality. And finally, global theorists may subscribe to the view that religious forces themselves contributed significantly to the development of patterns of universal order, so that the very notion of globality itself is suffused with religious connotations, although perhaps with religious sentiments which are no longer rooted in the particularistic organizational structures of extant denominational communities. And these options by no means exhaust all the possibilities. Whichever of these alternative views is ultimately adopted, the fact remains that it is incumbent on the analyst to make some judgment relative to the role of religious forces in the broader context of globalization processes.

No final resolution to this issue is registered among the papers constituting this collection. Clearly for some, the factors prompting a quest for global order derive, at least in part, from deep well-springs of religious sentiment and organizational structures. Researchers who hold to this presupposition typically subscribe to the correlative view that religion will probably continue to provide some measure of normative direction in the near future. Others take the alternative view that globalization is preeminently a secular phenomenon. This is not to say that societies participating in the emergent global order make no room for religion, but simply that religion's "place" is not prescribed nor can its enduring presence be taken for granted. And still other presenters have embraced a position separate from—but not intermediate to—these two extremes, a position which casts the role of religion in an entirely different mode by proposing that religion has been thematized in the contemporary era as a socio-cultural category which functions both as a mode of collective identity on the societal level and as a form of consumption on the level of individuals. Viewed in this way, meanwhile, religion emerges as a *genre* of expression, communication, and legitimation rather than simply an institutional enclave alongside political, economic, and familial entities, as was so commonly the image devised for it during the modern era.

Without question, the relation of religion to the globalization process is the major issue underlying the several essays collected in this volume. Moreover, there are also subtle indicators present in these discrete investigations that the conceptualization for the linkages between religion and global order not only needs to be, but in several prominent instances is being, recast. The stark distinction between religion and the world—or in this case, global order—no longer captures in sufficiently nuanced terms, either analytically or empirically, the sort of interconnection prevailing between these spheres in the postmodern age. Following the conceptual developments initiated by Parsons (1937; 1953; 1977; 1978) and extended by Münch (1987; 1988), one can with considerable cogency now describe the relations obtaining between religion and global order as instances of interpenetration, that is to say, instances wherein both opposed systems retain their differentiated identity and yet simultaneously attain an accommodated unity.

One of the present authors has written extensively on the place of religion in the emergent global system. Roland Robertson has argued in several instances that the role of religion is, at the present time, ambiguous with respect to its influence (see Robertson 1987; 1988a; 1988b; and for a fuller explication, see Simpson's and Robertson's chapters in this volume). Moreover, religion may be playing a different role outside Europe—and especially in Asia and Latin America—relative to the creation of unique accounts of the "place" various societies and civilizations are seeking to carve out with respect to world history.

Particularism versus Universalism

A secondary theme which resurfaced with unexpected regularity throughout these several essays pertained to the linkage between particularism and universalism or, on other occasions, under the related rubrics of part/whole and localism/cosmopolitanism. Whatever its specific form, however, the crux of the issue turned on how readily the exploration of seemingly specific matters led ineluctably to the consideration of more global concerns, and vice versa. It quickly became clear that micro and macro-level questions often enjoy an interconnection of quite intricate significance. Accordingly, a relatively obscure event or an apparently isolated theme can sometimes burst forth with enormous import, if analysts are sensitive to the larger ramifications which can accrue from discrete cultural patterns and are willing to pursue their implications.

Consider, for example, this illustration (which did not surface during the conference, but it demonstrates the sort of linkage we did encounter time and again). During the Ming dynasty, China was the most technologically advanced nation in the world. When William the Conqueror was invading England, China was already producing over 125,000 tons of iron per year—a level which England would not attain until the

INTRODUCTION

industrial revolution. In addition, the Chinese had developed the magnetic compass, paper money, movable type printing, gunpowder, cannons loaded aboard ships, and a skill in and knowledge of cartography unmatched anywhere in the world. The Ming navy in 1420 included 1,350 combat vessels with 400 floating fortresses and over 250 ships designed for long-range cruising. The Admiral Cheng Ho undertook no fewer than seven major voyages between 1405 and 1433, exploring as far as Ceylon and the Red Sea in ships that displaced over 1,500 tons and measured over 400 feet in length.

This navy could almost certainly have navigated around the Cape of Good Hope and explored West Africa and even Europe well before Europeans found their way to Asia. And it is not beyond the realm of possibility that the Chinese could have crossed the Atlantic to discover the Americas far in advance of Columbus, and, had she held colonial aspirations similar to later Western nations, China could easily have conquered the new world and established her cultural, political patterns there. Almost inexplicably, however, the resurgence of neo-Confucianism in the 1430s resulted in an Imperial edict of 1436 which halted Chinese exploration, prompted the scuttling of Cheng Ho's warships, and urged China to turn inward in order to protect her cultural heritage against contamination by foreign barbarians. So successful was this campaign that China experienced almost 500 years of scientific, technological, and cultural stagnation (Kennedy 1987: 4–9).

The point of this lengthy illustration is to suggest that a small group of *Literati* managed to convince the reigning Ming Emperor of the need to retreat from a role of global prominence in order to preserve what China had already achieved in terms of cultural development. Had the Emperor not complied, it is altogether likely that China would have been the nation to discover the Americas and fashion itself into a formidable global power well before Europeans were able to do so. Indeed, it does not overstate the case to claim that the whole of world history was irrevocably altered by that edict of 1436 which turned China in upon herself. This particularistic episode, in other words, had the effect of permanently altering the course of world affairs. And this is not the only such incident. One wonders what might have been the future of Marxism globally had not the *New York Daily Tribune* paid Marx handsomely for his journalistic contributions to that newspaper in emerging capitalist America, and at a time when Marx was desperately in need of money, so that he could devote his energies to writing *Das Kapital* (McLellan 1977: 284–289). Indeed, these serendipitous events lend something of a social scientific credibility to those arguments of chaos theorists in the physical sciences who contend that reality often takes inexplicable courses which no theoretical model can really anticipate with any measure of certainty.

Before we venture too far afield with this line of development, however, we need to recall that the more modest point to be registered at this juncture is that matters of seemingly limited import can—and perhaps not infrequently do—blossom forth into developments of world-shattering significance. And even when we cannot anticipate the in breaking of a crucial event, we can discern in retrospect momentous occasions, if we cultivate an historical sensitivity to precisely such micro-level incidents. Moreover, when the issues at hand pertain to questions of ultimate meaning, order, and purpose—as is routinely the case with religious considerations—there may well be more instances when micro-level developments press toward the opposite pole of universal applicability and scope.

We should hasten to add, however, that the connection between particularism and universalism is much more rich and complex a process than merely the isolated instance wherein a particular event develops into a consequence of global importance. Indeed, much more important is the realization that particularism and universalism enjoy an ongoing reciprocity which is becoming ever more pronounced in the present circumstance. For one of the salient characteristics of the global situation in which we currently find ourselves, or so we would argue, is that part/whole issues constitute one of the fundamental modalities for structuring the contemporary situation.

China, again, has provided a recent example of just this sort of dynamic. The recent student demonstrations in Beijing which were so brutally crushed by the People's Liberation Army were self-consciously patterned after the May Fourth movement of 1919 wherein students and intellectuals of that day pressed for modernization by subscribing to the motto, "Science and Democracy." The leader of the original May Fourth movement was Hu Shih, a recently returned graduate student from Columbia University who had studied under John Dewey. The meaning of "Science and Democracy" was, therefore, intimately informed by Dewey's conception of those terms (Fairbank 1979: 230–235; Chesneaux *et al.* 1977: 65–97; Han 1990: 129–194). Seventy years later a new cortege of activists took to the streets in pursuit of democracy and science (with the latter term now largely regarded as a euphemism for economic development). Few demonstrators really had a very clear idea of what democracy, in particular, entailed. The slogan from the original May Fourth movement prevailed, but the substantive significance had long since eroded away. Yet despite this difficulty, thousands were willing to risk their futures and their only lives in order

INTRODUCTION

to advance Chinese society toward the goal of attaining a democratic order. Or to put the issue somewhat more axiomatically, thousands—and perhaps millions—of Chinese have recently pledged their full measure of devotion to the universal goal of democracy, even though they had only a hazy understanding of what that meant for their particularistic circumstances.

The events in China, however, were only one part of the story. Perhaps more significant is the fact that people all around the globe followed the saga of the Chinese students with inordinant attention. And when the government crushed the movement with brutal force in Tiananmen Square and, then, put out the revisionist report that no students died there, students throughout China and people around the world knew better. Indeed, unlike the crushing of the original May Fourth movement in 1919, this time channels of communication were open through a global network. Students received fax machine reports from supporters outside China and from Western news media on an hourly basis. Television pictures from Tiananmen Square were beamed by satellite to a world-wide audience, and the BBC and Voice of America covered much of the nation with descriptions of the demonstrations from their first outbreak to their bloody conclusion.

The response of the government in Beijing to try to control the interpretation of history—which might have worked with some measure of success in 1951 or during the Cultural Revolution in the 1960s—played forth on the global scene as a pathetic attempt by old men to tilt with the windmill of modernized media surveillance. Willy nilly, Chinese society already participates in a global order of communication and political-economic relations which render the old tactics devised during the Communist revolution palpably obsolete. And perhaps no event in recent memory so clearly demonstrates the universal involvement of particularistic nations as the Chinese crisis of 1989.

For present purposes, this event also provides the context for making another crucial point. That is: universal participation is not only inevitable, but the development of particularistic identities—as nation-states, ethnic groups, language communities, religious enclaves—is also thrust intractably on specific groups as a necessary means of preserving their identity in face of their global participation. When pressure was brought on China in the form of economic sanctions, public rebuke, loss of diplomatic contracts, and the like, Chinese officials were all but forced to assert that no outsider would be allowed to influence Chinese decision-making relative to domestic or foreign policy. One manifestation of China's global involvement, in other words, was the insistence on her inviolate integrity as a nation-state. Indeed, one of the dangers inherent in the universalizing tendencies of globalization is that it may, in crucial instances, force individual groups to extreme actions in order to demonstrate their particularistic "place" amid the empirical pluralism of the international arena.

This conclusion stands as a stark reminder that the processes of globalization cannot be naively enjoined as wholly benign. Rather, the concurrent drive toward universalism and particularism should be expected to generate serious tensions, deep divisions, and often violent outbreaks as the historical process moves toward a new level of social organization for the planet. Anticipating and describing these pressure-points constitutes an important undertaking for seeking to foster their resolution. Otherwise, we shall be left to react in knee-jerk fashion to each new crisis as it overtakes us.

Possessing a perspective which provides a clearer comprehension of the complex nature of global tensions does not, of course, insure that we shall have the political, cultural, or economic wisdom to handle them more equitably and peacefully. Yet, it does appear to hold better promise for some sort of reasoned response than merely confronting each new crisis on the basis of outmoded conventional wisdom and political shibboleths. Clearly, however, our concern in this volume is not to resolve the sundry issues on the global agenda, but to begin to develop some preliminary schemes for making sense of the world into which we are rapidly moving at an almost frightening pace.

A Brief Introduction to the Content of This Book

The foregoing comments were designed to provide a context for the papers that are contained within this volume, papers generated by a conference whose theme was "Religion and the Quest for Global Order." Our intent in designing the conference was to encourage essays of a relatively broad historical and cross-cultural scope, while still attending to the central theme of globalization processes. We held no prescriptive assumptions about the sort of interplay between religious forces and world-system dynamics; and the various authors display quite varied points of view relative to this issue. Consensus did arise, however, over several of the critical concepts and processes particularly germane to the discussion of global matters, such as universalism/particularism or localism/cosmopolitanism.

The initial essay of this volume, by John H. Simpson, serves as a kind of introduction to the whole problem area. Simpson sets out in a generalized fashion some of the basic themes bound up in the larger globalization *Problemstellung*. The four subsequent chapters deal with

INTRODUCTION

different historical eras and the quest for global order unleashed in each one. Theodore Long examines Old Testament prophecy as an instance wherein particularistic concerns press toward a universal vision. Using recent archeological findings, James F. Strange documents the subtle ways in which early Christian communities were linked to the universal order of Greco-Roman culture through the first four centuries. The radical wing of the Reformation, and especially left-wing groups in the English civil war, provide the focus for William R. Garrett's contribution. The central theme of this piece is that the human rights commitments of the Levelers and other groups pressed toward acknowledging the common prerogatives pertaining to all persons *qua* persons. And finally, James Muldoon, an historian and canon law specialist, looks at the latent consequences of legal developments in preparing the path toward global order by Spanish colonizers of the Americas.

Several cross-cultural analyses follow next. Glenn Yocum details the rituals and temple structures attending two models of universal order in Tamil India. Stanley Johannesen provides something of a case study of Norwegian Pentecostal immigrants to New York City and the manner in which the Holy Ghost is invoked as a means of rationalizing their lifeworld. In sharp contrast, Mike Featherstone focuses on consumer culture and postmodernism in contemporary societies. Shifting to the Islamic world, politics and culture in Islamic globalism is explored by Bryan Turner. And Anson Shupe rounds out these cross-cultural studies with an analysis of the rise and significance of the new religious movement of Soka Gakkai in Japan.

The last quintet of contributions to this volume also address contemporary features of the globalization process. Eileen Barker provides an analysis and critique of the Unification movement in recent religious affairs. The role of American televangelism in the global communications network is delineated by Jeffrey Hadden. Lonnie Kliever searches for a mode of synthesizing radical monotheism and radical democracy through an assessment of the work of Karl Mannheim and H. Richard Niebuhr. The significance of religion in the emerging global order is probed by Frank Lechner through an investigation of another normative system, namely, international law. And the final chapter by Roland Robertson surveys the ambiguous position of religion in globalization and modernization processes.

References

Alitto, Guy S. 1979. *The Last Confucian*. Berkeley: University of California Press.
Arendt, Hannah. 1957. "Karl Jaspers: Citizen of the World." 539–549 in *The Philosophy of Karl Jaspers*, edited by Paul A. Schlipp. La Salle: Open Court Publishing Company.
Braudel, Fernand. 1981. *The Structure of Everyday Life*. New York: Harper & Row.
_____. 1982. *The Wheels of Commerce*. New York: Harper & Row.
_____. 1984. *The Perspective of the World*. Chesneaux, Jean et. al. New York: Harper & Row.
Fairbank, John King. 1979. *The United States and China*. 4th ed. Cambridge, MA: Harvard University Press.
Gay, Peter. 1967. *The Enlightenment: An Interpretation*, I: *The Rise of Modern Paganism*. New York: Knopf.
_____. 1969. *The Enlightenment: An Interpretation*, II: *The Science of Freedom*. New York: Knopf.
Han, Minzhu. 1990. *Cries for Democracy: Writings and Speeches From the 1989 Chinese Democracy Movement*. Princeton: Princeton University Press.
Kennedy, Paul. 1987. *The Rise and The Fall of The Great Powers*. New York: Vintage Press.
Kern, Stephen. 1983. *The Culture of Time and Space: 1880–1918*. Cambridge: Harvard University Press.
Martin, David. 1978. *A General Theory of Secularization*. New York: Harper & Row.
McLellan, David. 1977. *Karl Marx: His Life and Thought*. New York: Harper & Row.
Moore, Wilbert E. 1979. *World Modernization*. New York: Elsevier.
Münch, Richard. 1987. *Theory of Action: Towards a New Synthesis Going Beyond Parsons*. London: Routledge & Kegan Paul.
_____. 1988. *Understanding Modernity: Toward a New Perspective Going Beyond Durkheim and Weber*. London: Routledge & Kegan Paul.
Parsons, Talcott. 1937. *The Structure of Social Action*. New York: Free Press.
_____. 1966. *Societies: Evolutionary and Comparative Perspectives*. Englewood Cliffs, N.J.: Prentice-Hall.
_____. 1971a. *The System of Modern Societies*. Englewood Cliffs, N.J.: Prentice-Hall.
_____. 1971b. "Comparative Studies and Evolutionary Change." 97–140 in *Comparative Methods In Sociology*, edited by Ivan Vallier. Berkeley: University of California Press.
_____. 1977. *Social Systems and the Evolution of Action Theory*. New York: Free Press.
_____. 1978. *Action Theory and the Human Condition*. New York: Free Press.
_____ et al. 1953. *Working Papers in the Theory of Action*. New York: Free Press.
Robertson, Roland. 1987. "From Secularization to Globalization." *Journal of Oriental Studies* 26(1): 28–32.
_____. 1988a. "Modernity and Religion: Towards the Comparative Genealogy of Religion in Global Perspective." *Zen Buddhism Today* 6 (November): 125–133.
_____. 1988b. "Liberation Theology, Latin America and Third World Underdevelopment." 117–134 in *The Politics of Latin American Liberation Theology*, edited by Richard L. Rubenstein and John K. Roth. Washington, D.C.: Washington Institute Press.

Rosenstock-Huessy, Eugene. [1938] 1969. *Out of Revolution: Autobiography of Western Man*. Norwich, VT: Argo Books.
Stackhouse, Max L. 1989. "The Theological Challenge of Globalization." *The Christian Century*, May 3: 468–471.
Troeltsch, Ernst. 1931. *The Social Teaching of the Christian Churches*. 2 Vols. London: George Allen & Unwin, Ltd.
_____. 1958. *Protestantism and Progress*. Boston: Beacon Press.
Wallerstein, Immanuel. 1974. *The Modern World-System, I: Capitalist Agriculture and the Origins of the European World-Economy in the Sixteenth Century*. New York: Academic Press.
_____. 1979. *The Capitalist World-Economy*. London: Cambridge University Press.
_____. 1980. *The Modern World-System, II: Mercantilism and the Consolidation of the European World-Economy, 1600–1750*. New York: Academica Press.
_____. 1989. *The Modern World-System, III: The Second Era of Great Expansion of the Capitalist World-Economy*. New York: Academic Press.
Weber, Max. [1904–5] 1958. *The Protestant Ethic and the Spirit of Capitalism*. New York: Scribners.

1
GLOBALIZATION AND RELIGION
THEMES AND PROSPECTS
John H. Simpson

Introduction

AS THIS BOOK ATTESTS, THERE IS NOW CONSIDERABLE INTEREST in the problem of religion in global perspective. In some measure this interest—at least among sociologists of religion in the United States—has been spurred by the appearance of politically militant fundamentalism—Islamic, Christian, and Jewish—linked in various ways to the politics of oil, Reagan's socio-cultural politics of revitalization, and the struggle of the State of Israel to resist hostile encirclement. Sociologists with the help of historians, scholars of religious studies, and others have been quick to describe those movements and other formally similar developments outside the U.S.-Middle East orbit (Hadden and Shupe 1986; 1988; 1989).

At the same time, however, some sociologists with an interest in religion have attempted to place contemporary social and political movements within a frame of reference that goes beyond the socio-political dynamics of nation-states. In their view more is at stake than, simply, the adequate description of religio-social movements at the nation-state level. Furthermore, they eschew the notion that contemporary religious movements are of primary interest because they seem to constitute evidence against secularization theory. Contextualizing secularization, its putative reversal, and a host of other phenomena within the category of the globe as an emergent socio-cultural unit, this new perspective focuses on religion's role in globalization or "...the making of the world into a single place" (Robertson 1987a: 36).

At this point in its development the globalization perspective is best understood as a 'conversation'—sometimes covert, other times overt—between a number of theories and perspectives that posit an axiom of global singularity. Certainly, the best known of these is the world-systems approach of Wallerstein and his followers.[1] A chronologically earlier sketch is found in Nettl and Robertson (1968), an important precursor of the globalization perspective subsequently developed by Robertson.[2] What might be called the "Stanford School" of world-systems analysis constitutes a third major voice in the globalization conversation.[3] Among other things its members—who, clearly, factionalized—have independently thematized and developed certain elements found in Nettl and Robertson (1968), elaborated notions of state institutionalization and development in the global system, and applied Wallerstein's paradigm to the analysis of the post-World War II period. The application of appropriate formal models to test notions of institutional change, state development, and the distribution of wealth in the world-system constitute major contributions of the Stanford School to globalization research.[4]

It would, I think, be a mistake to reduce the conversation among theorists and researchers with a global perspective to an intellectual donnybrook between competing camps. Nevertheless, a cursory examination of the literature quickly reveals that there are major differences in emphases and theoretical strategies. The most vivid contrast is to be found between the conceptually simple yet historically rich arguments of Wallerstein who derives the modern world system from the spread of capitalism and the more variegated and sociologically complex arguments of Meyer and Robertson regarding the oneness of the world in terms of politics, states, and culture.

The purpose of this essay is to introduce the contrasting themes and approaches of the major voices in the globalization 'conversation' to a broad audience and, especially, to those with interests in the sociology of religion and religious studies. The globalization 'conversation' deserves attention because its participants are attempting to fill a major theoretical vacuum. Simply put, sociological thematizations of globality are attempts to come to grips with the discontinuity in sociological theory induced by the fact that the globe as one place is neither an integrated social system nor does it exhibit a focusing mechanism that resembles the state. In other words, the classic sociological types of order that were either taken for granted as a pre-condition for doing theory (Marx) or viewed as problematic to be thematized and solved (Weber, Durkheim, Parsons) do not exist at the global level. Yet there is an undoubted sense that the world has become one 'ordered' place. How is that possible sociologically speaking? How do we know/construct/invent the globe in such a way that we can claim that our discourse frames, grasps, and accounts for the "oneness" of the world. That is the problem addressed by theories of globalization.

Classical sociology is, essentially, an account of the changes that occurred in the West during the eighteenth century, nineteenth century, and early parts of the twentieth century, an account achieved by inventing such transitions as *Gemeinschaft* to *Gesellschaft*, feudalism to capitalism, agricultural formation to industrial formation, empire to nation-state, estate to society, etc. As Robertson (1985) notes, sociological discourse 'bared' and captured the sense of the great transformations that generated modern societies. As the accounts of classical sociology (society-based discourse) produced meaning—that is came to be viewed as adequate explanations for the changes rampant in the West in an earlier period—so the globalization conversation, today, is an attempt to grasp changes at the world level through a globe-based discourse.

As far as the sociology of religion is concerned, it should be recalled that religion as a socially based phenomenon and category was invented during the construction of classical sociology. The sociological invention of religion, that is the construction of religion as a social category, represented a solution to the problem of meaning within society-based discourse—an ambiguous solution, it might be added, as the notion of secularization makes abundantly clear. In the broadest terms the globalization phenomenon can be described as a crisis of meaning (that is, a theoretical crisis) at the global level thus begging the question—among other questions—of what it means to invent 'religion' as a globally based phenomenon.

Constructing the Oneness of the World

The notion that the world is one place is not a post-modern idea. Some pre-literate and traditional peoples have viewed the world as one place with range, habitat, and cosmology woven into a seamless, co-incident whole. Within the stream of historical/civilizational consciousness, however, there has always been a distinction between the mythological unity of the world and the empirical realities of difference, otherness, discontinuity of distance, and absolute boundaries erected on the basis of language, tribe, and what we would, today, call "culture." The notional, ideational oneness of the world is, clearly, embedded in the story frameworks of all the so-called "world religions." At the same time, however, they all thematize difference and otherness, that is the empirical disunity of the world. The obvious, familiar example is found in the Hebrew Bible.

The story of globalization in one sense begins with the great reversal called "science" which posits the empirical unity of the world (an atom of carbon in Papua, New Guinea is the same as an atom of carbon in Pittsburgh) and through technology reduces the palpable discontinuities in the world, thereby, bringing into sharp relief the 'non-empirical' differences that exist among the human species. The search for an adequate theory of globalization can be viewed in large measure as the search for a myth, of social oneness in a field of empirical continuity that, paradoxically, heightens the sense of socially constructed human differences.

Judged in terms of simplicity and narrative suppleness (but not necessarily adequacy), there can be little doubt that Wallerstein's world systems theory takes the prize among the various globalization perspectives. According to Wallerstein, the appropriate object of analysis in social science is the organization of the material base or mode of production of an entity or self-contained system. Since the dawn of history only three types of self-contained systems have existed: tribal/extended kin mini-systems, world-empires, and the world economy. Each system has a characteristic mode of production: reciprocal-lineage (mini-systems), redistributive-tributary (world-empires), and capitalism (the world economy) (Taylor 1985: 7).

The basic difference between the capitalist mode of production and other modes is that capitalist production is for exchange rather than use (by the producer or his/her kin) and is determined solely by the criterion of market profitability. Surplus (profit) accrues to the producer-seller and is not subject to redistribution on non-market grounds. From an analytical point of the view capitalism disentangles the economic sector from social or political structures where redistribution could occur on grounds other than profit, as is the case in mini-systems and world empires. The capitalist mode of production, then, is an autonomous self-reproducing system wholly determined by price competition in the market.

From its origin in Europe in the eighteenth century, capitalism has spread to a position of dominance such that, today, according to Wallerstein, the entire globe is a self-contained capitalist system. It is also a differentially structured system with marked variation between subunits in terms of the capacity to extract and accumulate surplus (capital) which determines whether a subunit is in the core, semi-periphery, or periphery of the world system. The core is defined by "relatively high wages, advanced technology and a diversified production mix whereas periphery processes involve low wages, more rudimentary technology, and a simple production mix" (Taylor 1985: 17). The semi-periphery is characterized by a mix of core and periphery processes where neither is dominant.

The core dominates the periphery and semi-periphery because the process of exchange generates disproportionate amounts of capital in the core. The favorable position of the core can be traced to the imposition of non-market biases in the exchange process (the political fixing of prices in colonial systems) and to the lower cost of labor in the periphery which results in exchanges that require disproportionate labor input in the production of peripheral commodities in order to achieve parity in terms of the value of labor expressed in core goods. Exchange, then, results in surplus value flowing to the core. Given that exchange proceeds on those terms, the core will always dominate the periphery, and the periphery will be dependent upon the core.

While the processes underlying the capitalist system are invariant, the system is dynamic in terms of the types of units that are exchanged and the location of units in the system. Thus, colonial systems have given way to a universal system of nation-states; and dominance in the core has passed from Dutch to British to American hegemony since the system's inception in the sixteenth century. Furthermore, a distinction can be drawn between redistributive processes within units and the location of units in the world system. All nation-states, whether they are internally capitalist, socialist, or communist, are externally subject to the process that defines capitalism: production for exchange in a market system. Thus, the major communist states, China and the old Soviet Union, have been classified as semi-peripheral in the world systems perspective. That is their location in the capitalist world system. At their boundaries even communist states are not independent of the world market and its capitalist mechanism according to Wallerstein.

Wallerstein finds oneness in the world because the world in his eyes is, essentially, a single capitalist system. Conflict in the system is thematized in terms of the great material disparities between core, semi-periphery, and periphery and the interests of units in maintaining or changing their positions. The system conforms, essentially, to the principles of micro-economics with significant biases, e.g. tariff protection, war, being introduced by core states when necessary in order to maintain hegemony and avert crises and by peripheral states where possible in order to attempt to obtain better terms of exchange. Is Wallerstein's construction of oneness adequate? Both Meyer and Robertson think not. Neither denies that the world is in part one because of its formation through the spread of capitalism. Both, however, reject the Wallersteinian notion that the singularity of the world is constituted simply and without remainder by a network of capitalist exchange relations. In other words, the oneness of the world, according to Meyer and Robertson, is more than the sensibility that a great chain of capitalist economic 'being' suffuses the global human population. Both reject mono-causal 'economism' in favor of models emphasizing the interpenetration of material, political, and symbolic factors that are expressed in global processes and structures.

However, Wallerstein, Meyer, and Robertson do have one thing in common: All three reject the model of development that was popular in the fifties and early sixties and posited the recapitulation of Western European—North American industrialization, democracy, and civil society in the new nation-states of the Third World (Rostow 1960). In his critique of developmentalism which, simultaneously, encompasses his finding of oneness in the world, Wallerstein assumes that there are three basic elements in the world system: a single capitalist market, a three-tiered structure of zones or units (core, semi-periphery, periphery), and a multiple state system. Ultimately, as noted above, the structure of zones or units and the major features of the state system—politics, diplomacy, war—are derivable from the nature of the global capitalist system.

Meyer rejects developmentalism by finding oneness in the world in terms of globally diffused normative 'myths' of rationalization, individuation, and progress which organize action independent of the degree of material development or industrialization in a particular context or locale. The powerful 'story lines' of modernity with their insatiable organizing capacities have found a universal hole, according to Meyer, in state and state-sponsored structures and transnational bodies.

Finally, in his alternative to developmentalism, Robertson argues that there are three elementary units—selves, nation-states, and the world system of nation-states that are bound together in a single system of reflexive and symmetric comparison processes. The global condition of simultaneous unity (one world) and diversity (many parts) is produced by the interaction of selves, nation-states, and the system of nation-states. A generalized notion of humanity/mankind serves as an ultimate point of reference for action with the perspectives of elementary units constrained by the cultural ingredients of tradition and modernity.

I have already noted above that Wallerstein's analysis assumes the framework of micro-economics biased by the self-serving intervention of powerful actors such as the state and those who control large pools of capital to skew markets in their favor. Neither Meyer nor Robertson deny the inequalities of wealth and the differential capacities to generate wealth that exist in the world system and are the object of Wallerstein's analysis. Both, however, go beyond Wallerstein by, essentially, overriding his objectivism in favor of system models that incorporate interpretive processes. Thus, Meyer, in his widely cited article, "The World Polity and the Authority of the Nation-State" (1980: 136), argues that there is a Global Polity defined by a set of rules that is exogenous to individual societies and legitimates "...the extension and expansion of authority of rationalized nation-states to control and act on behalf of their populations."

Viewing the world only in terms of exchange, Meyer contends, makes it hard to explain the viability and stability of the nation-state, especially in the peripheral zones of the world system. Were the world simply organized as a vast exchange network, it would, according to Meyer, exhibit much different social features than it does:

(1) Instead of an organizationally stable set of economically strong and economically weak states, weak states would be in a constant state of morphological flux, deformed and reformed to the advantage of the stronger states as happens among weaker economic organizations competing in a marketplace. That does not happen. Weak and strong states maintain their boundaries and organizational integrity.

(2) There would be a marked tendency for continuous increases in the division of labor between poor and rich countries. That does not happen. The rates of increase in production and service activities in both central and peripheral societies are "broadly similar" (114).

(3) Political entities in the world would be increasingly subordinated to economic units. That does not happen. Across the world government revenues tend to increase as a proportion of gross unit product.

(4) If the state were a mere reflection of the economic forces of commodity production, political differentiation in the world would increase. That does not happen. States in poor and rich countries alike tend to increase the rate of appropriation of the expanding economic resources of their societies.

(5) Poor peripheral countries should be less likely to adopt modern institutional arrangements than richer countries. That does not happen. Both rich and poor countries exhibit similar rates of expansion in the

development of a variety of institutional sectors: education, urbanization, communications, and state services.

In arguing as he does Meyer does not deny that gross material inequalities exist in the world system, inequalities that are based, essentially, on the world economy of commodity production. But those inequalities do not explain the structure and persistence of the nation-state and the global system of formally similar nation-states which incorporates both the rich and the poor nations. Meyer, in other words, adds the empirical generalization of formal state similarity to the empirical generalization of material difference and notes that one cannot explain the other. What, then, does explain formal state similarity across the globe?

According to Meyer, there is a world polity consisting of a set of rules that (a) defines the nation-state as the legitimate factor in the world system; (b) guarantees the sovereignty and autonomy of the nation-state through third party enforcement; (c) provides the nation-state with control of significant resources (and labor); (d) defines the pursuit of progress by the nation-state on behalf of its citizen population as normative; (e) mandates that the state be collectively organized in such a way that it can claim that purposes that are derivable from the notion of progress are immanent in its organizational apparatus; (f) empowers the state to create value which can be accounted as product in the service sector, thus enabling the state, independent of commodity production, to demonstrate that it is serving the purpose of progress inasmuch as one attribute of progress is the increase of gross product. That feature of the world polity is particularly crucial for peripheral zones that are marginal to the exchange of commodities in the global economic system as it allows them to create intra-societal value based on 'invisible,' socially defined commodities, e.g. education, organized social control, welfare services.

In considering Meyer's argument, it is important to keep in mind that he is arguing for the notion of functional similarity across nation-states in terms of norms and purposes and their organizational expression. All states, in his view, must incorporate the essential ingredient of modernity, the notion of progress. They are constrained to act in a progressive manner or risk being defined as deviant.

Meyer draws a sharp distinction between state, regime, and society noting that regime instability and one-party rule, particularly in peripheral zones, does not affect the purposes of the state as defined in the world polity. Furthermore, society, especially in peripheral zones, frequently becomes the object rather than the source of state action with the progressive purposes of the world polity immanent in the action of the state and in opposition to recalcitrant traditionalism embedded in society.

Meyer, then, finds oneness in the world in terms of the formal similarity of nation-states—rich and poor alike—which is attributable to a set of rules that define a common world polity, common in the sense that all actors (nation-states) subscribe to the rules or, where they don't, are subject to sanctions by significant coalitions of nation-states that may, as individual units, have vastly divergent national interests. For example, in the midst of the Cold War, the Soviet Union and the United States acting in coalition underscored the autonomy and sovereignty of the nation-state by supporting Egypt when it was attacked in the 1958 Suez Incident by old colonial powers—the United Kingdom and France—and Israel. The reassertion of the imperial model at the expense of Egypt's integrity as an autonomous and sovereign nation-state was opposed by the two strongest nation-states in the world who, otherwise, had little in common as far as national interests were concerned. While any commodity-based explanation of the Suez Incident seems hopelessly obscure and excessively ideological, the concerted action of the Soviet Union and the United States can easily be explained with reference to the exogenous constraining rules of the world polity as formulated by Meyer.

The oneness Meyer finds in the world avoids the economistic, one-dimensional perspective of Wallerstein and his followers by essentially positing a dialectical process where power, which may have a source in commodity exchange processes, leads to authority which, in turn, can take on a life of its own. Where incorporated within the bounds of the modern nation-state, authority becomes a means for defining value. That assumption, in the final analysis, separates Meyer from the Wallersteinian world systems perspective where value creation is attributed solely to the labor process of commodity production. In that regard there is considerable irony in Meyer's analysis since he argues, in effect, that the rules of the world polity are, essentially, socialist in nature. They constrain nation-states to act in a progressive manner toward their citizen populations and redistribute value—either state-created value or value derived from exchange in the world system—along their populations. In effect, then, Meyer argues that Wallerstein and his followers can't see the operative socialist 'forest' in the world polity because they can't seem to gaze beyond the 'trees' of industrialized 'Marco Poloism'—long distance trade for profit in primary resources, agricultural commodities, and manufactures, to newer sources of value, many of them state-created, in services (including the body-focused arts), social control, media, education, and other socially defined 'invisible' products.

Meyer constructs oneness from the putative immanence of norms of rationalization and progress in state structures around the world where value is created and accounted for by a variety of means including (but not limited to) commodity production. There is no doubt that Meyer's line of reasoning puts considerable distance between himself and Wallerstein. It also differs in certain formal and critical respects from Robertson's analysis of oneness in the world to which I now turn.

Robertson's earliest work in globalization theory (although it did not go by that name at the time) was done in association with J.P. Nettl (Nettl and Robertson 1968). In it we find a rather remarkable *fin-de-siècle* analysis by two British social scientists who are wrestling with the problem of how to understand a world in which Empire has given way to Commonwealth and where, paradoxically, old and new nations simultaneously exhibit both vigor and weakness, each in somewhat different ways. Nettl and Robertson reject the American model of developmentalism as an adequate analysis of what is happening or could happen to the nation-states outside the developed West. At the same time, however, they steer clear of neo-Marxian diagnoses of the state of the world and the obverse of those views: utilitarian, game-theoretical approaches to the world-system that were popular in the sixties.

Anticipating the cultural arguments that were to become popular some twenty years later, Nettl and Robertson elaborated the notion of modernization as the key to understanding the developing world-system. While in some respects similar to Meyer's neo-Weberian analysis, Nettl and Robertson's approach places less emphasis on the institutionalization of norms in state structures and underscores the sharing of norms among world elites—especially national political elites—regarding what constitutes the "good" progressive state. According to Nettl and Robertson, the pathos of the expanding world-system is found in the gap between widely shared normative goals among world-level elites and the capacities of new nation-states to realize those goals.

Regarded strictly from an analytic point of view, there are a number of ironic advances in the analysis of Nettl and Robertson. Among other things, they pay a great deal of attention to the problem of characterizing the processes and mechanisms whereby norms of progress become operative in the world system. Eschewing for the most part phenomenological approaches to the matter, they adopt the American social psychology of comparisons in order to account for the pathos of the world-system. The fundamental theoretical problem—essentially bracketed or dismissed by Weber and Marx—is how to characterize and account for the relationship between socio-cognitive 'contents' (notions, ideas, norms) and action. The 'European' theoretical problem is solved by Nettl and Robertson using 'American' means.

A second ironic advance in Nettl and Robertson—perhaps, less successful than their use of the social psychology of comparisons—involves embedding social comparison processes in a Parsonian action framework in order to elucidate the 'content' of those processes. I count that tactic as ironic since what we have are two British analysts employing a theory of the American mind spun-out by Parsons from nineteenth and early twentieth century European social 'self-reflexivities' and applied to the problem of action in a post-British Empire world.

In constructing his analysis of the global situation Robertson argues that a fundamental feature of the contemporary world-system is the tension between *Gemeinschaft* and *Gesellschaft* which accompanies the progressive press across the globe for rationalization in politics, economics, and society. Unlike Meyer and Wallerstein, however, Robertson is unwilling to simply bracket traditionalism and declare it, in effect, an 'error term' in the explanation of the global situation. Thus, Robertson insists that the developing global situation can only be understood in terms of the tension and dialectic between *Gemeinschaft* and *Gesellschaft*. Robertson, then, reads the emergent global situation as a process continuous with the rise of the modern West inasmuch as it can be thematized in *Gemeinschaft-Gesellschaft* terms. At the same time, however, Robertson views globalization as structurally and formally more complex than the situation that obtained with the modernization of the West which can be reduced for some theoretical purposes to the problematic of the individual and society. The complication of the global situation arises from the necessity to contextualize individuals and societies within an emergent system of interrelated nation-states where all three units (selves, nation-states, the system of nation-states) have simultaneous effects on one another. Thus, globalization represents a threefold leap in the number of relational paths between units that have to be considered in the construction of theory in comparison with the 'classic' case of modernization in the West.

Robertson achieves the Anglo-American turn in his analysis of globalization by arguing that the major process obtaining between units is "relativization." The press of emergent globalization forces units to take into consideration the actions of other units on a global scale where it becomes impossible to fortify one's interpretive claims against those of others in order to produce globally stable absolutes. Under globalization all absolutes are relative, which is not to deny that 'local' absolutes may find strength through self-definition vis-à-vis the global process of relativization, e.g., Albania, various religious fundamentalisms.

I characterize Robertson's positing of a process of relativization at the global level as an "Anglo-American" turn because it, essentially, sets globalization on a pragmatic, median base. Selves, societies, and the system of nation-states are autonomous, underwritten actors operating in a milieu of minimal formal constraint where, on the basis of taking the role of the other, moments of constitutional and procedural settlement are achieved. Empirically, the world as a system is, essentially, proto-associational and proceeds on the basis of *ad hoc* agreements between autonomous units. It is not a system controlled in any final or effective way by units that are superordinate to its constituent parts—selves, nations, and the system of nation-states.

While the world as an empirical system is proto-associational, conceptual responses to globality—that is projected images of desirable world order—are quite varied. According to Robertson (1991), images of world order that arise as cultural responses to globality may be classified in global *Gemeinschaft* or *Gesellschaft* categories with variants in each category determined by the symmetry, asymmetry, centralization, or decentralization of relations between the units in a category. For example, world order can be conceived of as a series of relatively closed societal communities (global *Gemeinschaft*). The symmetric version of global *Gemeinschaft* views such communities as relatively equal in terms of cultural and institutional heritages, while the asymmetric version views one community as better or more important than others. On the other hand, world order may be conceived of as a series of open exchanging societies (global *Gesellschaft*).

The symmetrical version of global *Gesellschaft* views all societies as worthwhile exchange partners, while the asymmetrical version pinpoints the dominance or hegemony of certain societies in the maintenance of world order. Robertson's implicit characterization of the empirical global situation as a proto-associational system composed of selves, nations, and the system of nation-states—all subjected to *Gemeinschaft-Gesellschaft* tensions—leads directly to a consideration of the role of culture and religion as ingredients in the making of a globalized world.

The theoretical justification for Robertson's insistence that the contemporary global situation cannot be fully understood without reference to culture/religion is three-fold. First, by positing tension and a dialectical relationship between *Gemeinschaft* and *Gesellschaft*, rather than subordinating *Gemeinschaft* to progressive transformation by assuming the irresistible diffusion and ascendance of *Gesellschaft* as the classical theorists did, Robertson builds the contents of tradition and the 'life-world' including religion into the process of globalization. In fact, Robertson's *Gemeinschaft-Gesellshaft* tension can be viewed as a social mode where the symbols, structures, and cultural elements of *Gemeinschaft* and *Gesellschaft* are so intertwined that a new typological social complex has been defined. That complex abandons both optimistic (Marxist) and pessimistic (Weberian) progressivism in favor of reading the present and the future in terms of ongoing tension between *Gemeinschaft* and *Gesellschaft*. By arguing that the defining moments of the globalization process are an admixture of the old and the new, the modern and the traditional, Robertson comes much closer to the so-called "post-modern sensibility" than either Wallerstein or Meyer.

Second, as far as religion goes, Robertson's theory sketch of the global situation implicitly recognizes processes of institutional differentiation. From an institutional point of view, a marked difference between modernization as classically described and globalization as described by Robertson is that the former brings about the autonomy of institutional sectors, while the latter may encourage the 'recombination' of autonomous institutions in some circumstances. For religion this means that it enters into the globalization process as a differentiated institution seeking institutional 'partnerships' in the global arena which, of course, from a formal perspective, is exactly the opposite of what transpired in the process of modernization where religion became a differentiated institution.

The third opening Robertson makes for religion in the globalization process underscores religion's functional possibilities in a field of interacting social units. Given the median field of interaction between selves, nations, and the system of nation-states that constitute the contemporary global situation, units find themselves pressed to establish and display their identities. That is especially true, Robertson argues, for nation-states where much of the recent world-wide tension between church and state can be interpreted as a response to identity-formation problems in the global arena.

Robertson, then, finds oneness in the world in terms of the diffusion of a field of action over the entire globe in which social units are increasingly constrained to compare and relate their points of view and behaviors with respect to one another. Although Robertson, thus, reads the world from a pragmatic perspective, he eschews the optimistic progressivism of 'classic' pragmatism by noting that relativization, in principle, can produce either the seeds of conflict or a basis for accommodation in any given situation. On those grounds Robertson's approach to globalization makes quicker sense of many contemporary global events where politics and religion or culture are deeply intertwined than either Wallerstein's approach or Meyer's approach.

A case in point is the Rushdie affair where the Iranian theocrat Khomeini, condemned the novelist Salman Rushdie to death for insulting Islam in his book, *The Satanic Verses*. The defense of Rushdie by the advanced western nations and the ensuing diplomatic crisis are difficult to account for in any immediate sense within a Wallersteinian exchange framework or a Meyersonian framework stressing the state implementation of progressive norms. (Although, certainly, the state's monopoly over violence was at issue.)

It is easy, however, to read the Rushdie affair as a provocative symbolic encounter where three points of view—each, in fact, encompassing an absolute—have been placed in the global media arena: a traditional high view of the Prophet, a secularized rendering of certain aspects of the Prophet's life, and the secular western norm of freedom of speech and the press. That the Rushdie affair virtually overnight redefined the relationship in very large mass populations between certain features of Islamic civilization and western secular civilization is consistent with the general frame of reference that Robertson proposes as the key to understanding the oneness that has descended on the globe.

Conclusion: Religion and the Global Situation

It is by no means clear at this juncture where the struggle to give theoretical meaning to the oneness of the world will lead us. As the review of Wallerstein, Meyer, and Robertson suggests, oneness can be thematized in a number of ways, there being no sense that a single approach in isolation provides a fully satisfactory account of oneness. Exchange processes, myths of progress, and logic of interaction and perception operating within an admixture of traditional and modern institutions that perforce lead to the direction of co-operative systems or systems governed by the tempered conflict of pluralism are each defensible as analytic perches for viewing and grasping the oneness in the world.

In raising the question of the place of religion as an analytic component in an adequate theory of the globe, it is tempting to dismiss approaches such as Wallerstein's or Meyer's in favor of Robertson's since he explicitly thematizes the role of religion in the contemporary global situation. Wallerstein and Meyer, on the other hand—each for somewhat different reasons—do not view religion in the common-sense meaning of that term as one of the necessary ingredients that must be taken into account in order to understand the making of the contemporary global situation. However, despite the obvious substantive differences between Robertson and Wallerstein or Meyer regarding the role and place of religion in a theory of the globe, it would, I think, be a mistake to dismiss Wallerstein and Meyer as providing no help in understanding how religion fits into the global complex. Both, in fact, generate formal clues regarding ways of thinking about religion and globalization which complement Robertson's approach.

When generalized, Wallerstein's analysis implicitly raises the question of the structure of the relationship between religion and other institutions. While Wallerstein's analysis—in the typical Marxist mode—treats religion and culture as structurally dependent upon or reducible to the analysis of exchange processes, it does pose the question of the necessity of that reduction and the possibility of variation in the relationship between religion and other institutions according to historical circumstances. The point is that Wallerstein, despite his Marxist reductionism, does encourage us in a derivative fashion to pursue the nature of the structural relationship between religion and other institutions at the global level.

Where generalized, Meyer encourages us to think about the organizing capacity of myths. Meyer, himself, views the myths of progress and science as possessing the greatest organizing capacity in the contemporary world. Despite that secular note, however, Meyer—like Wallerstein—implicitly suggests a line of analysis regarding religion to the extent that he raises the question of the conditions under which any kind of myth—religious or secular—will organize a context of action. It is, of course, possible to view Meyer's analysis as 'religious' to begin with in the sense that to talk about the organizing capacity of myth per se as a fundamental category in understanding human action is to approach the analysis of action from a 'religious' perspective. From that perspective the common sense understanding of some myths as religious and others as secular simply means that religious myths are specialized kinds of myths, but all myths are 'religious.'

Finally, it should be noted that Robertson's approach to the question of globalization is not a specialized approach that is built around the role of religion in the contemporary situation. It is the case that Robertson has paid a great deal of attention to religion in his writings about globalization but religion per se is not the primary focus of his analysis. Rather he thematizes religion as one source and, indeed, a major source of the frames of reference that enter into the construction of the identities of units and the perceptions of units in the field of global interaction. Like Wallerstein and Meyer, Robertson proceeds from a theoretically generalizable perspective.

While no theory of the globe based on a simple combination of the modes of analysis employed by Wallerstein, Meyer, and Robertson appears to be around the corner, it probably is the case that an adequate theory of the globe will have some roots in each approach and will blend developed views of the structure of institutions and their relationship to exchange processes, the varying capacities of different types of myths to organize action, and the dynamics of symbolic interaction between selves, nations, and the system of nation-states at the global level. The task seems enormous and it is hoped that sociologists with an interest in religion will take it seriously.

Notes

1. The basic references are Wallerstein 1974; 1979; 1980; 1983.
2. The basic references are Nettl and Robertson 1968; Robertson 1982; 1985; 1987a,b,c; 1989; 1991; Robertson and Chirico 1985; Robertson and Lechner 1985.
3. The basic references are Meyer 1980; Meyer and Hannan 1979; Bergesen 1980; cf. Chase-Dunn 1989.
4. Luhmann (1982) argues that modern society is a world society "… in a double sense. It provides one world for one system; and it integrates all world horizons as horizons of one communicative system. The phenomenological and the structural meanings converge. A plurality of possible worlds becomes inconceivable. The world-wide communicative system constitutes one world which includes all possibilities" (133). It is impossible to explore within the confines of this chapter whether Luhmann's systems analysis logically subsumes other globalization theories and is consistent with the empirical and historic specificities of the approaches that are explored here.

References

Bergesen, A. (ed.). 1980. *Studies of the Modern World System*. New York: Academic Press.
Chase-Dunn, C. 1989. *Global Formation: Structures of the World Economy*. London: Blackwell.
Hadden, J.K. and A. Shupe (eds.). 1986. *Prophetic Religions and Politics: Religion and the Political Order*. New York: Paragon House.
_____. 1988. *The Politics of Religion and Social Change: Religion and the Political Order*. New York: Paragon House.
_____. 1989. *Fundamentalism and Secularism Reconsidered*. New York: Paragon House.
Luhmann, N. 1982. "The World Society As a Social System." *International Journal of Social Systems* 8:131–138.
Meyer, J.W. 1980. "The World Polity and the Authority of the Nation State." 109–137

in *Studies of a Modern World-System*, edited by Albert Bergesen. New York: Academic Press.

Meyer, J.W. and M.T. Hannan (eds.). 1979. *National Development and the World System: Educational, Economic, and Political Change, 1950–1970*. Chicago: The University of Chicago Press.

Nettl, J.P. and R. Robertson. 1968. *International Systems and the Modernization of Societies: The Formation of National Goals and Attitudes*. New York: Basic Books.

Robertson, R. 1982. "Religion, Global Complexity and the Human Condition." 185–212 in *Absolute Values and the Creation of the New World, Vol. 1*. New York: International Cultural Foundation.

_____. 1985. "The Sacred and the World-System." 347–359 in *The Sacred in a Secular Age*, edited by Philip Hammond. Berkeley: University of California Press.

_____. 1987a. "Globalization and Societal Modernization: A Note on Japan and Japanese Religion." *Sociological Analysis* 47: 35–42.

_____. 1987b. "Church-State Relations and the World-System." 39–51 in *Church-State Relations: Tensions and Transitions*, edited by T. Robbins and R. Robertson. New Brunswick. N.J.: Transaction Books.

_____. 1987c. "Globalization Theory and Civilization Analysis." *Comparative Civilizations Review* 17: 20–30.

_____. 1989. "Globalization, Politics, and Religion." 10–23 in *The Changing Face of Religion*, edited by J. Beckford and T. Luckmann. London: Sage.

_____. 1991. "Globality, Global Culture and Images of World Order." In *Social Change and Modernity*, edited by Hans Haferkamp and Neil Smelser. Berkeley: University of California Press.

Robertson, R. and J. Chirico. 1985. "Humanity, Globalization, and Worldwide Religious Resurgence: A Theoretical Exploration." *Sociological Analysis* 46(3): 219–242.

Robertson, R. and F. Lechner. 1985. "Modernization, Globalization and the Problem of Culture in World-Systems Theory." *Theory, Culture and Society* 2 (3): 103–118.

Rostow, W.W. 1960. *The Stages of Economic Growth*. Cambridge: Cambridge University Press.

Taylor, P.J. 1985. *Political Geography: World-Economy, Nation-State and Locality*. London: Longman.

Wallerstein, I. 1974. *The Modern World System: Capitalist Agriculture and the Origins of the European World-Economy in the Sixteenth Century*. New York: Academic Press.

_____. 1979. *The Capitalist World-Economy*. Cambridge University Press.

_____. 1980. *The Modern World-System II: Mercantilism and the Consolidation of the European World-Economy 1600–1750*. New York: Academic Press.

_____. 1983. *Historical Capitalism*. London: Verso.

2
OLD TESTAMENT UNIVERSALISM
PROPHETIC SEEDS ON PARTICULARISTIC SOIL
Theodore E. Long

BOTH THE IDEA AND THE IDEAL OF GLOBAL ORDER rely on universalistic principles to provide a foundation for integrating diverse nations and peoples, at least in some minimal sense. Such universalism has deep religious roots, Weber (1963: 23) suggests, originating in the "Yahweh cult" of the Hebrew people, whose experience Parsons (1966: 95ff.) considers a fertile "seed-bed" of societal evolution. Because of its contribution to universalism, the Jewish religion has "world-historical importance" (Weber 1952: 4) for religious history, for the development of the modern world, and now for the emergence of global order. Those claims imply that a return to the religious roots of universalism will enable us to elaborate its meaning and its formative contribution to contemporary social evolution, in addition to displaying some of the distinctive underpinnings of the Judaic tradition itself.

Here I undertake such analysis, not as an initial foray into the field, but as an extension and specification of previous work by Weber (1952;

1963) and Parsons (1951; 1966), which exposed the connection of Hebrew religion, universalism, and the modern world. Their investigations into the development of universal ethical and legal principles as part of a covenant with a monotheistic god centered on the simple logical quality of inclusiveness without specifying the various dimensions along which such universalism was developed. In addition, they treated universalism in ideal-typical fashion without fully exploring its empirical imperfections and complications. And both scholars adopt what we might call a "separation thesis," which considers universalism to have gained historic import independent of its origins in ancient Israel. This paper offers a specification of several dimensions of universalism arising from the multiple elements of Hebrew religion and provides a more situated empirical analysis of the complex entanglements of universalism and particularism. In that light, I suggest that it may be difficult to sustain the separation thesis completely and consider lessons about universalism which we might learn from the Hebrew experience.

My analysis centers on the Old Testament, the canonization of which provides the primary resource for inserting Hebrew universalism into the world-historical process (Weber 1952: 4). There the basic character of universalism developed in the historic experiences of the Israelites, which provide the empirical grounding for elaborating the ideal type. Old Testament scholarship is extensive and quite disputatious at points, and I could not hope, nor do I want, to make claims on that territory. Instead of taking it as a topic, I use the Old Testament as a resource for the sociological exploration of universalism on the strategic site of ancient Judaism. As the founding cultural document of Judaism, the biblical record is of interest here primarily as an index of the nature and extent of universalism embedded in Jewish religion, regardless of the sources, character, quality or value of biblical texts themselves.

Consistent with Weber and Parsons, I approach the text with a spare conception of a universalistic trait as one applicable to all members of a class of phenomena, treating particularistic traits as those limited to a specific part or unit of the whole. Looking through those lenses, I examine six prominent themes in Old Testament religion: (1) the covenant, (2) the promised land, (3) monotheism, (4) the law, (5) justice, and (6) historicity. None of these themes is defined by its universalism or particularism alone, but the meaning of each is deeply implicated in the matter. Moreover, none of these themes is one dimensional; in all of them we find universalism entangled with particularism, in principle or in practice. Those diverse entanglements drive us to the conclusion that universalism is only partially realized in Hebrew religion. Its main themes contain seeds of universalism, but they are planted in very particularistic soil which limited their full growth and flowering.

In that sense, at least, Israel's history is the story of universalism's struggle to grow in somewhat unfavorable conditions. Nonetheless, the Hebrews do make some important contributions to the wider development of universalism by defining its main dimensions and directions of growth, by establishing a root system to nourish it, and by generating the means for extending and transplanting it. It was left to other religious traditions, particularly Christianity, to realize more fully those universalistic possibilities. To some extent, Christianity surely transcended Old Testament universalism theologically and ethically, but it is difficult to believe that it could overcome the complications of context and circumstance which limit the practical implementation of universal principles. In that sense, the empirical imperfections and limits of universalism we see in the Old Testament may be constitutive features of its application to human life.

Without cultivation, therefore, those seeds may not sprout at all in the rocky soil of historic societies. That universalism was able to take root and grow among the Hebrews was due primarily to the efforts of Israelite prophets, who sowed, nurtured, and protected it over the centuries. At several critical points in Israel's history, the prophets extended universalism as a way of preserving an Israelite society threatened by an overgrowth of particularism. Because the connection of ancient Judaism and universalism runs through them, we must not only analyze prophecy's role in establishing that relationship but also consider the extent to which prophecy defines it as well.

Universalism and Particularism in Ancient Judaism

At the center of Old Testament religion stand two primary organizing principles: the covenant and the promised land (Johnson 1987), each of which rests on a particularistic idea. Those principles provided the foundation on which the Israelites built their nation and elaborated the other themes considered below. But the historic uncertainty about realizing those particularistic claims created openings for and stimulated challenges from universalistic principles, even on the same ground. Eventually, the covenant became more universalistic and the promised land became a particularistic fantasy in the face of international realities.

The Covenant. God's promise to favor the Israelites in return for their allegiance and obedience helped form them into a people by setting them apart from others. Indeed, the covenant was formed originally with Abraham himself (cf. Genesis 15–18) and in perpetuity with his kin group. Over time, the circle was extended beyond kinship to the groups called tribes, but the promise was still something like a limited pact, neither available to nor applicable to everyone. Israel was formed as an elect nation, a chosen people destined for special purpose.

Their distinctiveness was not just theological, for the Israelites set themselves apart with numerous marks of election and limits on pretenders. The requirement of circumcision was most prominent among these, for it was unique and seriously discouraged adult conversion. As a virtual religious birthmark, it became "an indelible symbol of an historic covenant and membership of a chosen people" (Johnson 1987: 37). Other practices, such as the observance of the sabbath and dietary and cleanliness restrictions, also helped mark the Hebrews as an unusual, even strange, people.

Even so, the covenant contained alternate possibilities and resources which could be exploited for more universalistic ends. First, as Zeitlin (1984: 95) notes, while the covenant was made only with the Israelites, it was made with all of them rather than being reserved for a social elite or religious virtuosi. Within Israel, God's promises were given to everyone and made no distinctions among people. Second, the covenant could be construed rationally as a contract which established "ethical obligations" for both parties (Zeitlin 1984: xi). Now any one contract establishes a specific relationship, but a system of contractualism is universalistic, open to anyone who elects to strike a bargain and operating by impersonal principles, not the identity of specific persons or groups. Finally, the fact that this covenant formed a people around their relationship to God gave those who spoke for God a special status and power in Israel (Johnson 1987: 32ff.). As mediators of the covenant and interpreters of God's will, the prophets thus held a strategic position in the life of Israel and in the development of universalism.

At various points in Israel's history, prophets used their position to extend the reach of the covenant and to elaborate its universalistic possibilities. The establishment of Mosaic law, for example, marked a substantial step toward systematic contractualism in the definition of the covenant (Johnson 1987: 34). In addition, Isaiah's vision of a world at peace rests on an extension of the covenant to all nations and peoples (Zeitlin 1984: 226ff.). And over time, in such writings as Deutero-Isaiah and Ezekiel, the collective emphasis in the original covenant is challenged with an emphasis "on the individual as the bearer of faith, outside the claims of tribe, race, nation" (Johnson 1987: 76).

In principle, then, the meaning of the Israelites' covenant with God became relatively less exclusive and increasingly more inclusive. In practice however, they remained largely set apart, though somewhat less so as time went on. While there gradually evolved a kind of quasi-conversion by acceptance of the faith, ancient Israel still followed blood and birth to define membership, as exemplified in Ezra's separation of mixed marriages (Zeitlin 1984: 268-78). Even today, when conversion is institutionalized, Jews devote far less energy to proselytization than Christians, who implemented more systematically the individual, contractual principles articulated in early Judaism. And the persistent identification of Jewish religion with the Hebrew people testifies to the formidable particularism in which Judaism has been rooted from its beginnings.

The Promised Land. No other people has been so passionately attached to place as the Jews, yet few other peoples have been separated from their homeland so persistently throughout history. Every people has an affection for place, a sense of roots and rightness about land and location, but for Israel the promised land is a theological principle and ideological passion. And while their constant dispersions and sojourns throughout the world push Jews toward a more global orientation, it also intensifies their yearning for the land that God granted them originally.

Clearly the most potent element of place was God's promise to cede it to the Israelites. That promise elevated affection for the land to an entitlement, one secured by a transcendent power, not just human treasures. Furthermore, the promise was no vague general assurance that God would provide a dwelling place; it specified a particular geographic location, the land of Canaan at least (Genesis 17:8), and perhaps more (Genesis 15:18).

That promise established both a perpetual claim and a persistent interest in those Middle-Eastern lands. Because God granted it to them, the Israelites believed no other people could legitimately occupy it and they claimed rights over it even from a distance. In addition to that claim, the promised land held a compelling interest for the Hebrews because their relation to Canaan was a measure of their relationship to God. Their occupation of the land was God's fulfillment of his promise, and testified to his satisfaction with his people. Their separation from that place, on the other hand, signified a break in the covenant, usually by their own doing, but potentially also by God himself. Wherever else they might be, the promise of the land sustained the Israelite community.

Tied to the promised land even today, Judaism is grounded in a very particularistic principle. But the historic failure of that promise made the Israelites a global people and pushed them toward universalism for survival's sake. As an enclave, Israel was constantly vulnerable and often fell to outsiders. Even on the promised land, the promise only seemed to hold when Israel extended its territory or forged international ties, as in the reign of David. Outside Canaan, in their bondage and wanderings, in their captivity and exile, this peculiar people became worldly, learning to navigate and sustain themselves in alien lands. Religiously, they institutionalized the mobile God in their portable ark of the covenant, and when they were separated from the Temple (the geographical center of cultic life), they invented the prototype of the synagogue to sustain ritual and education without priests (Zeitlin 1984: 268–9).

In contrast to the covenant, which became ever more universalistic in principle but remained particularistic in its application, the particularistic principle of the promised land persisted long after the Israelites had accommodated themselves to geographic universalism in practice. Indeed, sustaining the promise provided a certain freedom and justification for worldly accommodation as an expedient to preserve them for renewing the covenant upon their return. And on strictly religious terms, prophets like Jeremiah suggested that submission to foreign powers was required as retribution for sin and a time of purification (Zeitlin 1984: 238ff.).

Monotheism. Judaism is widely celebrated for the development of monotheism, but there is still dispute over what true monotheism entails and when Israel embraced it. At the extremes, Zeitlin (1984) suggests that Israel was monotheistic from the outset while Weber (1952), following Wellhausen, concluded that monotheism was crystallized by the classical prophets. It appears reasonable to gather these diverse views around the notion that the Hebrews always worshipped a single God, but the nature and standing of that God, at least as they understood him, changed over time.

Based on Johnson's reading of Jewish history, we thus can identify at least three different versions of monotheism, which supersede one another and grow progressively more universalistic. First, the God of Abraham stands as the one God of Israel, but not of other peoples, who were attached to different gods. Consistent with Israel's own self-understanding as a peculiar people, their God was distinctly theirs, one of a multitude of particularistic gods. A second, stronger version of monotheism, which comes clearly into view with Moses and the Exodus, is the omnipotent God above gods. This is the mighty God who delivered the Israelites from Pharaoh, leads them through the wilderness to the promised land, and rules over their golden era of kings. By virtue of his omnipotence, this God transcended earthly limits and other Gods to become a much more universal presence.

The third version, what Johnson (1987: 76) describes as "pure monotheism," comes into focus with Deutero-Isaiah and the classical prophets, who conceive of their one God as the only God. Whereas the God of Moses enjoined the Israelites to place no other gods before Him, this ultimate God declared that no other gods existed. He alone created and governed the world, directing the actions not just of the Hebrews but of all other peoples as well—whether they recognized it or not. This pure monotheism emphasizes the "uni" in universal, establishing a single, common reference point around which all peoples could organize their lives on earth and to whom all would be subject.

Even on its own ground, that progression toward pure monotheism could not avoid particularistic challenges in the form of idols and pagan gods. Ancient Judaism pulsed with alternating currents of fidelity and allegiance to Yahweh and of indulgence in idolatry or deviation to the blandishments of other gods. At those critical times when idolatry and false gods threatened the covenant, Zeitlin (1984) emphasizes, prophetic voices called the people to return to Yahweh and to extend his domain. To be sure, the priests of the Yahwist cult institutionalized and sustained monotheism, but it was the prophets who pushed it toward universalism as a way of reestablishing the covenant and of extending God's claims in changing historical circumstances.

The Law. Hebrew law was a snake pit of intricate and complex regulations, which together constituted a virtually impossible regimen and served to reinforce the peculiar exclusiveness of the Israelite community. Far from abstract, most of them required very specific and concerted action to produce strictly defined outcomes, not general principles to guide action in various circumstances. Along with their ceremonial counterparts in the ritual cult practices of Temple life, these particularistic rules established and preserved group loyalties rather than ethical reflection about moral action in diverse circumstances.

The prophets took two giant steps toward the establishment of legal and moral universalism in Israel. The first, unmistakably, was the formation of Mosaic law, which reconstructed the moral life of Israel around a small number of general principles applicable to a broad spectrum of life, civil and religious. As a lawmaker and judge, Moses engineered "a mighty framework to enclose in a structure of rectitude every aspect of public and private conduct" (Johnson 1987: 27). Absolute and even-handed, Mosaic law subjected everyone to continuous moral accountability. No one was exempt, and no one could substitute for another; all were answerable at any time and in any situation.

The second step toward legal and moral universalism was taken by the classical prophets. In addition to reinforcing the idea that Israel will be judged by her moral conduct, these later prophets emphasized individual moral accountability. Love of God and knowledge of the law created a subjective moral guidance system capable of successfully applying principle to practice and gave people the motivation to do so. Failure to do so was a breach of the covenant, but now one attributable to individual spiritual failings. In its bulk, then, Old Testament law particularizes, but in principle and philosophy it comes to embody universalism by holding all individuals personally accountable to abstract rules of conduct.

Justice. Perhaps the classical prophets are best known for their thundering critique of injustice in Israel, for it dramatizes the most unambiguously universalistic theme in Old Testament religion. Simply put, the ideal of justice requires equality for all, an even distribution of goods among them; and the prophets railed at any substantial failure of that principle. Because it sets people apart from one another, some with special advantages and others with distinct disadvantages, inequality embodies particularistic distinctions. There are times when Israel achieved a rough justice, such as its early democratic egalitarianism, but it is most notable for its failures to realize that ideal in practice. Ironically, justice reached its peak when the covenant was most problematic (outside the promised land without its bounty) and broke down most completely when the nation of Israel was successfully established in the land of Canaan under the rule of David.

As elaborated in the Old Testament, the general principle of justice included four specific forms ranging from other-worldly to this-worldly, the latter being most corruptible. Religious justice was equality in the eyes of God, which actually became more certain during Hebrew history as the covenant and monotheism became more universalized. Moral or legal justice was equal application of Hebrew law, which vacillated according to the individual making judgments even after law was universalized. Political justice was the equal distribution of power, as in democracy, which was systematically undermined with establishment of a Israelite political kingdom. And economic justice was an equal distribution of wealth, which failed both in times of plenty and at the behest of power. The breakdown of justice in Israel, especially of the last two types, marked a corruption of the people which threatened their covenant with God. The prophets' call to abandon privilege for the sake of the poor struggled against powerful human and social forces, but it nonetheless established the principle of justice as a basic standard of ethics and polity.

Historicity. Judaism is an historical religion, in the sense that it entails the protection of future goals, developmental change toward their realization, and a memory of the past. The covenant with Israel not only assumed a future in which the parties were to act to fulfill their promises but literally created history by forging a new relationship between God and his people. That God himself is often described as the God of history who visits his people at different times to help or chastise them. His constancy over time sustains them through the changes they experience at specific times, and his faithfulness through their sojourn in the past is the memory which sustains them in facing the future. As the agents of historicity, what the prophets did was to remind people about their covenant history with God and either lead them forward to realize a promise or call them back from their infidelity to renew the covenant.

Within a temporal world, such historicity qualifies as universalistic because it applies to all times. The particularistic counterparts to that are unitemporal systems, human simulations of eternity which in principle recognize only a constant present without past or future, such as Egyptian religion. Such unchanging systems may recognize time and change in principle but simply get stuck in a particular time, failing to achieve or cope with historical development. From time to time, the Israelites seem to have become stuck in their cultic ways, and eventually Judaism went into an historical holding pattern waiting for the messiah. For the most part, however, ancient Judaism's historicity has been sustained by strategically timed prophetic voices.

Old Testament Universalism in Sociological Perspective

Having worked my way through those major elements of Hebrew religion and their specific links to universalism, I now draw together the threads of this argument in more systematic analytic terms. First, I summarize the meaning of universalism as it emerges in the Old Testament. Second, I consider the nature and degree of universalism in Israel as a case of partial or incomplete universalism because of its grounding and entanglement with particularism. Third, I assess the significance of Old Testament prophecy for the nature of universalism and its limits. Finally, I suggest several implications of the analysis for the possibilities of universalism in a global order.

Elaborating the Meaning of Universalism

Table 2-1 systematizes the multiple meanings of universalism and particularism which emerge from the foregoing review. Working from the rudimentary definition of universalism as an emphasis on the inclusion of all members of a class, we can now specify several sociological dimensions along which such universalistic patterns develop. As construed by Weber and Parsons, universalism was defined morally as a universalistic ethic, itself grounded in monotheism. Even as it specifies those cultural dimensions of universalism, though, the study of Hebrew religion also shows that they are buttressed by the contextual dimensions of space and time and the organizational dimensions of membership and distribution, along each of which we find a different expression of the universalist principle.

TABLE 2-1
Dimensions of Universalism and Particularism in Hebrew Religion

O.T. Religion	Dimension	Particularism	Universalism
Promised Land	Space	Local	Cosmopolitan
Historicity	Time	Unitemporal	Multitemporal
Monotheism	Meaning	Incommensurate	Shared
Law	Morality	Loyalty	General Rules
Covenant	Membership	Exclusive	Inclusive
Justice	Distribution	Unequal	Equal

The contextual significance of universalism is expressed in terms of spatial and temporal distribution. Spatial universalism means broad geographic relevance, which I have characterized as cosmopolitan. When the applicability of things is localized in one or few places, as in the theme of the promised land, we would call it particularistic. Likewise, temporal universalism means broad distribution in time, like the historicity of Hebrew religion, while its particularistic counterpart has only narrow applicability in time. For want of more elegant terms, I have described these simply as multitemporal and unitemporal, respectively.

Culturally, universalism entails distinct patterns of meaning and morality. Along the dimension of meaning, developed in Israel around the monotheistic principle, universalism refers to a unified or common system of understanding for all people(s), while particularism is characterized by diverse or incommensurate systems of meaning understandable only to a segment of people. Note that this is not merely a matter of categorical definition but of power to define and organize cognition as well. The moral dimension of universalism developed in Old Testament law, consistent with such analytic conceptions as Parsons', involves a system of abstract rules to which all individuals can be held similarly accountable across diverse situations. In contrast, particularistic morality is organized and defined around concrete loyalties, applicable only to a specific individual or group and variable according to the identity of those involved in a situation.

The organizational dimensions of universalism apply to the issues of membership as raised by the covenant, and distribution which arose from prophetic preachments on justice. Universal membership, which Lechner (1987) has analyzed in terms of solidarity, is broadly inclusive of people, while the particularistic organization of membership excludes significant portions of a population. Distribution is an issue of balance, such that an equally balanced distribution of goods (moral or material) counts as universalistic, while an unequal distribution could qualify as particularistic.

Old Testament Universalism. The identification of these various dimensions already marks a substantial achievement of Old Testament religion in establishing the meaning of universalism. Moreover, by committing their story to writing, the Hebrews provided a resource for sustaining and extending universalism, and their own commitment to and practice of universalistic principles established roots that have nourished universalism to this day.

As I have already suggested, though, their achievements were incomplete and inconsistent because of the very particularistic ground in which the seeds of universalism were planted. In some cases, there appear to be limits to Israel's capacity to embrace universalism, even in principle, without abandoning its religious heritage. Those are not necessarily limitations on universalism itself (though that is not precluded) but rather on Israel's capacity to fully incorporate universalistic traits. The central limits are established by the covenant and the promised land, which cannot be fully universalized while remaining true to Yahweh in any substantial sense. The strictest limit on inclusive membership is practical, for while the covenant can be extended quite far in principle, it would be difficult to actually incorporate large numbers of non-ethnic Jews without abandoning the idea of a chosen people. On the other hand, even the extensively practical cosmopolitanism of the Hebrews and Jews cannot underwrite a universalization of Israel's territorial ideals, for that would undermine the covenant, faith in God's power, and perhaps even the future hopes of the Jewish people. The other noticeable limits on Hebrew universalism in the actualization of universal law and justice may reflect in part the intrinsic difficulty of achieving those ideals. But they also derive from the limits imposed by the covenant and the promised land, where particularism exports localism and exclusiveness.

We also find regular differences between the development of a universalistic ideal and its actual implementation. Even in ideal terms, the Hebrews did not fully embrace universalism, but in practice, universalism is quite a problematic and incomplete achievement. Notice first that four of the six Judaic principles were initially defined and actualized in particularistic terms. In the two cases formulated more universalistically, justice and historicity, the actualization of those ideals remained problematic, especially in the case of justice. To the extent that Judaism is universalistic, that fact must thus count as an historical achievement, not a given. And as we can see, those accomplishments themselves are uneven in the degree to which they have moved into alignment with universalism.

Finally, Israel vacillates in its commitment to universalism over time, sometimes championing it, other times forsaking it. At a minimum that vacillation implies that universalism and particularism are not dichotomous variables but poles of a continuum along the various dimensions identified above. Moreover, such wavering reflects an ongoing struggle between the two over their actual implementation, with each pole exercising sufficient pull that a society's position along the continuum is rather unstable. In Hebrew religion at least, universalism is rarely secure in practice, even when it finds support in principle, for the power of Israel's particularistic origins and habits is formidable. It is possible as well that this struggle displays an inherent instability in universalism, and we can at least begin to speculate about that by looking at the role of the prophets in mediating universalism.

The Prophetic Mediation of Universalism. The connection between Judaism and universalism runs through the Hebrew prophets. Understanding their role will therefore contribute to defining and explaining that connection. Prophecy is "the charismatic proclamation/demonstration of divine claims and judgments on human life or institutions by one called to that mission" (Long 1986: 14). In contrast to priests, prophets are neither institution-builders nor administrators but revolutionaries whose charisma transcends established orders and permits them to proclaim utopian and absolutist messages of God. In some cases those messages are meant to purify a sullied principle, in others to articulate a new command or ideal. Sociologically, then, the prophet can disrupt but not order, idealize but not actualize, initiate but not complete. Prophets are thus an important social resource for connecting, or reconnecting communities with the transcendent. They gain their greatest relevance precisely when established order is uncertain, for whatever reason.

In view of those traits, it is easier to understand both the attractions and the imperfections of universalism. Universalism engages people's sentiments because it offers to reconstitute a fractured situation. Above all, Weber (1963: 59) notes, these universalizing prophets provide a "unified view of the world" against the possibility of social disintegration. On the other hand, the seeds of universalism appear to have limited potential. To the extent that it is carried by prophets, universalism is a temporary ideal that often runs against the grain and has little institutional grounding or support.

In Israel, it is important to note that prophets of all varieties almost invariably come to the fore at times of international crisis, when the Hebrew people are threatened by alien powers. Two of the most terrible of such occasions, the Egyptian bondage and the destruction of the Kingdom, called forth the most prominent universalists, first in the person of Moses and then the classical prophets. Their appearance is pivotal for the Hebrew community, not only because of the danger to Israel but also because they are connected to Israel's source of being and power, Yahweh. The danger simultaneously represents a threat to the particularistic principles on which Israel was founded and the insufficiency of that particularism. To sustain the community thus required both an affirmation and a modification of that particularism.

Prophetic universalism satisfied both requirements because it embodied particularism while advocating universalism. The prophets' charisma marked them as thoroughly unique, and as mediums for God they provided a revelation of his distinctive character. As advocates of universalism, however, they suggested not a reconstruction of Israel's faith but extensions of it sufficient both to preserve and strengthen the community among the peoples of the world. Indeed, within the limits of the known world, they were advocates of a form of "global order" built around an international federation for settling disputes (Gottwald 1964). That their most ambitious principles were not realized is to be expected in view of the prophets' utopianism and the compromises endemic to the institutions which must carry any community past its crises to everyday life.

The Possibilities of Universalism. What, then, may we conclude or suggest about the character of universalism and its social possibilities? How we answer that question depends in large measure on our orientation to the "separation thesis" propounded by Weber and Parsons. Guided by that hypothesis, the most they might say is that this examination of Old Testament religion extends and elaborates the ideal-typical meaning of universalism in the directions outlined in Table One. But the experience of the Hebrew people, while interesting in itself, would not appear especially useful to them in assessing the possibilities of universalism today, which would be defined by the manner in which our contemporaries had appropriated the idea of universalism and by their level of commitment to it.

Surely there is something to their view, for it simply restates the established principle that culture (in this case the meaning and morality of universalism which Weber and Parsons emphasize) has a life of its own independent of its formative context. At the same time, though, acknowledging the relevance of the contextual and organizational dimensions of universalism exposed in Israel's experience would seem to establish limits on such independence and open the way toward recognizing some other complications for universalism. First, recognizing those other dimensions makes universalism less pliable, more grounded in material realities and the practical considerations of social life. To some extent, therefore, it cannot be separated from its setting but is defined by it. Second, it is along those other dimensions that universalism encountered its greatest limits and became most problematic in biblical times. There is thus some warrant for balancing the separation thesis with the axiom that the Hebrew experience with universalism is in part constitutive of its character. From that perspective, we might suggest several ways that Old Testament universalism could be instructive for today.

Consider the possibility that universalism and particularism are interdependent or jointly constructed. To an extent, universalism is defined against a background of particularism, taking somewhat variable shape relative to the historically specific character of particularism, but always dependent upon it for a contrast which gives it life. More than contrast, it could even be conflict which interlocks the two tendencies, each establishing its own character by its challenge to the other. Thus, universalism may flourish by challenging particularistic prejudices or loyalties but flounder when required to build a society on its own, as we discovered in the struggle over civil rights.

More specifically, it may be that societal profiles on the various dimensions of universalism will always balance relatively strong universalistic traits with some firmly rooted particularistic features, as the Israelites did. Empirically, it could be that universalism arises from a particularistic root that nourishes and sustains its identity. If so, we might wonder about the possibility of universalism as the particularistic ground of a global order gradually diminishes. Another type of balancing act is displayed today where universalistic principles are employed to protect the particularistic integrity of diverse subcultures. Or perhaps no society can fully institutionalize universalism for some reason or another and particularism always finds a way to sustain itself or undermine universalism in practice. Whatever the reason(s), some such balance may be typical if the two tendencies are interdependent.

A third way the interdependence of universalism and particularism may find expression is in the alternating rhythms of social life. Taking a cue from the prophetic experience, universalism may be most prominent in transition periods, when communities are reconstituting themselves, while particularism becomes the habit of tranquility. But we might just as well imagine that certain types of societies, particularly modern ones, could reverse the roles, being ordered primarily by universalistic principles and challenged by particularistic ones, as we see to some extent in fundamentalist movements.

Not all the specific possibilities raised above are implicated directly in the Old Testament case, but they emerge from joining the separation thesis with the plausible hypothesis that the specific patterns of Hebrew universalism display some common traits of universalism—and particularism—in general. In so doing, we can also see the potential complications and limits of global order, which will rest just as surely on some particularistic traits as on the universalistic ones it will claim as founding principles. How that partnership is organized, and whether the inherent tension between the partners will prove destructive or energizing, will be among the most interesting questions for sociological analysis of the emerging global order.

References

Gottwald, Norman K. 1964. *All the Kingdoms of the Earth: Israelite Prophecy and International Relations in the Ancient Near East.* New York: Harper & Row.
Heschel, Abraham J. 1962. *The Prophets: An Introduction.* New York: Harper & Row.
Johnson, Paul. 1987. *A History of the Jews.* New York: Harper & Row.
Lechner, Frank. 1987. "Modernity and its Procontents: Societal Solidarity in Comparative Perspective." Paper presented at the annual meetings of the Association for the Sociology of Religion and the American Sociological Association, August, 1987, Chicago.
Lindblom, J. 1962. *Prophecy in Ancient Israel.* Philadelphia: Fortress.
Long, Theodore E. 1986. "Prophecy, Charisma and Politics: Reinterpreting the Weberian Thesis." 3–17 in *Prophetic Religions and Politics: Religion and the Political Order,* edited by J. Hadden and A. Shupe. New York: Paragon House.
Mays, James Luther and Paul J. Achtemeier (eds.). 1987. *Interpreting the Prophets.* Philadelphia: Fortress.
National Council of Churches. 1953. *The Holy Bible: Revised Standard Version.* New York: Nelson.
Parsons, Talcott. 1951. *The Social System.* New York: Free Press.
_____. 1966. *Societies: Evolutionary and Comparative Perspectives.* Englewood Cliffs, N.J.: Prentice-Hall.
Petersen, David L. (ed.). 1987. *Prophecy in Israel: Search for An Identity.* Philadelphia: Fortress.
Weber, Max. [1952] 1967. *Ancient Judaism.* Translated and edited by Hans H. Gerth and Don Martindale. New York: Free Press.
_____. [1922] 1963. *The Sociology of Religion.* Translated by Ephraim Fischoff. Boston: Beacon.
Zeitlin, Irving M. 1984. *Ancient Judaism: Biblical Criticism from Max Weber to the Present.* Cambridge: Polity Press.
Zimmerli, Walther. 1965. *The Law and the Prophets: A Study of the Meaning of the Old Testament.* Oxford: Blackwell.

3

TWO ASPECTS OF THE DEVELOPMENT OF UNIVERSALISM IN CHRISTIANITY

THE FIRST TO THE FOURTH CENTURIES

James F. Strange

SCHOLARLY STUDY OF THE MOVEMENT FROM SECT TO CHURCH in the first three centuries has proceeded with vigor since Harnack.[1] Yet, in spite of the great quantity of publications in this area, it seems unlikely that we will advance materially unless we alter our questions. It seems appropriate, therefore, to pause in our current deliberations and research to pose a new question, or perhaps an old question phrased in a new way, which is the question of the means of the movement of Christianity towards a universalist position.

Of course it is tempting to insist on a definition of universalism in order to pursue the inquiry. That is the usual course. Yet, in this case, it seems more fruitful simply to cultivate one relatively undeveloped idea and then to conjoin it with another rather better understood idea. Then we may be in a posture to speculate along lines that have yielded suggestive ideas before. That is the design of this paper.

It may be worthwhile to begin by reviewing this situation out of which Christianity emerged in our attempt to understand how this most unpromising of world religions shifted from local to universal in its self-understanding. In this analysis, then, it is imperative to remind ourselves that Christianity developed out of biblical religion, in which the wick of universalism had long burned (Eichrodt 1950: Part I, 63f., 88f.; Part II, 13f.).

For example, as others have pointed out before, may I respectfully point out that the Bible does not legislate what a good Israelite was to do in order to be acceptable to God. Rather the statement is that a person will do thus and so in order to be acceptable before God, particularly in prophetic circles. Thus Micah (6:8) can ask, "What does the Lord require of thee, oh man, but to do justice, to love mercy, and to walk humbly with thy God" (Eichrodt 1950: Part I, 51f.; Heschel 1962).

It also happens to be the case, as Neusner (1972: xxi) has reminded us, that post-biblical Judaism took precisely the same broad view. Nowhere in the post-biblical literature of the first three centuries C.E. is there an insistence that a Jew must do thus and so, only that one must do thus and so.

Therefore, it is no surprise that Christianity should embrace universal ideas and elements from the very beginning. It was the founder of Christianity, namely, Jesus of Nazareth, whom tradition credits with transmitting and transmuting this stance so visible in Isaiah, Micah, and other prophets in what we have come to call the Sermon on the Mount. Here the gospels record that he taught, "Blessed are the meek..." and so forth, giving articulation to a universalist position himself.[2]

However, what were the other elements in the local and regional culture that supported a movement toward universalism? The answers to this question have been obvious for at least five generations. First, Jewish culture was itself moving in this direction, specifically in the opinions of the house of Hillel (Urbach 1981). Second, Greek culture as early as the fifth century B.C.E. had articulated the position that Zeus was he who was known by many names (e.g., in Cleanthes, "Hymn to Zeus"). Perhaps the real denouement of this movement can be seen in the self-conscious creation of the god of Serapis in Alexandria by committee.[3] Third, Roman culture was officially syncretistic, sometimes recognized as a form of political universalism (Nock 1972: v. II, 551–58).

Another element in Greek culture, but especially in Roman culture, that aided and abetted the movement toward universalism, was the official policy of urbanization in the Roman empire[4] (Avi-Yonah 1977). It was the city where diverse populations had to develop at least a rudimentary form of tolerance in order to survive. And survive these populations did, for Romans founded their multilingual and multinational cities as far afield as Britain and Syria (Rykwert 1976: 84).

At this juncture, it is important to declare and underscore our crucial, first point, namely, that Christianity at its very beginnings emerged in an urban environment, not in the romantic, peasant villages of Ernst Renan's *Life of Jesus* (1863). In other words, Galilee was itself urban.

Scholars have had access to the archaeological and literary evidence for this assertion for nearly a century. Recent excavations and surveys have added to that evidence and reinforced the portrait of a Galilee with a rural infrastructure, but with a strong overlay of urbanism. For example, in recent years excavations at Tiberias and at Hammath-Tiberias have confirmed them as cities (Levine 1981: 63–69, 157–59; Shanks 1979: 119–20; *Excavations and Surveys in Israel 1982* 1984: 110; *Excavations and Surveys in Israel 1983* 1984: 103; Dothan 1983). Furthermore, a survey at the probable site of the city of Bethsaida suggests that our old estimates of its size were far too small (Urman 1985: 120–21). Recent excavations by the author and by the Duke University/Hebrew University expedition at Sepphoris in the virtual geographic center of lower Galilee have furnished even more telling data (Strange and Longstaff 1984a, 1984b, 1985, 1986; Meyers, Netzer, and Meyers 1986). Also within the past ten years scholars from the Biblicum Franciscanum in Jerusalem have conducted important archaeological excavations at Magdala within the Franciscan property there (Corbo 1974). Other excavations in the port city of Acco-Ptolemais have provided us with notable information (Dothan 1976; Kindler 1978; Raban 1983).

Consider Josephus and the gospels. According to the New Testament, three of Jesus' disciples were from Bethsaida in Gaulanitis, a city, not a village or a small town (John 1:44). According to Josephus one of the sons of Herod the Great, Herod Philip, founded Bethsaida just across the Jordan from Galilee and on the northeast shores of the Sea of Galilee. He named it Julias in honor of the daughter of Augustus, (*Jewish Wars*: II, 168). This was a city imposing enough that Herod Philip was himself buried there in a monument that he had commissioned (*Antiquities*: XVIII, 108; Schuerer 1979: 171–72).

On the western shore of the same lake stood the large cities of Tiberias and Magdala, both capitals of monarchies (*Jewish Wars*, II, xiii–2), the latter evidently the home city of Mary Magdalene. Magdala was large enough to have a stadium, fortifications, a synagogue, and an aqueduct (*Jewish Wars*: II, 21, 3—599). This suggests that Magdala, or Taricheae as it was otherwise known, was an imposing, walled city (Strange 1976: 561). Tiberius, hardly five Roman miles south of Magdala, was also a walled city. It functioned as an important regional, urban center with two grain markets, a palace of Herod Antipas, a stadium, and its own aqueduct. Tiberias exercised the right to mint its own coins. Tiberius controlled the eastern half of lower Galilee as its city territory (*Antiquities*: XVIII, 2, 3—36–38; *Jewish Wars*: II, 9.1–168); (Schuerer 1979: 178–83).

Furthermore, just as Magdala and Tiberius (and perhaps Bethsaida) bracketed Galilee on the east, so the city of Ptolemais-Acco bracketed Galilee on the Mediterranean coast. This was a booming port city with a long Canaanite and Hellenistic past. Ptolemais-Acco controlled the entire Mediterranean coast of Galilee by the first century C.E. (Avi-Yonah 1976: 89).

Even the tiny village of Nazareth—and the full impact of this point has not yet been fully realized—did not lie outside an urban territory. Hardly six Roman miles north of Nazareth, or about one and one-half hour's walk, stood the great, walled city of Sepphoris, the first capital of Galilee under Herod Antipas, but also a major city of his father, Herod the Great. Nazareth lay within the city territory of Sepphoris and relied upon Sepphoris for its court system, security, and government services. Sepphoris minted its own coinage and had its own wet and dry measures (Ben-David 1974: 341). Sepphoris had a theatre, the regional law courts, and the regional markets. It was a great Jewish intellectual center, certainly from the Second Jewish Revolt of 135 C.E. and probably earlier (Schuerer 1979: 172–76; Tsuk 1987).

In order to form a picture of this urban center within which Nazareth lay, let us turn to a bit of its Roman history. Sepphoris certainly was a walled city as early as 103 B.C.E., for it endured a siege on the part of Ptolemy Lathyrus, king of Cyprus, who was at war with Alexander Yannai, king of Judea (*Antiquities*: XIII, 12.5). There is additional historical information about the city only in 55 B.C.E., when Aulus Gabinius, Proconsul in Syria, recognized *de facto* the strategic importance of Sepphoris and located one of the five Roman Councils of Judea there, and the only one for Galilee (*Antiquities*: XV, 5.4—91; *Jewish Wars*: 1.8.5—170). Sixteen years later Herod the Great seized Sepphoris during the civil war (*Antiquities*: XIV, 15.4; *Jewish Wars*: 1.16.2). Herod retained the city as his northern headquarters for the remainder of his reign, which gave the city a royal patron.

Sepphoris presumably served Herod well, but not necessarily willingly. Judah ben Hezekiah commanded the Sepphoreans in revolt immediately upon the death of Herod the Great shortly before Passover in 4 B.C.E. The Roman governor of Syria, Varus, reacted in characteristic Roman fashion, swiftly and with deadly force. He marched to Sepphoris with both of his Roman legions and with Nabatean auxiliary troops. He sacked Sepphoris, reduced the city to ashes, and sold its inhabitants as slaves (*Antiquities*: XVII, 10.9—271; *Jewish Wars*: II, 5.1).

Herod Antipas inherited the destroyed city from his father, Herod the Great. He now had the opportunity to refound and rebuild this city exactly as he wished. He had grown up in Rome as a Roman, not in Galilee as a Jewish prince (*Antiquities*: XVII, 1.3). Antipas employed craftsmen from the villages and cities all over Galilee. Josephus would hail the result of his refounding of Sepphoris as the "ornament of all Galilee" and "the strongest city in Galilee" (*Antiquities*: XVIII, 27; *Jewish Wars*: II, 511).

The works of Herod Antipas at Sepphoris included a theatre that seated 4,000[5] (or he rebuilt his father's theatre), his palace, and an upper and lower city, each with markets. The upper city or citadel was predominantly Jewish by the time of the Second Revolt and surely earlier (*b. Yoma* 11a). A higharch commanded the "old fort" (always called by the Latin plural "*castra*" by the rabbis *m. Arakin* 9.6). There was an archive building (*m. Kidd.* 4.6), and Josephus relates that Rome ordered the archives brought from Tiberius to Sepphoris in the days of Nero (*Life* 9—38). The Romans later replaced the "old archives" with the "new archives" (Miller 1984). Antipas elevated the city to his capital (*Antiquities*: XVIII, 2.1).

Other information about this Roman provincial city of mixed population also comes from the rabbis of the first to the third centuries C.E. They knew the upper and lower markets (*b. Erub.* 5b), a fortified upper city or citadel, a colonnaded street in the middle of the city (*j. Ketub.* I.25d), a city wall (*b. Bab. Bat.* 7b–8a), a city gate (*Eccl. Rab.* 3.2 par. 3), many spice shops (*Baraita Baba Batra* 75a), inns, synagogues, schools or academies (*j Pea* 20b, 27–31), private dwellings with upper stories and sometimes with a Roman-style dining room or "triclinium" (*Lev. Rab.* 16.2), and "the wheels of Sepphoris," evidently referring to water wheels that lifted water to the upper city or citadel (*Eccl. Rab.* 12.6 par. I). There was a flowing spring below the city (*m. Ket.* 1.10).

According to the coins of Sepphoris of the second century, the city contained a temple dedicated to the Capitoline Triad of Jupiter, Juno, and Minerva. These coins also bear the Greek name of the city,

Diocaesarea. Another coin of Antoninus shows a temple to Zeus. Yet a third coin may present a temple of Serapis or a city goddess[6] (Hill 1965: xi–xiii, 1–4, and pl. I.1–7; Meshorer c1985).

The rabbis asserted that the territory of Sepphoris extended sixteen miles in every direction and flowed with milk and honey (*b. Ket.* 111b; *b. Meg.* 6a). Water ran down to the city on two aqueducts from springs at Abel three miles to the east (*m. Erub.* 8.7). The aqueducts first emptied into a huge underground reservoir nearly 165 m. long that was hewn out of the bedrock about one Roman mile east of Sepphoris. Stadia with Roman towers and a "Syrian monument" marked the eighteen miles of road from Tiberius to Sepphoris (*j. Erub.* 6.31b).

The destruction of Sepphoris by Varus and its rebuilding by Antipas marked its transition from a Hellenistic city to a loyalist Roman city. The rabbis of the Common Era remembered the "old government" of Sepphoris (*m. Kid.* 4.5). After this period many Latin and Greek names appear in the record, including the names of Jews (*Sifre Dt.* 13; *Mid. Tannaim* 7.2; *t. Bab. Metzia* 3.11). Therefore the city was certainly of Jewish and Gentile population.

Pharisaic families do not appear in Sepphoris in Jewish literature of the first century. Instead we find references to families with some sort of priestly connection or who discharged priestly duties. Sepphoris was therefore surely a priestly city. For example, Jose ben Illem of Sepphoris substituted for the High Priest Matthias in Jerusalem on the Day of Atonement. A certain Arsela of Sepphoris led the scapegoat from the Temple into the desert on the Day of Atonement (*m. Yomah* 6.5). It is even important to know that a certain priest of Sepphoris bore the sobriquet "ben haachin" because of his greed (*t. Sota* 13.8). Finally we find praise for the women of Sepphoris who were exceptionally faithful in attending the temple (*y. Ber.* 3 6b; *t. Taan.* 1 end: *y. Yoma* 6.43c; *y. Maas. Sh.* 5.56a). In this regard it is important that, after 70 C.E. and the destruction of the Second Temple, the second priestly course of Jedaiah settled at Sepphoris (*Mishmarot* 2).

Ya'akov Meshorer has recently found that Sepphoris honored Vespasian on its coins a full year before he was proclaimed emperor. This event strongly suggests that Sepphoris was fully Roman, even if its citizens were fully Jewish. Furthermore, that the city honored Vespasian is evidence that the city did not become Romanized only after the first revolt[7] (Meshorer 1979).

Furthermore, Meshorer has discovered that coins of the city of Sepphoris under Caracella (212–217 C.E.) seem to presuppose a treaty of peace between the city council of Sepphoris and the Roman Senate. If so, then this city continued to have a unique relationship with Rome that was likely formative for the whole of Galilee[8] (Meshorer 1979: 169).

Therefore, Nazareth and other villages of lower Galilee lay immediately within and participated directly in the urban culture of the Roman empire. These villages could not and did not escape Rome's policy of urbanization. It is therefore useful to remind ourselves that Roman provincial cities had become focal points of the local and regional culture with a strong overlay of the dominant Greco-Roman culture. Or, to put it the other way around, we may regard Roman provincial cities as veritable concentrations of Roman culture and ideas laid over the local customs and laws (Coulanges 1956: 360–88; Jones 1971: xiii–xiv). Therefore, these Galilean cities functioned as the same regional centers of Roman culture[9] (Goodman 1983: 135–54). A second important point is that these regional centers therefore became vehicles for the preservation and transmission of Roman culture, Roman public policy values, and symbols of Roman power, such as Roman architecture[10] (Avi-Yonah 1977: 127–29; Jones 1931).

Those who use central place theory and other kinds of network theory have pointed out that a city, town, or village comprises a major node in a trade and communication network[11] (Hodder and Orton 1976: 68–71). Therefore, to the extent that Christianity threw in its lot with the urban centers of the Roman empire, it had placed itself in an optimal communication setting. St. Paul is, of course, the most signal example of one whose communication strategy took him from city to city.

However, there is no guarantee that Paul's or any other Christian preacher's participation in the informal, Roman communication network would ensure that his religion would develop into a universal movement, one adaptable to virtually any sub-culture of the Roman empire. Other factors were at work.

The ideas of earliest Christianity had to have certain characteristics in order to survive within the network. These are surely traits compatible with the dominant culture of Rome. First, the ideas that would survive had to be transportable. Therefore, it would have been quite impossible for Christianity to have remained a religion that simply identified itself with a certain land, with a local god, with a certain people, or with a specific social pattern (Snyder 1985: 1–2). These attributes of primitive Christianity, had they remained permanent, would have effectively blocked survival of these ideas after transmission throughout the network of Roman urban centers.

Earliest Christianity in general articulated itself in broader categories. The Didache, on the other hand, preserves the self-expression of a form of rural Christianity that apparently did not survive (Theisen 1977).

Second, the Christian movement, later the Christian church, had to tell its story in the specific linguistic medium of the eastern urban empire, or Hellenistic Greek. The importance of Greek as the universal medium may be exaggerated, but it is difficult to understand how it could be. The surprise may be how much and how early Christianity took to the other imperial language, namely Latin, in the western empire[12] (Snyder 1985: 169–70). Note that other forms of Christianity are identified by their linguistic medium, namely Syriac, Armenian, Coptic, and Georgian Christianity, to mention only those for whom we have material evidence in Palestine. These forms of Christianity lingered on as regional, even local, surely at least partially because they did not continue in the prime linguistic media of the Roman empire and because of their ethnic specificity.

Third, the basic ideas of earliest Christianity had to become universal in some fundamental sense. That is, they already must exist in universal terms at Christianity's inception, or there must already have existed a ready, similar idea in the receiving culture (Nock 1972: 74–91). This universalism is part of what makes these ideas transportable, as discussed earlier. To be more specific, it is not enough that universal elements were present among the basic ideas, the ideas themselves must be universal. This is true for ideas like atonement, inheritance, and redemption, not to mention sacrifice, resurrection, and "son of God."[13] Since these ideas come to expression in the earliest strata of Christian literature, but appear in philosophical form in Justin Martyr, Athenagoras, and Minusius Felix, they evidently met that requirement, though surely in varying degrees (Windelband 1956: 352–65).

Therefore, it seems clear that earliest Christianity had two elements that seemed to assure its eventual rise as a religion that championed a wide, if not global, order. By the fourth century the third element emerged that pushed Christianity forward as a political element to be reckoned with. This was royal patronage (Grant 1978: 13–43).

With the identification of the new religion as the emperor's own, the stage was finally set, the foundation finally laid. Now it was only a question of time before this new, royally sanctioned religion, borne forward on Roman urban culture, would continue to take root in the local, ethnic cultures of the Roman empire and beyond. That stage is not yet over.

Notes

1. For a convenient summary of recent research see Markus (1980).
2. For the contrary position cf. Albright and Mann (1971), 45ff.; on the role of Paul in the universalization of Christianity, see, e.g., Nock (1972: 69–74).
3. Prumm (1954: 272–75) stresses that Isis, Serapis, and Harpocrates form a *Gotterdreiheit*. Tinh (1982: 10–17) emphasizes that the spread of the worship of Isis and Serapis was mainly by private initiative.
4. On the Greek *polis* as the dominating force of human life at the time, see Detienne (1975: 49–78). The role of ancient Greek educational systems in Roman cities in forming the Christian idea of faith appears in detail in Kinneavy (1987).
5. Waterman (1937: 6–12) estimated that the theatre sat 3,000, but it seems closer to 4,000, following his drawing and allowing 60 cm. per person.
6. An alternative interpretation of pagan divinities on coins as merely conventional symbols of political loyalty that cannot be used to prove the presence of temples is in Klimowsky (1974: 88).
7. Legends of the coins in question read as follows: Obv: LDI NERONO KLAUDIOU KAISAROS or "Year 14 (A.D. 68) of Nero Claudius Caesar." Obv. EPI OUESPASIANOU EIRENOPOLI NERONIAS SEPPHOR [IS] or "In Honor of Vespasian" or "In the time of Vespasian, City of Peace, Neronias." Hendin (1976: 100) has interpreted the EPI OYESPASIANOU series in the sense of "By Vespasian," that is, as issued by Vespasian as governor. Even if this were so, it would not challenge the point of Sepphoris as a loyal Roman city.
8. Legends of the coins in question read DIOKAISARIAS IERAS ASULOU AUTONOMOU PISTES [PHILIA] SUMMACHIA IERAS BOULES SUGKLETOU KAI DEMOU ROMAION or "Diokaisaria the Holy, City of Shelter, Autonomous, Loyal, [a treaty of] Friendship and Alliance between the Holy Council and the Senate of the Roman People."
9. A similar point from the perspective of Greco-Roman educational systems appears in Kinneavy (1987: 68–70) on Tiberias and Sepphoris.
10. For possible influence of the urban center of Sepphoris on Jesus' proclamation see Batey (1984).
11. On communication network theory see Rogers and Kincaid (1981), especially Chapter 6 on predicting social change from village connectedness and Chapter 7 on spacial determinants in network links.
12. See Kinneavy (1987) for a convenient summary of the question of the extent of Greek in Roman Palestine.
13. This is true of the earlier, popular ideas with which Christianity expressed itself, such as Jesus as miracle worker, Jesus as Philosopher, alienation-deliverance, and peace. See Snyder (1985: 163–65) and Nock (1972).

References

Albright, W.F. and C.S. Mann. 1971. *Matthew: A New Translation and Commentary*. The Anchor Bible. Garden City: Doubleday.

Avi-Yonah, Michael. 1976. *Gazetteer of Roman Palestine*. Qedem: Monographs of the Institute of Archaeology, The Hebrew University of Jerusalem, 5. Jerusalem: The Hebrew University of Jerusalem.

———. 1977. *The Holy Land from the Persian to the Arab Conquest (536 B.C. to A.D. 640): A Historical Geography*. Grand Rapids: Baker Book House.

Batey, Richard A. 1984. "Jesus and the Theatre." *New Testament Studies* 30:563–74.

Ben-David, Arye. 1974. *Talmudische Okonomie: Die Wirtschaft des judischen Palastina zur Zeit der Mischna und des Talmud*, vol. 1. Hildesheim: Georg Olms Verlag.

Corbo, Virgilio C. 1974. "Scavi Archeologici a Magdala (1971–1973)." *Studii Biblici Franciscani, Liber Annuus* XXIV:1–37.

Coulanges, Fustel de. [1956]. *The Ancient City: A Classic Study of the Religious and Civil Institutions of Ancient Greece and Rome*. Garden City: Doubleday.

Detienne, Marcel. 1975. "Les chemins de la deviance: Orphisme, Dionysisme et Pythagorisme," in [*Atti del Quattordicesimo*] *Convengno di Studi sulla Magna Grecia: Orfismo in Magna Grecia*. Naples: Arte Tipografica.

Dothan, Moshe. 1976. "Akko: Interim Excavation Report First Season, 1973/4." *Bulletin of the American Schools of Oriental Research* 224:1–48.

———. 1983. *Hammath-Tiberias: Early Synagogues and the Hellenistic and Roman Remains*. Series: Ancient Synagogue Studies. Jerusalem: Israel Exploration Society, University of Haifa, and the Department of Antiquities and Museums.

Eichrodt, Walther. 1950. *Theologie des Alten Testaments*, Parts I and II. Berlin: Evangelische Verlagsanstalt.

Excavations and Surveys in Israel 1982. 1984. vol. 1: English Edition of *Hadashot Arkheologiyot*, Archaeological Newsletter of the Israel Department of Antiquities and Museums, Numbers 78–81. Jerusalem: Israel Department of Antiquities and Museums.

Excavations and Surveys in Israel 1983. 1984. vol. 2: English Edition of *Hadashot Arkheologiyot*, Archaeological Newsletter of the Israel Department of Antiquities and Museums, Numbers 82–83. Jerusalem: Israel Department of Antiquities and Museums.

Goodman, Martin. 1983. *State and Society in Roman Galilee, A.D. 132–212*. Series: Oxford Centre for Postgraduate Hebrew Studies. Totowa, New Jersey: Rowman & Allanheld.

Grant, Robert M. 1978. *Early Christianity and Society: Seven Studies*. London: Collins.

Heschel, Abraham J. 1962. *The Prophets: An Introduction*. New York: Harper & Row.

Hill, George Francis. 1965. *Catalogue of the Greek Coins of Palestine (Galilee, Samaria, and Judaea)*. Bolgona: A. Forni.

Hendin, David. 1976. *Guide to Ancient Jewish Coins*. New York: Attic Books.

Hodder, Ian and Clive Orton. 1976. *Spatial Analysis in Archaeology*. Series: New Studies in Archaeology I. Cambridge: Cambridge University Press.

Jones, A.H.M. 1931. "Urbanization of Palestine." *Journal of Roman Studies* 21:78–85, with one map.

———. 1971. *The Cities of the Eastern Roman Provinces*, revised by M. Avi-Yonah, *et al.* Oxford: Clarendon.

Kindler, Arie. 1978. "Akko, A City of Many Names." *Bulletin of the American Schools of Oriental Research* 231-51, 252-55.

Kinneavy, James L. 1987. *Greek Rhetorical Origins of Christian Faith: An Inquiry.* New York and Oxford: Oxford University Press.

Klimowsky, Ernest W. 1974. *On Ancient Palestinian and Other Coins: Their Symbolism and Metrology.* Series: Numismatic Studies and Research, vol. VII. Tel Aviv: Israel Numismatic Society.

Levine, Lee I. (ed.). 1981. *Ancient Synagogues Revealed.* Jerusalem: The Israel Exploration Society.

Markus, R.A. 1980. "The Problem of Self-Definition: From Sect to Church." 1-15 in *Jewish and Christian Self-Definition*, vol. 1: *The Shaping of Christianity in the Second and third Centuries*, edited by E.P. Sanders. Philadelphia: Fortress Press.

Meshorer, Ya'akov. 1979. "Sepphoris and Rome." 159-71 in *Greek Numismatics and Archaeology: Essays in Honor of Margaret Thompson*, edited by O. Morkholm and N.M. Waggoner. Belgium: Cultura Press.

———. c1985. *City of Coins of Eretz-Israel and the Decapolis in the Roman Period.* Jerusalem: Israel Museum.

Meyers, Eric M., Ehud Netzer, and Carol L. Meyers. 1986. "Sepphoris—'Ornament of All Galilee.'" *Biblical Archaeologist* 49, 1:4-19.

Miller, Stewart. 1984. *Studies in the History and Tradition of Sepphoris.* Series: Studies in Judaism in Late Antiquity 37. Leiden: E.J. Brill.

Neusner, Jacob. 1972. *Invitation to the Talmud: A Teaching Book.* New York: Harper & Row.

Nock, Arthur Darby. 1972. *Essays on Religion and the Ancient World*, selected and edited by Zeph Steward, 2 vols. Cambridge: Harvard University Press.

Prumm, Karl. 1954. *Religionsgeschischtliches Handbuch fur den Raum der Altchristlichen Umwelt.* Rome: Papstliches Bibelinstitut.

Raban, Avner. 1983. "The Biblical Port of Akko on Israel's Coast." *Archaeology* 36, 1:60-61.

Rogers, Everett M. and D. Lawrence Kincaid. 1981. *Communication Networks: Toward a New Paradigm for Research.* New York: The Free Press.

Rykwert, Joseph. 1976. *The Idea of a Town: The Anthropology of Urban Form in Rome, Italy, and the Ancient World.* Princeton: Princeton University Press.

Schuerer, Emil. 1979. *The History of the Jewish People in the Age of Jesus Christ (175 B.C.-A.D. 135)*, vol. II. A new English version revised and edited by Geza Vermes, Fergus Millar and Matthew Black. Edinburgh: T. & T. Clark.

Shanks, Hershel. 1979. *Judaism in Stone: The Archaeology of Ancient Synagogues.* New York: Harper & Row.

Snyder, Graydon F. 1985. *Ante Pacem: Archaeological Evidence of Church Life Before Constantine.* Macon: Mercer University Press.

Strange, James F. 1976. "Magdala." 561 in *Interpreters' Dictionary of the Bible, Supplementary Volume.* Nashville: Abingdon Press.

Strange, James F. and T.R.W. Longstaff. 1984a. "Sepphoris (Sippori), 1983," Notes and News. *Israel Exploration Journal* 34:51-52.

———. 1984b. "Sepphoris (Sippori)—Survey, 1984," Notes and News. *Israel Exploration Journal* 34:269-70.

———. 1985. "Sepphoris (Sippori) 1985 (II)," Notes and News. *Israel Exploration Journal* 35:297-99.

———. 1986. "Sepphoris (Sippori) 1986," Notes and News. *Israel Exploration Journal* 37.
Theisen, Gerd. 1977. *Sociology of Early Palestinian Christianity*. Philadelphia: Fortress Press.
Tinh, Tran tam. 1982. "Sarapis and Isis." In *Jewish and Christian Self-Definition*, vol. 3: *Self-Definition in the Greco-Roman World*, edited by Ben F. Meyer and E.P. Sanders. Philadelphia: Fortress Press.
Tsuk, Tsvika. 1987. *Sepphoris and Its Site*. Tel-Aviv: Society for the Preservation of Nature (Hebrew).
Urbach, Ephraim E. 1981. "Self-Isolation or Self-Affirmation in Judaism in the First Three Centuries: Theory and Practice." 269–98 in *Jewish and Christian Self-Definition*, vol. 2: *Aspects of Judaism in the Greco-Roman Period*, edited by E.P. Sanders, et al. Philadelphia: Fortress Press.
Urman, Dan. 1985. *The Golan: A Profile of a Region During the Roman and Byzantine Periods*. BAR International Series 269. Oxford: British Archaeological Reports.
Waterman, Leroy, et al. 1937. *Preliminary Report of the University of Michigan Excavations at Sepphoris, Palestine, in 1931*. Ann Arbor: University of Michigan Press.
Windelband, Wilhelm. 1956. *History of Ancient Philosophy*. New York: Dover.

4

THE REFORMATION, INDIVIDUALISM, AND THE QUEST FOR GLOBAL ORDER

William R. Garrett

AGAINST THE BACKDROP OF NUMEROUS INTERPRETATIONS of the Reformation, the argument developed in this essay proposes that the organizational fragmentation and legitimation of individualism achieved by Protestant groups ultimately fostered a new quest for universal order among the left-wing sectarians of the English Reformation. Specifically, these groups—including the Baptists, Levellers, Diggers, and the like (especially those with millennial expectations)—pioneered in the construction of a theory of god-given, unalienable human rights which included liberty of conscience and a whole succession of other legal prerogatives. This line of argument logically led toward the conclusion that all persons by virtue of their very humanity participated in a universal order and that in this order they enjoyed rights by divine decree which no political order could legitimately infringe upon or abrogate.

Although these claims were not sustainable politically in the muddled aftermath of the English Civil War, they did attain institutionalization when the new nation of the United States was formed. The paper concludes with several questions pertaining to the cultural credibility of the human rights perspective in a time when the emerging global culture encompasses a wide variety of religious, political, and economic structures and processes.

Countervailing Interpretations of the Reformation

The Reformation and Counter-Reformation have attracted scholarly attention from theologians, historians, and social scientists on a scale almost unmatched by other events in the course of Western civilization. From these sundry and erudite research ventures, we know with a great deal more accuracy now what transpired empirically across the continent of Europe with respect to the leading participants of both Protestant and Catholic communions. Yet all this has failed to silence the debates over what caused the Reformation and what were its most enduring consequences. Contemporary reinterpretations must reckon perforce with a diverse array of explanatory claims, each alleging with greater or lesser degrees of elegance to have unsealed the hidden mysteries of this salient event that irrevocably sundered the organizational unity of the church.

Perhaps the most famous attempt to delineate one long range consequence of the Reformation from a sociological perspective was Weber's, *The Protestant Ethic and the Spirit of Capitalism* (1958). His nuanced argument relative to the role of Calvinism in stimulating the take-off of modern rational capitalism as a latent function of the peculiar mentality framed by the traits of the Protestant ethic immediately precipitated a heated controversy (Winckelmann 1972) which continues to rage over three-quarters of a century later (Zaret 1985; Collins 1986). Although Felix Rachfahl ([1910] 1972: 216) characterized the Protestant Ethic thesis as a *"kollektivarbeit"* jointly produced by Weber and Troeltsch, a characterization which considerably irritated Weber ([1910] 1972) and called forth a clarification from Troeltsch ([1910] 1972: 188–192), the fact remained that these two Heidelberg colleagues ultimately stood some distance apart in their relative assessment of the long term significance of the Reformation. Certainly, Troeltsch (1931: 644–650; 915–918) concurred with Weber that the development of "inner worldly" asceticism within a "calling" released energies that directly furthered capitalist economic activity, but he (1958: 43–57) drove a sharp wedge between early Protestantism of church-type Lutheranism and Calvinism and modern Protestantism with its Baptist, Quaker, and spiritualistic sects. Indeed, the distinctive traits of neo-Protestantism derived more from the "external onslaught of modern secular culture" than from inherently religious forces, in Troeltsch's view (Morgan 1977: 44).

Meanwhile, another of Weber's economic contemporaries, Werner Sombart ([1911] 1962) challenged the Protestant Ethic thesis from a quite different vantage point. Sombart argued that the rationalization which Weber had discerned as crucial to the modern capitalist enterprise derived not from Protestantism, but from an older orientation toward the world-carried by the religious tradition of Judaism. Sombart's ([1911] 1962: 187) qualification of Weber was not so much a refutation of the Puritan-capitalist connection as it was a contention that the influence of Judaism was at once older, more pervasive, and consequently far more significant. Thus, among Weber, Troeltsch, and Sombart, three quite varied perspectives on the Reformation and the influence of Protestantism on modern economic and social development are critically explicated.

Working within the tradition of Weber and Troeltsch, Talcott Parsons (1967: 402–412) proffers yet another interpretation of the salient contribution of Reformation movements with respect to the advent of modernity. Accentuating the Lutheran-Calvinistic notions of *sola fide*, personal regeneration, the priesthood of believers, and the concept of vocation as a vehicle for expressing one's ethical responsibility to God, Parsons (1967: 402) adduced the conclusion that the essential change introduced by the reformation was the religious "enfranchisement" of the individual. By this he meant that Protestantism emancipated the self from corporate church structures insofar as saving grace was concerned and thereby set the individual in direct relation to God. The latent effect of this substantive religious change was to bequeath a sense of grandeur, dignity, and sanctity to the individual personality which traditional society of the high middle ages could never have comprehended, even among Renaissance theorists. To be sure, individualism would be greatly intensified during the later denominational phase (which roughly corresponds to Troeltsch's construct of modern Protestantism), but the groundwork was clearly laid, to Parson's mind, during the age of the Reformation.

An almost diametrically opposed point of view arises from the neo-Marxist historiography of Braudel ([1979] 1986, II) and the world-systems theory of Wallerstein (1979). Braudel confesses to a certain "allergic" reaction to the "confusing method of argumentation" developed by Weber and proposes instead that the innovative instruments of capitalism—such as double-entry book-keeping, bills of exchange, endorsements, discounting, stock exchanges, and the like—were all developed in southern Europe well before the Reformation. Indeed, the reformation succeeded in converting persons to Protestantism, according to Braudel (1986: II, 566–570), outside the geographical area once dominated by the Roman empire, that is to say, in regions less civilized, urbanized, and internally developed—with the exception, of course, of the episodic Roman occupation of Britain (although Christopher Hill [1986: 140] finds it difficult to understand how one can brush aside five hundred years of Roman occupation as episodic). Nonetheless, the materialist interpretation propounded by Braudel views the Reformation as a movement relegated to the periphery of economic culture during the sixteenth century, with the effect that Reformation ideology became a kind of rallying point among lesser-developed societies.

Despite Braudel's recourse to a geographic argument relative to the Reformation debate, the major dimension along which he typically analyzed development was temporal, given his professional status as a historian. Wallerstein, by contrast, predicates his analytical interpretation on the dimension of space (see Braudel's [1986: III, 69–70] gentle criticism on this score). Not only has Wallerstein been concerned with tracing out the process by which the whole world has been integrated into an international capitalist system, but he has also sought to clarify the shifting "centers" in this world economy and their relation to a multitude of peripheral regions. "Capitalism has been developed," he (1979: 140) declares, "by the extension in space of its basic framework and within that by the progressive 'mechanization' of productive activity." The argument against Weber, from this point of view, is that he pinpoints the transition to capitalism too narrowly. Such a massive social transformation as that occasioned by the growth of the capitalist world system simply cannot be so neatly confined, in Wallerstein's judgment, to those geographical, ideological, and temporal forces affiliated with Puritanism. Weber's failing was to select one fragment of the transformation process and mistake it for the total picture.

A final challenge to the Weber thesis worth considering within the perimeters of those concerns addressed in this brief essay bears somewhat on the Wallersteinian notion of the development of the capitalist world-economy, but then veers in a decidedly different direction. We have in mind Randall Collins' (1983) attempt to locate the source of modern rational capitalism in a religious movement predating the Reformation by some four hundred years or so. Succinctly put, Collins maintains that the monastic orders coming to prominence in Roman Catholicism between 1100 and 1450 pioneered in the development of rational, capitalist agrarian practices and, given the strategic linkages among houses of the same order, they could readily shift labor, capital, or commodities to take advantage of market forces or economic needs. Accordingly, it was in the monasteries where rational technology, the entrepreneurial organization of capital, free labor, and mass commodity markets first came into prominence. And it was from this source that the foundation was laid and the model perfected for modern capitalist expansion.[1]

Reconciling these divergent points of view—and, indeed, merely subjecting each one to critical evaluation—cannot be undertaken in this brief space. The more limited aim to the survey above has been to demonstrate that the significance of Protestantism relative to the attainment of a global order is very much in dispute. Weber's provocative essay on the Protestant Ethic assigned a crucial role to the Calvinistic wing of the Reformation insofar as it triggered not only a rationalization of economic conduct, but also of law, art, politics, and secular culture generally. Sombart and Collins countered by crediting other religious communities with capitalist innovations, namely, Judaism and monastic Catholicism, respectively. Braudel and Wallerstein downplayed religious factors in the emergence of the capitalist world-system by opting for neo-Marxist explanations that stressed the inherent, expansive character of capitalism as a social system. And finally, Troeltsch and Parsons, each in their own way, agreed and modified the original Weberian argument. Parsons accentuated the legitimation of individualism which flowed from the Reformation controversy, while Troeltsch remained convinced that the modern world was less a consequence of early Protestantism than of secular forces arising out of the Renaissance, secular forces with which later Protestantism had to effect some sort of compromise.

Early Protestantism and the Rise of Religious Tolerance

The veritable panoply of socio-historical analyses for understanding the Reformation provides a contemporary interpreter with a wide open field for constructing a recrudescent model for indicating the globalizing influence of certain patterns arising from Protestant sources. The thesis to be explored in this writing takes its clues from Troeltsch's research endeavors, and especially his juxtaposition of early and modern Protestantism. The precise argument to be developed below holds that the sorts of changes introduced by early Protestantism served to set the stage for the emergence of a radically reworked notion of the nature and dignity of the self arising out of the Free Church tradition, particularly in opposition to such collective forces as the state and the established ecclesiastical order.

Indeed, it will be our claim that it was the third wing of the Reformation—that is, the sectarians of various persuasions from millenarians to rationalists—who ultimately contributed most dramatically to the development of a modern conception of individualism. This was not their primary objective, of course, since most did not apprehend the sort of role they were playing willy-nilly on the stage of Western cultural development. From their perspective, most were simply lobbying for those legitimate rights which they felt they ought to enjoy as human beings, rights that were confirmed in their calling as regenerate believers. To establish this claim for the ultimate significance of the Reformation, we must begin at the point of Luther's separation from the Roman communion. Troeltsch is certainly correct to assert from a sociological point of view that the momentous change introduced by Protestantism was the wresting of the means of salvation from the ministrations of the institutional church. Placing the self in direct communion with God had the effect of elevating individual dignity in a manner that could not have been replicated in other institutional contexts. To be sure, both Luther and Calvin anticipated that individual salvation would invariably occur within the tender confines of the reformation church, but their disparagement of the institutional church as the *depositum fide* and necessary vehicle for salvation had the effect of placing the individual soul on an altogether different plane of religious significance.

Even where established churches prevailed in Protestant territories after the Reformation—and this was everywhere normative until the colony of Rhode Island obtained its charter in 1640 that prohibited an established church—they had to contend with an alternative source of legitimated authority in the form of individual conscience. The Anglican Church with Puritanism was not the first to feel the sting of internal criticism; it had already appeared on the Continent in the form of various guises of Anabaptism. The Mennonites and many of the early spiritualist sects on the continent withdrew from contacts with the state and secular culture generally in their endeavor to preserve individual and congregational purity. Anglo-American and low-country Protestants marched to a different drummer, however, for they refused to adopt a passive attitude toward secular authorities. Rather than exhibit tolerance toward the state, they were committed to extracting a recognition of tolerance toward their views from the state. This turnabout signaled the advent of a whole new era in church-state, self-society, relations.

Orthodox Lutheran and Calvinist thought had, of course, paved the way for the ideas of the radical reformers. Ironically, it was Luther (1962: 77–129) who drastically devalued the secular state in his doctrine of the two kingdoms—wherein the church stood supreme in the kingdom of God as the sole agency of salvation—while it was Calvin (1960: 1518–1521)[2] who devised the notion of legitimate revolution against repressive regimes; and it was Calvin's distant followers among the radical sectarians who later manifested a stronger willingness to challenge state authority in the name of a higher center of value.

Indeed, it is a matter of some interest that Lutheranism produced off-shoots of pietism which, in their passive orientation toward secular life, largely avoided any form of political confrontation (Fulbrook 1983), while Calvinism spawned numerous sectarian movements whose involvement in political affairs was at once activist and committed to basic structural changes within societal systems. This would seem to suggest that there was something inherent in the Calvinist symbol system which prompted its adherents to risk the ethical scandal of too close an affiliation with affairs of this world in order to usher in a renovated social order predicated on biblical principles or, at least, respective of religious precepts. That quintessential feature of Calvinist religiosity, which Weber perhaps intuitively discerned, was the commitment to transform the contemporary world in light of a transcendental image of the kingdom of God.

Whereas Luther was more or less prepared to leave the kingdom of this world in its present state, Calvinism was dedicated to recreating the empirical world into as near a likeness as could be achieved of the world to come. Therefore, the transformational ethic of Calvinism unleashed a powerful force oriented toward the renovation of the world which did not hesitate to attack the most powerful political structures in the realm, the combined force of the church and the state.

A cardinal point which church historians seldom elucidate with sufficient adequacy is that, wherever sectarian Protestantism waged a campaign against repressive state structures, it was almost always in opposition to main-line Protestant regimes. Catholic-Protestant clashes did arise with considerable violence in France and the Low countries, as well as in England during the brief tenure of Queen Mary, and wars of religion decimated large sections of Europe as nation-states vied for religio-political dominance, but the compromise formula, *cujus regio, ejus religio*, effected at the Peace of Augsburg (1555) between Catholic and Lutheran delegates, largely deleted the possibility of further conflicts internal to European societies between Protestants and Catholics. By the same token, however, the stage was set for future religious conflict to occur between competing segments of the same religious tradition—that is, between Lutherans and pietists, orthodox Calvinists and Puritan or sectarian dissenters.

Because Lutheranism gave rise to sectarian movements that were primarily concerned with the cultivation of the inner religious life and mysticism (Steeman 1984: 92), their subsequent impact on political-cultural affairs was decidedly limited. Calvinism was an entirely different matter. It managed to generate in the Free Church tradition, and especially within the English context, enormous creative energies that were channeled through a wide variety of ecclesiastical organizations. The proliferation of divergent religious bodies within both Lutheranism and Calvinism signaled, in Troeltschian terms, the disintegration of the very idea of a church-type unity to Christian civilization.

The declension of church-type religiosity left in its wake a fragmented ecclesiastical order. The medieval synthesis so painstakingly constructed by Catholicism and which early Protestantism had so diligently tried to preserve against its own inherent sectarian tendencies eventually gave way to a new form of organized Christianity, replete with a succession of now competing proto-denominational bodies. The exclusive claim to be the representative of God's order on earth could still be maintained by Tridentine Catholicism—and, indeed, it was precisely this claim which led Counter-Reformation Catholicism to repress all sectarian movements within it and channel potential challenges to its hegemony into the formation of new religious Orders (Troeltsch 1931: 700). But Protestantism had to reckon with a radically altered organizational environment wherein no single church could any longer assert authority over dogmatic definitions and ecclesiastical practices. The problem of religious authority in the formulation of belief became, according to Spitz (1985: 348), the Achilles heel of Protestantism. Although this judgment may be somewhat overdrawn, nonetheless, the alternate sociological principle upon which Protestant unity might be predicated remained frustratingly elusive during the first century or so after the Reformation.

Out of sheer desperation and on the basis of political expediency, as we have already mentioned, the initial response of Protestant bodies was to turn toward their respective secular princes as guarantors of physical protection and religious unity within each of their discrete domains. Lacking in profound religious warrant, however, this solution became increasingly problematic, especially in the face of rising incidents of internal dissent and renewed pressures for additional reforms. The conventional interpretation of how Protestantism finally reacted to its troublesome fragmentation in belief and social structure has typically held—by Troeltsch (1931: 671–673) among others—that the principle of toleration was endorsed as a mechanism for restoring some measure of harmony among conflicting religious bodies. To be sure, toleration intrinsically failed to address the issue of disunity that constituted the heart of the Protestant dilemma; at best, it merely provided some degree of respite from internecine warfare.

Troeltsch (1931: 671–672) regarded the pleas for religious tolerance penned by Milton and Locke as the keystones in that effort to evolve an adequate social theory for a maturing Protestantism. Today, the role of these two theorists must be assessed somewhat differently. Certainly, Milton urged toleration of his own views and evinced a liberal attitude toward the acceptance of religious practices for Jews, but he remained woefully bigoted with respect to Catholics, Presbyterians, or even sectarians who counseled a political strategy from the pulpit which differed from his own stance on government (Wolfe 1963: 87). Locke's theory of toleration stemmed from a latitudinarian Deism that essentially devalued religion, and hence he found it difficult to comprehend why there could be bitter conflicts over dogmatic issues. Neither Milton nor Locke, however, even came close to embracing the radical position of Roger Williams or the Levellers on religious tolerance. For the tolerance proclaimed by these latter thinkers was designed to protect liberty of conscience, that is to say, their position took with utmost seriousness the individual integrity of believers. Although Milton and Locke were Protestant individualists, they failed in the final analysis to carry that line of development to its fuller elaboration by endorsing universal religious toleration such as their comrades to the left embraced. And for that reason, both Milton and Locke represent peripheral figures to the internal dynamic of Protestant thought, at least in comparison to the radical sectarians, Troeltsch to the contrary notwithstanding.

Individualism, Millenarianism, and Unalienable Rights

The enfranchisement of the individual was a trend unleashed by Luther and Calvin as the foremost theologians of the Protestant Reformation. Milton and Locke laid greater stress on individualism than had the founding fathers of the Reformation, yet they were not the culminating point for this line of development. The purest forms of Protestant individualism were articulated by extremists who subscribed to a notion of the unalienable right to freedom of conscience. And this claim swiftly swelled into a whole panoply of rights—freedom of assembly, freedom of speech, freedom of the press, the right to due process, and so forth—which radicals beginning with Roger Williams and the Levellers of the English Civil War proclaimed as their inherent possession by virtue of a grant from God. Moreover, the originality of their position inhered primarily in their assertion that even the state could not with equity invade this private sphere of personal prerogative. Although Shapiro (1986: 277) has recently argued that "the notion of private-law rights of exclusive dominion having force against the state first achieved currency with Locke and the Whigs during their radical phase in the early 1680s...," the fact remains that such ideas initially surfaced during the Putney and Whitehall debates of Cromwell's New Model Army in the 1640s (see Woodhouse 1974) and, in the New World, this conception of the inviolability of individual rights was formally incorporated into the Plantation Agreement at Providence in 1640 (Commager 1963: 24–26).

Concomitant to the emergence of a view that individuals were endowed with God-given rights was the correlative notion that the state was perforce a wholly secular institution. In other words, these Protestant extremists were among the first political thinkers in the Western intellectual tradition to strip the state of any supernatural warrant, while they simultaneously accorded selves a succession of guaranteed rights that possessed religious legitimation. The upshot of this stance, as I (1987: 28–31) have argued elsewhere, was to erect an institutionalized wall of protection around the construct of individualism and thereby vouchsafe the self with its aggregate of inherent rights in a "moral space" shielded from external interference by functionaries of other social institutions, and especially the state. Thus, the human rights tradition that arose from the ranks of the radical sectarians during the 1640s—as opposed to the secular natural rights perspective of Locke and Rousseau—not only brought to fuller completion the intrinsic presuppositions of Protestant individualism, but it also provided substantive depth to the construct of the self well in advance of enlightenment philosophy and political theory.

Devising an explanation that accounts for the development of an unalienable rights point of view immediately leads one into some wily interpretive thickets. Certainly, it can be suggested that the empirical context of historical circumstances in which Williams, the Levellers, and later New World figures such as Isaac Backus were situated must have contributed significantly to their efforts to safeguard individual rights. Such a structuralist sort of explanation cannot suffice on its own, however, in answering what is essentially a question pertaining to the causal forces responsible for the emergence of the audacious claim to

God-given prerogatives redounding to discrete individuals. A central component of the ideational logic undergirding radical concepts of the self and its attendant rights can be discerned in the various manifestations of millennial thought which flourished in the seventeenth and eighteenth centuries both in New and Old England.

Indeed, millennial theologies of widely divergent types informed the writings and religious practices of Roger Williams (Gilpin 1979); the Ranters (Hill 1972; Coppe [1649] 1973); the Levellers (Lilburne [1639] 1971); Diggers (Hayes 1979); Fifth Monarchy Men (Wolfe 1949: 3); scholars such as Newton, Mede, Richard More, Brightman, and others (Hill 1975), as well as left-wing sectarians of Baptist, familist, Brownist, and other persuasions (Cragg 1975: 157) during the years of mounting crisis surrounding the English Civil War. For the most part, Anglo-American millennialism stopped well short of the chiliastic tendencies typical of the more extreme segments of continental millennialist thought, such as those of the Muensterites and John of Leyden (Cohn 1970). Nevertheless, they were at one in the view that a critical new era was dawning, that the prophetic utterances of the Book of Revelation were coming to fruition in the tumultuous events of the 1640s, and that the Kingdom of God was breaking into history with accompanying cataclysmic social processes.

Given the social location of the millennarians within the "middling-to-meaner" strata of Civil War England, it is not at all surprising that Leveller/Digger rhetoric swiftly took on starkly class-based complaints. Indeed, in a manner reminiscent of contemporary Liberation theology, the Diggers, Fifth Monarchy Men, and certain lower-status adherents of Leveller principles averred that the hope for English redemption and social reform was firmly anchored in the efforts of "the poor" and "the humble common folk" who represented the vanguard of that liberating force ushering in the Kingdom of God (Hayes 1979: 8–12; Woodhouse 1974: 98–100; Hill 1972: 91–111). Wealth corrupted piety by fueling a desire for power, privilege, and material prosperity rather than righteousness. Lacking these worldly interests, the poor could more readily lead the way toward liberty, equality, individualism, and democracy.

Moreover, the urgency to radical social reconstruction hinged on the stalwart belief among the millennarians that their reforms constituted a crucial precondition for the emergence of the coming new order. The saints came to the conclusion that not only were they to enjoy salvation in the world to come, but also that they would very shortly assume sovereignty in this world as well (Haller 1957: 269). Hence, the utopian vision of the millennarians, far from fostering an other-worldly withdrawal from civil affairs in rapt expectation of the coming eschaton, prompted instead a redoubled commitment to inner-worldly activism which had as its goal the swift transformation of the social structure of revolutionary England in light of the imminent millennial order poised just beyond the historical horizon. To be sure, the "rule of saints" as understood by the Presbyterians and Independents in England or the Standing Order Churches of the New England way in the New World likewise entertained a claim to power in the world as currently constituted.

Yet their view of proper sovereignty stopped well short of the democratic, universalist, individual rights perspective of the millennarians. The Presbyterians and Independents—as well as members of the standing order churches in New England—were decidedly less elitist than the previous regimes of Tudor and Stuart England, but they remained quite unwilling to entrust to the "rabble" and lower-status common folk the serious business of helping direct the affairs of state. And they remained similarly unsympathetic to notions that claimed God-given rights for all members of the populace, regardless of their social position.

For the most part, the millennialists of the Revolutionary era subscribed to what contemporary scholars now label premillennial thought (Davidson 1977: 28). That is to say, premillennialists regarded the second coming of Christ as the event which would inaugurate a thousand-years reign of peace and prosperity. Only later in the eighteenth century did postmillennial theories arise which asserted that Christ's physical return would occur at the end of the millennium—perhaps the chief American exponent of this view was Jonathan Edwards (see Heimert 1966: 66–70). Both perspectives lent an important ideological justification to world transforming action, however, for both accorded to their respective historical periods a sense of urgency and expectancy. Indeed, the fateful era of the 1640s proved to be such a potentially pregnant period in English social experience primarily because there came together in one limited time-frame structural opportunity for radical change, a lively expression of material interests (especially but not exclusively on the part of lower-status social actors), and a vibrant articulation of ideological religious interests in the form of millennarian utopianism.

To be sure, the radical agenda for societal transformation introduced by the left-wing sectarians never attained empirical realization. The debates over how to put English society back together again after the Revolutionary War were finally silenced by Cromwell's assumption of the Protectorate (Hill 1970). The claim to God-given rights appertaining to all citizens *qua* citizens was ultimately repudiated in favor of a Lockean version of legislatively enacted civil rights (Jellinek 1901). And English constitutional history after the Restoration and Glorious

Revolution, by consequence, proceeded in a markedly different direction than that followed by the fledgling colonies struggling to become the United States (Lovejoy 1972; Jennings 1966). By a circuitous historical route, many of the aspirations of the Levellers and other sectarians in England during the 1640s subsequently attained institutionalization, partially in the American colonial charters during the seventeenth century, and more completely in the American Declaration of Independence and Bill of Rights in the eighteenth century.

Although Jefferson invoked the language of Locke in the Declaration of Independence relative to the "unalienable rights to life, liberty, and the pursuit of happiness," the signification attaching to this phrase was far more in keeping with universal human rights proposed by the Levellers and Williams than the Whig version of Lockean political theory. For the national Bill of Rights made clear—as the Bills of Rights contained in many state constitutions had already done—that citizens enjoyed private-law rights which the state could not infringe upon or abrogate. And once this political position was established in the United States and the French Declaration of the Rights of Man and of Citizens, it has served as a significant model for other political entities around the globe, including the Universal Declaration of Human Rights adopted by the General Assembly of the United Nations in 1948.

Conclusion: The Human Rights Tradition and Global Order

Whether the success of the human rights tradition—which we have traced back to the agitations afflicting the Anglo-American domains during the 1640s—can be sustained in the decades ahead remains today a question very much blowing in the wind. There are, however, two relevant observations which need to be drawn with respect to the argument developed in this brief essay.

The first observation pertains to the peculiar nature of that quest for universalism which arises out of this perspective. Essentially the basic argument spun out in this interpretation claims the following: The individualism spawned by the Protestant Reformation, along with the subsequent fragmentation of the organizational unity of the church, appears at first blush to preclude the development of any notion of global order arising from the ranks of what Roman Catholics nowadays refer to as "the separated brethren." The thesis advanced herein is that it was precisely at the level of individual selves that a new conception of global order was initiated. That is to say, all persons could be conceived as participating in the global order of humanity by virtue of their common inheritance as recipients of God-given rights. Thus, the universalism proposed by the radical sectarians pressed well beyond the boundaries of the institutional church to embrace, at a deeper level, the whole of humankind.

Indeed, it was this logic which propelled Roger Williams to argue for religious toleration not only for other Protestant persuasions, but also for Jews, Catholics, and Turks (Woodhouse 1974: 280–281; Polishook 1967: 93; Morgan 1967: 129). And it was a similar logic which encouraged English dissenters and American revolutionaries corresponding in the eighteenth century during the Revolutionary War to expand their conception of liberties held by British subjects to liberties appertaining to all persons everywhere (Bonwick 1977). For once one invests individuals *qua* individuals with rights, there is no way to curtail the universal implications of this point of view, short of denying the status of humanity to selected groups of persons.

Perhaps the more pressing question today, however, pertains to whether the ideational legitimation which once undergirded the human rights tradition can be sustained in a post-modern age. Does the appeal to divine action constitute a sufficient warrant for maintaining commitment to human rights for humanity at large? Or are we in need of an alternative set of legitimating ideas more in concert with the thought-forms prevalent in a multi-religious, politico-economic global order? And if so, what would be the likely source: Enlightenment philosophy, a theory of justice a la Rawls, or some recrudescent version of international law? Or finally, is this the appropriate time to scuttle all claim to a universal human rights paradigm redounding to individuals in favor of a Rousseau-Marxian alternative which accords unalienable rights to the collectivity?

The answers to these questions not only hold crucial consequences for the world's cultural future, but they also will reveal a great deal about how much ideational continuity is possible between critical epochs in global history. Certainly, it appears likely from our current historical vantage point that millennial thought-forms will no longer be able to be very persuasive in the decades ahead—and yet millennialism continues to persist, arising from such varied sources as Jerry Falwell to Unification theology. Perhaps we shall discover from our research on the emerging global culture of today that it is not so much the millennial, as it is the utopian, aspect of religious ideas which affords them such creative power and formative influence. Or perhaps we will discover—as Weber suggested with respect to the Protestant Ethic thesis—that religious ideas are only important at the "break-through" point of cultural transformations and, thereafter, cultural traditions can enjoy secular success without ongoing religious legitimation.

My own hunch—for what its worth—is that the Weberian alternative will not be borne out in subsequent research, and that the view that religious ideas are somehow culturally specific to the pre-modern and modern mentality, but foreign to the post-modern world, is simply a mistaken vestige of enlightenment reflection. If so, this would mean that we should expect to discern some sort of ongoing linkage between religious ideas and secular cultural forms in the global processes currently underway. And such a conclusion would certainly add greater distinction to one of Troeltsch's more profound observations, namely, that "religion is the soul of culture."

Notes

1. This intriguing thesis by Collins runs afoul of a number of troublesome historical problems. Not the least of which is the fact that by the tenth century only one monastic order was centrally administered and its several houses under the authority of the head abbot of the mother house. Indeed, it was the organizational skills of the Cluniac order which provided the model for Cistercian development in the next century (Walker 1959: 199–200; 255–227; Garrett 1987: 6). Of considerably larger consequence, however, is the fact that Collins (1983: 211–213) has underestimated the role of canon law in providing the legal infrastructure for the subsequent development of commercial, manorial, urban, and royal law (Berman 1983). Without the groundwork laid by legal changes, the sort of economic developments Collins describes could never have come to fruition.
2. It is, perhaps, worth noting that Calvin articulated a theory of revolution against unjust political authorities in the last two sections, of his last chapter, of the *Institutes*. The very placement indicates his own reluctance to countenance a radical solution to political problems. His followers, however, were considerably less fearful than he in challenging political authorities, especially those within the left-wing, sectarian branch of the Calvinist tradition.

References

Berman, Harold J. 1983. *Law and Revolution*. Cambridge, MA: Harvard University Press.

Bonwick, Colin. 1977. *English Radicals and the American Revolution*. Chapel Hill, N.C.: University of North Carolina Press.

Braudel, Fernand. [1979] *Civilization and Capitalism: The Wheels of Commerce*, 1986, vol. II. New York: Harper & Row.

_____. [1979] *Civilization and Capitalism: The Perspective of the World*, vol. III. New York: Harper & Row.

Calvin, John. 1960. *Institutes of the Christian Religion*, 2 vols. Philadelphia: Westminster Press.

Cohn, Norman. 1970. *The Pursuit of the Millennium.* Rev. ed. New York: Oxford University Press.
Collins, Randall. 1983. "The Weberian Revolution of the High Middle Ages." 205–225 in Albert Bergesen, ed., *Crises in the World-System.* Beverly Hills, CA: Sage Publications.
_____. 1986. *Max Weber: A Skeleton Key.* Beverly Hills, CA: Sage Publications.
Commager, H.S., ed. 1963. *Documents of American History*, vol. I, 7th ed. New York: Meredith Publishing Co.
Coppe, Abiezer. [1649] 1973. *A Fiery Flying Roll.* Exeter, England: The Rota at the University of Exeter.
Cragg, Gerald R. 1975. *Freedom and Authority.* Philadelphia: Westminster Press.
Davidson, James West. 1977. *The Logic of Millennial Thought.* New Haven, CT: Yale University Press.
Fulbrook, Mary. 1983. *Piety and Politics.* New York: Cambridge University Press.
Garrett, William R. 1987. "Religion, Law, and the Human Condition." *Sociological Analysis* vol. 47, No. S:1–34.
Gilpin, W. Clark. 1979. *The Millenarian Piety of Roger Williams.* Chicago: University of Chicago Press.
Haller, William. 1957. *The Rise of Puritanism.* New York: Harper.
Hayes, T. Wilson. 1979. *Winstanley the Digger.* Cambridge, MA: Harvard University Press.
Heimert, Alan. 1966. *Religion and the American Mind.* Cambridge, MA: Harvard University Press.
Hill, Christopher. 1970. *God's Englishman.* New York: Harper & Row.
_____. 1972. *The World Turned Upside Down.* New York: Viking Press.
_____. 1975. *Change and Continuity in 17th Century England.* Cambridge, MA: Harvard University Press.
_____. 1986. *The Collected Essays of Christopher Hill*, vol. III. Amherst, MA: University of Massachusetts Press.
Jellinek, Georg. 1901. *The Declaration of the Rights of Man and of Citizens.* New York: Henry Holt and Company.
Jennings, W. Ivor. 1966. *The British Constitution.* New York: Cambridge University Press.
Lilburne, John. [1639] 1971. *Come Out of Her My People.* Exeter, England: The Rota at Exeter University.
Lovejoy, David S. 1972. *The Glorious Revolution in America.* New York: Harper & Row.
Luther, Martin. 1962. *Luther's Works*, vol. 45. Philadelphia: Muhlenberg Press.
Morgan, Edmund S. 1967. *Roger Williams: The Church and the State.* New York: Harcourt, Brace, and World, Inc.
Morgan, Robert. 1977. "Introduction." 1–51 in Robert Morgan and Michael Pye, eds., *Ernst Troeltsch: Writings on Theology and Religion.* Atlanta: John Knox Press.
Parsons, Talcott. 1967. *Sociological Theory and Modern Society.* New York: Free Press.
Polishook, Irwin H., ed. 1967. *Roger Williams, John Cotton, and Religious Freedom.* Englewood Cliffs, N.J.: Prentice-Hall.
Rachfahl, Felix. [1910] "Nochmals Kalvinismus und Kapitalismus." 216–282, Johannes Winckelmann, ed., *Die Protestantische Ethik II.* Hamburg: Sibenstern Taschenbuch Verlag.

Shapiro, Ian. 1986. *The Evolution of Rights in Liberal Theory*. New York: Cambridge University Press.
Spitz, Lewis W. 1985. *The Protestant Reformation, 1517–1559*. New York: Harper & Row.
Sombart, Werner. [1911] *The Jews and Modern Capitalism*. New York: Collier 1962 Books.
Steeman, Theodore M. 1984. "Troeltsch and Modern American Religion." *Archives de Sciences Sociales des Religions*, vol. 58, No. 1:85–116.
Troeltsch, Ernst. [1910] 1972. "Die Kulturbedeutung des Calvinismus." 188–215 in Johannes Winckelmann, ed., *Die Protestantische Ethik II*. Hamburg: Siebenstern Taschenbuch Verlag.
———. 1958. *Protestantism and Progress*. Boston: Beacon Press.
Walker, Williston. 1959. *A History of the Christian Church*, rev. ed. New York: Scribners.
Wallerstein, Immanuel. 1979. *The Capitalist World Economy*. New York: Cambridge University Press.
Weber, Max. [1910] 1972. "Antikritisches Schlusswort zum 'Geist des Kapitalismus.'" 283–345 in Johannes Winckelmann, ed., *Die Protestantische Ethik II*. Hamburg: Siebenstern Taschenbuch Verlag.
———. 1958. *The Protestant Ethic and the Spirit of Capitalism*. New York: Scribners.
Winckelmann, Johannes. 1972. *Die Protestantische Ethik II: Kritiken und Antikritiken*. Hamburg: Siebenstern Taschenbuch Verlag.
Wolfe, Don M. 1963. *Milton in the Puritan Revolution*. New York: Humanities Press.
———. 1967. *Leveller Manifestos of the Puritan Revolution*. New York: Humanities Press.
Woodhouse, A.S.P., ed. 1974. *Puritanism and Liberty*. 2nd ed. Chicago: The University of Chicago Press.
Zaret, David. 1985. *The Heavenly Contract: Ideology and Organization in Pre-Revolutionary Puritanism*. Chicago: University of Chicago Press.

5

THE CONQUEST OF THE AMERICAS
THE SPANISH SEARCH FOR GLOBAL ORDER
James M. Muldoon

DISCUSSION OF A CHRISTIAN GLOBAL ORDER appears comparatively late in Christian thought. Christians always took for granted the universal nature of Christ's message and obeyed His injunction to teach all nations. This did not, however, generate any formal theological or philosophical discussion of the nature of a Christian world order.

Indeed, because Christianity first emerged in conflict with the society around it, early Christians tended to think of the world as an arena within which believers battled unbelievers. Instead of seeing religion as a part of the overall social order, Christians often thought of their relation to the social order in terms of the conflict between Church and State. Conflict, not cooperation, was the usual Christian view of global order. Christians sought withdrawal from the world, not a role in shaping its direction.

Not until Christianity became a dominant force in European society during the Middle Ages did Christian thinkers begin to consider a positive role for Christianity in the global order. To the extent that medieval thinkers did consider the nature of a Christian world order, they often looked to an idealized Roman Empire. Since the pagans had created, if not a global order, then at least a structure, the Roman Empire, that included all the then-known civilized world, should not Christians be able to create a similar order based on the true faith? By 1200, the hope of creating a Christian world order based on the medieval Roman Empire was only a political fantasy indulged in by romantics. The rulers of the emerging national kingdoms within Europe had rejected any form of subordination to the Holy Roman Emperor other than granting him an honorific precedence (Ladner 1954). Lawyers began developing explanations of why territories once part of the ancient Roman Empire were no longer so (Post 1964: 453–482).

The development of these sovereign national kingdoms could lead inevitably to a kind of international anarchy. To counter such tendencies, a line of popes beginning in the mid-eleventh century began to assert papal headship of the increasingly politically Christian Europe. Although papal leadership in purely spiritual matters was never in dispute, the application of spiritual leadership to political situations was always a matter of debate, if not actual conflict. At the beginning of the thirteenth century, Pope Innocent III (1198–1216) attempted to reinforce the papal leadership role by advancing the policy of placing the pope at the heart of the several feudal hierarchies that formed the various national kingdoms of Europe. The policy of papal feudal overlordship went back to the eleventh century, but Innocent III was the first pope to employ it as a basis for a European Christian order. Innocent III's program for a European Christian order under papal leadership failed. Secular rulers rarely heeded papal calls for arbitration in political disputes unless it was clearly in their interest to do so. The everyday realities of medieval political life exceeded the papal power to do anything about them.

If the papacy was unable to impose its conception of order on Christian society, it should come as no surprise that it showed little interest in considering the nature of a global order. Such an order would require the papacy to deal with the schismatic Greeks at Constantinople, the Mongols who were assaulting north-eastern and central Europe, and the Moslems whose conquests bordered Christian Europe from the Middle East, along the North African coast and on into Spain. Beyond these immediate neighbors of Christian society were other, virtually unknown, infidel societies. Given the political situation in which medieval European Christians found themselves, it should be no surprise that they tended to conceive of relations with those beyond Europe in terms of the just war of defense.

During the mid-thirteenth century, however, there emerged a small indication of the way in which a Christian theory of global order might develop. In commenting upon a letter of Innocent III concerning the vows taken by crusaders, Pope Innocent IV (1243–1254) raised the question of the right by which the Church could authorize a war against the Moslems at all. Rather than focusing on the just war of defense as the keystone of a discussion of Christian-infidel relations, Innocent IV began by asserting the right of all men to organize societies and to govern themselves as they saw fit. As a consequence, Christians had no right to attack and seize the lands of non-believers simply because they were not Christians. In the case of the Holy Land, Christians could legitimately wage war to regain it because it was taken from its Christian inhabitants by the Moslems in an unjust war. Other lands that the Moslems occupied could not be seized because they were legitimately occupied by the Moslems. The same was true for other infidel societies as well. Social organization and government were the natural rights of all men and did not depend upon being in the state of grace (Muldoon 1979: 5–14).

To the extent that Innocent IV's argument supported the natural right of all societies to exist, presumably in peace, it provided a basis for determining how these societies could live together in some kind of harmony. He did not stop, however, however, at asserting the right of all societies to exist. He suggested a potential global order based on Christ's statement that He possessed other sheep not of this flock. Traditionally, the Christians were seen as Christ's flock with the pope acting as shepherd in the place of Christ. Christ's reference to His having other sheep meant to Innocent IV that those who were not members of the Church were nevertheless subject to the jurisdiction of Christ and therefore of His vicar, the pope. The consequence of this argument was that the pope had judicial authority over all men. He judged Christians according to Christian law, Jews according to Mosaic law and infidels according to the natural law (Muldoon 1979: 10–11).

Taking Innocent IV's arguments as a starting point, it would be possible to develop a theory of global order based on the papal obligation to judge all men according to the law that governed their behavior. Christian rulers would enforce papal decisions using armed force where moral suasion failed to achieve the goal of ending evil practices. The kind of order that this could engender would not be one with which modern western men would be comfortable. It would make European Christians the rulers of the entire world, at least in theory. Only those societies that lived according to the Christian conception of the natural law could live at peace with Christian societies. Infidel societies would exist at the sufferance of Christian society. The implications for Christian society itself are not all that comforting either. Innocent IV had no objection to employing the secular arm to repress heretics and schismatics, and he certainly did not see Jews and Moslems as full members of Christian states possessing and exercising the same rights as Christians. Innocent IV's conception of a global order is essentially a religious one.

In the long run, the most important contribution of Innocent IV to the development of a theory of global order acceptable in twentieth-century terms is his argument that all men have the right to organize and govern themselves as they see fit, subject to the principles of natural law. In a sense, his arguments echo Thomas Aquinas' (1970: 3–9) arguments about the natural right of men to organize and govern themselves, suggesting the extent to which natural law justifications for the social order were becoming widespread in the thirteenth century. Innocent IV's arguments were restated and employed by canonists and others for the next two centuries, but his ideas were not given further development and refinement. His assertion of the natural right of all men to govern themselves became the *communis opinio* among the canonists, gradually displacing the argument that *dominium*, the right to possess property and political power, was, since the birth of Christ, based on being in the state of grace. This would have meant of course that only Christians could legitimately possess land and power. If *dominium* depended upon being in the state of grace, then Christians, presumably being in the state of grace, could legitimately conquer the entire world and impose a Christian order on it (Muldoon 1979: 16–17). While Innocent IV did indicate that there were legitimate occasions when Christians could conquer infidel nations, he was clear that his theory was not a blanket invitation to world conquest and global order.

It was not until the sixteenth century that Christian thinkers began to consider the issue of political order on a global scale. The establishment of the Spanish overseas empire in the century following Columbus' voyages saw the parallel development of preliminary concepts of international order based on some kind of international law and also on the assumption that peaceful relations were possible between Christian and non-Christian societies. The fundamental reason for the development of these theories was that the peoples of the New World whom the Spanish were encountering did not fit the traditional mold that the theory of the just war provided for dealing with non-Christian societies. Unlike the Mongols and the Moslems who threatened medieval Europe, the inhabitants of the New World were at peace with Europeans, if only because they were separated from them by several thousand miles of ocean. For Europeans to deal with these people, it was first necessary that the Europeans sail overseas to encounter them. In those terms, if anyone was the aggressor, it was the European seaman who claimed possession of the New World for his king.

The Spanish discovery of the New World occurred in conjunction with what R. Trevor Davies ([1937] 1954: 280–284) has termed "The Golden Age of Spanish Scholasticism," the period in which Spanish intellectual life reached its peak and in which Spanish thinkers played a major role in shaping the European intellectual outlook. As a consequence, a great deal of attention was paid to the moral and legal implications of the discoveries. Furthermore, the imperial government was interested in justifying its control of the newly discovered lands. The result was what Lewis Hanke ([1949] 1965) termed *The Spanish Struggle for Justice in the Conquest of America*, an attempt to deal with the inhabitants of the New World justly, according to Christian teaching. While this struggle had a number of aspects, the basic issue was the nature of the relationship between the Spanish, Christian, Hapsburg Empire and the infidel societies of the Americas. Although the Spanish never claimed global domination, the territories over which they claimed jurisdiction certainly comprised the largest amount of territory ever ruled by a single ruler. As a result, Spanish thinkers were among the first to consider the problem of order on something approaching a global scale.

Two Spanish priests, the Dominican Francisco de Vitoria (1486–1546) and the Jesuit Francisco Suárez (1548–1617), were the pioneers of Spanish thinking on international law and relations. Numerous Spanish theologians, philosophers, and lawyers contributed to the effort in what became a major collaborative work that went on well into the seventeenth century. The work of these Spanish thinkers stands as a bridge between medieval thinkers, such as Innocent IV, and modern thinkers on international law, such as Hugo Grotius (1583–1645). The work of Vitoria and Suárez provided a foundation that enabled theorists to move from a medieval, religious basis for international law and relations to a modern, secular basis. In part, at least, the reason that Grotius's views on these issues were significantly different from the views of Innocent IV was that by the time the Dutch theorist was writing, he had the work of the Spanish thinkers to assist him in breaking from the narrow confines of medieval just-war thought and beginning the development of a broader basis on which to rest the relations among nations (Muldoon 1972).

Francisco de Vitoria began his discussion of global order with an analysis of the problems associated with the discovery and conquest of the New World. The question of the legitimacy of the conquest was important to the Spanish monarchs. For two centuries, Iberian rulers had engaged in the early stages of overseas exploration, sending ships down the coast of Africa, discovering the Atlantic Islands, and colonizing some of them, tasks that contributed to their ability to discover and colonize the Americas. This work was always done under papal license. Papal Bulls outlining Portuguese and Castilian responsibilities in the Atlantic Islands and along the coast of Africa go back to the fourteenth century. The papal letters outlined regions in which the Portuguese or the Castilians had responsibility for the conversion of the native population. Several popes had specified distinct spheres of spiritual jurisdiction for each kingdom, but because neither ruler could support missionary activity in the sphere of the other, these papal letters created not only areas of spiritual jurisdiction but of political and economic jurisdiction as well. The profits of these activities were to underwrite the cost of missionary activity.

The most famous of these papal bulls were those that Pope Alexander VI (1492–1503) issued following Columbus' first voyage. These bulls, subsequently modified, divided the newly explored regions of the Atlantic into Portuguese and Castilian spheres of missionary jurisdiction. The pope did not, as is often said inaccurately, simply arrogantly divide the world between the two Iberian powers, as if he had the right to deprive the infidels of their lands and power simply because they were infidels. Obviously he could not do that, and the Castilians and the Portuguese knew it very well. The pope as the universal shepherd, however, could authorize particular Christian rulers to support and maintain the work of missionaries and that is what Alexander VI's bulls accomplished (Muldoon 1978).

From the beginning the issue of the extent to which force could be used in pursuit of missionary goals arose. The theory of the just war was expanded to deal with these new situations. Under what, if any, circumstances could Christian rulers use troops in the course of fulfilling their responsibilities? During the first half-century of the conquest of the New World, the legitimacy of the work troubled a number of Spanish thinkers and public officials. In 1550, a conference was held under imperial sponsorship at Valladolid, at which both the defenders and the critics of the conquest were represented (Hanke [1949] 1965: 117–32).

The result of this conference was inconclusive, not because the government was uninterested in the moral and legal implications of the conquest but because the issues appeared to be so intractable. Although Vitoria was dead by the time that the Valladolid conference took place, and his discussion of the conquest of the New World did not appear in print until 1557, his ideas were well represented at the Valladolid conference through the presence of his students. As a result, Vitoria's ideas came to play a major role in the Spanish discussion of the legitimacy of the conquest and, in the long run, in the discussion of the possibility of a Christian global order.

The basis for Vitoria's ([1917] 1964) entire treatment of the Spanish presence in the Americas appeared at the beginning of his first *relectio*, an extended discussion, of what he termed the problem of the "Indians Lately Discovered." He opened the discussion with a line from the New Testament. "Teach all nations, baptizing them in the name of the Father and Son and Holy Spirit." (Matthew 28:19) This narrow statement of spiritual mission was the basis upon which Vitoria based his discussion of the Spanish occupation of the Americas.

The first question he posed sprang logically from this charge. Is it possible, he asked, that "the children of unbelievers may be baptized against the wishes of their parents...." (Vitoria [1917] 1964: 116) This issue then gave rise to a series of related questions: "By what right these Indian natives came under Spanish sway... What rights the Spanish sovereigns obtained over them in temporal and civil matters... What rights these sovereigns or the Church obtained over them in matters spiritual and touching religion...." In Vitoria's view, the presence of Spanish missionaries in the Americas could not be discussed without consideration of the political implications of that presence, as well as consideration of the spiritual responsibilties of the Church.

Furthermore, Vitoria's ([1917] 1964: 119) approach to the issue was more than theoretical. He was aware of the evils and injustices that the conquerors were inflicting on the Indians. Although he did not say so directly, the fundamental issue here was the issue of worldwide order. What were the implications for the political order of the Church's obligation to teach all men?

After considering a variety of arguments supporting the legitimacy of the conquest in this first discussion of the issues involved, Vitoria ([1917] 1964: 128) concluded that "the aborigines undoubtedly had true dominion in both public and private matters, just like Christians, and that neither their princes nor private persons could be despoiled of their property on the ground of their not being true owners." In terms of global order, this meant that non-Christians need not automatically fear conquest by Christians because Christians must recognize the legitimacy of infidel property and political rights. This conclusion would suggest the possibility of a global order consisting of autonomous societies that worked together in harmony based on their natural right to exist rather than on some religiously based principles.

The second of Vitoria's discussions of infidel rights dealt with the assertion that there was a single ruler who was at least *de jure* the lord of the world. If this argument was accepted, then there could exist a global order under a single ruler whose position would most likely rest on the ability of his armies to force those who rejected his claim to world domination to accept it by force. There were two traditional candidates for this role, the Holy Roman Emperor, in this case Vitoria's own sovereign, Charles I of Castile who was also the Holy Roman Emperor Charles V (1519–1555), and the pope.

Vitoria ([1917] 1964: 130–134) rejected all the arguments that lawyers and theologians had advanced in support of these claims. He admitted that Roman law did, in one place, describe the emperor as the *Dominus mundi*, the lord of the world, but he rejected that claim as being little more than a rhetorical flourish. In historical fact, as the Dominican pointed out, even when the Roman Empire reached its peak in the first century after Christ, it did not include all of the known world. The coming of Christ and the eventual Christianization of the Roman Empire made no difference (Vitoria [1917] 1964: 132).

Vitoria also gave short shrift to the claim that the pope was the *de jure* temporal head of mankind. Citing numerous authorities, including Pope Innocent IV, Vitoria pointed out that the pope had no right to claim such temporal power. Papal power was spiritual, not temporal. Vitoria ([1917] 1964: 146) was even skeptical of any papal claim to a kind of indirect power in temporal matters, denying Innocent IV's argument that the pope could order Christian secular rulers to punish infidels who violated the natural law. In this case, rather than following the opinion of Innocent IV, as he usually did, Vitoria looked to Thomas Aquinas for guidance. According to his thirteenth-century Dominican predecessor, "prelates have received power over those only who have submitted themselves to the faith." At this point, Vitoria appears to have had doubts about the possibility of knowing the natural law. This is not because the Indians were unintelligent but because of the inherent difficulties in knowing what it contained. In effect, Vitoria ([1917] 1964: 147) argued that natural law provided no basis for papal-based world order. If failure to accept Christianity did not justify conquering the Indians, their failure to understand the natural law did not either.

Vitoria's discussion of the conquest could lead one to conclude that the traditional arguments about conquest and the potential of those arguments for developing a theory of global relations were not relevant in the sixteenth century. The reader might well conclude that there was no basis for a global order, at least no just basis, only conquest. Vitoria did not, however, feel that way. Even though traditional arguments based on Roman imperial domination or on papal spiritual jurisdiction did not apply, Vitoria was able to develop other approaches to the issue, approaches that were more in line with the actual development of a world society, if not world order, approaches that were essentially secular in nature.

Having recognized the right of infidels to possess property and political power and having denied the existence of any papal right to order the punishment of those who violated the natural law, Vitoria went on to demonstrate a basis for armed Christian intervention in infidel societies. This argument was founded on a conception of world order. Christians and infidels alike possess a natural right to travel freely throughout the world, a right founded in "natural society and fellowship." As a result, the "Spanish have a right to travel in the lands in question [i.e. the Americas] and to sojourn there, provided they do no harm to the natives, and the natives may not prevent them." This right to travel freely is founded in "the law of nations (*jus gentium*), which either is natural law or is derived from natural law..." (Vitoria [1917] 1964: 151). Interestingly enough, the first example of this right to travel that Vitoria ([1917] 1964: 152) gave was not the obvious case of Christian missionaries. He pointed instead to the right of merchants to travel.

Should the Indians fail to act peacefully toward the Spanish merchants and travelers who have come to the New World, then, and only then, did the Spanish have the right to resort to defensive force in order to protect them. Resort to arms should be the last resort. If "reason and persuasion" fail to move the natives, argued Vitoria ([1917] 1964: 154) and if "the barbarians decline to agree and propose to use force, the Spaniards can defend themselves and do all that consists with their own safety...."

Only after determining the existence of a right to travel freely for the purpose of trade did Vitoria ([1917] 1964: 157) consider the situation of the Christian missionary. The answer to the question of the missionary's right to travel precisely paralleled the answer given in the case of the merchant.

> If the Indians...prevent the Spaniards from freely preaching the Gospel, the Spaniards, after first reasoning with them in order to remove scandal, may preach it despite their unwillingness and devote themselves to the conversion of the people in question, and if need be they may then accept or even make war, until they succeed in obtaining facilities and safety for preaching the Gospel.

In the final analysis, Vitoria provided some justifications for the Spanish domination of the New World, but these justifications were not the traditional religious ones. He seems to reveal a good deal of skepticism about arguments based on natural law, even though the justification that he does employ, the right to travel freely throughout the world, is rooted in the natural law by way of the *jus gentium*. Perhaps the difference is that while the natural law is an abstract concept, the law of nations dealing as it does with what men actually do, is evidence of widespread acceptance of a right to travel in peace. Within the Europe of Vitoria's time, the right to travel freely was widely accepted. Thousands of people went on religious pilgrimages each year. As far back as the thirteenth century, the Magna Carta contained a clause, chapter 41, that expressly protected foreign merchants travelling in England, indicating the importance of the right to peaceful travel (*Magna Carta* 1972: 179). If one combines Vitoria's views about the right of all men to self-government with his views about the right to travel freely and his opinion about "the natural society and fellowship" that characterized mankind, one would have some of the basic elements needed to construct a theory of global order. Such a global order would, however, be based on natural premises, not on religious or spiritual ones.

As Vitoria dominated Spanish thought on the problem of international law in the first half of the sixteenth century, so Suárez dominated it during the last half of that century and on into the seventeenth century. Suárez's work was founded on the work of Vitoria. At the same time, Suárez was also forced to consider some new aspects of international relations that his predecessor did not have to treat. One result of the changed circumstances of the world within which the Jesuit lived was that he had to consider the nature of relations between Catholic states and Protestant states, as well as to consider the older problem of relations between Catholic and infidel states. The problem of Catholic-Protestant relations had been only beginning when Vitoria died, but by the end of the century this issue became crucial to any Catholic theory of international order.

The permanent establishment of Protestant states posed a new problem for Catholic thinkers on international relations because, as heretics, Protestants were, according to canon law, subject to ecclesiastical punishment. In the sixteenth century, popes had ordered Protestant rulers deposed and released their Christian subjects from obedience to them. In 1570, for example, Pope Pius V (Bettenson 1963: 339) issued the bull *Regnans in excelsi*, declaring "we deprive the said Elizabeth of her pretended right to the realm [of England]...and we enjoin and forbid all and several the nobles etc....that they presume not to obey her and her admonitions, commands, and laws." This letter did not lead to the deposition of Queen Elizabeth I (1558–1603). Indeed it did not even lead to any significant opposition, Catholics even being very active in opposing the Spanish Armada in 1588. Nevertheless Pius V's bull posed a serious problem for Catholics and Protestants interested in the European political order (Allen [1928] 1960: 106). Could Catholics be loyal subjects of a Protestant ruler and could Protestants assure Catholic rulers that they would be loyal in spite of religious differences?

Suárez came to the issue of Catholic-Protestant relations by way of a work that Elizabeth I's successor, James I (1603–1625), published in 1609. His *Apologie for the Oath of Allegiance* as a defense of the legal requirement that all the English king's subjects take an oath of allegiance that included the words (Suárez [1944] 1964: v. 2, 705):

> I do further swear that I do from my heart abhor, detest and abjure, as impious and heretical, this [damnable] doctrine and position; that princes which be excommunicated or deprived by the pope, may be deposed or murdered by their subjects or any other whatsoever.

The *Apologie* required a Catholic response; and in 1613 Suárez published one, *A Defence of the Catholic and Apostolic Faith*, that dealt with, among other points, the issue of papal claims to supremacy over secular rulers. In a larger sense, Suárez dealt with the issue of whether a Christian secular ruler was or could be completely free of all subordination to the pope in temporal matters. Under this heading he considered the question of whether the pope was supreme in temporal affairs.

Suárez ([1944] 1964: v. 2, 669) began his discussion with the observation that some defenders of papal power, especially priests, had claimed that "in the whole Catholic Church there exists but one supreme temporal prince, who holds, *per se* and directly, supreme civil power over the entire Church; and that this supreme prince is the pope...." After discussing the basis for this assertion, Suárez ([1944] 1964: v. 2, 671) concluded "that Christian kings do possess supreme civil power within their own order" and they recognize "no other person...as a direct superior...." The consequence was that "there exists within the Church no one supreme temporal prince over that whole body, that is to say, over all the kingdoms of the Church...."

Having disposed of the notion that there was a supreme temporal ruler over all the Christian rulers of Europe, neither the pope nor the Holy Roman Emperor being able to claim such jurisdiction, Suárez went on to discuss the power of the pope to intervene in the operation of a kingdom even though he was not the temporal overlord of that kingdom. James I of England had criticized the papacy on this very issue, according to Suárez ([1944] 1964: v. 2, 685). If James I had his way, the pope would be deprived "of every remedy against heretical princes," a theory that Suárez associated with the thirteenth-century Italian political thinker, Marsilius of Padua (d.1343), whose *Defensor Pacis* was a wholesale attack on the theory that the Church could intervene in the secular order under any circumstances. Could there be a stable international order within Europe if the pope could legitimately call upon the Catholic subjects of Protestant rulers to rebel and to replace their heretical rulers with orthodox ones? The crucial issue for Suárez was not the papal right to declare a ruler a heretic. That was what Suárez termed "directive power." The dangerous part was the pope's claim to possess "coercive power," that is the power to impose sanctions, even calling for rebellion, in order to implement his "directive power."

Defining a ruler as a heretic, a spiritual matter clearly within the papal sphere of jurisdiction, obviously had important ramifications in the temporal order. As the Suárez ([1944] 1964: v. 2, 685) saw things, the pope did possess "coercive power over temporal princes who are incorrigibly wicked, and especially over schismatics and stubborn heretics," because without "this coercive weapon...directive force is inefficacious...." Suárez ([1944] 1964: v. 2, 689) went on to point out that throughout the history of the Church "the popes have certainly made frequent use of the said form of censure when opposing emperors and kings." As Suárez ([1944] 1964: v. 2, 699-700) saw matters, the papacy had an especially strong reason for insisting upon the right to employ coercive power against secular rulers when their actions warrant it.

He argued that: "The sins of princes—especially those sins which are opposed to the faith and to religion—are more pernicious [than the sins of other Christians]; for princes easily lead their subjects to imitate them, whether by their [bare] example, or by favors and promises, or even by threats and intimidation." The role of the pope then was to defend the subjects of "a bad king, and especially one who is schismatic and heretical" because such a ruler "places his subjects in grave danger of perdition...." Suárez ([1944] 1964: v. 2, 701) was careful to point out that "the pope has not power to punish an un-baptized and heathen king for infidelity or other sins," but, as in the case of a heretical or schismatic ruler, the pope could free such a ruler's Christian subjects "from their subjection to their ruler, on the ground that they are in evident peril of moral destruction."

So far, then, Suárez's views did not bode well for a religiously divided Europe. Ironically, his arguments would hold more promise for Christian-infidel relations than for the relations between Catholic and Protestant powers. As long as the pope claimed the right to order Catholic subjects of Protestant kings to rebel, there was no serious possibility of peaceful, orderly international relations within Christian Europe.

Turning finally to the specific oath that James I required of his subjects, Suárez ([1944] 1964: v. 2, 725) concluded that the oath was a wrongful assertion of the temporal power's superiority over the spiritual realm. In the first place, he argued, it is wrong to assert, as the oath does, "that the pope is not endowed with power to depose a heretical or schismatic king who is dragging or perverting his kingdom to the point where it will embrace the same schism or heresy." In the final analysis:

> ...it is implicit in the very substance of the oath...that a temporal king may even exact of his subjects a sworn belief in regard to those matters having to do with the doctrines of the faith and with the renunciation of heresies.... And all this is surely equivalent to declaring that a temporal king holds primacy in spiritual—or ecclesiastical—affairs.

In Suárez's terms, James I of England has simply arrogated to himself and other secular rulers the power to intervene in spiritual matters while condemning the pope for asserting the right to intervene in secular matters, thus turning the papal view of the right order of things upside down. From the perspective of international order, however, James I's position had much to commend it. If the secular ruler is to be the ultimate judge of religious matters within his own kingdom, then an internal order would exist within a kingdom. On the basis of this internal order an international order of sovereign nations could be erected without reference to religious belief. Just as the principle of *cuius regio eius religio* became the solution to the religious struggle within the Holy Roman Empire, allowing each principality's ruler to determine the religion of that constituent element of the Empire, thus ending the religious wars that had nearly destroyed Germany, an international order could be erected on the principle of *cuius regio eius religio* as well. The German rulers within the Empire were to ignore the pope when they agreed on the principle of *cuius regio eius religio* in the Peace of Westphalia (1648), and James I was already suggesting the possibility of creating an international order without the pope (Randle 1973: 379–92).

In this way, Protestant rulers could negotiate with Catholic rulers safe in the knowledge that the Catholics of their own kingdoms would not be ordered to rebel against them; and Catholic rulers could be assured that their Protestant subjects would not be encouraged to rebel either. As Suárez may well have recognized, what James I and his fellow monarchs were actually doing was to make religion a matter of personal devotion, subject to the needs of public order as determined by the ruler (Allen [1928] 1960: 292–96). If this could be done at the national level, there is, theoretically, no reason to doubt that it could work on the international level. This view of religion as a private matter subject to governmental limitation was contrary to the teachings of the Catholic Church and to most Protestant denominations as well. It was, however, a view of the place of religion in the public order that developed from the bitter experience of the religious wars that accompanied the Reformation.

In other writings, those dealing with the conquest of the Americas, Suárez considered in greater detail the possibility of peaceful relations between Catholic and infidels. He discussed this issue in a series of lectures on the theological virtues of faith, hope, and charity, giving an indication of where his priorities lay. While these lectures had been presented in the classroom over the years, they appeared in print only in 1621 and so they contained the most complete discussion of the nature of Christian-infidel relations in Suárez's work. One of Suárez's ([1944] 1964: v. 2, 739) lectures was devoted to the topic: "On the means which may be used for the conversion and coercion of unbelievers who are not apostates." Under this heading, he began with a consideration of the Church's claim to possess the right to preach everywhere without hindrance. On this point, reasonably enough, Suárez ([1944] 1964: v. 2, 740) concluded "that the Church has that power by which it may legitimately preach the Catholic faith everywhere and to all kinds of unbelievers."

In terms of international relations, of course, the central issue was not the right of the Church to preach, but, rather, the Church's right to employ force in the implementation of that right. Following Vitoria and others, Suárez ([1944] 1964: v. 2, 742) argued that "the Church has the right of defending its preachers, and of subduing those who by force and violence hinder or do not permit this preaching." Suárez supported this conclusion with a variety of arguments, some of which gave a slightly different twist to old arguments.

For example, one argument he employed to justify the use of troops where a ruler sought to prevent the entrance of missionaries was similar to an argument he had used to justify the use of force against Protestant rulers. In both cases he argued that a ruler who did not allow Catholic missionaries to enter his kingdom was doing an injury to his subjects and the Church therefore had a right to employ force to protect such a ruler's subjects from this kind of injury as well as to protect the right of its missionaries to preach freely. A ruler who prevented the entry of preachers "does the gravest injury to many who perchance might have been converted if they had heard" the Gospel (Suárez [1944] 1964: v. 2, 743).

Thus, the use of force is defensive in a twofold sense. It defends the Church's right to preach and the subjects' right to hear the Gospel. The second line of argument that Suárez employed to support his argument about the use of force involved comparing missionaries to ambassadors. As temporal governments have the "right of protecting...ambassadors and of avenging an injury if they are ill-treated," so, too, the Church has "this right with respect to her own ambassadors who are the preachers of the faith...."

Having demonstrated the Church's right to use force in the defense of missionaries and of potential converts, Suárez then turned to the question of who can exercise this right and under what circumstances. He concluded, reasonably enough, that the pope alone has the responsibility of defending the "universal rights of the church." No secular prince has the right to act in these situations without papal approval because this is a spiritual matter not a temporal one. Secular rulers would be required for the actual exercise of force in these cases because the Church is not allowed to use force. Again following Vitoria and his predecessors, Suárez ([1944] 1964: v. 2, 746) added that "the pope can distribute among temporal princes and kings the provinces and realms of the unbelievers...in order that they may make provision for the sending of preachers of the Gospel to those infidels, and may protect such preachers by their power, even through the declaration of just war, if reason and a rightful cause should require it." Furthermore, the pope has the power to "mark off specific boundaries for each prince" as did "Alexander VI in the case of the kings of Portugal and of Castile." In this way, the potential converts would in effect bear the cost of their own conversion.

In Suárez's ([1944] 1964: v. 2, 747) opinion, the purpose for papal demarcation of areas of missionary activity was to insure that the missionary efforts "should be conducted in an orderly manner" while also insuring that "peace among Christian princes" was maintained and that "the welfare of the people committed" to each ruler's care was assured. In this stage of the argument, Suárez provided some basis for a theory of global order under papal direction, an order resting on religious motives and European armies.

In connection with the problem of defending the right of the Church to protect the preachers of the Gospel and the right of subjects to hear that preaching, Suárez had assumed in the case he had previously used that the ruler and his subjects were at odds on the issue. What if the ruler and his subjects were agreed in their opposition to Christian missionaries, could the Church still insist upon its right to use arms to insure their admission and their safety? In responding to this point, a point of some significance in the modern world where rulers are elected and, therefore, presumably reflect their constituents' views, Suárez ([1944] 1964: v. 2, 756) returned to the right of travel provided by the *ius gentium*: "...I think that they may be forced to permit the preachers of the Gospel to live in their territories; for this tolerance is obligatory under the *ius gentium* and cannot be impeded without just cause." At this point, Suárez appears to have been echoing Vitoria's discussion of the natural human community that included all men who thus have the right to travel everywhere in peace and security. The right to preach the Gospel becomes, in this case, an application of this natural right.

In another part of these lectures, Suárez dealt with the argument that the pope has the right to act as universal judge, specifically raising the issue of whether the pope has the right to order the destruction of idols. The Spanish Jesuit noted here that it was important to distinguish between what the rulers of Christian kingdoms should do within their own kingdoms and what they should do regarding idols worshipped by those who were not subject to them in temporal matters. Within his own kingdom, a Christian ruler has the right, even the obligation, to eliminate pagan rites if they are contrary to natural reason. According to Suárez ([1944] 1964: 769) infidels who are not subject to Christian rulers, however, "cannot normally be forced to change their errors and their rites" because "the Church has no jurisdiction over the unbelievers in question, and that coercion or punishment without jurisdiction is unjust." As a result (Suárez [1944] 1964: v. 2, 769–70), "an infidel state, supreme in its own order," cannot "be punished by the Church on account of its crimes, even if those crimes are contrary to natural reason; and consequently, it may not be compelled to give up idolatry or similar rites."

Suárez ([1944] 1964: v. 2, 780–81) did consider one case in which an infidel ruler could be deprived of his office by the Church. This situation, an example used in similar discussions reaching back to the thirteenth century, involved a ruler whose subjects had become Christians while he remained an infidel. In such circumstances "the Church may indirectly deprive" the non-Christian ruler of his power over his Christian subjects "if the welfare or defence of the latter makes this necessary." Here again, the argument for papal intervention rested upon the Church's right to defend its members, rights, and interests everywhere. If it could protect the Christian subjects of Christian rulers from the tyrannical actions of such rulers, the Church could certainly protect its members who were the subjects of an infidel ruler who was acting against their spiritual interests.

At the same time, Suárez did not encourage rebellion or invasion under such circumstances. He advised the Christian subjects of a wicked infidel ruler to "change their domicile and pass over to the realm of Christian princes." If their infidel ruler "attempts to prevent his Christian subjects from thus transferring their domicile, he may be forcibly resisted by Christian princes, and justly subdued in war in defence of these subjects, because they are being deprived of their right which they wish to exercise," that is the right to travel freely from one place to another. Yet again, what might appear to others as a form of Christian aggression against an infidel ruler is, according to Suárez, simply another example of the just war of defense.

Finally, and only briefly, Suárez considered the nature of relations that should exist between Christians and non-Christians. The bulk of this discussion dealt with the nature of such relations when non-Christians lived within a Christian society and under a Christian ruler. Virtually all of Suárez's ([1944] 1964: v. 2, 787–95) discussion considered Christian-Jewish relations, an issue long-debated in Spain. The theme of this brief discussion was that Christians were to be careful in their intercourse with non-believers lest their faith be undermined. At this point, Suárez might have gone on to consider such relations on the international level, but he did not.

The death of Suárez coincided with the beginning of the end for Hapsburg and Spanish power. In the year following his death, the Thirty Years War (1618–1648) began. By the end of the war, the Spanish Hapsburgs were bankrupt; and the Austrian Hapsburgs retained the imperial title but at the price of seeing it reduced to a shell of itself (Holborn 1959: 361–74). Furthermore, the Catholic Church, having been battered by the Reformation, withdrew into itself, condemning the modern world but having nothing with which to replace it except, perhaps, a return to an idealized and romanticized Middle Ages.

As late as the nineteenth century, Pope Pius IX could issue the *Syllabus of Errors* ([1864] 1954: 282–85) in which he catalogued all the intellectual and moral evils of the modern western world. Even when Leo XIII began to engage the Church with the modern world and its distinctive problems, he could only do so through a medieval prism. He not only began to consider social issues in *Rerum Novarum*, but he had also earlier issued *Aeterni Patris* ([1879] 1981: 187). In that letter, Leo XIII stated that among "the scholastic doctors, the chief and master of all, towers Thomas Aquinas" who "is rightly esteemed the special bulwark and glory of the Catholic Faith." The work of Vitoria, Suárez, and their colleagues simply fell into disuse in Catholic circles after the Thomist revival of the twentieth century. As a consequence, the only Catholic thinkers who tried to come to grips with the problem of global order in the modern world have been neglected in Catholic philosophical work.

The value of Vitoria and Suárez in the task of developing an intellectual basis for a concept of world order was rediscovered in the twentieth century by James Brown Scott, a Protestant lawyer who was active in the Carnegie Endowment for International Peace's campaign for world peace through world law (Muldoon 1972: 486–490). Scott encouraged the publication of a series of works on the origins of international law which included selections from the writings of Vitoria and Suárez which, he argued, were important building blocks for the subsequent, and more highly regarded, work of Grotius and his successors. The list of authors in the series, *Classics of International Law*, illustrated one of James Brown Scott's major points, namely that while Catholic writers began the development of modern international law, the work was later taken over and transformed into modern international law as a result of the Protestant thinkers who were more capable of dealing with the modern world.

James Brown Scott's conclusions about Catholic thinking on the issues of international law and relations bring us to the end of this discussion of sixteenth-century Catholic thinking on these issues. On the basis of the discussion presented here, what can be said about the contribution of Catholic thought to the issue of global order? My conclusion is pessimism about such a contribution unless there are some significant developments in Catholic social and political thought. Any modern liberal theory of global order must be based on an acceptance of the pluralistic nature of the modern world and an acceptance of differing views of the moral basis of society. No one really believes that every single form of social behavior can or must be accepted and tolerated. One would have to be morally invertebrate, not liberal, to tolerate human sacrifice or *suttee*. It is also hard to believe that even the most liberal westerners would really accept polygamy or child marriage. The issue is not absolute toleration but, as the medieval writers made clear, the degree of toleration to be exercised. In practice, modern men tend to believe in a kind of modified law of nations, what people generally do, rather than in an abstract law of nature, a fixed notion of what they ought to do, something they have in common with the Spanish international writers of the sixteenth and seventeenth centuries.

Catholic thought, based on Aquinas's teachings, still rests on the natural law basis of order. In the modern, pluralistic world this means that Catholic thought is often at odds with contemporary values. In itself, that is certainly not a bad thing. The difficulty arises when Catholics seek to participate in pluralistic societies. To what degree can they participate and to what degree must they withdraw from participation? In the contemporary world, this often presents dilemmas for many American Catholics. On the one hand, for example, their bishops recently issued a pastoral letter very critical of nuclear arms. On the other hand, the bishops have also taken a strong anti-abortion position. What is the voter to do when faced with a choice between a candidate who supports legal abortion and opposes nuclear arms and a candidate who takes the opposite positions? As the political position of President Reagan demonstrated, this is a real and immediate dilemma, not some neo-scholastic *reductio ad absurdum*. Modern pluralistic societies present these dilemmas all of the time. If this sort of dilemma exists on the national level, what greater possibilities for such dilemmas must exist at the international level. At the moment, Catholic thinking does not provide any but the most general contribution to the development of global order. It does, however, provide a number of dilemmas.

If Catholic thinkers wish to contribute to the debate within a pluralistic world about global order, about nuclear weapons, about the economy, and about issues such as abortion, they will have to go beyond the work of Aquinas. This is not to denigrate Aquinas. He was indeed the greatest and most inclusive of Catholic thinkers, but his thought reflected the circumstances of his own world. Later figures, like Vitoria and Suárez, began the task of developing Aquinas's principles to meet new circumstances. If Catholic thinkers wish to deal with contemporary problems within a Catholic tradition, they should at least consider beginning with Aquinas but then moving on through the critics of Aquinas and to the sixteenth-century continuators of the Thomistic tradition. Vitoria and Suárez did, after all, begin to wrestle with the problem of co-existence with infidel societies, one of the fundamental issues involved in the development of the modern pluralistic global order.

If there is to be a reconsideration of Catholic thought on global order, indeed reconsideration of global order from virtually any perspective, there can be no better time than the present. The forthcoming celebration of the five hundredth anniversary of Christopher Columbus' first voyage will soon be upon us. Although medieval writers had begun the discussion of the nature of a global order in a rudimentary fashion, the issue had little practical significance until Columbus' voyages made the New World a part of the European consciousness. Once he had encountered the inhabitants of the Caribbean islands, Columbus began the discussion of global order. How were these people to be treated? Were they valid possessors of the lands that they inhabited? Was it the moral responsibility of the Spanish to baptize and Christianize these people? If so, could or should force be used to protect the missionaries who went to preach to the Indians? Did European Christians have an obligation to stop practices that violated the natural law? Was the conquest of the Americas justified in order to stop cannibalism and human sacrifice?

All of these questions touching upon the relations between the Christian Old World and the pagan New World emerged within a few years of Columbus' voyages. In addition to all the other consequences of Columbus' voyages, economic, social, political, biological, as Lewis Hanke ([1949] 1965: 1) pointed out, the conquest of the Americas also gave rise to "one of the greatest attempts the world has seen to make Christian precepts prevail in the relations between peoples."

There will be a number of commemorations of Columbus' first voyage in the next several years. There will be parades of tall ships, recreations of Columbus' landing on one or another Caribbean island, and other such activities. For religious organizations, a fitting commemoration would be serious consideration of the moral consequences of that voyage and their implications for the contemporary world.

References

Allen, J.W. [1928] 1960. *A History of Political Thought in the Sixteenth Century*. London and New York: Metheun and Barnes & Noble.
Aquinas, Thomas. 1970. *Aquinas: Selected Political Writings*, edited by A.P. D'Entreves. Oxford: B. Blackwell.
Bettenson, Henry (ed.). 1963. *Documents of the Christian Church*. 2nd ed. London: Oxford University Press.
Davies, R. Trevor. [1937] 1954. *The Golden Age of Spain*. London: Macmillan.
Hanke, Lewis. [1949] 1965. *The Spanish Struggle for Justice in the Conquest of America*. Boston: Little, Brown.
Holborn, Hajo. 1959. *A History of Modern Germany: The Reformation*. New York: Knopf.
Holt, James C. (ed.). 1972. *Magna Carta and the Idea of Liberty*. New York: John Wiley.
James, I. 1918. "Apologie." 71–109 in *The Political Works*, edited by C.H. McIlwain. Cambridge: Harvard University Press.
Ladner, G.B. 1954. "The Concepts of 'Ecclesia' and 'Christianitas' and Their Relation to the Idea of Papal 'Plenitudo Potestatis' from Gregory VII to Boniface VIII." *Mescellanea Historiae Pontificiae* 18:49–77.
Leo XIII. [1879] 1981. "Aeterni Patris." In *One Hundred Years of Thomism: Aeterni Patris and Afterwards*, edited by Victor B. Brezik, C.S.B. Houston: Center for Thomistic Studies.
Muldoon, James. 1972. "The Contribution of the Medieval Canon Lawyers to the Formation of International Law." *Traditio* 28:483–97.
_____. 1978. "Papal Responsibility for the Infidel: Another Look at Alexander VI's *Inter Caetera*." *Catholic Historical Review* 64:168–84.
_____. 1979. *Popes, Lawyers, and Infidels: The Church and the Non-Christian World, 1250–1550*. Philadelphia: University of Pennsylvania Press.
Pius IX. [1864] 1954. "Syllabus of Errors." In *Church and State Through the Centuries*, edited by S.Z. Ehler and J.B. Morrall. London: Burns & Oates.
Post, Gaines. 1964. *Studies in Medieval Legal Thought: Public Law and the State, 1100–1322*. Princeton: Princeton University Press.
Randle, Robert F. 1973. *The Origins of Peace*. New York: Free Press.
Suárez, Francisco. [1944] 1964. *Selections from Three Works*, edited by Gladys L. Williams, Ammi Brown, and John Waldron. New York: Oceana.
Victoria (Vitoria), Franciscus de. [1917] 1964. *De Indis et de Ivre Reflectiones*, edited by Ernest Nys. New York: Oceana.

6

THE GODDESS AND THE GURU

TWO MODELS OF UNIVERSAL ORDER IN TAMIL INDIA

Glenn E. Yocum

THIS PAPER TAKES A VERY DIFFERENT APPROACH to the topic of religion and the quest for global order from the other essays collected in this volume. Its data, namely, sacred geography and ritual activity oriented around two Hindu temples, require that "global order" and the quest for such order be differently construed from what they are in the other essays. Beyond distinctive data and attendant interpretive constraints, however, I would argue that this discussion of Hindu materials adds a useful perspective on the topic.

We live in a world where global order is certainly a pressing concern, especially as we can no longer ignore the consequences of rapid worldwide industrialization and population growth. It is more and more difficult to be enamored of "progress" or even, I think, to affirm linear historical thinking about human activity in the last few millennia as a privileged way of understanding where we humans have been and are headed. The Hindu data presented here, though the product of a premodern society, are not irrelevant to thinking about how to live in a post-modern world. Polycentric universal orders that expand outward to include more than just humankind in their orbits of interest may very well hold some keys to how humans might survive in a world that contains a plurality of human cultures and religions and, even more urgently, requires the existence of life forms other than their own.

The Abrahamic monotheisms have periodically given rise to historical movements impelled by prophetic leadership aiming at the achievement of comprehensive global order. Hindus, on the other hand, at least for the last millennium and a half, have expressed their concern for universal order in quite different terms. The result in India has typically been the creation of complex spatio-temporal symbolic ensembles integrating all aspects of reality—divine, human, physical, natural. To highlight by exaggeration the differences between the Hindu tradition and the monotheisms of West Asian origin, the Hindu quest for global order has typically sought stasis, harmony, and hierarchy rather than dynamic change, revolution, and egalitarian brotherhood.

This paper focuses on two places, Madurai and Avadayarkoil, both of which represent Hindu attempts to create models of universal order; both center around Saiva temples; both lie within the sphere of influence of the pre-modern Pandyan Kings; and both attained their current level of articulation about 300 years ago during the time of Nayak rule in Madurai. The city of Madurai itself and its focal Minaksi-Sundaresvara temple express a vision of universal order centered on a divine queen and king and their union in marriage. The hinterlands town of Avadayarkoil and its sprawling Atmanatacuvami temple revolve around an ascetic guru-god who initiates disciples into a career of world renunciation. In these two instances one encounters yet again the classic Hindu polarity of *dharma* and *moksa*, though the idiom of expression, namely, that of universal order centered on a temple, is the same in both cases.

Madurai and the Minaksi Temple: The Goddess as Cosmic Linchpin

The city of Madurai in southern peninsular India has been the center of Tamil culture for at least the last 2,000 years, particularly so in view of the city's association with earliest stratum of extant Tamil literature, the Cankam poems stemming from the early centuries of the Christian era. But Madurai is more than a long-lived cultural center; it is also a city whose very design and annual ritual cycle exhibit a strong concern with cosmic order. At the heart of the city lies the grand stone palace (*koyil*—literally, "King's dwelling," but also the most common Tamil word for "temple") of the goddess Minaksi and her husband Sundaresvara, the local manifestation of Siva.[1] Spreading out from the temple's central shrines, one housing a stone image of Minaksi, the other representing Sundaresvara's presence in the form of *sivalinqam* (the god's most typical emblem, a vaguely phallic-like stone column), are Madurai's major streets, concentric waves rippling from the divine energy at the city's center. Indeed, the city's spatial pattern is based on a *mandala*, a sacred diagram mirroring an ordered universe in which gods and humans have their proper place and role.

At the center of a Hindu temple stands the *garbhaqrha*, the "womb-house," the *sanctum sanctorum* containing the fixed stone representation (*mulastanam*—"root place") of the principal deity. After either its discovery (Sundaresvara's *sivalinqam* in the Minaksi temple, for example, is a "self-existent" *svayambhu linqam*) or after its sculpting and ritual consecration, this stone representation is not just an "image" but an embodiment of god, a divine "real presence," to borrow a phrase from Christian sacramental theology.

The Minaksi temple, as already noted, has two contiguous but separate central sancta, one of the goddess (the *"amman* temple") and one for her spouse (the *"cuvami* temple"). The forms enshrined there receive ritual homage at various set times during the day. These rituals performed by the temple's Brahmin priests are ministrations to the deities' bodies, e.g., bathing, clothing, fanning, feeding, providing entertainment, putting the deity to sleep, waking the god in the morning, etc. Hence, the temple is understood to be a dwelling whose divine occupants take up residence among their human—and non-human—subjects. In the case of the Minaksi temple, Minaksi and Sundaresvara are quite explicitly identified with royalty, particularly with the Pandyan dynasty. They are literally king and queen of Madurai, situated at the center of their kingdom, protectors of the realm.

Each of the central sancta is surrounded by two walled *prakarams* (courtyards) that devotees use for circumambulation of Minaksi's and Sundaresvara's shrines. (See the map of the Minaksi temple on page 90, reproduced from Fuller 1984.) These *prakarams* also house images of various intermediate divine beings and saints. Outside these *prakarams*, but still within the temple's high outer wall, is the third *prakaram*, part of which is also counted as the innermost of the streets that orbit around the central shrines. This *prakaram* also contains a number of ancillary buildings, particularly on its east side, some used for specific rituals (e.g., the Kalayana Mantapam—the "wedding pavilion"), others functioning as temple offices, storerooms, stables for the temple elephant and camels, and shops selling various religious and ritual paraphernalia. Also within the temple's walls are the Golden Lotus Tank, a

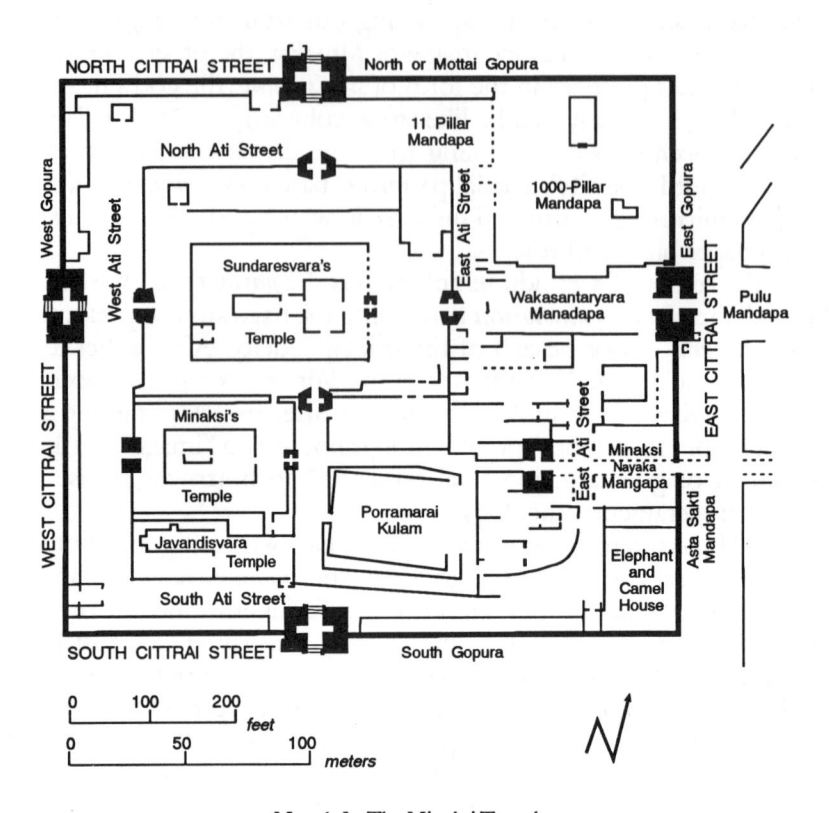

Map 6-1. The Minaksi Temple

small pond where devotees bathe; the temple kitchens, where food for the deities is prepared; and the *sthala vrksa*, the sacred "tree of the place," a common feature in temples in Tamil Nadu.

The Minaksi temple, as is true of most south Indian Hindu temples, is oriented toward the east. Minaksi and Sundaresvara both face east, and their images are located at the western terminus of two east-west running streets that thus, theoretically at least, afford both deities an unobstructed view of the rising sun on the eastern horizon. The major entrance to the temple is through a gate in the outer wall aligned with Minaksi's shrine, an indication of her preeminence at the temple. The temple's outer walls are surmounted by four high towers called *gopuram*-s situated at the cardinal points of the compass; these are visible throughout the city and beyond. The *gopuram*-s are themselves covered with images of the gods, allowing those outside the temple, particularly those "impure" castes denied entry to the temple in pre-Independence times, a vision of the gods who are more fully and efficaciously visible within the precincts. Beyond the Minaksi temple's outer wall, four more sets of streets run parallel to the temple boundaries—Cittarai Street, Avanti Mula Street, Maci Street, and Veli Street. (See map of Madurai on page 92, reproduced from Fuller 1984.)

Within the area marked off by Veli Street—the city limit of Nayak-period Madurai and site of a moat that a British administrator ordered filled in 1837—lie the palace of the Nakak kings near the southeast corner of the enclosed area and, in the southwest, the temple of Kutalalakar, a local form of the Visnu. Thus, traditional Madurai was home to all the principal custodians of Hindu dharmic order—the three major Hindu deities (Siva, Visnu, and the goddess) and a king, not to mention the Brahmins whose houses occupied the area in the immediate vicinity of the temple.

The Minaksi temple's square *mandala*-design is one shared by other large south Indian Hindu temples. The key concept at work in the layout of the temple—and by extension of the city as well—is that of the *vastumandala* or *vastuprursamandala*, a term that clearly connects the temple and its environing city to the ideology of Vedic sacrifice. Preparatory to the Minaksi temple's major annual festival, described below, the temple priests ritually draw a *vastumandala* on a floor within the temple. The *mandala* itself is then worshipped. This ritual in effect recreates the proper relations among the gods and among men, renewing the order to which the architectonics of the temple and the city give such vivid expression.

The various subareas of the *vastumandala* are conceived to be the domains of particular deities, cosmic forces, demons, and humans:

> Brahma in the center; Vedic gods from each of the three levels of the cosmos; the *naksatras* (constellations); and guardians of the cardinal and intermediate directions. The diagram becomes, in short, the sacred cosmos made manifest in both space and time.... Onto this plan, the spirit or *purusa* of the site is projected. This *purusa* is anthropomorphically conceived to be a person lying with elbows and knees spread out within the delimited site. The cosmos created by the assignment of deities to plots is coextensive with the body of the *purusa*, and it is this *purusa* that enlivens and organizes the disparate elements, powers, and beings of the cosmos conceived, by virtue of the anthropomorphism, as an organic whole.

> One of the types of *mandalas* contained in the texts is identified as "southern." This *mandala* has Brahma in the center surrounded by three concentric enclosures. Starting from the center and moving outward, there are enclosures allocated to gods (*daivaka*), human beings (*manusa*), and demons (*pisaca*). Dramrisch identifies this plan with that which lies at the root of the *prakarams*

92   GLENN E. YOCUM

MADURAI
OLD CITY CENTER
Only main streets are shown

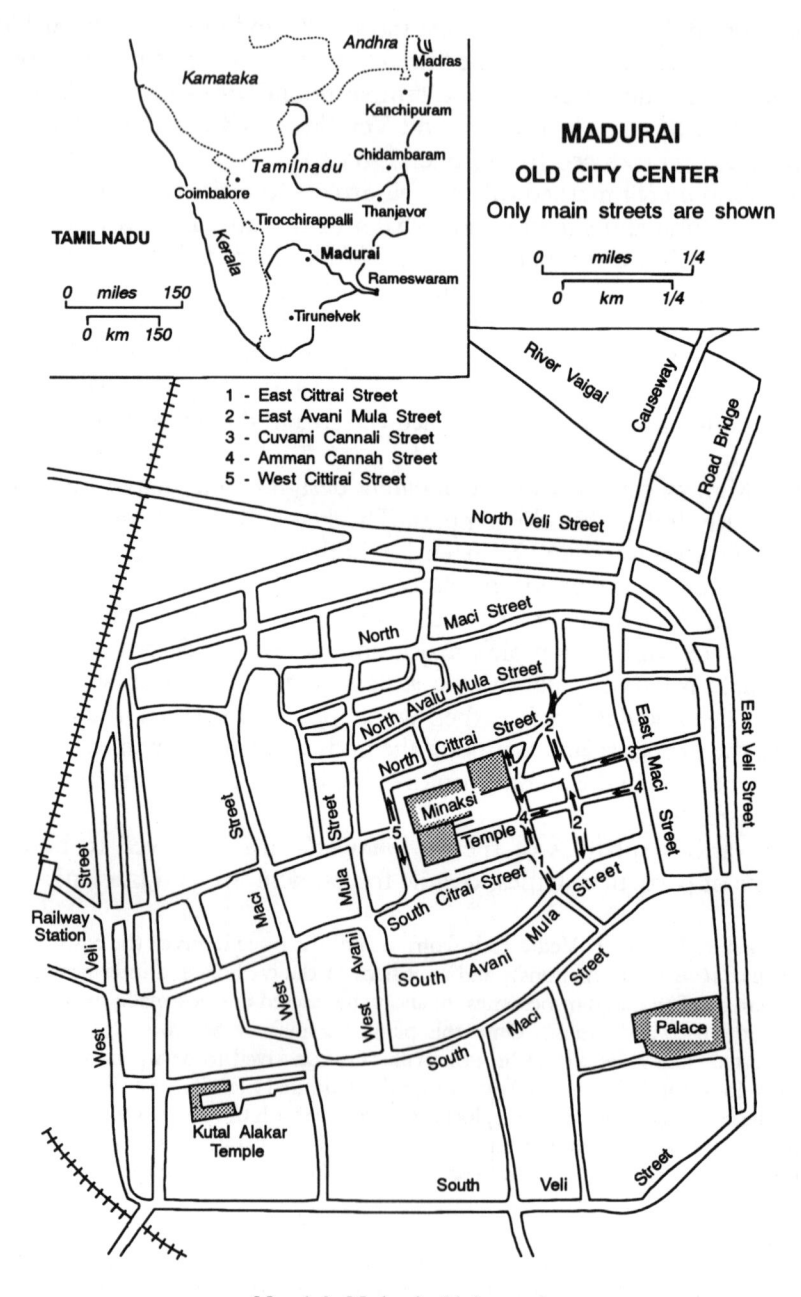

1 - East Cittrai Street
2 - East Avani Mula Street
3 - Cuvami Cannali Street
4 - Amman Cannah Street
5 - West Cittirai Street

Map 6–2. Madurai: old city center

of South Indian temples.[2] The enclosures, it should be noted, are allocated hierarchically to various types of beings according to their distance from the center. As applied to town planning, this triple enclosure scheme is to govern the assignment of castes and occupational groups. Allocation of people is also supposed to proceed in consideration of the deities assigned to plots within the square *mandala*.... What is clear...is that a city is conceived to be an integrated whole proceeding from and undergirded by a sacred geometry, oriented to the four cardinal directions about the sacred center established architecturally by the temple (Reynolds 1987: 172–173).

The parallels between temple/city and the body of a person (*purusa*) resonate strongly with one of the great speculative hymns of the *Raveda*. The Purusasukta ("the *purusa* hymn"), *Raveda* 10.90, imagines the creation of the cosmos proceeding from the sacrificial dismemberment of a primeval man.[3] From specific parts of his body are born various elements of the cosmos, e.g., sun from his eye, wind from his breath, the moon from his mind, etc. But of particular interest to us here is the correlation of an organically conceived social order with parts of the *purusa's* body:

> 1. When they divided the Man *purusa*, into how many parts did they apportion him? What do they call his mouth, his two arms and thighs, hands and feet?
> 2. His mouth became the Brahmin; his arms were made into the Warrior, his thighs the People, and from his feet the Servants were born.
> 3. The moon was born from his mind; from his eye the sun was born. Indra and Agni came from his mouth, and from his vital breath the Wind was born.
> 4. From his navel the middle realm of space arose; from his head the sky evolved. From his two feet came the earth, and the quarters of the sky from his ear. Thus they set the world in order (O'Flaherty 1981: 31).

This is the first mention in the Vedic corpus of the four *varna*-s, the four classes of the ideal dharmic society: Brahmins, Ksatriyas, Vaisyas, and Sudras. Worthy of comment here is that these social groups are symbolized hierarchically and organically—together they function like a body. Furthermore the entire cosmos is conceived to be a body-like organism. The design of the Minaksi temple and city of Madurai thus clearly exemplify a mode of conceptualizing universal order that is at least 3000 years old in the Indian subcontinent.

But clearly the sacred order that radiates out from the Minaksi temple to encompass a city and its inhabitants is not established merely—or even mainly—by architectonics. At least as important to Madurai's position as the center around which an ordered universe is established is its mythic history. That history is not merely narrated in a *sthalapurana* ("sacred history of the place") but is also painted on the temple walls, condensed into easily recognized plastic icons, and enacted annually in the ritual calendar of the Minaksi Temple, especially in its festivals and most particularly in the "Cittirai festival" that takes place in the month of Cittirai (April–May), Madurai's *sthalapurana*, the *Tiruvilaiyatal Puranam* ("the history of the sacred sports"), tells the story of 64 "sports" Siva performed in Madurai.[4]

It is beyond the scope of this paper to summarize all or even most of these divine activities. Suffice it to say that they recount instances when Siva-Sundaresvara manifested himself in Madurai and its environs, thereby establishing the sacrality of the place. Some depict him as a divine protector who defeats demonic forces, thus rendering the place safe for human habitation. Others tell of his connection with the Pandyan dynasty, thus providing the early kings of Madurai with a divine pedigree. Still other of the "sports" are sectarian and narrate how devotees of Siva superseded the Jains in the city. Not a few of the stories show the god as something of a trickster and are characterized by a humorous, sportive quality.

The stories from the *Tiruvilaiyatal Puranam* that have the most direct bearing on the Cittirai festival, which is the high point of Madurai's ritual year and also the most vivid enactment of the city's sense of order, concern Minaksi. These can be capsulized as follows: The Pandyan king, whose father had built the city of Madurai, and his queen were without offspring. They petitioned Lord Sundaresvara for an heir. The result of their efforts was not the desired son but a daughter with three breasts whom the parents named Minaksi ("she with the fish eyes"). Sundaresvara told the parents not to worry about the girl's physical irregularity and instructed them to raise her as if she were a son, assuring them that her third breast would disappear when she met the man who would be her husband.

Trained in the military arts, Minaksi proved to be a fearsome warrior. Upon the Pandyan king's death, Minaksi was crowned queen of Madurai. Thereafter she undertook a campaign of universal conquest with her army of female attendants and vanquished the Lords of the Eight Directions. Then Minaksi engaged the army of Lord Sundaresvara. While she was able to defeat Sundaresvar's army, when the god himself appeared, Minaksi's third breast disappeared and her demeanor turned modest; she now comported herself as *dharma* would require a wife to behave in the presence of her husband. A wedding was soon scheduled. In attendance were an impressive array of human and divine guests. Brahma chanted mantras and Minaksi's brother, Visnu, poured the sacred water over the joined hands of the bride and the groom. In due course Minaksi had a son who became king of Madurai. Minaksi and

Sundaresvara then retired to their temple shrines where they still reside, passing on temporal authority to the ongoing line of Pandyan kings.

What in the popular mind has come to be called the "Cittirai festival" includes more than the twelve-day *brahmotsava* ("major festival") of the Minaksi temple that culminates in the wedding of Minaksi and Sundaresvara. The Cittirai festival also encompasses the nine-day journey festival of Lord Alakar, a form of Visnu resident in a temple at Alagarkoil twelve miles to the northeast of Madurai. Originally the two festivals did not overlap, but in the mid-seventeenth century Tirumala Nayak, the most powerful of the Telegu-speaking Nayak rulers of Madurai, moved the date of Minaksi's wedding so that it partially overlapped Alakar's journey festival.

Today the vast majority of the huge crowd that gathers in Madurai for the Cittirai festival understand the two celebrations to be parts of one grand ritual drama, even though the puranic texts and temple priests maintain that the festivals are independent of each other. The official reason for Alakara's journey from his temple at Alagarkoil to the bed of the Vaigai river just beyond the northeast corner of Veli Street is so that Alakar can grant release to one of his devotees, an ascetic who had fallen under a curse and assumed the form of a frog. But in the popular explanation Alakar comes to Madurai to attend the wedding of Minaksi, who is his sister. However, by the time Alakar reaches the river bed Minaksi's wedding has already taken place. Thus, he does not enter the city but returns to his temple at Alagarkoil angry at having missed the wedding.

In ritual fact the wedding is attended by another form of Visnu whose image is brought to Madurai—along with that of the god Murakan—from Tiruppankunram, a village a few miles to the southwest of Madurai. Alakar-Visnu from Alagarkoil, however, is a very important god for many of the people who inhabit the countryside to the northeast of the city, and thus it is Alakar's attendance at the wedding upon which popular imagination fastens. In fact, the circumstances surrounding Alakar's journey and the social composition of his worshippers provide clues about Tirumala Nayak's possible motives in rescheduling Minaksi's wedding so that it overlaps Alakar's journey. Many of Alakar's devotees are members of the Kallar caste, whose traditional occupation was thieving and serving as village guards, though today most Kallar are engaged in agriculture. The Kallar are traditional devotees of the deity who guards Alakar's temple and whose shrine is on the doors of the *gopuram* on the east wall of the Alagarkoil temple.

This god, called Karuppanacuvami ("the black lord"), eats meat and possesses some of his devotees. In short, he is a non-Brahmanical god, but his worshippers through their devotion to him are thus also devotees of his lord, viz., Lord Alakar. Furthermore, when Alakar undertakes his journey to Madurai he dresses as a Kallar in deference to Karuppanacuvami's devotees through whose territory he passes. And for the entire course of the journey he is accompanied by Karuppanacuvami's priest who presides at the door shrine in Alagarkoil. Thus, by coordinating the two festivals Tirumals Nayak was able ritually to integrate a cast notoriously difficult to control into the ritual order of his kingdom. And whereas specific groups or individuals may be devoted to Sundaresvara-Siva or to Alakar-Visnu-Karuppanacuvami, all are united in their allegiance to Minaksi.

Another possible motive for moving the wedding to the month of Cittirai (it had probably been a month or two earlier in Maci or Pankuni before Tirumala Nayak changed its schedule) relates to another change instituted by Tirumala Nayak. It was during his reign that huge wooden "cars" were built to carry Minaksi's and Sundaresvara's metal festival images in regal procession through Madurai's streets on the day after their wedding. But, as anyone who has seen a south Indian temple car knows, it requires substantial manpower to pull these huge structures. Before Tirumala Nayak changed its date, the wedding had fallen during the harvest season. In Cittirai the harvest is over and the hot season has arrived. Farmers from the countryside are thus free at this time of the year to attend festivals and to undertake the traditional service and honor of pulling the cars.

To summarize briefly the course of the Cittirai festival:[5] On the day before the wedding festival formally begins, the *vastumandala* is drawn within the Minaksi temple. Thus, the sacred order of the temple and city is ritually renewed before the dramatic reenactment of its most formative events. On the morning of the first day of the wedding festival, as is common in Saiva temples in south India, a flag is raised marking the beginning of the festival. From the evening of the first day through the evening of the seventh day, images (*utsavamurti*-s—"festival images," movable images made of metal) of Minaksi and Sundaresvara along with those of several attendant figures (their sons Vinayakar and Murukan, and the saint Candikesvara) are pulled through the city streets, usually around Maci Street, on various vehicles every morning and evening.

Such processions thus have five vehicles, one for each of the above-named figures in the following order: Vinayakar (i.e., Ganesa), Murukan (i.e., Skanda, Subrahmanya, Kumara), Sundaresvara accompanied by small images of Minaksi and Skanda (i.e., Somaskanda), Minaksi, and Candikesvara. The processions, beginning from the east side of the temple, circumambulate the center in a standard clockwise direction

THE GODDESS AND THE GURU: TWO MODELS OF UNIVERSAL ORDER 97

(*pradaksina*), always keeping the temple on the right. These processions are occasions for the deities to survey their kingdom, re-sanctify the ordered universe outlined by the *mandala* of Madurai's streets, give *darsan* (auspicious vision) of themselves to their devotees outside the temple, and also to receive ritual homage from the city's inhabitants. Such processions stop frequently so that the priests accompanying them can present the offerings of worshippers to the deities; and typically the deities will stop at some prearranged resting place, often a hall sponsored by a family or a caste or a pious association.

The first day of the month of Cittirai falls on the fifth day of the wedding festival. Since Cittirai is the first month of the Tamil year, the Cittirai festival thus has added associations of cosmic renewal typical of new year celebrations. In fact, one of the ritual activities that takes place within the Minaksi temple on this day is the reading of the astrological forecast for the new year.

On the evening of the eighth day, before the evening procession, Minaksi undergoes a coronation ceremony (*pattapisekam*) in the sanctum of her temple. On the text day Minaksi's conquest of the Lords of the Eight Directions is enacted during the evening procession at the corner of North and East Maci Streets. Represented on this occasion by a young girl, Minaksi finally encounters Sundaresvara, played by a boy, and is defeated by him. Early the next morning, on the festival's tenth day, images of Visnu and Murukan arrive from Tirupparankunram to attend the wedding, and later that morning Minaksi and Sundaresvara are married in a grand wedding ceremony in the Kalyana Mantapam ("wedding pavilion") of the Minaksi temple. Admission to this event is by ticket only; in 1970 tickets were available at 10, 5, and 3 rupees (Harman 1981: 306). The procession on the following morning is the car festival that attracts huge crowds when Minaksi and Sundaresvara are pulled around Maci Street on two enormous cars. On the twelfth day of the wedding festival the images of the deities are bathed in the Golden Lotus Tank; a ritual reenacting the god Indra's original discovery of Sundaresvara's shrine is performed; and the images of Visnu and Murukan, who came for the wedding from Tirupparankunram, depart. The festival flag is lowered, and the Minaksi temple's part of the Cittirai festival draws to a close.

Meanwhile the nine-day festival of Alakar's journey has already begun. For the first three days—identical to the eighth, ninth, and tenth days of the wedding festival—Alakar receives special worship in his temple at Alagarkoil. On the fourth day Alakar, dressed as a Kallar, sets forth on his journey—to give release to the saint Sutapas, according to the textual tradition; to attend his sister Minaksi's wedding, according to popular explanation. This is the same day as the car procession takes place in Madurai, the day after the wedding. En route Alakar stops at pavilions in Kallar villages and receives the homage of his devotees. On that evening he reaches the bank of the Vaigal just opposite Madurai. The next day Alakar enters the Vaigal river bed, and throughout the next three days he appears on various vehicles and in various guises much to the delight of his numerous devotees. During the fifth day of his journey festival Alakar meets the image of Lord Kutalalakar, another form of Visnu whose temple is located in Madurai, in the dry river bed of the Vaigai. Popular lore claims that it is then that he learns he has missed the wedding of his sister Minaksi. The next morning, proceeding on a snake vehicle, Alakar journeys up the Vaigai and grants release to the saint who was trapped in the body of a frog. Throughout that night he gives a special *drsan* of his ten incarnations at the Ramarayar Mantapam on the bank of the Vaigai. Early on the morning of the eighth day, again dressed as a Kallar, Alakar retraces his route back to his temple at Alagarkoil, stopping at the same resting places he visited on his way to the Vaigai. On the morning of the ninth day Alakar reaches his temple, and the Cittirai festival is over for another year.

These festivals through their many elements—the dramas they stage, the routes of their processions, and not least the large and diverse crowds they attract—ritually articulate a social order and a polity, albeit not one without tensions (Lord Alakar does, after all, miss the wedding). They are graphic annual demonstrations that Madurai is a city whose order centers on the goddess Minaksi and her temple. Both the city's design and its ritual calendar bespeak the creation of an ordered universe. To inhabit Madurai is thus to live in an ordered universe expressed through the architectonics of the city and the rhythms of its ritual-civic cycle.

As Reynolds aptly puts it:

> Though the political and economic systems, formerly part of a unitary worldview which included religion, are dramatically different in contemporary Madurai—and indeed have been since at least the time of British rule—the unity forged by the ritual process set into motion by Tirumala Nayak especially, still remains today. And though the city's boundaries extend far beyond those delimited by the walls of former years, the old boundaries of the core city remain relevant to the ritual life of Madurai. It would not be going too far to say that the *mandala* on which the city is predicated remains relevant, too. There are smaller centers within the city—each shrine and temple founds a world—but no center has developed in the expanded Madurai municipality to challenge the Mihaksi-Sundaresvarar temple as the center. In light of the vigor with which the Cittirai festival is performed even today, it seems safe to say

that the city continues to speak to the many urban and rural inhabitant-devotees, still functions, though in a less encompassing way, as a symbol of and a process for achieving cosmic, moral, and social order. Madurai is a place, and a sacred place at that: the product of an architectural rite; but it is also a process, a ritual process, in which both the sacred history and sacred geometry of the city continue to unfold each year (Reynolds 1987: 185).

In its creation of order through an ensemble of religious symbols and practices, Madurai is hardly unique among cities and towns in south India. Another south Indian example of spatial-ritual order will provide comparative perspective on Madurai's example, one centered, however, not on a goddess, her royal consort, and a brother-in-law and his low-caste devotees, but rather on an ascetic guru and his chief disciple, an erstwhile minister of the Pandyan King in Madurai.

Avadayarkoil and the Atmanatacuvami Temple: The Disappearing Guru at the Center of the Universe

About six miles east of Madurai as the crow flies, not far from the seacoast, is the small town of Avadayarkoil in Arantangi Taluk, Pudukkottai District. Far removed from a major urban center, its ambience is very different from that of Madurai. Avadayarkoil is located in what was a border region between the old Pandyan kingdom centered in Madurai and the Chola Kingdom whose heartland was the Cauvery delta to the north of Avadararkoil. Local traditions connect the place both with the Pandyans and Madurai as well as with the Chola king and the great Chola temple at Chidambaram, about 100 miles to the north. Today by far the most impressive feature of the town and region, otherwise a relatively remote and impoverished area by contemporary Tamil Nadu standards, is a large temple at the center of the town, the temple of Atmanatacuvami, a local form of Siva. The Atmanatacuvami temple's architecture and exquisite stone sculpture exhibit a variety of styles, indicating that construction took place over many centuries under the patronage of various kings—Pandyans, Cholas, Nayaks, and the Setapatis of Pudakkottai, among others (Raghavan 1984: 31ff.).

The oldest parts of the Atmanatcuvami temple probably were built about 1,000 years ago, but many of the structures and sculptures outside of the temple's inner core (e.g., various *mantapam*-s and the temple *gopuram*) are similar in style and apparent provenance to those sections of Madurai's Minaksi temple that stem from the Nayak period of keen building activity about 300 years ago. Though epigraphic evidence is wanting, it appears that Avadayarkoil's big temple experienced an efflorescence in construction at about the same time the Minaksi temple underwent major expansion, though the principal patrons, given local stories I have heard, may well have been the rajas of Ramnad and Pudukkottai rather than—or as well as—the Nayaks of Madurai. More significant for our purposes than identification of the dynasties responsible for building specific parts of the temple is the fact that for at least the last few centuries the Atmanatacuavmi temple has been under the control of the Thiruvavadutharai Adheenam, a non-Brahmin Saiva monastic foundation located in Thiruvavadutharai, a village in the heart of the Cauvery delta about 76 miles to the northeast. The ownership and management of the temple by this institution headed by a celibate ascetic guru is quite appropriate given the temple's distinctive symbolism, as will soon become apparent.

The Atmanatacuvami temple's basic design is like that of the Minaksi temple: sanctum surrounded by several walled *prakaram*-s with streets outside the walled enclosure running parallel to the temple walls. (See map on page 101.)[6] The first street outside the temple walls—actually a narrow lane—is counted as the fourth *prakaram*, and here, immediately outside the temple walls around the temple's north, east, and west sides, there are houses inhabited by Brahmins, many of whom have a family member engaged in service in the temple. The fifth and outermost *prakaram* is, in fact, Avadayarkoil's main street where route buses make their way through the town, stopping just outside the main entrance to the temple on the south side where several small shops are also clustered. These streets are the ones used for processions at festival times, including the car procession, and are consequently referred to as the "Car Streets." The temple office is located in a building on South Car Street that also functions as a guest house of the Thiruvavduthurai Adheenam, used by officials or monks of the "mutt" (i.e., Sanskrit *matha*—a monastic foundation) when visiting Avadayarkoil.

Also, a short distance back a side lane from South Car Street lies the grave (*samadhi*) of one of the gurus of the Thiruvavduthurai Adheenam who died in Avadayarkoil while on pilgrimage. These then are the major spatial features of Avadayarkoil, creating an ordered universe similar in basic design to that of Madurai. Closer inspection, however, reveals some noteworthy differences, virtually all of which can be accounted for in terms of the nature of the deity enshrined here, for at Avadayarkoil Siva does not appear as a Pandyan king married to a powerful local goddess but as an ascetic teacher quite distanced from women and mundane affairs. In fact this ordered universe, somewhat paradoxically perhaps, is centered on renunciation and liberating instruction rather than on marriage and royal power.

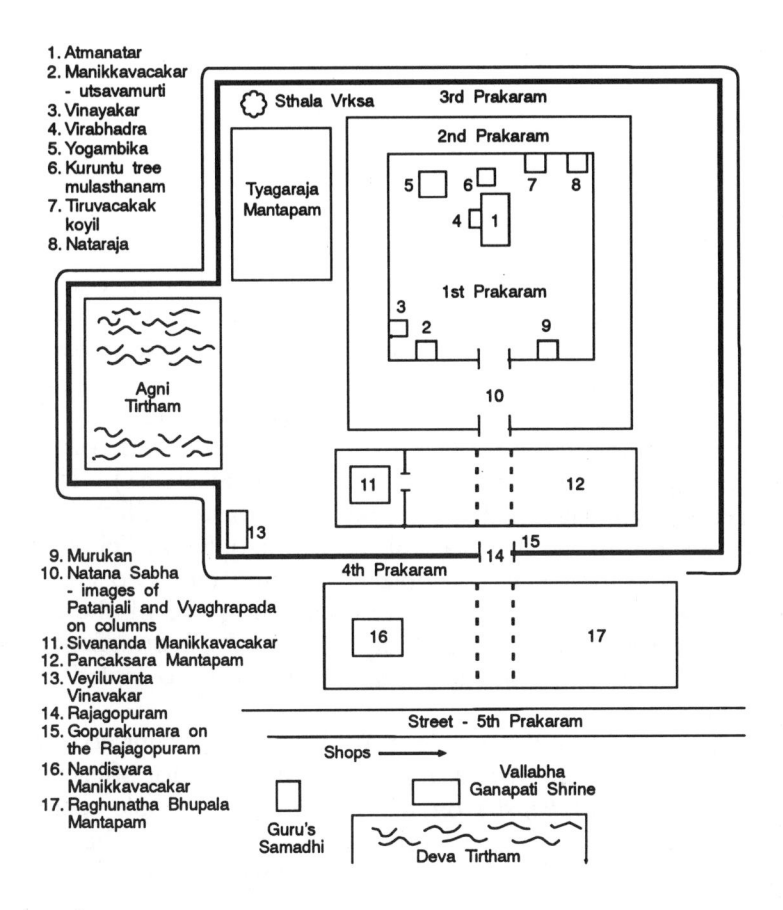

THE GODDESS AND THE GURU: TWO MODELS OF UNIVERSAL ORDER 101

```
1. Atmanatar
2. Manikkavacakar
   - utsavamurti
3. Vinayakar
4. Virabhadra
5. Yogambika
6. Kuruntu tree
   mulasthanam
7. Tiruvacakak
   koyil
8. Nataraja

9. Murukan
10. Natana Sabha
    - images of
    Patanjali and Vyaghrapada
    on columns
11. Sivananda Manikkavacakar
12. Pancaksara Mantapam
13. Veyiluvanta
    Vinayakar
14. Rajagopuram
15. Gopurakumara on
    the Rajagopuram
16. Nandisvara
    Manikkavacakar
17. Raghunatha Bhupala
    Mantapam
```

Map 6–3. The Atmanatacuvami Temple

An obvious difference from the Minaksi temple is that Atmanatar's temple opens to the south, a rather striking peculiarity given the eastward orientation of most south Indian temples. However, this clearly associates Siva at Avadayarkoil with yogis and teachers, who are said to face south; witness, for example, Siva's image at Daksinamurti ("south-facing form"; *daksina* also denotes the fee paid to a priest or teacher) which is typically found on the outer southern wall of Saiva temple sanctums in south India. More unusual still, at this temple there are none of the usual movable festival images (*utsavamurti*-s) for Siva. In fact, apart from an *utsavamurti* for Murukan, which is processed on monthly Karitikkai days and on other special celebrations for Murukan, the Atmanatacuvami temple's only processional image is that of

Manikkavacakar, a famous Tamil poet-saint whom Atamanatar initiated at Avadayarkoil. (See below.) When the temple's two major annual ten-day *brahmotsava*-s are celebrated in Markali (Dec.–Jan) and Ani (June–July) months, this image of Manikkavacakar, decorated to appear as different manifestations of Siva, is the single icon take around the *prakaram*-s through the Car Streets in the daily morning and evening festival processions.

Siva's name at Avadayarkoil is related to some of the temple's peculiarities. Atmanatar/Atmanatcuvami means "the Lord of the Self" (the less Sanskritic Uyirnatan and Uyirkku Uyir ["the soul of the soul"] are also sometimes used). Atmanatar does not appear in the temple *garbhagrha* in the customary *linqam* form. Local informants and the *Tirupperunturai Vilakkam*, a Tamil chapbook pilgrim's guide, stress that Siva's appearance at Avadayarkoil is *aruvam* (Sanskrit *arupa*—"formless," and a *rahasyam*—a "mystery") (Venkateswara Iyer 1925: 60–61).[7] The latter term echoes language used to describe the way Siva manifests himself at Chidambaram. As we shall see, this is not the only parallel between Avadayarkoil and the Nataraja temple at Chidambaram, two sites connected by the career of Manikkavakar, one the place of the saint's initiation and the beginning of his "holy utterances" (*Tiruvacakam*), the other the site of his consummation of the *Tiruvacakam's* completion and canonization.

While the sanctum of the temple at Avadayarkoil contains no *linqam*, there is a large low *pitam* (Sanskrit *pitha*—altar, plinth for offerings) in the center of the *garbhagrha* on which some local people claim are imprinted the footprints of the divine guru Atmanatar. The temple priests, however, insist that Siva is strictly "formless" at this place. The "mystery" of the "non-image" is compounded by the fact that the center of the *pitam* is hidden by a gold *kavacam* (an armor-like metal covering used to decorate images in south Indian temples) here called the *suvarnakkuvalai* and said to have been installed by Manikkavacakar himself (Venkateswara Iyer 1925: 51, 60–61). This *kavacam* is only removed for a special brief moment at the Ardra Darsanam festival in Markali month, and then, as at all other times, in keeping with standard practice in south Indian temples, worshippers other than priests must remain outside the door to the sanctum. So the "mystery" is preserved.

As anyone familiar with temples of Siva in contemporary south India knows, it is frequently the goddess shrine within the temple that most seems to draw worshippers to the shrine—understandably so given the concern of the majority of the temple-goers with the problems of health, marriage, progeny, prosperity, education, and employment, problems that the goddess is understood to care about and be willing to help with more than the rather aloof lord. Furthermore, the best-known local myths of many Saiva temples focus on the relationship between Siva and his spouse.

As is true in Madurai, it is commonly some aspect of the goddess's behavior that serves to explain the site's sacredness. Her persona usually projects a distinctively local character. She is thus the one who frequently "locates" the temple. Festivals often culminate in—or at least include—a marriage ceremony uniting Siva and the goddess. At Avadayarkoil there is no wedding to celebrate, although there is a goddess, but her significance is much reduced compared to most other temples. Her name Yogambika, "the mother of yoga" (variously Yoganayaki, Sivayoganayaki), reveals her unusual character. Her modest shrine in the first *prakaram* also contains no typical image, and its entrance is barred by a cage. It is as though this "temple for *jnani*-s [strivers after wisdom] and *sannyasi*-s [renouncers]," to quote one of the temple chanters (*otuvar*-s), must give some expression to the goddess's presence, but here this is a presence that needs to be graphically delimited, indeed a power under strict control, caged.

One of the few additional iconographic themes to which the goddess has a small part at Avadayarkoil focuses on Siva's dance. Parallel to the five *sabha*-s (halls) of the Nataraja temple in Chidambaram are the six *sabha*-s at Avadayarkoil. The area on the south side of the second *prakaram* is called the Natana Sabha (or Nirutta Sabha), the "dancing hall." Although Patanjali and Vyaghrapada came here to witness Siva's dance—and their images are there on the pillars—Siva dispatched them to Chidambaram to have *darsan* dance at that place instead, explaining that at Avadayarkoil he is without form (Venkataswara Iyer 1925: 59).

However, Siva did rehearse his dance here at midnight with the goddess as his only witness, and this gave rise to the proverb "Only after dancing at home should one go to a public hall" (*araiyaile atiya pinnare ampalattirku vara ventum*) (Muttukkumaracami Cervani 1972: 116). This is the most intimate contact the goddess enjoys with Siva at Avadayarkoil. The *Tirupperunturai Vilakkam* reports that the temple has a *palliyarai* ("bed chamber")—which I have neither seen nor heard mentioned by anyone in Avadayarkoil—but, consistent with the temple's wider symbolism, it is also stated that the lord and his lady do not go to the *palliyarai* as they do in other temples (Venkateswara Iyer 1925: 73).

The usual relationship with Siva's divine family undergoes further modification at Avadayarkoil due to the sannyasic symbolism that dominates there. In the third *prakaram* there is a shrine to Ganesa, here called Veyiluvanta Vinayakar ("Vinayakar who likes heat") or Atupa Ganapati ("heat Ganapati"). And on the *rajagopuram*, the tall *gopuram* that crowns the southern entrance in the wall bounding the third *prakaram*, there is a frequently venerated image of Murukan called Goporakumara or Gopuravelavan. The myth which explains these two shrines is interesting (Venkateswara Iyer 1925: 66). Since Atmanatar has surrendered all his honors (*cirappu*) and festivals at Avadayarkoil to Manikkavacakar, his two sons became angry. Therefore Vinayakar stood in the heat, and Murukan threatened his father by saying he would jump from the mountain. Then Siva pacified his two sons.

A further aberration at Avadayarkoil is the absence of a shrine to Siva's attendant-devotee Candikesvara. This, too, can be related to the temple's jnanic-sannyasic preoccupations. In most Tamil Saiva temples there is a Candikesvara shrine in the inner *prakaram* on the north side of the sanctum. During a typical circumambulation of the sanctum, after having *darsan* of the *linqam*, a worshipper will pause at Candikesvara's shrine and announce his presence by clapping his hands or snapping his fingers. This is because either Candikesvara is meditating (an explanation favored by priests) or is deaf (the more commonly stated reason). In any case, Candikesvara is regarded as the temple record keeper who notes who has worshipped and how often, thus ensuring that the meritorious action will not go unrecognized. Furthermore, Candikesvara's *utsavamurti* comes last in the daily morning and evening processions during festivals at Saiva temples in Tamil Nadu. In processions Candikesvara functions as a kind of "rearguard." But in the festivals celebrated at Avadayarkoil, as already mentioned, Manikkavacakar-Siva traverses the streets unattended. Symbolically, Candikesvara's absence bespeaks a jnanic-sannyasic rejection of merit accumulation as a proper motive for visiting this temple and also reflects a distinctive tendency at Avadayarkoil to reduce the royal symbolism evident in festival processions at many other south Indian shrines.

It is striking that most of the Atmanatacuvami temple's distinctive elements enumerated here have to do with features that are absent, subtractions from the symbolic ensemble of more standard temples. Despite four subsidiary shrines to Manikkavacakar within the temple[8] the most sacred spot involving the saint—debatedly the holiest location in the entire temple, competing with the *pitam* in the sanctum—is the shrine of the *Kuruntu* (wild lime) tree in the first *prakaram* just outside the northwest corner of Atmanatar's sanctum. Although there is a large thriving *kuruntu* tree in the northwest corner of the third *prakaram*, which is the temple's *sthala vrksa* but is generally ignored by worshippers, *the kurutu* tree, the one under which Atmanatar is said to have sat when he initiated Manikkavacakar, is situated at the above-mentioned site in the *prakaram* behind the sanctum sanctorum. Here one sees what appears to be a stone column about three to four feet in height, much worshipped and besmeared with palm oil, situated on a platform itself about three feet higher than the rest of the *prakaram*. The *lingam*-shaped column is sculpted in low relief to show a teacher, facing south, sitting at the base of a tree giving his blessing to a figure who crouches in worshipful posture at his feet. The details of the sculpture are best seen on festival occasions when a gold *kavacam* which highlights these features covers the *vigraha* (immovable image). The "tree," said to be the trunk of the original *kuruntu* tree,[9] is covered by a *mantapam* that one of my informants claimed was the original hall built by one of Atmanatar's disciples on the occasion of Manikkavacakar's initiation.

Following the same pattern of discussion here as was used for Madurai in the first section of this paper, it remains to summarize the principal myth that establishes Avadayarkoil's sacredness and to sketch the scenario of its culminating ritual in the temple's major festival, the Ardra Darsanam festival in December–January. The major event that locates the sacredness of the Atmanatacuvami temple, already mentioned several times, is the poet-saint Manikkavacakar's formal initiation (*upatacam*, Sanskrit *upadesa*) into saving wisdom and an ascetic way of life at the hands of Atmanatar, appearing in the guise of a Saiva guru. The story is told at some length in both the *Tiruvatavurar Puranam*, a hagiography that recounts Manikkavacakar's life, and in the *Tiruvilaiyatal Puranam*, since Madurai and the Pandyan King also figure prominently in the story.

In a nutshell, what happened is this: Manikkavacakar, the Brahmin chief minister of the Pandyan king in Madurai, was dispatched by his master to Perunturai (i.e., modern-day Avadayarkoil) to buy horses. On entering the town, he saw an ascetic teacher seated underneath a *kuruntu* tree holding a book in his hand, the *Civananapotam*. Manikkavacakar quickly concluded that this was the guru of his heart's desire—indeed recognized that the guru was none other than Siva himself—and sought initiation as his disciple.

The initiation, performed beneath the *kuruntu* tree, involved Siva's teaching Manikkavacakar a mantra and resulted in the dramatic transformation of the erstwhile royal Brahmin into an ascetic disciple of the guru, a fact repeatedly depicted in temple sculpture and painting. It also transformed money for horses into money for the guru, much to the displeasure of the king back in Madurai. This teacher—not one of those gurus whose fancy is conveyances—used the money to have a temple constructed on the site of the initiation and to endow rituals for this place of worship.

Meanwhile, back in Madurai, when the king learned what had happened to his chief minister, he summoned Manikkavacakar to return immediately. The guru commanded his newly initiated disciple to go back, promising that he would bring the horses himself at a later date. When Manikkavacakar arrived in Madurai *sans* horses, *sans* money, the king had him jailed and tortured. But Siva kept his promise; he disguised himself as an irresistible horse groom, rounded up all the jackals in the forest outside Perunturai, transformed them all into the most handsome horses imaginable, and drove them off to Madurai. When the king saw these fine animals, he relented and had Manikkavacakar released from prison. But that very night the horses reverted to being jackals, causing near panic in the city. Back to prison went Manikkavacakar. Then Siva caused the Vaigai to flood, and after some more antics, stemmed the flood, revealed his true nature to the now repentant Pandyan, who released Manikkavacakar from his service (but only after offering him his kingdom!), free to return to his guru at Avadayarkoil.

When Manikkavacakar arrived back in Perunturai, he fell at the feet of his teacher. The guru's attendants, former inhabitants of Mt. Kailasa in the Himalayas, now pleaded with Siva to return to his heavenly abode, for they desired to see his divine form again. The guru then directed them to build an altar (*pitam*) in the shade of the *kuruntu* tree on which they were to inlay his footprints (*Tiruvatavurar Puranam* 1925: 332).[10] He further told them that a great fire would appear in a nearby tank. When this happened they were to throw themselves into the fire. This would end all their suffering and they would return to him at that time. Having said this, the guru set out for Kailasa.

But Manikkavacakar followed him and fell at his feet. Siva then said that he would always be available beneath the *kuruntu* tree to show his grace and remove the karma of his devotees. Manikkavacakar could remain at Perunturai with Siva's devotees until the fire appeared, but he was not to enter the flames with the rest. Rather the teacher instructed him to leave Perunturai at that time for Uttarakocamankai. Then he should proceed to other Saiva temples where he would worship the lord, ultimately reaching Chidambaram, at which place Manikkavacakar would defeat Buddhists in a debate and be granted the supreme knowledge of Siva and union with the god. After further explaining the glories of Chidambarum, the guru disappeared, and Manikkavacakar returned to assist the teacher's disciples in constructing the *pitam* beneath the *kuruntu* tree.

Manikkavacakar worshipped in Perunturai with the others and began to sing the hymns that would later be collected in the *Tiruvacakam*.[11]

After spending a number of days in this manner, the fire Siva had foretold appeared and all of the other disciples plunged into the burning tank (the Agni tirtham on the west side of the third *prakaram* of the contemporary temple). Siva and his spouse Parvati then appeared in the heavens riding the bull Nandi, and the devotees who had just entered the flames surrounded the divine couple as the adoring heavenly host. The god then vanished. Manikkacacakar sat down under a cassia tree and did yogic meditation before breaking into tears and singing a song of separation. Then he left the tank, worshipped Siva's feet, sang another hymn of praise, and bid farewell to holy Perunturai, remembering the guru's instructions to go to Uttarakocamanaki. So ends the story of the saint's activities at Avadayarkoil.

Of all the unusual features of the Avadayarkoil temple, the most striking is the absence of the standard festival images of various Saiva gods and saints, since here they are condensed into a single metal processional image, that of Manikkavacakar himself. During the two annual ten-day festivals at the atmanatacuvami temple this image is attired for morning and evening processions to make it appear as various manifestations of Siva (e.g., Nataraja, Bhiksatana). Local temple lore, both printed and derived from interviews, insists that at his place Siva bestowed on Manikkavacakar all the god's customary rights (*urimai*) and reputation (*perumai*) (Muttukkamarcami Cervai 1972: 116); for what the initiation effected was the oneness of guru and disciple, of god and man. The foundation (*potam*) of wisdom (*nana*) is that *civam*, the one immovable essence, pervades both Siva and his devotee.[12] Or to make the same point by translating a line from Manikkavacakar's *Tiruvacakam* that appears on the popular print available at the temple office:

The father [i.e. Siva] took charge of me
and I was transformed into *civam*.
O wonder! Who but I knows such grace!

(Tamil, *civamakki enaiyanta attan enkkaruliyavaru ar peruvar accove—Tiruvacakam* 51:1; Manikkavacakar 1968: 967.) Thus the entire festival sequence focused on Manikkavacakar's image—but especially the *upatecakkatci* ("*darsan* of the initiation," i.e., the ritual reenactment of the initiation; see below)—is a showing (*darsan*) of the unity of reality, dramatized in the "mixing together" (*irantar kalattal*, a phrase used by several informants) of a god-teacher and a human devotee.

But enough theological commentary. I must rehearse the ritual enacted at the temple's heart that, as it were, pumps life into its stone limbs.[13] At about five o'clock in the morning of the tenth day of the

Ardra Darsanam festival (actually the eleventh day, but counted at the climactic end of the tenth and final day in the printed festival program),[14] a ritual begins at the temple sanctum that will culminate about one hour later with Manikkavacakar's initiation underneath the *kuruntu* tree just outside the sanctum in the first *prakaram*. Since the performance sequence was virtually identical in 1985 to what it had been three years earlier in 1982, unless I note otherwise, what follows is true of both instances observed.

Manikkavacakar's festival image, bejewelled and dressed in fine silks, is brought directly before the doorway to the sanctum of the temple, so that he will have the best location for the special *darsan* that is about to occur. On this occasion Manikkavacakar's image represents not Siva (as it had on previous days of the festival) but Manikkavacakar himself come to Perunturai as the Pandyan's chief minister. After Manikkavacakar's image has been properly situated, a curtain hanging in the doorway of the sanctum is very briefly pulled aside three times in quick succession while a priest waves a lamp over the *pitam*. This is the only time during the year when the *pitam* is not hidden by its customary covering. Human devotees crowd the area outside the sanctum doorway to the left and to the right, leaving the privileged vantage point directly in front of the sanctum to Manikkavacakar. Assuming some typicality in my own experiences in 1982 and 1985, the *rahasyam* seems certain of continued mysteriousness; for the curtain is drawn very quickly; the *pitam* lies at least fifteen feet away from the door through which only priests may pass; and the shoving and straining of the crowd outside the door make a sustained view of anything nearly impossible.

After this special *darsan* is over, two further lamp-wavings occur in the sanctum. Following the second of these—after the worshippers have dispersed somewhat from the area immediately outside the temple sanctum—one of the senior priests, heavily garlanded with *rudraksa* beads (*rudraksa* berries are sacred to Siva) and crowned with a fantastic *lingam*-shaped *rudraksa* headgear—emerges from the sanctum, does a brief *puja* (ritual homage) to the image of Manikkavacakar, and then turns to the right to begin a circumambulation around the inner *prakaram* of the temple. He represents Atmanatar come to initiate Manikkavacakar. Since the Atamanatacuvami temple is oriented toward the south, the priest representing Atmanatar is clearly homologous to Siva as Daksinamurti coming down from the northern heights of his Himalayan abode to teach liberating wisdom.

Manikkavacakar's image follows the priest playing Atmanatar in procession outside the east wall of the sanctum in the inner *prakaram*. The assembled worshippers follow the two main actors in this ritual drama.

Brief stops for *diparadhana* (the waving of lamps) are made at the shrines of Vinayakar (Ganesa), Virabhadra, and Yogambika. After worship at the goddess shrine, the procession reaches the *kuruntu* tree. It is next to the *kuruntu* tree shrine that the *upatecam* is reenacted. The priest playing Siva climbs a temporary wooden platform set up next to the *kuruntu* shrine. Here he murmurs a number of Sanskrit mantras, displays several *mundra*-s, and does some *pranayama* (yogic breath control) exercises. Invested with the power of the mantras, the priest playing Atmanatar later told me, he at this point fully incarnates the god. Manikkavacakar's image is then brought beside the guru-priest-god, and both are wrapped in a red cloth. It is now that Siva "teaches" Manikkavacakar. While wrapped in the cloth, he whispers the *pancaksara mantra* in Manikkavacakar's ear. The *pancaksara*'s sacred "five syllables" are the well-known Saiva formula *name civaya* ("obeisance to Siva").

While the initiation was occurring in 1982, one of the temple *otuvar*-s (chanters of Tamil hymns) intoned a lyric in praise of *civa*, *nana*, and *potam*. The removal of the cloth wrapping the figures marks the high point of *upatecakkatci*, for now one catches his first glimpse of the transformed Manikkavacakar. In 1985 a new touch was added to this ritual, one straight out of Tamil hagiography. A cardboard box filled with flowers had been rigged to the ceiling above the initiation platform. At the moment the figures were unveiled, the box opened to shower flowers on Siva-Atmanatar and Manikkavacakar. Flowers typically rain from the sky at auspicious climaxes in the stories about the Tamil Saiva saints. It is also at this point that the *otuvar* stops his singing and leads all those present in a chant of the *pancaksara mantra* that then leads into antiphonal singing of the first hymn of Manikkavacakar's *Tiruvacakam*, whose opening line begins "*names civaya vaalka.*" ("Hail to *name civaya!*") The *otuvar* sings half a line, and the worshipers repeat it.

Siva and Manikkavacakar remain on the platform, and both have lamps waved before them by the temple priests. After this, *prasadam* is distributed by the priest playing Siva. First, temple and mutt officials, dignitaries, and special guests are presented with sections of the garlands that had adorned the two images (i.e., Manikkavacakar's *utsavamurti* and the priest embodying Atmanatar). Then *vibhuti* (sacred ash) is distributed to the remaining people present.

Finally, the *pradaksina* (clockwise circumambulation) of the inner *prakaram* continues with stops for lamp-waving at the Talvallan (i.e., Nataraja) and Murukan shrines at the northeast and southeast corners respectively. Thereafter the procession moves through the door separating the first and second *prakaram*-s, and just outside this door (thus directly south of the sanctum) in the second *prakaram*, a rather lengthy *puja* is done before Manikkavacakar's image. This includes the *otuvar's* chanting verses from the *Tiruvacakam*. Here Manikkavacakar's image is turned toward each of the four directions and lamps are waved before him while he faces north, east, south, and west. Informants say that he does this in order to bless all the devotees in the world. Clearly, it is also symbolic of sovereignty. The former chief minister has been transformed into a universal ascetic lord.

It is worth pausing at this point to note that of all the Tamil Saiva saints, Manikkavacakar is the only one whose standard iconographic form displays him in an attitude of teaching (Raghavan 1984: 70–71), the right hand in a gesture with thumb and forefinger joined, variously called *jnanamudra*, *vyakhyanamudra*, or *cinmudra*, representing realization of liberating wisdom and explanation of the truth, the left hand (*pustaka hasta*) holding a palm-leaf book (viz., the *Tiruvacakam*).[15] Other Tamil saints are typically shown with hands clasped in adoration (*anjali mudra*). Of them all, so far as I know, only Manikkavacakar undergoes formal initiation. Only he is transformed into a divine teacher himself.

The *puja* in the second *prakaram* concludes *upatecakkatci*, and with it the Ardra Darsanam festival at Avadayarkoil reaches its conclusion. The only remaining ritual connected with the festival occurs in the private space of the temple office on South Car Street. Here temple functionaries from the priests to musicians to carpenters to peons—everyone who had a role in mounting the festival—are presented with betel nuts and leaves in the order of their ritual ranks. The highest ranking temple or mutt official present distributes the betel on this occasion. Whereas the priests distributed honors at the *kuruntu* tree after the *upatacam*, with officials of the temple and the Thiruvavaduthurai mutt receiving theirs first, now the roles are reversed: temple or mutt officials distribute the tokens of status with Brahmin priests as the first recipients. What one sees here then is a rather clear ritual condensation of the complementarity and separation between Brahmins and "Saivas" (i.e., "pure" non-Brahmin *sudra*-s, principally of agriculturalist castes) that undergirds and pervades much traditional south Indian temple culture, not to mention the wider culture as well.

Avadayarkoil's sacred order is expressed in the same symbolic language as that of Madurai, but the message in this case is significantly different. Renunciation, guruship, and *moksa* rather than marriage, royal sovereignty, and *dharma* govern this universe. The marginality of the place—near the seacoast, in a hinterland—serve to underscore the social marginality of the renouncer and the marginality of *moksa*'s transcendence of the mundane world. Indeed, the *samadhi shrine of the guru on the south side of South Car Street rearticulates the marginality of the renouncer, itself situated outside the sacred precincts marked by the Car Streets.*[16] If as Reynolds claims (1987), Madurai is a *koyil nakar* par excellence, a temple-cum-palace city, then it is tempting to call Avadayarkoil a *samadhi nakar*, a "city of transcendent awareness and liberation."

But lest we become enamored with one-dimensional interpretation of Avadayarkoil's universe—one based on what is, to be sure, the clearly primary ascetic and liberation-oriented symbolism of the place—two further observations should provide some balance. One finds some devotees in Avadayarkoil who direct their devotion to "Lord Manikkavacakar" (in Tamil, *manikkavackar peruman*) and clearly hope for—sometimes receive—boons from him that are not unlike those granted to some devotees of Minaksi, Sundaresvara, and Alakar.

At least in some minds it would seem that the notion is deeply rooted that gods who reside in stone temple palaces and travel on splendid vehicles accompanied by a host of human retainers are really quasi-feudal lords, no matter how much iconographic subtraction or how many *rahasyam*-s there may otherwise be. And, second observation, even if the goddess at Avadayarkoil is the unmarried austerities-practicing "mother of yoga" and lives in a cage, it does not prevent the women of the town from flocking to monthly Laksmi Pujas designed to ensure a happy, prosperous, and fertile married life, rites held in the temple in the inner *prakaram* immediately in front of Yogombika's shrine, conducted moreover by temples priests, for a fee set by temple-mutt authorities. The messiness of the world does intrude on the symbolic elegance of the place. Perhaps humans can only tolerate so much order and integration, especially the ascetic, other-worldly kind.

Concluding Comments

I began this paper with some broadly comparative comments about the tendency of the monotheistic traditions to spawn historical movements of universalization, transformation, and revolution. India, of course, also has a history, though not one always very easy to construct, and India has not been without movements that have sought and produced change. But much Hindu ideology and ritual practice have tended to ignore or even to deny that change—the very stuff of history—has much significance or even "reality." Indeed, a chief function of the kinds of symbol, practices, and institutions with which this paper has been concerned is to create a stable world—stable at least in the minds of those who live in its cultural orbit. To live in Madurai or Avadayarkoil—or numerous other villages and towns and some cities in Hindu India—is potentially to live in a complete world—a universal, global world.

But unlike the monotheistic tendency to shift the focus of sacrality from a visible, physical world to the sphere of morals and politics—and hence of historical movement—Madurai and Avadayarkoil are virtually pervaded by sacred, physical space and action.[17] Madurai and Avadayarkoil are cities of what Redfield and Singer call the "moral order" (1954; cited by Reynolds 1987: 166) whereas the majority of the cities of the modern West, especially those of post-Columbian North America, are cities of the "technical order," their design and style dominated by concern with production and trade. Indeed, several of the large Indian cities created by British mercantilism (e.g., Calcutta, Bombay, Madras) are also primarily cities of the "technical order." Ironically perhaps, these modern cities in India or elsewhere throughout the world, whose design is clearly not an expression of a symbolic moral order, are among the most visible effects of globalizing economic and political movements whose ideological origins lie in European Protestantism.

Two more points remain to be made. One relates to the fact that the symbolic universal orders of Madurai and Avadayarkoil achieved their fullest flowering under the Madurai Nayaks—or possibly in the case of Avadayarkoil under the even more local Pudukkottai Setupatis and rajas of Ramnad. The political-military reach of all these rulers—Nayaks, Setupatis, or Ramnad rajas—was at best modest. Thus, these two globalizing visions of a local place were not creations of great imperial powers but of "little kings," who themselves may have been feudatories of other kings probably only slightly less little themselves.

The Hindu sense of universal order is not significantly correlated with the relatively few periods in India's long history when empires have created political unity in the subcontinent; the examples of subcontinental empire that come readily to mind are few—the Mauryas, the Guptas, the Mughals, the Raj, and the current Nehru dynasty. In fact none of these, with the possible exception of Lutyen's and Baker's New Delhi, created very striking models of universal order that begin to rival those of decidedly regional dynasties of the peninsula and of Indianized southeast Asia. One might indeed claim that the genius of the Hindu sense for universal order lies in its regionalism and localism, its capacity for concertizing the universal in a specific locale. The high points of India's civilization are not necessarily times of empire and political integration, a lesson historians have only recently begun to teach us.[18] What Madurai and Avadayarkoil show is that cultural integration is not dependent on large-scale political units, but that one of the key ingredients of Hindu cultural integration is a quite remarkable capacity for universalizing and sacralizing local space and time.

THE GODDESS AND THE GURU: TWO MODELS OF UNIVERSAL ORDER   113

This capacity for comprehending the universal in the local is not unrelated to another widespread Hindu norm—the turn inward, the identification of the ultimately real with the innermost but also universal self, the *atman*. Thus, the final point I want to suggest is that, unlike the prophet who seeks to externalize his vision of global order in a transformation of society, the Hindu tradition's propensity for localizing the universe is correlated with the tradition's longstanding habit of seeking ultimate transformation within. Perhaps nowhere is this correlation more obvious than at Avadayarkoil where the "Lord of the Self" dwells in mysterious formless form in the sanctum of the temple. And perhaps nowhere has the connection between the temple and its sacred topography, on the one side, and the inward turn toward the transcendental self, on the other, been better expressed than in David Shulman's study of Tamil Saiva temple myths, a passage with which I will conclude:

> What is the pilgrim's experience in this land of temples? There is often, to begin with, the long, uncomfortable journey to the shrine, which may be defined as a form of asceticism, *tapas*. The journey is, however, only the prelude to a deeper sense of self-sacrifice. Once the pilgrim arrives at the shrine, he sees before him the towering *gopuras* or gates set in the walls that enclose the sacred area. He leaves his shoes outside the gate; he will also usually undergo an initial purification by bathing, which prepares him for contact with the powerful forces inside. Once the pilgrim is through the *gopura*, the real journey begins. This is a journey into the self, and backwards in time. The tall *gopuras* of the south Indian temple create a sense of dynamism, of movement away from the gate and toward the center, which is locked inside the stone heart of the main shrine. There lies the sacred force contained within the walls, rendered accessible only through the strong ties that bound it, and through the ritual ordering of the universe within. The worshipper first circles around the temple compound, offering obeisance at minor shrines, always keeping the main sanctuary on his right; he circumscribes the center in an individual act of demarcation, just as the stone walls forever mark its limits. At length he will penetrate into the recesses of the main shrine and come to rest before the *garbhagrha*, where the image of the deity is located. Here he has arrived at the farthest reach of his wandering; hidden away in stone and darkness, as in a cave in the bowels of the earth, lies the symbol of the god, which is imbued with the divine power whose deeds are narrated in [the temple's] myths. Knowledge, or truth, is, in the eyes of the Hindus, by nature esoteric; it is buried, lost, to be recovered from the depths of the sea or from the darkness of the earth. The temple expresses in its very structure this search for hidden wisdom: the *gopuras* point us inward, to the cave. But the *garbhagrha* is, literally, a "house of the womb"; at this spot the pilgrim is conceived afresh, to be reborn without taint, with all the powers latent in the newborn child (Shulman 1980: 18–19).

Notes

Primary research in India on which much of this paper is based, especially the sections on Avadayarkoil, was made possible by a Senior Research Fellowship of the American Institute of Indian Studies in 1981–82 and by a grant from the Graves Foundation in the Humanities (Pomona College) in 1984–85. Regarding my research on the Atmanatacuvami temple I am much indebted to many generous and hospitable people in Avadayarkoil, especially to Sri S. Apukkalai Iyer, Vedic bhattar at the temple, and to Thiru S.V. Ganapathi, temple manager. Individuals at the Thiruvavaduthurai Adheenam, which owns and manages the Atmanatacuvami temple, have greatly facilitated my study on Avadayarkoil, particularly Sri-la-Sri Sivaprakasa Pandarasannadhi Avl., the head of the Thiruvavaduthurai Adheenam, and Thiru B.E. Subramanian, former Adheenam manager.

1. The information in the following description of Madurai's spatial arrangements and of the "Cittirai festival" is derived from the following sources: Reynolds (1987), Elder (1978), Fuller (1980 and 1984), Hudson (1978 and 1982), and Harman (1981). In this section I will note only direct quotations and interpretive/analytical points from these works. My description of the Minaksi temple and Madurai's spatial pattern also relies upon my own observations made during five brief visits to Maurai in 1968, 1973, 1980, 1982, and 1985.
2. Reynolds here refers to Stella Kramisch's definitive study of the Hindu temple (vol. 1, 60), which explores the meaning of the temple mainly in terms of *vastupurusamandala* as described in a number of Sanskrit texts (see Kramrisch 1976).
3. For a very competent introductory discussion of the Purusa Sukta, see Hopkins (1971: 22–25).
4. For discussion of the *Tiruvilaiyatal Puranam* and its contents, see especially Harman (1981), Dessigane *et al.* (1960), and Loud (1982).
5. For complete schedules of the Cittirai festival, translated from festival programs issued by the Minaksi and Alagarkoil temples in 1970, see Harman 1981: 294–322.
6. A fuller description of the Atmanatacuvami temple, its myths and rituals, can be found in a previous article of mine (Yocum 1986). Much of this section reproduces and condenses information presented there.
7. The *Tirupperunturai Vilakkham* also says that Siva's form at Avadayarkoil is light (*joti*) (Venkateswara Iyer 1925: 24, 26).
8. There are two large Manikkavacakar shrines in the outer *prakaram*-s of the temple: in the fourth *prakaram* the Nandisvara Manikkavacakar *mulastanam*, and in the third *prakaram* a sanctum to Sivananda Manikkavackar. The sanctum and ambulatory walls of the latter shrine are covered with murals depicting the saint's life. These paintings are probably about 100 years old. In the first *prakaram* is the shrine for Manikkavacakar's festival image and a small shrine which houses a palm leaf manuscript of the *Tiruvacakam*, one of three copies reputed to have been made by Siva himself when he came to Chidambaram at the end of the saint's life and requested Manikkavacakar to dictate his songs while the god in the guise of a scribe wrote them down.
9. The 1961 Census reports that "to avoid the ravages of nature the trunk of this tree has been copperplated and preserved" (Chockalingam 1971: 429). The "tree" seemed to me to be stone rather than covered with copper.

THE GODDESS AND THE GURU: TWO MODELS OF UNIVERSAL ORDER 115

10. According to informants in Avadayakoil, this *pitam* marks the place where Siva sat beneath the *kuruntu* tree.
11. Twenty of the *Tiruvacakam's* fifty-one hymns are said to have been composed in Perunturai. *Tiruvavatavurar Puranam*, 354–358 and 368, mention twenty-one hymns, one of which is not found in the *Tiruvacakam*.
12. Here I am echoing language from the description of Manikkavacakar's initial encounter with the guru in the *Tiruvatavurar Puranam* by Katavulmamunivar (1967: vs. 83–84). When Manikkavacakar first saw the guru, the teacher had a book in his hand. Manikkavacakar asked what book it was and received the reply that it was the *Civananapotam*. When the chief minister inquired further about the meaning of *civam*, *nanam*, and *potam*, he got a terse answer from the guru that *civam* is the one immovable reality, knowledge of this is *nanam*, and experience of this knowledge is *potam*. But this was enough for Manikkavacakar, as he immediately begged the teacher to make him his disciple.
13. This metaphor that compares the Atamanatacuvami Temple to a living body is not something I supplied in order to make explicit parallels to the *vasutupurusamandala* at Madurai or to classical Hindu theories about temples. Rather it was repeatedly used by my chief informant at Avadayarkoil, Sri S. Appukkalai Iyer, Vedic bhattar at the temple.
14. That the *upatecakkatci* is the climax and essential part of the Ardra Darsanam festival at Avadayarkoil is indicated by the radical attenuation of the festival in the years 1983–85. This was a time of drought in the Avadayarkoil area, and income from temple-owned lands was severely reduced. Consequently, the ten-day festival was curtailed to a single day during this three-year period. What had been a ten-day celebration in January 1982, with morning and evening processions on each day, was limited at the Ardra Darsanam in 1985 to a special evening *puja* in the temple followed by the *upatecakkatci* early the next morning. There were no processions outside the temple in the Car Streets during this festival in 1985. Clearly, the essential core of the festival is the initiation.
15. On the meanings of this *mudra*, see Liebert 1976: 61–61, 113–14, and 347–48. For a contemporary appropriation and explanation from a Saiva Siddhanta perspective of the *cinmudra* see Ramachandran 1985: iv–v.
16. Cf. the relationship at Tiruvannamalai between the big central temple and the Ramanan ashram and *samadhi* on a slope outside the town. Tiruvannamalai has one of the largest, most classically regular Siva temples in Tami Nadu.
17. Cf. the rather different but nonetheless very physical and concrete way sacrality is expressed in a complex of sacred topoi in the Hindu holy city of Banaras, the subject of an important book by Diana Eck (1982).
18. On this point, see the perceptive comments of Harvey Alper (1987: 31).

References

Alper, Harvey P. 1987. "Order Chaos and Renunciation: The Reign of Dharma in Modern India." 24–59 in *The Terrible Meek: Religion and Revolution in Cross-Cultural Perspective*, edited by Lonnie D. Kliever. New York: Paragon House.
Chockalingam, K. 1971. *Census of India 1961: vol. IX—Tamil Nadu; Part XI D—Temples of Tamil Nadu; vol. VII(i) Thanjavur*. Madras: Census of India.

Dessigane, R., P.Z. Pattabiramin and J. Filliozat. 1960. *La Légende des Jeux de Civa à Madurai d'après les Textes et les Peintures*. 2 vols. Pondichery: Institute Francais d'Indologie.

Eck, Diana L. 1982. *Banaras: City of Light*. New York: Alfred A. Knopf.

Elder, Joseph W. 1978. "Wedding of Goddess: Parts I & II." South Asian Film Series. Madison: South Asian Area Center, University of Wisconsin.

Fuller, C.J. 1980. "The Divine Couple's Relationship in a South Indian Temple: Minaksi and Sundaresvar at Madurai." *History of Religions* 19, 4:321–48.

———. 1984. *Servants of the Goddess: The Priests of a South Indian Temple*. Cambridge: Cambridge University Press.

Gould, Harold A. 1987. *The Hindu Caste System: The Sacralization of a Social Order*. Delhi: Chanakya Publications.

Harman, William P. 1981. "The Sacred Marriage of Maturai: Myth, Ritual, and Devotion in a South Indian Temple." Ph.D. dissertation. University of Chicago.

Hopkins, Thomas J. 1971. *The Hindu Religious Tradition*. Encino, CA: Dickenson Publishing Company.

Hudson, D. Dennis. 1978. "Siva, Minaksi, Visnu—Reflections on a Popular Myth in Madurai." 107–18 in *South Indian Temples: An Analytical Reconsideration*, edited by Burton Stein. New Delhi: Vikas.

———. 1982. "Two Citra Festivals in Madurai." 101–56, in *Religious Festivals in South India and Sri Lanka*, edited by Guy R. Welbon and Glenn E. Yocum. New Delhi: Monohar.

Katavulmamunivar. 1967. *Tiruvatavuraratikal Puranam*. Edited by Pu. Ci. Punnaivanananta Mutallyar. Madras: South India Saiva Siddhanta Works Publishing Society.

Kramrisch, Stella. 1976. *The Hindu Temple*. 2 vols. Delhi: Motilal Banarsidass reprint.

Liebert, Gösta. 1976. *Iconographic Dictionary of the Indian Religions: Hinduism-Buddhism-Jainism*. Leiden: E.J. Brill.

Loud, John A. 1982. *Sports of Siva (Madurai)*. Madurai: Distributed by Mrs. P. Shenbagavally.

Manikkavacakar. 1968. *Tiruvacakam*. Edited by Cuvami Citpavanantar. Tirupparaytturai: Sri Ramakirusna Tapovanam.

Muttukkumaracami Cervai Ca. 1972. "Araikuvi Vitarulum Atmanatan." *Tirukkoyil* 15, 3:115–17.

O'Flaherty, Wendy Doniger, trans. 1981. *The Rig Veda: An Anthology*. Harmondsworth: Penguin Books.

Raghavan, Prema. 1984. "Observations on Some Unusual Features at Avudaiyar Kovil (A Temple in Tamil Nadu)." M.A. thesis. University of Baroda.

Ramachandran, T.N. 1985. "Editor's Note." *Journal of the International Institute of Saiva Siddhanta* 1, 1:iii–v.

Redfield, Robert and Milton Singer. 1954. "The Cultural Role of Cities." *Economic Development and Cultural Change* 3, 1:53–73.

Reiniche, Marie-Louise. 1985. "Le Temple dans la Localité: Quatre Exemples au Tamilnad." 75–119 in *L'Espace du Temple I: Espaces, Itinéraires, Médiations*, edited by Jean-Claude Galey. Paris: Editions de l'Ecole des Hautes Etudes en Sciences Sociales.

Reynolds, Holly Baker. 1987. "Madurai: *Koyil Nakar*." 160–92 in *The City as a Sacred*

Center: Essays on Six Asian Contexts, edited by Bardwell Smith and Holly Baker Reynolds. Leiden: E.J. Brill.

Schomerus, H.W., trans. 1925. *Sivaitische Heilegenlegenden* (Periyapurana und Tiruvatavurar-purana). Jena: Eugen Diederichs.

Shulman, Daid Dean. 1980. *Tamil, Temple Myths: Sacrifice and Divine Marriage in the South Indian Saiva Tradition*. Princeton: Princeton University Press.

Venkateswara Iyer V. 1925. *Tirupperunturai Vilakkam*. Pattukkottai: Sri Nadiamman Press.

Yocum, Glenn. 1986. "Brahmin, King, Sannyasi, and the Goddess in a Cage: Reflections on the 'Conceptual Order of Hinduism' at a Tamil Saiva Temple." *Contributions to Indian Sociology* (n.s.) 20, 1:15–39.

7

THE HOLY GHOST AND THE ORDERING OF THE WORLD

Stanley Johannesen

THE FOLLOWING ESSAY CONCERNS A FORM of radical Protestant piety which may be the fastest growing movement of Christianity in the world, and the one least bound to national and ethnic limitations. I speak of the form of piety and ecclesiology that has grown out of the Pentecostal revival of 1906. This growth itself suggests some relevance to the theme of world order. Is Pentecostalism a portent of the form of a world religion? What world order would be the concomitant or declared objective of such a world religion?

The word "world" is itself problematic in such a context. The sectarian world-view, however numerous or successful the sect, is set against the world, both in its sumptuary ethics and its eschatology. World order, if it refers to anything, can only refer to the reign of anti-Christ. Nevertheless, piety is among other things a map of the world, drawn in affective rather than propositional terms, derived from an experience of the world, however limited or local. What I have done in this essay, then, is to turn the question around. If the Pentecostals do not have a world order in mind, they do have a characteristic way of ordering the world, a way of expressing their experience of the main constituents of world order: ethnicity, territory, power. The example that follows is extremely local, atypical in many ways. I believe, however, that the example demonstrates a central issue in the effective ethos of Pentecostalism and of radical Spirit pieties, namely an ordering of the world that is also a disordering of its constituent parts.

In the course of research and reflection for an essay on a Norwegian Pentecostal Church (Johannesen 1988)—the church I grew up in the 1940s and 1950s in Brooklyn—I was led to ponder anew the nature of Christian piety, and in particular those highly variable ways of living in the world, responding to the world, imaginatively figuring the order of the world, that correspond to variations in the religious experience. These Norwegian immigrants, like other Pentecostals the world over, rationalized their experience largely in the terms of the writer of Luke-Acts, with his emphasis on miracles and lay evangelization in a church to whom the Holy Ghost had come as promised by Jesus (Hollenweger 1972: 503; Quebedeaux 1976: 131). The social condition of rapid urbanization and uprooting, of consciousness of spiritual impoverishment, in a climate of global awareness and eschatological urgency, produced both in the first-century and the twentieth-century forms of piety that stressed miracle-working power and other charismatic gifts, conferred directly by the Holy Ghost, for the sake of building churches and evangelizing the world.

Pentecostalism is now an established revitalization movement in contemporary religious life. It is also clear that the emergence and evolution of Pentecostalist groups conform in interesting ways to the classic models of sectarian formation (Quebedeaux 1976; Flora 1976). From both of these points of view it is perhaps not a paradox, but a predictable commonplace that such groups simultaneously protect the boundaries of group identity with jealous fervor, and project their experiences outward into the world with aggressive zeal.

The Brooklyn church that I am studying was intensely preoccupied with keeping out the world, and equally intensely preoccupied with saving the world, even at long distances, supporting several missionaries, as was common among Pentecostal churches in the Scandinavian tradition, entirely out of the resources of local congregations (Pethrus 1973: 67–74, 161). Missionary zeal was not unique to Pentecostal churches, and in some respects the conceptualization of foreign mission, and its organizational strategies, were merely taken over from the older evangelical churches, as these gave over to more liberal, ecumenical attitudes toward the world. It is not, however, in classical foreign mission, itself so redolent of the culture-bound premises of nineteenth century Protestantism, that the Lukan church primarily reveals itself.

The Lukan church reveals itself in its distinctive relationship to the Holy Ghost, and in its corresponding views of the self and the world.

What does it mean for people to discover the power of the Holy Ghost? I don't mean in an individual psychological or spiritual way, but collectively, as the felt power of an experience of association?

Most Norwegians are Lutherans. Until the Reformation, they were Catholics whose religious traditions were derived to a great extent from Celtic and Anglo-Saxon sources (Willson 1903; Undset 1934). One of their leading saints was an Irish princess shipwrecked and martyred on the coast of Norway. Another was Saint Olav, the king who succeeded in imposing Christianity across the entire Norwegian land, also martyred. Pagan practices died hard, but in the Celtic fashion left a rich profusion of popular beliefs in fairies, elves and the like. Although Olav, and other Christianizers before him, converted people by force and extortion and trickery, there is no question that Latin Christianity nativized itself in the population as a civilizing and enriching force. Unlike the Saxons, who were Christianized by the foreign sword of the Frankish Charlemagne, the Norwegians, being Christianized by their own sword, so to speak, made a saint of their own conqueror. Olav, in other words, was a native saint, thereby sanctifying national community in his own relics.

The Reformation in Norway, on the other hand, was imposed by a Danish king in a lightning coup, at the precise moment of the deepest political humiliation in the nation's history, leaving moral and intellectual scars that persist to this day. Whereas the Lutheran Reformation in Germany expressed the lack of a sense of sanctity in society, and indeed deepened and institutionalized this sense, the Lutheran Reformation in Norway stripped away the sense of the connection between the population and its patron saint, also called, tellingly, "king in Norway forever." Norwegian historiography traditionally spoke of the next three hundred years as the dark night of the nation and can scarcely produce even an intelligible account of the Reformation, so foreign, swift, and degrading an experience it had been (Christopherson 1972). Popular religious expression, by the nineteenth century, found vent in waves of pietism and revivalism, not unlike the similar enthusiasms of the contemporary American frontier—and out of a similar condition of spiritual impoverishment and neglect. In both these societies, so radically different in virtually all other respects, an enthusiastic religion of heart-searching, emotional outpouring, lay preaching, and anti-clerical sentiment found fertile ground.

The Pentecostal revival came to Norway directly from the American awakening in the first decade of the twentieth century (Hollenweger

1972; Barratt 1907). T.B. Barratt, the English-born Methodist bishop, who came into contact with Pentecostals in New York City, preached the so-called Baptism in the Holy Ghost in Oslo, from whence it spread to Germany, Sweden, and Brazil, through men like Jonathan Paul, Lewi Pethrus, and Daniel Berg, who had come to Norway to investigate Barratt's claim and to hear his preaching. It is perhaps not coincidental that this extraordinary revival in Norway took place at exactly the time that Norway finally experienced full independence after nearly four hundred years, and embarked on an ambitious cultural program to reform the language and establish the cultural foundation of a distinct Norwegian nationality. That is, while Norwegian society was preoccupied with finding its own language, a significant number of Norwegians found evidence of the operation of the Holy Ghost in the practice of speaking in an unknown language.

Glossolalia has of course been reported at many times and places, by no means exclusively in Christian contexts, and appears to have surfaced in ecstatic religious movements in earlier centuries (Quebedeaux 1976). However, the twentieth-century revival of these practices has established itself as a religious revolution, and was reported, nearly simultaneously, not only among black Holiness and Methodist congregations in the United States, and among Norwegian Free Church groups, but among similar sectarian denominations in South Africa, Wales, and India. Could it be that these were places having in common powerful feelings of alienation that were largely cultural in content and symbolized in particular by language issues? Under such conditions, the Holy Ghost created involuntary membership in liturgical (i.e., publicly confessed) community as a solution for some people of the problem of voluntary membership in linguistic communities that were either alien and humiliating, or invented and lacking roots, or despised by significant others.

That is, in addition to the usual definition of deprivation in speaking of inducements to sectarian membership, we should also investigate this particular form of collective deprivation. For some people, clearly, to surrender the voice and the body to a power which is by definition irresistible is not only no loss of honor, it is an anodyne against other losses of honor. For those Norwegians who found this power irresistible it was possible to abandon the sanctification of the Norwegian state altogether and still be profoundly Christian. The Norwegians I knew understood their nationality in more-or-less pagan terms in terms of Vikings, peasant folklore, nature romanticism, the revived monarchy (but without Saint Olav), while at the same time defining their Christian association in terms of the world-wide network of local churches established by the power of the Holy Ghost. From its beginning in the mid-nineteenth century, the center of Norwegian settlement followed the expansion of the docks and the dock trades, from lower Manhattan across to Brooklyn and around the shoreline from Brooklyn Heights out toward the Narrows: Red Hook, Park Slope, Greenwood and Sunset Park, and finally Bay Ridge, were the centers of successive generation of Norwegian communities (Jonassen 1948). When people scattered to the suburbs in large numbers in the 1950s and 1960s, Norwegians formed similar loose clusters in Staten Island, New Jersey, Long Island, and upstate New York.

Two features set this pattern apart from other immigrant pattern in the city. One of these is the curious absence of communal tradition in relation to this peregrination. Nothing resembling the sense of origin that Jews associate with the Lower East Side, or that Italians associate with Italian Harlem. When Salem—the name of the Norwegian Pentecostal church, which stood at 4th Avenue and 54th Street, in the heart of Sunset Park—bought a church building in Red Hook for the purpose of mission work among derelicts, there was not, to my recollection, the slightest sense of the historical and social significance of this for communal memory. The church in Red Hook had been one of about five different church buildings occupied by the Bethelship Norwegian Methodist Church—perhaps the oldest Norwegian congregation in the city—in its progress across the city with the flow of its constituency. The redundancy of this building was recognized by the Pentecostals as a providential opportunity to evangelize unfortunates, who were in fact mostly Norwegian men. What was missing was a sense of formerly occupied and now abandoned communal territory. Nothing remotely like nostalgia attached to this, or to any other area of early settlement—although the suburbanites sometimes feel this about the most recent centers of settlement in the city: Sunset Park and Bay Ridge. But this is of course because they are losing ethnic characteristics altogether.

The other quality that set the Norwegian settlement pattern apart from other groups in the city, was a quality we might describe as social diffidence. There was a weakness of lateral communal affect somewhat akin to the weakness of communal memory. Norwegians were divided between the drinkers and the church-goers, between the high Lutherans and the "free" groups. The Pentecostals were in a league apart. Furthermore, Norwegians appeared to prefer settlement in densities where they were always a minority. No Norwegians lived in dense clusters, as did the Fins in Brooklyn. Instead they were surrounded by a Catholic majority: Irish, Italians, Poles, and later Puerto Ricans. This had something to do with the low tolerance of Norwegians for interference and the preference for formality in social exchanges, even among close friends. Coffee and sweets, served formally, were the social glue. Drinkers were saloon drinkers and got drunk and nasty. Norwegian families were patriarchal, but not *domus* centered. When married children set up on their own they were wholly independent and usually lived at some remove from their parents, whom they treated with some formality and even coldness.

There are many ways to interpret, much more to experience, such a society. It is not my purpose here to make judgments about the quality of emotional life in this Norwegian immigrant community. What I would like to point out is the character of the emotional path along which the experience of the Holy Ghost traveled for Norwegian Pentecostals. In this particular instance, what is remarkable is the absence of emotional impediments to a radically new principle of association, I mean a principle of liturgical practice and a principle of charisma distinguished by the absence of discernible ethnic or other cultural features—indeed the absence, to the knowledge of the communicants in this liturgical community, of any proximate historical precedent for their religious experiences. Norwegian immigrants to New York City in the late nineteenth and early twentieth century had inherited the truncated piety of their ancestors. They found neither the secular nationalism of their contemporaries in the old country, nor the social practices of the isolated farms of Norway of an earlier day, really suited to new-world conditions, and yet, perhaps by virtue of the individualism and emotional discipline enforced by these conditions, were economically successful, rising in a few generations from the class of skilled artisans, to entrepreneur builders and contractors, to full access to the professional and managerial classes in American life. Deprivation, in other words, if that is what it was, and if it helps explain the extraordinary appeal of the Pentecostal movement among Norwegians, was a communal deprivation, a deprivation of collective memory and of religious symbols of collective life. Neither Lutheranism nor the quasi-pagan Norwegian national idea provided mechanisms for the sanctification of communal memory, or places of settlement, or social structures. Norwegians were suspended between the Shorter Catechism and the trolls, between rote Christianity and fragments of a debased folklore. The Holy Ghost flooded this arid plain, because having no personal or ethnic features Himself, and speaking a language not ever heard on Earth, He gave positive value to deracination.

Robert Orsi's recent book on Italian immigrants in New York makes an instructive comparison with these Pentecostal Norwegians in Brooklyn (Orsi 1985). We have already noticed obvious differences in pattern of settlement and in the emotional density of social life, between Norwegians and South Italians in New York City. But there are also similarities. In both communities, a significant number of people turned to emotionally charged religious expression as an outlet for the pain of uprootedness and change. In both cases popular religious expression had an anti-clerical tinge to it, occasioned by a deep collective mistrust of the elitism and the rationalism of the official church. The most useful way to describe the profound difference between these modes of piety is not, therefore, to play on the difference between churches and sects, voluntary and involuntary membership, orthodoxy and dissent, and so forth, for in both cases we are dealing with popular forms of piety that were never quite respectable, created in congregation and parish by the needs and impulses of ordinary people.

The most economical way to phrase the difference between these forms of piety is in terms of the presence or absence of an attitude we may call devotional. The supplicant or devotee of the Virgin is stimulated by an image to a large but finite round of association. The Virgin's powers are vast; but they are employed along lines that correspond to the known facts of her sex, her experience, her sympathies, and the social circumstances of her earthly origin in Mediterranean culture and customs. These qualities furthermore are idealization of the social characteristics of her devotees, inspiring feelings of affection, respect, and confidence that are marks of the attitude of devotion.

Mary has powers of mobility that are superior to the saints, who are attached to locales and other specialized situation and functions and sometimes to the vicinity of their relics. Mary left no bones, and therefore appears in visions and in images exclusively, making her the ideal patron of populations of wide territorial extent, of dubious native sanctity, or in precarious cultural affinity with Catholic culture. The vouchsafing of visions of herself in these condition has often seemed to legitimize—or in the language of religious legitimation, to sanctify—the territorial expansion of the church. But also to serve the religious needs of people not wholly comfortable with the official church. The Virgin of Guadalupe, the Black Virgin of Poland, Our Lady of Fatima, and the Madonna of 115th Street, are instances of Mary's peregrinational facility, but it is both a stately and an entirely public processional, cultic practices surrounding her devotion replicating the solemnity and the deliberation of the Virgin's own original self-disclosure, as images are paraded through streets, and monuments of great durability are erected at the sites of her appearance. Devotion therefore is a principle of loyalty and bonding necessarily suffused with a strong sense of place, of territorial boundary (the Virgin is not everywhere) and of visual experience.

It is not possible to be devoted to the Holy Ghost in this sense. Although in the hierarchy of celestial beings in the Christian pantheon, the Holy Ghost might be taken to be a patron of the widest possible territory, a competitor with the Virgin in territorial conquest; in fact such a supposition would miss entirely the qualitative disjunction between these two principles. Both devotion and territory suppose distance: in the first instance, psychological and moral distance between devotee and object of devotion; in the second instance, distance of dignity and honor between the sanctifying patron and the sanctified territory. The Holy Ghost knows neither type of distance, being everywhere already: in the moral subject and in every site, occupied or unoccupied. One does not speak of the honor of the Holy Ghost, as one does of Mary, but rather of his power. The Holy Ghost is the principle of the holy which is a state of being; and not of the sacred which is a structure of exchanges and transference based on rules. The Holy Ghost is at once too remote to be associated with any recognizable culture, and too near to be distinct from the self.

The institutional and intellectual background of the Pentecostal movement is informative here. The canonical episode for the Pentecostal movement as a whole has been the revival, with Baptism in the Holy Ghost and speaking in tongues, at the Azusa Street mission in Los Angeles in 1906. What is sometimes obscured is that the groundwork was laid for the doctrine of a second experience of infilling of the Holy Ghost after Salvation, by the American Holiness denominations, which, building on Wesleyan perfectionism, posited a stage of entire holiness, or sanctification, a condition of virtual sinlessness, attainable by a definite, one-time experience. The problems with holiness doctrines are inherent: first, maintaining the rigors of a doctrine of sinlessness in a popular religious movement; and second, identifying the marks of the definite experience—if it is a step beyond the mere assent of the revivalistic doctrine of salvation.

Classical Pentecostalism solved these two problems at a stroke. The Baptism of the Holy Ghost empowered the superior form of the Christian life, and speaking in tongues was the outward sign. The issue of holiness remained an awkward one, some groups actually maintaining a three-stage view, with both holiness and the Baptism in the Holy Ghost; others quietly abandoning the requirement of sanctification as a definite experience, for a gradual perfectionism assisted by the Holy Ghost. By such casuistry the Pentecostal denomination rationalized a set of doctrines to accompany a radical revolution that ultimately had little to do with old-fashioned Wesleyan perfectionism, but a great deal to do with power. Holiness, in the Pentecostalist lexicon, is basically not an ethical issue (even though superficially it is connected with a great deal of rule-oriented behavior and petty scrupulosity), because ethics, like devotion, requires distance from random feelings. Holiness, being a state, is its own measure, every feeling is equally relevant, and only feelings are relevant.

Consider in detail the setting and the practice of Pentecostal piety. I have already described how, in the case of Norwegian immigrants in New York City, the shape of settlement itself indicated a looseness of attachment to particular places. Pentecostal practices deepened this indifference to a virtual counter-principle. The less sanctified a place the more likely it was that a religious feeling impressing itself there was an authentic visitation of the Holy Ghost. Neither of the buildings that Salem occupied as a congregation was built as a church building. The first one, on Seventh Avenue in Sunset Park, had been a movie house. The second one, on Fourth Avenue, was purchased from a Jewish congregation whose members had left the area, and was left largely unchanged, except for building a baptismal tank and placing the name "JESUS" in bold gothic script at the front of the auditorium.

Within the church itself the ostensible function of various architectural features of the building, that made it in appearance a "religious" building, were persistently perverted. Although the church had ample room in the main sanctuary for the typical practices of North American revivalistic services—an "altar," benches suitable for extended praying and worshipping—the most important and solemn occasions, the seeking of Baptisms in the Holy Ghost, which frequently required extended prayer, weeping and bodily prostration, was undertaken in what was called the "prayer room," a windowless, dingy room without any ornamentation, at the end of a dark corridor behind the furnace room.

As if this were not enough of a repudiation of the attitudes of devotion associated with sacred space: People reminiscing, even after many years, about their own Baptisms, will say that they received it "under the piano," or some such place, or will talk about the joy and the power of their experiences driving them right out of the church, down into the subway station, as one man described it to me.

One effect of such practices is to make the liturgical element of community consist in the telling of such experiences. Piety has shifted from devotion to witnessing, from the beholding of a sacred image to the recounting of an experience of power. From autobiographical recounting, the Lukan church moves toward specialization of involuntary experiences of power, called the gifts of the Spirit, or the charismatic gifts, that are themselves mostly acts of telling and showing. These are miraculous but nonetheless routinized episodes of Holy Ghost power operating to prophesy, or interpret tongues, or provide wisdom, or heal bodies, through individuals who are known to "possess" the gifts pertaining to these powers.

What is important to note is that the gifts of the Holy Spirit are not conferred by ordination, or by collective decision-making. The fact of their possession by people is known in the evidence of their exercise, making the church itself curiously passive in its piety: the audience of a performance, rather than the custodian of an image. "Charisma" here belongs neither to things nor to persons, but to function.

A final consequence of the mode of piety I have been describing is that the world is also equally a function of perception. The world may be conceived in the usual geo-political sense, as a mission field, as the arena of the struggle of godly forces and ungodly forces, but the "world" in the language of Holy Ghost religion is also whatever is unholy in the self. Where there is no transference of sanctity possible, by image or by sacrament, or by progressive territorial investment, then there is clearly no permanent or enduring condition of the world. The world is, paradoxically, coextensive with the Holy Ghost. This is played out most extensively in the body itself, which in the language of Scripture is conceived to be the "temple" of the Holy Ghost. It is thus that dress codes and behavioral prescriptions such as those involving dancing, smoking, drinking, attending movies, have clearly to do with elaborate pollution fears that are not dispelled by the indwelling of the Holy Ghost at Baptism, but are rather intensified by it. The conscience—that is the feeling of the body as containing holiness, a sensory rather than an ethical faculty—is sensitized by the Holy Ghost to everything that occupies the same sensory medium. This is why every critical survey of Pentecostal movements notices that, while the movements are global in scope, they are everywhere preoccupied with a conception of the world that is localized in selves (Flora 1976; d'Epinay 1969). This "boundary maintenance" is not only social in the usual sense, but also deeply personal, as a crisis of embodiment. The self is not merely torn, as in classical spiritual dilemmas, between God and the world, between the flesh and the things of the spirit; the self must rather choose between not knowing where the world ends and the self begin, and not knowing where the Holy Ghost ends and the self begins. Changing the world is equivalent to achieving purity in the body. Being baptized into the Holy Ghost is to make the tongue and the body His.

Let us say that there are two contrasting sets of correspondences governing contrasting Christian life worlds: In one there is a correspondence between devotion to an image such as that of the Virgin Mary—in which the devotee seeks a transfer of sanctity from the greater fund to the lesser—and a conception of territoriality in which the world is progressively brought into the realm of sanctity by the extension of the patronage of powerful celestial personages. In the other, a piety of the experience of holiness corresponds with a conception of the world as a substance rather than a place. It may be possible to place in these contrasting structures other opposing principles with greater or lesser degrees of persuasiveness. Might we say, for example, that a civil ethic corresponding to the first set consists in obligation, and that such an ethic corresponding to the second is the rule of law?

We need not go so far, in order to establish the principle I have been trying to approach in this essay. Namely, that there is a powerful interlocking correspondence between the precise nature of invoked supernatural beings and the fundamental bonding and other purpose and agreement-reaching mechanisms of a society. The advantage of considering Pentecostal movements in this light is both that the piety in question is an extremely archaic Christian piety of radical social and spiritual implication, and that it provides an example of Christian piety that is not modern in the Weberian sense, and yet is so characteristically a product of the twentieth century. The Norwegian experience is useful for a similar reason: It stands apart from our ordinary understanding of the relationships between such terms as Reformation, saints, nation, popular piety, Christianization, and allows us to see these things in longer and less usual perspective.

Can we move from these marginal cases to more central, more global aspects of modernity? My own interest in Norwegian-American immigrants, and in Pentecostalism, came out of efforts to understand several main currents in American cultural and religious history: for example, the unprecedented emphasis in American theology and in American popular piety on the person and operation of the Holy Ghost. In many respects, Pentecostalism is only the final mass-movement phase of a Calvinist "moment" that has been Christianizing mobile, commercial, and frontier populations since the sixteenth century, most dramat- ically and typically in America. The narrowing of a piety of the Holy Ghost to the mimesis of the church in Acts is perhaps only the predictable outcome of the steady decline in America of the clerical control of revivalist and experiential religion, including both the Calvinist awakenings and Methodist spiritual discipline, and the rise of Fundamentalism as a reaction to science and modernity.

Calvin stands squarely at the head of the processes I am describing here, and the roots of a piety based on the Holy Ghost lie in Calvin's sacramental theology (Rothkrug 1988). His rejection of the Real Presence, his insistence on maintaining that the physical body of Christ remained in Heaven, meant that the Holy Ghost was invoked as the carrier of spiritual grace in the sacrament. It also meant the most complete and radical break in Western culture with a politico-religious principle that had characterized the Christian West since late antiquity: namely, that the physical presences of celestial and sanctified beings stood literally in the territories of which they were the titular patron and guardians. Calvin rejected the presence of Christ in the Host in much the way that Protestants in North America would reject the idea that the Madonna came to 115th Street. With the rejection of the link between sacred persons and sacralized territory followed all those practices that are characteristic of Puritanism, and of the revivalist and Pietist tradition that followed: churches as voluntary associations, the reliance on personal testimony for accreditation, the religious accommodation to mobility, wealth, secular pursuits, life among strangers, pragmatic and republican institutions of government.

These are well-understood and commented-on phenomena of modernization. What I have tried to suggest in this paper, however, is that where the Holy Ghost is invoked we may expect to find, along with these Weberian rationalization of life worlds, also a dissolving of the territorial character of the world. In its place is a conception of the world as a medium, flowing unimpeded in and through the self, and extending the will of the self by unmediated stages or progressive territorial conquest to its heart's desire anywhere in the world. When this medium is held, in Fundamentalist fashion, to be literally and truly the habitat of the Holy Ghost, we can see clearly the ground of the evangelical energy and success of the Pentecostal movement. The corresponding sense of political virtue, conceiving of the world as continuous from the desires of the self to all the imaginable needs of the world, is a fair description of the piety of that other institutional legacy of Calvin's war on medieval Christianity, the American Republic. In both cases the absence of an ideology of world order cannot conceal the way in which the religious ordering of the world has immense effects by altering the very building blocks of world order.

References

Barratt, Thomas Ball. 1907. *Da jeg fik min pintsedaab og tungemaalsgaven*. Oslo. Reprinted as *When the Fire Fell: And an Account of My Life*. 2nd ed. Larvik. 1927.
Christopherson, Kenneth E. 1972. "Norwegian Historiography of Norway's Reformation." Ph.D. dissertation, University of Minnesota.
d'Epinay, Christian Lalive. 1969. *Haven of the Masses: A Study of the Pentecostal Movement in Chile*. London: Lutterworth.
Flora, Cornelia Butler. 1976. *Pentecostalism in Colombia: Baptism by Fire and Spirit*. Rutherford: Fairleigh Dickinson University Press.
Hollenweger, Walter J. 1972. *The Pentecostals*. Minneapolis: Augsburg.
Johannesen, Stanley. 1988. "The Holy Ghost in Sunset Park." *Historical Reflections/Réflexions Historiques* 15:543–77.
Jonassen, Christen T. 1948. "The Norwegians in Bay Ridge: A Sociological Study of an Ethnic Group." Ph.D. dissertation, New York University.
Orsi, Robert. 1985. *The Madonna of 115th Street: Faith and Community in Italian Harlem, 1880–1950*. New Haven: Yale University Press.
Pethrus, Lewi. 1973. *A Spiritual Memoir*. Plainfield, N.J.: Logos.
Quebedeaux, Richard. 1976. *The New Charismatics: The Origins, Development, and Significance of Neo-Pentecostalism*. Garden City: Doubleday.
Rothkrug, Lionel. 1988. "German Holiness and Western Sanctity in Medieval and Modern History." In *Culture, Society and Religion in Early Modern Europe: Essays by the Students and Colleagues of William J. Bouwsma*, edited by Ellery Schalk. Waterloo, Ontario: Historical Reflections.
Undset, Sigrid. 1934. *Saga of Saints*. London: Sheed & Ward.
Willson, Thomas B. 1903. *History of the Church and State in Norway: From the Tenth to the Sixteenth Century*. London.

8

CONSUMER CULTURE, POSTMODERNISM, AND GLOBAL DISORDER

Mike Featherstone

ONE OF THE NOTICEABLE FEATURES OF SOCIOLOGY in the 1980s has been the growth of interest in the cultural dimension of social life which has propelled the sociology of culture from a marginal position towards the center of the sociological field (Robertson 1988; Featherstone 1989b). At the same time a reverse process seems to have taken place which has seen the sociology of religion move towards a more marginal and isolated place within the field (Fenn 1982; Beckford 1985; Robertson 1985). Save for a few notable exceptions there has generally been little interest in religious phenomena on the part of those engaged in theorizing the contemporary cultural complex.

Yet we hardly need to recall that the classic sociological theorists Weber and Durkheim, whose writings have long been held up as exemplary texts for the sociology of culture, both treated religion as central to the understanding of the structure and development of social life. Indeed the progressive demise of the influences of religion in social life, which can be related to the processes of industrialization, rationalization, urbanization, and social differentiation, has been held by some to have provoked a peculiarly modern crisis of meaning or crisis in the effectiveness of the social bond, which could only be adequately allayed through the creation or emergence of some new meaning complex. The decline of religion and the erosion of its institutional bases within society then is often held to have left behind a vacuum with deleterious effects for both the individual and society.

Yet for some, the dissipation of religion into numerous quasi-religious and non-religious meaning complexes, which supply individuals with the knowledge to help them cope with the intractable existential questions of ultimate meaning, the sacred, birth, death, sexuality, etc., has merely rendered religion invisible. Max Weber's famous metaphor in *The Protestant Ethic* of religion striding into the market place of worldly affairs and slamming the monastery door behind it, becomes further transformed in modern society with religion placed very much in the consumer market place alongside other meaning complexes.

Here we think of the writings of Peter Berger (1969) and Thomas Luckmann (1967) with individuals able to select from a plurality of suitably packaged bodies of knowledge in the supermarket of lifestyles. Individuals' sense of fulfillment, happiness, and ultimate life-meaning become located in the private sphere where "man is free to choose and decide on his own what to do with his time, his home, his body, and his gods" (B. Luckmann 1971). (See also Hammond 1986 and Turner 1983 on the market model of religion.)

If the tendency in modern western societies is for religion to become a private leisure-time pursuit purchased in the market like any other consumer culture lifestyle, then we need to ask a number of questions about the effect of this shift on religion. Has this brought religion close to other consumer commodities and experiences, does it have to present itself as a way of life and meaning complex which offer similar kinds of emotional refreshment to other leisure pursuits? Have other leisure-time experiences such as consumer culture spectacles taken on the aura of the sacred? How significant are questions of ultimate meaning, of belief, in the habitual day-to-day practices and power balances individuals are enmeshed in? What effective practical knowledge is provided by religious, quasi-religious, and non-religious meaning-complexes? Are questions of meaning and belief more relevant to particular social groups and classes, e.g. the intellectuals? How does the "choice" of particular types of religious and quasi-religious meaning complexes relate to other cultural taste and lifestyle pursuits which can be mapped onto the universe of tastes and lifestyles which operate with a specific society?

In addition to a discussion of religion in relation to consumer culture we need also to speculate about the possible role of religion in relation to a postmodern culture. Consumer culture can clearly be located as arising within modernity, yet it displays tendencies which point towards the *post*-modern. The postmodern and its derivations, postmodernity, postmodernism, and postmodernization, are as yet an ill-defined family of terms which have been stretched to encompass phenomena ranging from epochs and artistic movements to everyday cultural practices and experiences (for a preliminary attempt to define the family of terms arising from the modern and postmodern see Featherstone 1988a).

At the same time the term *postmodernism* is used to point to a major metatheoretical shift, a rejection, transcendence, and break with the dominant modes of investigation and evaluation employed in the arts, humanities, and social sciences. *Postmodernity* refers to an epochal shift which points to a transcendence of modernity. Habermas (1984) for example following Weber (1948) has argued that modernity entails the progressive rationalization and differentiation of the traditional worldview into separate and autonomous scientific, artistic, and ethical cultural value spheres.

Postmodernity, then, which Habermas (1987) wants to resist from the perspective of completing the enlightenment project of modernity to deliver the rational society, entails the elevation of the aesthetic value sphere already expanding within modernity through the development of autonomous art which in its interchange with consumer culture results in the over-production of images and signs which further the stylization of life—beyond the competing claims of the other spheres.

Some would want to speak of this shift in terms of a de-coupling of the cultural sphere from the technico-economic sphere (e.g. Bell 1976). Others would point to more radical and far-reading break in the constitution of the social world which has entailed the triumph of signifying culture and the end of the social. Baudrillard (1983a; 1983b), for example, suggests that a major consequence of the mass media has been a profusion of floating signs without empirical referents which leads to a simulational world in which we live in an aesthetic hallucination of reality. This growth of the power potential of the aesthetic sphere and the anesthetization of life which has developed symbiotically alongside the rise of consumer culture has been perceived as particularly threatening for religion and moral integration (Bell 1976; 1980). In Weber's (1948) terms the increasing valuation of art and eroticism produces a rival form of this-worldly salvation to religion.

The movement towards a postmodern culture then suggests a double shift: on the theoretical level it offers anti-foundational aesthetic models and justifications for the reading of texts and experiences, undermining the validity claims of scientific, philosophical, and other theoretical systems or metanarratives; on the practical level it offers aesthetic models for life (the aestheticization and stylization of life, the artist as hero, art as the good life, the valuation of eroticism and immediate sensory experience). While one has sympathy with those who want to rule out the whole discussion of postmodernity as far too speculative, imprecise, and faddish, its very formulation sensitizes us to some intriguing tendencies within contemporary culture.

Of course more detailed research is needed to establish and record the nature of the precise practices and experiences which are designated postmodern, as well as to document its visibility (the sites and locations) and generality (who is producing and consuming postmodern cultural goods and experiences?). As yet postmodernism can be regarded as a term used strategically within the avant-gardist and neo-avant-gardist struggles taking place within the artistic and intellectual fields (Featherstone 1988a; 1989a; 1989b). Yet it also points to something more: to cultural contents, practices, and experiences, and a broader sense of culture becoming an unstable field and suggests that we are entering what DiMaggio (1987) refers to as a phase of "cultural de-classification." Of course for some of those who detect and advocate postmodernism the shift is more than a mere phase and points to a new condition, or ultimate stage, in which culture becomes overloaded and overcharged with signs and images to move us beyond the possibility of stable symbolic hierarchies and a stable cultural order.

We must therefore also face the possibility that the various indications of postmodern culture are the harbingers of postmodernity. Here postmodernity suggests a movement beyond modernity which merely transcends it in an ironic, parotic, and capricious way: the notion of a higher integrated society based on some form of rational and just consensus gives way to pluralism, the celebration of otherness, fragmentation, the play of differences and cultural disorder. We must also of course inquire into the status of the assumed universality of the modernity-postmodernity distinction and ask how far the process is merely a Western one. Despite the celebration of cultural disorder and local knowledge, there is the tendency on the part of theorists of postmodernism, e.g. Lyotard (1984), to provide a narrative account of the move to postmodernity to which they give a universal thrust. We therefore need to locate the universalizing claim and advocacy of de-universality (local knowledge, otherness) in the context of the interests and strategies of particular groups of specialists in symbolic production (artists, intellectuals, academics, and their relationship to wider audiences and publics under changing conditions which are producing a de-monopolization and de-classification of culture).

In addition we need to locate these tendencies within the emergent global order in terms of the inter-state and inter-civilizational conflicts and the process of globalization. We need to disentangle the grand questions about the universalizability of (western) modernity and its summation and negation into the generalized particularity of postmodernity from notions of immanent logic or *fin de millennium* pathos—the fate of modernity—and endeavor to relate them to the actual struggles which take place between groups of people on an intra-societal level and the changing inter-societal power balances between nation-states and civilizational complexes.

Consumer Culture and the Sacred

Consumer culture is generally presented as being extremely destructive for religion in terms of its emphasis on hedonism, the pursuit of pleasure here and now, the cultivation of expressive lifestyles, the development of narcissistic and egoistic personality types. Before we examine some of the ways in which religion has accommodated to consumer culture and consumerism continues to support a religious dimension, it would be useful to outline briefly some of the salient features of consumer culture. The term, as it suggests, refers to the culture of the consumer society. It is based on the assumption that the movement towards mass consumption was accompanied by a general reorganization of symbolic production, everyday experiences, and practices. A number of studies have traced its origins back to the eighteenth century for the middle classes in Britain (McKendrick *et al.* 1982) and to the nineteenth century for the working classes in Britain, France, the United States, with the development of advertising, department stores, holiday resorts, mass entertainment and leisures, etc. (Bailey 1978; Ewen and Ewen 1982; Williams 1982).

Other studies emphasize that the inter-war years in the United States saw the first sustained development of a consumer culture with new tastes, dispositions, experiences, and ideals publicized through advertising, the motion picture industry, the fashion and cosmetic industries, mass-circulation tabloid newspapers and magazines, and mass spectator sport (Susman 1979, 1982; Ewen 1976; Bell 1976). It is often alleged that consumerism led to spiritual impoverishment and hedonistic selfishness with its "live now pay later" philosophy which ran directly counter to the ascetic regimes, industry, foresight, and thrift which religion in general, and the Puritan heritage in particular, taught. Malcolm Cowley (1951) writing in the 1930s drew attention to what he called the new "consumption ethic" which was initially developed by bohemian artists and intellectuals in Greenwich Village as an overt attack on the business-Christian ethic. The new consumption ethic which was taken over by the advertising industry by the late 1920s celebrated living for the moment, hedonism, self-expression, the body beautiful, paganism, freedom from social obligations, the exotica of far-away places, the cultivation of style and the stylization of life.

It is evident that one of the central features of consumer culture is the availability of an extensive range of commodities, goods, and experiences which are to be consumed, maintained, planned, and dreamt about by the general population. Yet this consumption is far from being just the consumption of utilities which are addressed to fixed needs (Adorno 1967; Jameson 1979; Leiss 1983). Rather, consumer culture through advertising, the media, and techniques of display of goods, is able to destabilize the original notion of use or meaning of goods and attach to them new images and signs which can summon up a whole range of associated feelings and desires. The overproduction of signs and loss of referents, which we have already spoken of in the context of postmodern culture, is therefore an immanent tendency within consumer culture. Hence within consumer culture the tendency is to push culture towards the center of social life, yet it is a fragmented and continually re-processed culture which does not cohere into anything like a dominant ideology. Of course we need to beware of treating culture on the level of sign and image systems without asking the questions: How are they are used in everyday practices, and who is engaged in their production and dissemination?

To answer the second question will entail a discussion of the role of specialists in symbolic production and various cultural intermediaries who handle, circulate, and purvey cultural goods and this will be discussed shortly. To answer the first question points to the significance of the active cultivation of lifestyle within the imagery of consumer culture. That is, individuals are encouraged to adopt a non-utilitarian attitude towards commodities and carefully choose, arrange, adapt, and display goods—whether furnishings, house, car, clothing, the body and leisure pursuits—to make a particular stylistic statement which expresses the individuality of the owner (see Featherstone 1987b).

The concern with constructing an expressive lifestyle, to achieve some sense of satisfying order from the commodities and practices that surround the individual generates a constant demand for information about lifestyles. For the individual who has only one life to live there is a vast array of interpretations of cultural goods, experiences, and lifestyles, all of which point to the capacity for self and lifestyle transformation. Warren Susman (1979: 220) has suggested that one of the key changes in identity formation which took place with the move towards consumer culture occurred with a shift from the proclamation of the virtues of character to that of personality. He quotes advice manuals from the early decades of the twentieth century to point to this transition. O.S. Marsden for example wrote a book entitled *Character: the Greatest Thing in the World* in 1899 which stressed the ideals of the Christian gentleman: integrity, courage, duty, and the virtues of hard work and thrift. In 1921 he published a new advice manual, *Masterful Personality*, which emphasized "the need to attract and hold friends," "to compel people to like you," to develop "personal charm," and "fascination."

This type of advice manual was of course hardly restricted to the development of consumer culture. The manners books examined by Norbert Elias (1978b; 1983) and his discussions of the taming of the medieval knights and the emergence of a court society in which the nobility became specialists in the art of consumption point to the care individuals had to take with fashion, demeanor, style of presentation, as well as in developing the skills to read the appearance of others in order to survive in the fluctuating power balances of the court figuration. These types of status games (which contrary to Sennett [1976] were anything but playful games) led to an emphasis upon distinctions and differences which has been adopted within consumer culture and is the central focus of one of the major recent analyses of consumption practices, tastes, and lifestyles (Bourdieu 1984).

Distinctions should not blind us to the existence of the counter-tendency which mass consumption and democratization favored, the tendency towards equalization and the diminishing of contrasts (Gellner 1979; Turner 1986). Consumer culture here seen as part of a process of functional democratization offered the transcendence of sumptuary laws and was accompanied by a greater levelling-out of balances of power (between the classes, men and women, parents and children) as the less powerful were for the first time able to emulate, within the limitations of mass fashion, the consumption practices and styles of the more powerful.

The tendencies towards emulation, equalization, and imitation on the one hand and differentiation, individuality, and distinction on the other have been noted by Georg Simmel (1978) as central to the dynamic of fashion which is seen as a compromise between adherence and absorption into the social group and individual differentiation and distinction from other group members. Simmel relates fashion to the fragmentation of modern life, the neurasthenia, the over-stimulation, and nervous excitement which accelerated with the growth of the metropolis. The modern individual is confronted by a feverish change of fashion and bewildering plurality of styles. Yet the peculiar stylishness of the times manifest in the objective culture, the visible public culture, was for Simmel compensated for by the stylization of the interior by which individuals sought to express their subjectivity (Frisby 1985: 65).

Two other points of interest can be drawn from Simmel's turn of the century discussion of fashion which are relevant to our understanding of consumer culture. First, he regards fashion as most closely associated with a particular social strata, the middle classes, and a specific location, the metropolis. Second, the stylization of everyday household objects, part of the project of the *Jugendstil* movement in Germany (in Britain there was the parallel movement known as Aestheticism) can be related to a larger project of the "stylization of everyday life" and the "beautification of life." Both point to a close relationship between art, fashion, and consumer culture and the various producers, consumers, audiences, transmitters, and intermediaries within sectors of the middle class which developed similar dispositions, tastes, classificatory schemes, and lifestyle practices, despite the apparent quest for individuality and distinction which seemingly distanced artists and their lifestyles from the more worldly commercial, design, and retail occupations.

They further point to the need to investigate the long-term process involving the growth of specialists in symbolic production and the growth of separate intellectual artistic disciplines, institutions, and movements which has taken place since the late eighteenth century. This process which involved the development of movements such as Romanticism, Aestheticism, Modernism, Dadaism, and the constant avant-gardist negation and re-creation of the artists' oppositional bohemian lifestyle, entailed the transmission of aesthetic dispositions and sensibilities, with notions such as "the artist as a hero" and "the stylization of life" to a larger audience. It also fed into consumer culture in a host of different ways which changed the design of everyday objects, commodities, and the fabric of the urban industrial landscape so that it is possible to speak of (to use the title of James Allen's [1983] book) *The Romance of Commerce and Culture*.

Hence there is a good deal of interest in highlighting the antinomian, out-to-shock and transgressive qualities of artistic counter-cultures (e.g., Bell 1976). Yet we should be careful not to just look at texts and art objects and assume that their meanings are self-evident and can be read off, but inquire into how they are used practically in everyday activities. There is a danger of over-estimating the significance of beliefs which are produced, classified, and discussed primarily by symbol specialists and underestimating the significance of practical knowledge, taken-for-granted, commonsense classificatory schemes and dispositions which do not operate as norms, but are called upon as social life unfolds practically by individuals held together in various shifting power balances with other people (see Bourdieu 1977; Elias 1978a). Here we would want to emphasize power balances and the practical uses of knowledge, because power exists as an aspect of every human relationship from the fact that people, groups, or individuals have the capacity to withhold or monopolize what other people need—food, love, meaning, protection from attack, knowledge, etc. (Elias 1984: 251).

Daniel Bell (1976), for example, tells us that "The real problem of modernity is the problem of belief." Secular systems of meaning have proved illusory solutions to the spiritual crisis once the anchorage of society in religion has been severed and only a religious revival is capable of restoring the continuity of generations and producing images of cosmic order, humility, and caring which can satisfactorily address our sense of the existential predicaments. Rather than dealing with the question in terms of a void in belief which needs to be filled to produce some meaningful moral order and adequate social bonding, a void which, for Bell (1976: 156) the aesthetic justification of life with its emphasis upon hedonism and self-expression is incapable of filling, we need to inquire into the specific ways in which beliefs, especially those produced by specialists in symbolic production such as priests, intellectuals, and artists, played a central role in holding together everyday life.

There is a tendency arising out of the practical day-to-day use and valuation of beliefs and ideas for symbol specialists (artists, intellectuals, priests) to over-value the importance of coherent belief systems as relevant guidelines structuring activities in everyday life. Indeed, there is also a tendency noted by (Bourdieu 1983) for intellectuals and artists to set themselves up as "uncreated creators" in the sense that they draw upon what Bourdieu calls the "ideology of charisma," "talent," and "giftedness" which should rather be seen as arising from the gradual sedimentation of dispositions and practice aptitudes which is reinforced within institutional contexts. Hence there is the tendency for artistic and intellectual pursuits such as writing or producing works of art to be regarded as creative and not to be understood as practices involving sedimented dispositions, institutional frameworks, and power-balances. In short artists and intellectuals have an interest in parading their own disinterestedness, in that their contempt for material things in the world (economic capital, money, property) their apparent disinterestedness, may conceal their interest in accumulating cultural capital in which status and prestige accumulation act effectively as an alternative form of currency and power.

To understand the changes in belief in modernity we therefore need to examine the long-term processes which led to a shift in the balance of power away from religious knowledge specialists to favor the growth of scientific, artistic, and intellectual knowledge in various institutions and practices (cf. Elias 1983: 262). This would entail an investigation of the development of the emergence of a relatively separate cultural sphere since the eighteenth century which paralleled the struggle to overturn the church authorities' monopoly hold on the societal fund of knowledge (see Featherstone 1988b). Therefore while it is possible to conceptualize one strand of this process as taking place on the level of belief we also have to consider the practical use of beliefs in relation to group alliances, interests, and struggles.

Although it is possible for specific sets of beliefs or ethical complexes to generate intense emotional fulfillment and commitment on the part of specific groups it is generally noted that: a) such phases are difficult to sustain in the long run and b) the commitment may be stronger on the part of certain groups or class fractions who may be predisposed more to taking ideas seriously and rarely applies universally across a society, although it may be possible that particular groups of carriers may sustain it as a long-term project. Hence Cowley's (1951) and Bell's (1976: 63) references to the propulsive force of a "consumption ethic" and that it became realized must be treated with caution. The term "consumption ethic" also features in Colin Campbell's (1987) book *The Romantic Ethic and the Spirit of Modern Consumerism*. Campbell (1987: 8) takes as his model the cultural approach Weber adopted in *The Protestant Ethic and Spirit of Capitalism* in which an assumed affinity between a particular ethic and spirit gave rise to psychological impulses which gave direction to an individual's everyday life. Yet in his later writing Weber (1968) developed a much stricter sociological account of the relationship between religious beliefs and the status and power structure of groups in society. He emphasized that status groups will endeavor to preserve and enhance their present style of life by maintaining a social distance and closing off economic opportunities to outsiders (see Bendix 1959: 258ff.).

In addition to the monopolization strategies of established groups to maintain visible differences in style of life, we can add that outsider groups will endeavor to de-monopolize, to adopt usurpatory tactics to break down exclusivity and privilege (cf. Elias 1965; Bourdieu 1980; Parkin 1979). In doing so of course they may claim to have wider ambitions then to join the established and emphasize the sincerity of their beliefs, their disinterested return to fundamentals in a quest to address their particular field or even the fate of a people or humanity in general.

An objection then to approaches which see modernity as entailing the replacement of religion by art to fill a vacuum in belief, or which would like to explain consumer culture in terms of an ethic is that they tend to rely on a view that society needs, or that individuals operate through, basic beliefs. Of course, under certain circumstances specialists in symbolic production may have an interest in increasing the circulation and demand for new symbolic and intellectual goods. Some groups then have an interest in dealing with men and women as "cultural beings," and form alliances with other groups who have an interest in becoming cultivated, in treating life as a learning project; yet we cannot assume this applies equally across the social structure. Still other groups may effectively dilute, transpose, and integrate articulated meaning complexes such as religion into their existing everyday mundane practices more on their own terms. "Big culture" then may have a different impact and practical relevance for different groups (cf. Robertson 1978: 80). For the intellectuals a central concern may be to search for coherence and to universalize their particular interpretation of the world to the extent that the disorder within culture is eliminated.

Bell's (1976; 1980: 333) definition of culture as the modalities of responses to the core existential questions—love, death, tragedy, obligation gives his view of culture and religion an intellectualist bias (Douglas 1982: 7). When religion is defined as providing the most coherent set of answers to these core existential questions, a decline in religion must necessarily be seen as providing a threat to social integration and the social bond, and this is Bell's verdict on the culture of modernism.

Yet such perspectives should also consider the extent to which culture diversity and disorder occurred both in pre-modern and modern societies. There is the danger that we will accept what Margaret Archer (1988: 1ff.) has referred to as "the myth of cultural integration" which became prevalent both in anthropology and German historicism. In doing so our sense of cultural coherence may be derived from assumed exemplary literary texts to the extent that we read-off popular practices from intellectualist accounts and neglect the integrity and diversity of popular traditions.

If we look at popular mainstream culture we may find little of the penetration of adversarial cultural modernism which so worries Bell. Rather it tends to be retained within its cultural enclave to be consumed by specialist, if expanding, audiences and publics. Popular mainstream culture, the soap operas, films, television advertisements, newspapers, magazines, etc., are generally much freer from cultural exploration, criticism, and protest. Here we frequently find a concern for respectability, cleanliness, good food, clothes, service, concern for law, order, and property and individual success (Douglas, 1980: 1b).

In addition mass consumption is rarely the endless modernist round of cultivation of new pleasures and sensations which Bell stresses. Mary Douglas argues that "To the consumer themselves, consumption is less like a pleasure for its own sake and more like a pleasurable fulfillment of social duties." Before pronouncing about the danger which art and intellectual pursuits represent to culture and social integration we need to investigate the actual everyday practical uses of culture by different social groups which directs us to the way in which culture interrelates with social structures and cannot be regarded as an autonomous sphere. If we do not there is a danger that we will follow mass society theorists and read-off mass consumption from mass production and miss the diverse ways in which cultural meaning and commodities can be reworked and de-commodified.

The ways in which new sets of ideas, be they religious or modernist, which are articulated by a cultural elite, influence large numbers of people must be demonstrated and not assumed. This applies as much for Protestantism in seventeenth-century England as for modernism in the United States in the twentieth century. A great deal of high culture may develop with little or no influence on the people. Weber's *Protestant Ethic* essay also demonstrates a caution about the extent to which the reformed doctrines successfully bridged the gulf between high culture and everyday behavior (Bendix 1970: 147). Seventeenth-century Puritan divines in England were concerned about the spiritual slumber of their flocks and evidence suggests that there was a continuing tradition of skepticism and irreligion (Reay 1985b: 101). The "theatre and counter-theatre of popular culture" with its charivaris, mock church ceremonies, ritual of popular protest, and festivals was still strong (Reay 1985a: 8). Indeed as Reay (1985a: 16) reminds us "the carnivalesque was surprisingly strong in early modern England." The carnivals, festivals, and fairs in early modern Europe celebrated transgressions of the classical and official culture with symbolic inversions and promotion of grotesque bodily pleasures. They provided sites of "ordered disorder" in which otherness and desire could be explored (Stallybrass and White 1986; Featherstone 1989c).

While it is possible to follow Bell (1976) and consider the diffusion of cultural modernism into the consumer culture of the lower classes, it is also important to examine the ways in which the liminal symbolic repertoires, the transgressions, inversions and celebration of otherness made its way from the carnivalesque and popular traditions to be taken up both in the art works and lifestyles of the burgeoning bohemians which became sites of cultural modernism in the large cities of the nineteenth century.

It is therefore important to avoid the temptation of the strand in current sociology which seeks to "retreat into the present" (Elias 1987) and avoid projecting backwards from our self-designated troubled times to some point of order and stability, a pre-industrial organic unity which existed prior to 1750. Daniel Bell's (1976; 1980) concern about the deleterious effects of cultural modernism can also be related to the German tradition of societal rationalization and *Kulturpessimismus* (Kalberg 1987) in which contemporary mass consumer society is perceived as atomized, impersonal, and bereft of meaningful social bonds and means of integration. It is therefore not surprising that Bell has been accused of nostalgia in seeking to advocate a religious revival to restore the social bond apparently endangered by cultural modernism (O'Neill 1988).

In summary then to understand contemporary culture and the place of religion within it we need to adopt a broader definition of culture than does Bell, one which allows us greater sensitivity to cultural diversity and disorder. Those groups which are disposed to take ideas seriously may be restricted to specific locations within the class structure (e.g. symbol specialists and cultural intermediaries within the middle class). On the other hand, other groups may exhibit a disregard for formal beliefs. It is possible that particular national state formation processes may give rise to a range of outcomes in which different societies develop a range of orientations towards beliefs and religions and intellectual goods. In some state formation processes in which the aristocracy plays a minor role, the particular conjunction of symbol specialist (e.g., Puritans) and economic specialists within the middle classes may help to produce a national culture and character structure which favor the importance of beliefs. It is possible to regard middle class culture in the United States from this perspective (see Bellah *et al.* 1985). Finally the attraction of belief systems may differ historically, with a temporary diffusion of particular sentiments to a wider population taking place at certain points in time. It is to such a Durkheimian perspective that we now turn.

Durkheim (1974: 92) emphasized that societies experience moments of collective ferment and enthusiasm. Such moments are however difficult to sustain both over time and across the span of social groups within a differentiated society. Durkheim emphasized the deep and enduring layer of affectivity at the heart of society which is manifest in symbols which embody social sentiments, collective representations, and rituals

(Tiryakian 1978). From this perspective modernity, with its processes of rationalization, commodification, secularization, and disenchantment, does not lead to the eclipse of religious sentiments, for while formal religions may decline, symbolic classifications and rituals, practices which embody sacred/profane distinctions, live on at the heart of secular social processes. As Durkheim pointed out, any thing can become sacred, so why not the "profane" goods of capitalism? If we focus on the actual use of commodities it is clear that in certain settings they can become de-commodified and receive a symbolic charge (over and above that intended by the advertisers) which makes them sacred to their users. It is therefore possible for mundane consumer goods to become transformed into cherished possessions (see Rochberg-Halton 1986: 170).

Modern society, then, is far from being a symbolically impoverished, mundane, material world in which commodities, goods, and things are regarded as mere "utilities." As we have argued, consumer culture produces a vast shifting web of signs, images, and symbols and these symbols cannot be conceptualized as merely profane. Alexander (1988: 189), building on Durkheim's later work, argues in modern society "social symbols are like sacred ones, in that they are powerful and compelling; the conflict between social values is like the conflict between the sacred and profane, or pure and impure sacredness; political interaction is like ritual participation in that it produces cohesion and value commitment."

This is not to imply that social symbols are harmonious and integrating. They may be contested and subjected to competitive processes. Here one thinks, for example, of the way in which the cultural dimension of the state formation process, with its legitimate moral regulation and unifying collective representations, must be seen as a product of an ongoing struggle to discredit and exclude alternative cultures and traditions (Corrigan and Sayer 1985). Alexander's (1988) own study of the Watergate crisis in the United States in the early 1970s is a good illustration of the outcome of the struggle between differentiated elites which led to the creation of a ritual *communitas* via the televised hearings affirming the sacred democratic myths of American civic religion.

From one perspective television within consumer culture can be regarded as trivializing the sacred in its capacity to put out a flood of information and arrive at bizarre juxtapositions as once sealed-off signs and symbols are now placed in contiguity. Yet it can also be argued that televised ceremonies, events and spectacles are also capable of generating a sense of festive occasion (Dayan and Katz 1988). Such events (for example, coronations, royal weddings, state funerals, and even rock concerts and sports championship finals) may heighten the sense of the sacred to generate and reaffirm the moral consensus which underpins social conflicts and competition. Because in modern societies we are made more aware of attempts to invent tradition, to manufacture charisma and the sacred, to manipulate consensus through television, it should not blind us to those events in which a new sense of the sacred is generated for successive generations.

As Durkheim pointed out such occasions generate intense feelings, excitement, "liquid emotion," and are reinforced in the accompanying communal activity by chants, dancing, ritual gestures. The 1960s can be regarded in this way with its happenings, music festivals like Woodstock, and general sense of excitement and effervescence. Such festive moments in which the everyday routine world becomes transformed into an extraordinary sacred world enabled people to temporarily live in unison, near to the ideal (Tiryakian 1978; Durkheim 1974). Subsequent gatherings often incorporate rituals which re-invoke the aura of the sacred of the original events and in effect act as "batteries" which charge up the liquid emotion which can be carried over to sustain people in the more mundane everyday world (Collins 1988: 111). Televised rock music spectacles such as the Band Aid, Food Aid, the Nelson Mandela concert, and other transnational link-ups may also invoke a more direct sense of emotional solidarity which may re-awaken and reinforce moral concerns such as the sense of common humanity, the sacredness of the person, human rights, and more recently the sacredness of nature and non-human species.

We have been arguing, then, that consumer culture has not resulted in the eclipse of the sacred by a debased materialism. This is in contrast to theorists who want to restrict the definition of culture and religion to the coherent answers to core existential questions (birth, sickness, death, love). Rather we can take a wider definition of culture which will focus not only on formal religious institutions and movements but also those social processes and practices which generate and regenerate sacred symbols: be it the ceremonies of the state, rock concerts, or the little sacred rituals which convey solidarity in small groups, or between friends and lovers. Hence we need to move away from approaches which read off consumption as a derivative of production and seek to dismiss it as mass consumption. Instead we have to acknowledge that while consumerism results in an inflation in the quantity of goods in circulation, this does not result in a general eclipse of the sacred, something which is evident if we focus on the symbolism which goods have in practice.

Postmodernism and Cultural Disorder

In this final section we will inquire into some of the changes which have been taking place since the 1960s in western societies which encourage some commentators to suggest that the beginning of a shift is taking place towards a postmodern culture. We will examine the relationship of these tendencies to consumer culture in general and more specifically examine those changes taking place within intellectual and artistic circles, and their relation to other groups which are altering the means of transmission, circulation, and reception of symbolic goods. In short, if a postmodern culture is emerging we need not to just ask the question "what is postmodern culture?" but "where is postmodern culture?" and "which groups have an interest in making it a reality?" through building upon more general sensibilities that may be emerging to educate and create larger audiences.

We also, in a more speculative vein, need to relate these changes to wider shifts in the global order, to shifts in the balance of power between nation-states taking place on inter-societal levels. The notion of a postmodern culture is clearly derived from a western context with the assumption that it represents a non-positive transcendence, a dramatic break with what was long regarded as the developmental trajectory of western modernity. We need to ask the questions how far and in what ways will this alleged sensitivity to polyculturalism, to the integrity and "otherness" of different cultural traditions, meet imminent tendencies in these other traditions halfway to produce a more open and pluralistic global circumstance with some tendencies towards cultural disorder, and how far this is merely a temporary pause or relaxation in the struggle for dominance, with the prospect of an intensification of the power struggle and economic elimination contests taking place between states holding out the prospect of changing trajectories for different cultural traditions and new orders of cultural dominance.

It is apparent that there is a good deal of ambiguity in the usage of the family of terms which derive from the postmodern. The initial focus of the terms postmodernity, postmodernism, *postmodernité*, and postmodernization is to suggest a relational move beyond the modern, with the accent more on what has been left behind than a positive depiction of what is to come. For our purposes here the terms of most immediate interest are postmodernity, which suggests an epochal shift beyond modernity and postmodernism, which points to the emergence of new artistic and intellectual movements in the cultural sphere which move us beyond artistic modernism. *Postmodernity* is usually associated with a movement towards a post-industrial age based upon the primacy of information. Yet few theorists have examined this idea of postmodernity in other than the most schematic terms (e.g. Lyotard 1984; Baudrillard 1983b). *Postmodernism* is a term which is easier to locate empirically as there have been definite artistic and intellectual movements since the 1960s with a specific set of practices which claim to move them beyond modernism.

There is a further term, the French term *postmodernité*, which is related to Baudelaire's emphasis upon the experience of newness and presentness in the modern city. *Postmodernité* points to the experience people have of the new cultural forms, practices, and experiences which are deemed postmodern such as are found in the simulated environments of theme parks, redeveloped downtowns, shopping centers, malls, etc. (For a fuller discussion of these terms, see Featherstone 1988a.) The approach we wish to follow here is to neither dismiss the postmodern as a short-run fad or to indulge in the heady excitement with which the term is often greeted whether in the form of a *fin de millennium* pessimism which wants to sweep away the modern for an eternal return or the optimism of the post-industrial theorists who are eager to usher in what they take as signs of a new order.

Rather we need to approach the postmodern in a more detached manner so that we can explore the problems of theoretical definition and examine the empirical evidence carefully. If this is done, it is clear that a degree of reflexivity is necessary so that we focus upon the specialists in symbolic production (artists, intellectuals, academics, and the various cultural intermediaries who disseminate their symbolic goods to wider audiences). This takes us away from the epochal speculations which point to cultural changes in terms of diffuse notions of mood or ethos. We should, then, initially focus upon postmodernism and examine the carriers and publics which help to detect, shape, and thematize the new experiences (*postmodernité*). It can be argued that only through a growth in their power potential could postmodernism be regarded as the herald of postmodernity.

If we ask the question who are the producers and carriers of postmodern cultural goods our attention is first drawn to changes which have taken place within various artistic and intellectual fields: the fields of art, literature, architecture, music, criticism and the academy. It was within such fields that the term was first used in the 1960s and 1970s to suggest a movement beyond the literary and artistic modernism which was seen as having reached both its formal exhaustion as well as the end of its oppositional and avant-gardist impulse through its canonization by academies, museums, and galleries which made it acceptable and a part of the syllabus in higher education institutions.

The problem with attempting to define postmodernism is that it means different things within each particular field. Yet the role of critics and cultural intermediaries in circulating information between fields is in the process of creating a common sense of what the term means. This furthers its usage by various specialists in symbolic production such as artists, novelists, intellectual, and academic commentators and researchers who use the term to interpret and frame a particular set of everyday experiences and cultural artifacts and modalities. From this perspective it is possible to isolate a number of features of postmodernism.

First, postmodernism involves an attack on autonomous, institutionalized art to deny its grounds and purpose. Art cannot be seen as a higher form of experience deriving from the creative genius or special qualities of the artist. Everything is already seen and written, the artist cannot achieve uniqueness but is doomed to make repetitions, which he/she should do without pretention. This move beyond the creative work of art, the artwork, or master text which becomes iconified in the museum, entails a blurring of the distinction between art and everyday life. In effect art is everywhere: in the street, the refuse, the body, the happening. There is no longer a valid distinction possible between high or serious art and mass, popular, art and kitsch.

Second, postmodernism develops an aesthetic of sensation, an aesthetics of the body which emphasizes the immediacy and unreflexiveness of primary processes, what Lyotard refers to as the *figural* as opposed to the *discursive* which has its basis in secondary processes (Lash 1988). It is, therefore legitimate to subvert narrative into a series of flows, to dwell on the sonority as opposed to the meaning of the spoken word (Artaud's theater), to focus on the body (interior as well as exterior) as art.

Third, in the literary, critical, and academic fields postmodernism implies an anti-foundational critique of all metanarratives, be it in science, religion, philosophy, humanism, marxism, or other systematic body of knowledge. Instead of the *grand récits* (metanarratives) Lyotard (1979) emphasizes *récits*. Hence "local" knowledge in terms of the *pagus*, the space inhabited by the "pagan," which takes on the cast of an anti-theological knowledge disputing its pretensions to global knowledge, is valorized (Doherty 1987: 15). Knowledge henceforth should be nomadic and parotic. It should playfully emphasize the discontinuities, openness, randomness, ironies, reflexivity, incoherences, and multiphrenic qualities of texts which can no longer be read with the intention of extracting a systematic interpretation. Our inner-worldly condition and entrapment in an opaque symbolic web means that we should not speak of the end of history or the end of society in an epochal sense, rather there has always already been the end of history.

Fourth, on the level of everyday cultural experiences, postmodernism implies the transformation of reality into images, and the fragmentation of time into a series of perpetual presents (Jameson 1984a: 15). Postmodern everyday culture is therefore a culture of stylistic diversity and heterogeneity, of an over-load of imagery and simulations which leads to a loss of the referent or sense of reality. The subsequent fragmentation of time into a series of presents through a lack of capacity to chain signs and images into narrative sequences leads to a schizophrenic emphasis on vivid, immediate, isolated, affect-charged experiences of the presentness of the world of *intensities*. Here the channel-hopping MTV viewer's fragmented view of the world is presented as the paradigm form.

Fifth, postmodernism, then, favors an aesthetization of the mode of perception and the aestheticization of everyday life. Art and aesthetic experiences therefore become the master paradigms for knowledge, experience, and sense of life-meaning.

Clearly at best these features we have isolated can be regarded as tendencies within small sectors of the academic and intellectual fields. In the first place it should be emphasized that these features are not themselves historically new or unique to the post-1960s phase. To take the second and fifth factors, for example, it is clear that a sense of the figural aesthetic and the aestheticization of everyday life can be traced back as far as the carnivals, festivals, and fairs of the Middle Ages. The sensory overload, flood of jumbled signs and images, collapse of symbolic hierarchies, symbolic invasions, and transgressions can clearly be detected in the carnivalesque of the lower orders. It is interesting to note that this tradition became a source of fascination for the middle classes, some of whom incorporated features of the carnivalesque and its transgressions into both the products and lifestyles of the artistic and literary bohemians which developed in the nineteenth century. This is of course the source of the artistic avant-garde which become concerned with constantly shifting the parameters of artistic modernism (see Featherstone 1989c). What would appear to be different with the emergence of the postmodern is: the extent and proliferation of these sensibilities: the carnivalesque in the Middle Ages was a relatively circumscribed liminal enclave of short duration. Today the numbers of symbolic specialists and potential audiences both via artistic and consumer culture markets is much larger. Yet there are therefore grounds for assuming that the development of these perceptions themselves may be indicators of more basic cultural changes taking place within society. If this is the case, then we need to look more closely at the constituency for the aestheticization of life, the basis for wider audiences who may become attuned and educated into postmodern sensibilities.

It can be argued that in recent years a new enlarged market has developed for intellectual, cultural and symbolic goods which is manifest in the expansion in numbers of specialists in these areas engaged in production, circulation, and transmission of these goods in the new middle class. There are long debates about the rise and composition of the new middle class which there isn't the space to go into here (Burris 1986), save to note the lack of agreement in terminology manifest in terms such as "the knowledge class," "the new class," "the new petit bourgeoisie," and "the service class." What social scientists do agree upon is that in a phase of increased unemployment this has been an expanding strata. The sectors of greatest interest for our particular concerns are the intellectuals, artists, academics, and what Bourdieu (1984) refers to as "the new culture intermediaries," which includes marketing, advertising, public relations, radio and television producers and presenters, magazine journalists, fashion writers, the helping professions (social workers, marriage counsellors, sex therapists, dieticians, play leaders, etc.). The new cultural intermediaries like academics, intellectuals, and artists typically invest in education and culture: they effectively adopt a learning mode towards life, yet often display the self-consciousness of the auto-didact, who is moving within the social space. They tend to be fascinated by identity, presentation, appearance, and the cultivation of a lifestyle with their models taken from intellectual and artistic circles. They actively promote and popularize the intellectuals' lifestyle to a larger audience, as well as help to break down the exclusivity of intellectual knowledge and the range of pursuits and fields intellectuals can be induced to comment on. This helps to collapse some of the old barriers and symbolic hierarchies which were based on the high culture/mass culture distinction. It also helps to educate and create a larger audience for intellectual and artistic goods and experiences which are receptive to some of the sensibilities manifest in phenomena like postmodernism.

As we have suggested earlier, the origins of these sensibilities should be regarded as part of a long-term process of numeric growth and increase in the power potential of specialists in symbolic production which can be traced back to the Romantic movement. Artists in particular, and specialists in symbolic production and intermediaries in general, are more disposed to a greater emotional exploration both as part of their work and lifestyle. This aspect was particularly evident in the 1960s in which a large cohort moving into higher education and the expanding service occupations become identified as a "counter-culture" which attacked emotional restraint and favored a more relaxed and informal style manifest in styles of dress and presentation. In effect this process of informalization (Wouters 1986) which became noticeable in the 1960s and 1970s, while presented as a dangerous and naive emotional regression in some circles, in fact depended upon greater self-control, a decontrolled control of the emotions which involved a relaxation and a higher level of control in being able to confront previously repressed emotions.

It has also been presented as having dangerously self-centered narcissistic implications in the 1970s (Lasch 1979). Yet it can be argued that the less strict canons of behavior and relaxation of codes which accompanied informalization and emotional exploration demanded that individuals show greater respect for each other (Wouters 1987). This may well be the case in some of the new religious movements and awareness therapies. The more widespread changes in organizational structures towards less authoritarian modes of management through negotiation (most noticeable in education and the helping professions, but by no means absent from other industrial and administrative organizations) also furthered greater flexibility in role performance and command structure (Haferkamp 1987).

In addition we should note that broader changes have occurred which have increased the number and general respectability of art occupations. In the Soho district of New York this has brought together city officials, business leaders, and developers, resulting in the gentrification of inner-city areas with greater new middle-class and upper-class users brought into contact with artists, intellectuals, cultural intermediaries. Hence there has been a growth in the public and audiences for symbolic goods which even in the recession of the 1980s, with the resurgence of conservative and traditional petit bourgeois values (e.g. Thatcherism), has been sustained.

Postmodernism then has to be understood against the background of a long-term process involving the growth of a consumer culture and expansion in the number of specialists and intermediaries engaged in the production and circulation of symbolic goods. It draws on tendencies in consumer culture which favor the aestheticization of life, the assumption that the aesthetic life is the ethically good life, and that there is no human nature or true self, with the goal of life an endless pursuit of new experiences, values, and vocabularies. While this may be a particularly threatening and restrictive paradigm for social science research, there are not the same grounds for making the same assertion about its role in everyday life. The aesthetic justification for life must be examined dispassionately, and if this is carried out it may show that the controlled de-control of emotions and absence of a centralized, coherent religious belief system does not lead to nihilism and social disintegration, rather the shift to aesthetic criteria and local knowledge may just as possibly lead to mutually expected self-restraint and respect for the other.

This does not necessarily lead to the end of the sacred; indeed, as we have argued, the sacred is able to sustain itself outside of organized religion within consumer culture. There are, however, if we are to follow some theorists of the postmodern, tendencies which would threaten the sacred. Baudrillard (1983a), for example, in drawing attention to the overload of information, signs, and images in the society where "TV is the world" argues that this overload threatens our ability to chain signs into narrative sequences.

Instead we gain aesthetic pleasure from the surface experience of the intensities of the flow of images: we do not seek coherent, lasting meaning. This then would entail the end of the symbolic as signs would be free to take on whatever associations and elisions of meaning the accidental and bizarre juxtapositions of consumer culture could throw up. In effect we would move towards cultural disorder. Yet if we move away from notions such as "TV is the World" (the closest example would be a twenty-four hour monadic MTV), where television is conceived as a sort of "moving wallpaper" to the actual practices of watching television, we note a collapsing of the public and private.

This is especially the case when we have collective viewing in which viewers, far from being passive, may actively participate in the religiosity of events, spectacles, and ceremonies and indeed may even ritualize watching by dressing up (Dayan and Katz 1988: 162). Hence once we move away from such notions such as information overload, in which the form of information determines the content and reception, to considering active viewing by embodied persons, then the symbolic and sacred dimension of social life can be sustained. In effect the practical aspect of cultural reproduction demands that people will attempt to stabilize signs into classificatory schemes which possess a practical coherence and symbolic dimension without, as we have stressed, seeking the logical and rational consistency and plausibility which is more central to the practices of symbol specialists.

Finally, there is the question of how consumer culture and postmodernism can be related to the global order. It is often assumed that consumer culture on a global scale parallels the expansion of the power of the United States over the world economic order (Mattelart 1979). Here consumer culture is seen as destined to become a universal culture which destroys each country's own national culture. Yet studies of the effect of television reception emphasize the importance of national differences in reading and de-coding messages. In effect the messages embedded in television programs only make sense to those socialized into the codes, so that different nationalities and social classes will view internationally popular television programs through inappropriate codes. It can also be argued that the tendency we have referred to within consumer culture to produce an over-load of information and signs would also work against any coherent, integrated universal global belief on the level of content. However, the prevalence of images of "the other," of different nations, previously unknown or only referred to through narrow stereotypes may effectively help to put the other, and the sense of a global circumstance, on the agenda.

With reference to postmodernism the loss of the sense of "the other" as alien or exotic, as a stereotype, flowing from a loss of faith in the metanarratives which underlay such interpretations, here one thinks of the work of Said on orientalism, produces a further crisis in the authority of interpreting different cultures or traditions from a center point or foundation. This crisis is beginning to emerge in theorization throughout the social sciences and can be related to changes in the perception of the global circumstance. The openness to otherness and the previously ignored, or the once felt threatening disorder of different cultures, itself represents a shift in the power balances between nations. To seek to know the other in its own terms, to seek to glimpse behind the narrow and over-bearing stereotypes, registers the hermeneutic turn in cultural methodology. This movement towards cultural de-classification and the de-construction of long-held symbolic hierarchies points to a world in which the chains of interdependencies between nations and cultures are lengthened and more densely interwoven.

In anthropology, for example, the postmodern-induced acceptance of the particularity and integrity of various bodies of local knowledge has been taken a stage further in which the anthropological subjects not only dispute the authority and validity of anthropologists' interpretation but seek to speak for themselves. The anthropologist is left to tell a story about his own experience (Friedman 1987). These changes taking place on an inter-societal level, which push academics and intellectuals towards a polyculturist perspective, are compounded by changes on an intra-societal level, some of which we have referred to which have on the one hand reduced the power of the intellectuals' authority through inflation in the intellectual field. This has resulted in greater numbers of new intellectuals and a de-monopolization of the power of established intellectuals to define symbolic hierarchies; and, on the other hand, there is a pull from the consumer marketplace with an increasing demand for symbolic goods on the part of new cultural intermediaries to cater to the thirst for new cultural experiences, sensations, etc. Effectively the intellectual is reduced to the role of an interpreter, packaging particularities, and unable to offer legitimate universal knowledge with any prospect of a legislative or practical effect (Bauman 1985).

From one perspective postmodernism can be understood as a cultural image, a talismanic concept which incorporates images of disorder, dissolution, relativism, and fragmentation which opens up a space beyond the hypnostatizations of the systematically and universalizing conceptual arsenal of modern. Its proponents find this attractive: the re-emergence of images of cultural disorder, which have themselves been an adversarial and transgressive sub-theme within the Western tradition, yet which remained largely enclaved with the liminal carnivalesque and its artistic recuperation. Such images themselves may have a wider appeal not only through intra-societal changes in the class structure which push to the fore new markets for symbolic goods and new opportunities for symbolic specialists, but also in terms of inter-societal and global processes. Indeed there is a sense in which, given the identification of the modern with the universalizing project of Western culture, the use of the term postmodern can act to orientate us to the changing circumstances in which the world is seen as one place in which different competing images of the globe come to the fore (Robertson 1991).

References

Adorno, T. 1967. "Veblen's Attack on Culture." In *Prisms*. London: Spearman.
Alexander, J.C. 1988. "Culture and Political Crisis: 'Watergate' and Durkheimian Sociology." In *Durkheimian Sociology: Cultural Studies*, edited by J.C. Alexander. Cambridge: Cambridge University Press.
Allen, J. 1983. *The Romance of Commerce and Culture*. Chicago: University of Chicago Press.
Archer, M. 1988. *Culture and Agency*. Cambridge: Cambridge University Press.
Bailey, P. 1978. *Leisure and Class in Victorian England*. London: Routledge and Kegan Paul.
Baudrillard, J. 1983a. *In the Shadow of the Silent Majorities*. New York: Semiotext(e).
_____. 1983b. *Simulations*. New York: Semiotext(e).
Bauman, Z. 1985. "On the Origin of Civilization." *Theory, Culture and Society* 2 (3).
Beckford, J. 1985. "The Insulation and Isolation of the Sociology of Religion." *Sociological Analysis* 4, 6 (4).
Bell, D. 1973. *The Coming of Post-Industrial Society*. New York: Harper.
_____. 1976. *The Cultural Contradictions of Capitalism*. London: Heinemann.
_____. 1980. *Sociological Journeys*. London: Heinemann.
Bellah, R.N., et al. 1985. *Habits of the Heart*. Berkeley: University of California Press.
Bendix, R. 1959. *Max Weber: An Intellectual Portrait*. London: Heinemann.

____. 1970. "Culture, Social Structure and Change." In *Embattled Reason: Essays on Social Knowledge*. New York: Oxford University Press.
Berger, P. 1969. *The Social Reality of Religion*. London: Faber.
Berman, M. 1983. *All That Is Solid Melts Into Air*. New York: Simon and Schuster.
Bourdieu, P. 1977. *Outline of a Theory of Practice*. Cambridge: Cambridge University Press.
____. 1980. "The Production of Belief: A Contribution to the Economy of Symbolic Goods." *Media, Culture and Society* 2(3).
____. 1983. "The Philosophical Institution." In A. Montefiore (ed.), *Philosophy in France Today*. Cambridge: Cambridge University Press.
____. 1984. *Distinctions*. Cambridge, MA: Harvard University Press.
Burris, V. 1986. "The Discovery of the New Middle Class." *Theory and Society* 15.
Campbell, C. 1987. *The Romantic Ethic and the Spirit of Modern Consumerism*. Oxford: Blackwell.
Collins, R. 1988. "The Durkheimian Tradition in Conflict Sociology." In J.C. Alexander (ed.), *Durkheimian Sociology: Cultural Studies*. Cambridge: Cambridge University Press.
Cowley, M. 1951. *Exiles Return*. New York: Viking.
Corrigan, P. and D. Sayer. 1985. *The Great Arch: English State Formation as Cultural Revolution*. Oxford: Blackwell.
Dayan, D. and E. Katz. 1988. "Articulating Consensus: The Ritual and Rhetoric of Media Events." In J.C. Alexander (ed.), *Durkheimian Sociology: Cultural Studies*. Cambridge University Press.
DiMaggio, P. 1987. "Classification in Art." *American Sociological Review* 52(4).
Doherty, T. 1987. "Theory, Enlightenment and Violence, Postmodern Hermeneutics as a Comedy of Errors." *Textual Practice* 1(2).
Douglas, Mary. 1980. *The World of Goods*. New York: Pantheon.
Durkheim, E. 1974. "Value Judgments and Judgments of Reality." In *Sociology and Philosophy*. New York: Free Press.
Elias, N. 1965. *The Established and the Outsiders*. London: Cass.
____. 1978a. *What is Sociology?* London: Hutchinson.
____. 1978b. *The Civilizing Process Volume I: The History of Manners*. Oxford: Blackwell.
____. 1983. *The Court Society*. Oxford: Blackwell.
____. 1984. "Power and Knowledge: An Interview with Peter Ludes." In N. Stehr and V. Meja (eds.), *Society and Knowledge*. New Brunswick: Transaction Books.
____. 1987. "The Retreat of Sociologists into the Present." *Theory, Culture and Society* 4 (2–3).
____. and E. Dunning. 1986. *Quest for Excitement*. Oxford: Blackwell.
Ewen, S. 1976. *Captains of Consciousness: Advertising and the Social Roots of the Consumer Culture*. New York: McGraw-Hill.
Ewen, S. & S. Ewen. 1982. *Channels of Desire*. New York: McGraw-Hill.
Featherstone, M. 1987a. "Consumer Culture, Symbolic Power and Universalism." In G. Stauth and S. Zubaida (eds.), *Mass Culture, Popular Culture and Social Life in the Middle East*. Boulder, Colorado: Westview.
____. 1987b. "Lifestyle and Consumer Culture." *Theory, Culture and Society* 4 (1).
____. 1988a. "In Pursuit of the Postmodern." *Theory, Culture and Society* 5 (2–3).

_____. 1988b. "Cultural Production, Consumption and the Development of the Cultural Sphere," paper presented at the 3rd German-American Theory Group Conference, Bremen.

_____. 1989a. "Postmodernism and the New Middle Class," paper presented at the IAPL Conference on Postmodernism, Lawrence, Kansas. Revised version re-titled "Postmodernism, Cultural Change and Social Practice," in D. Kellner (ed.), *Jameson/Postmodernism/Critique*. New York: Maisoneuve Press.

_____. 1989b. "Towards a Sociology of Postmodern Culture." In H. Haferkamp (ed.), *Culture and Social Structure*. Berlin: de Gruyter.

_____. 1989c. "Postmodernism and the Aestheticization of Everyday Life." In S. Lash and J. Friedman (eds.), *Culture and Modernity*. London: Hutchinson.

Fenn, R.K. 1982. "The Sociology of Religion: A Critical Survey." In T. Bottomore, S. Nowak, and M. Sokolowska (eds.), *Sociology: The State of the Art*. London: Sage.

Friedman, J. 1987. "Prolegomena to the Adventures of Phallus in Blunderland: An Anti-anti-discourse." *Culture and History* 1(1).

Frisby, D. 1985. "Georg Simmel, First Sociologist of Modernity." *Theory, Culture and Society* 2 (3).

Gellner, E. 1979. "The Social Roots of Egalitarianism." *Dialectics and Humanism* 4.

Habermas, J. 1984. *Theory of Communicative Action, Volume I*. London: Heinemann.

_____. 1987. *The Philosophical Discourse of Modernity*. Boston: Beacon Press.

Haferkamp, H. 1987. "Beyond the Iron Cage of Modernity: Achievement, Negotiation and Changes in the Power Structure." *Theory, Culture and Society* 4(1).

Hammond, P.E. 1986. "Religion in the Modern World." In J.D. Hunter and S.C. Ainlay (eds.), *Making Sense of Modern Times: P.L. Berger and the Vision of Interpretive Sociology*. London: RKP.

Hutcheon, L. 1987. "Beginning to Theorize Postmodernism." *Textual Practice* 1(1).

Huyssen, A. 1984. "Mapping the Postmodern." *New German Critique* 33.

Jameson, F. 1979. "Reflection and Utopia in Mass Culture." *Social Text* 1(1).

_____. 1984a. "Postmodernism: or the Cultural Logic of Late Capitalism." *New Left Review* 146.

_____. 1984b. "Postmodernism and the Consumer Society." In H. Foster (ed.), *Postmodern Culture*. London: Pluto Press.

Kalberg, S. 1987. "The Origin and Expansion of *Kulturpessimismus*." *Sociological Theory* 4 (Fall).

Kroker, A. 1985. "Baudrillard's Marx." *Theory, Culture and Society* 2 (3).

Lasch, C. 1979. *The Culture of Narcissism*. New York: Norton.

Lash, S. 1988. "Discourse or Figure? Postmodern as a Regime of Signification." *Theory, Culture and Society* 5(2–3).

Leiss, W. 1983. "The Icons of the Marketplace." *Theory, Culture and Society* 1(3).

Luckmann, B. 1971. "The Small Life Worlds of *Modern Man*." *Social Research*.

Luckmann, T. 1967. *The Invisible Religion*. London: Macmillan.

Lyotard, J.F. 1979. *Instructions painnes*. Paris: Galilee

_____. 1984. *The Postmodern Condition*. Manchester: Manchester University Press.

McKendrick, N., J. Brewer, and J.H. Plumb. 1982. *The Birth of a Consumer Society*. London: Europe.

Martin, B. 1981. *A Sociology of Contemporary Cultural Change*. Oxford: Blackwell.

Mattelart, A. 1979. *Multinational Corporations and the Control of Culture*. Brighton: Harvester P.

Megill, A. 1985. *Prophet of Yesterday*. Berkeley: University of California Press.
O'Neill, J. 1988. "Religion and Postmodernism: the Durkheimian Bond in Bell and Jameson." *Theory, Culture and Society* 5 (2–3).
Parkin, F. 1979. *Marxism and Class Theory: A Bourgeois Critique*. London: Tavistock.
Reay, B. 1985a. "Introduction." In *Popular Culture in Seventeenth Century England*. London: Croom Helm.
_____. 1985b. "Popular Religion." In *Popular Culture in Seventeenth Century England*. London: Croom Helm.
Robertson, R. 1978. *Meaning and Change*. Oxford: Blackwell.
_____. 1985. "Beyond the Sociology of Religion?" *Sociological Analysis* 46.
_____. 1987. "Globalization Theory and Civilization Analysis." *Comparative Civilizations Review* (Fall).
_____. 1988. "The Sociological Significance of Culture: Some General Considerations." *Theory, Culture and Society* 5(1).
_____. 1991. "Globality, Global Culture and Images of World Order." In *Modernity and Social Change*, ed. by N. Smelser and H. Haferkamp. Berkeley: University of California Press.
_____ and J. Chirico. 1985. "Humanity, Globalization and the Worldwide Religious Resurgence: A Theoretical Exploration." *Sociological Analysis* 46.
Rochberg-Halton, E. 1986. *Meaning and Modernity*. Chicago: University of Chicago Press.
Shusterman, R. 1988. "Ethics and Aesthetics Are One: Postmodernism's Ethics of Taste." *Theory, Culture and Society* 5 (2–3).
Sennett, R. 1976. *The Fall of Public Man*. Cambridge: Cambridge University Press.
Simmel, G. 1978. *The Philosophy of Money*. London: RKP.
Stallybrass, P. and A. White. 1986. *Transgression*. London: Methuen.
Susman, R. 1979. "Personality and the Making of Twentieth Century Culture." In J. Higham and P.K. Conkin (eds.), *New Directions in American Cultural History*. Baltimore: Johns Hopkins University Press.
_____. 1982. *Culture and Commitment 1929–1945*. New York: Braziller.
Tiryakian, E.A. 1978. "Emile Durkheim." In T. Bottomore and R. Nisbet (eds.), *A History of Sociological Analysis*. London: Heinemann.
Turner, B.S. 1983. *Religion and Social Theory*. London: Heinemann.
_____. 1986. *Equality*. London: Tavistock.
Weber, M. 1948. "Religious Rejections of the World and their Directions." In H.H. Gerth and C. Wright Mills (eds.), *From Max Weber*. London: RKP.
_____. 1968. *Economy and Society*, 3 vols. Totowa, N.J.: Bedminster Press.
Weiss, J. 1985. "Wiederwerzauberung der Welt." *Kolner Zietschrift fur Soziologie und Sozialpsychologie*.
Williams, R. 1982. *Dream Worlds, Mass Consumption in Late Nineteenth Century France*. Berkeley: University of California Press.
Wouters, C. 1986. "Formalization and Informalization: Changing Tension Balances in Civilizing Processes." *Theory, Culture and Society* 3(2).
_____. 1987. "Developments in the Behavioral Codes Between the Sexes." *Theory, Culture and Society* 4(2–3).

9
POLITICS AND CULTURE IN ISLAMIC GLOBALISM

Bryan S. Turner

FROM THE PERSPECTIVE OF SOCIOLOGY OF RELIGION, there are two separate but related processes in modern Islamic cultures. The first is the emergence of a global Islamic political system and the second is the cultural reaction of Islamic fundamentalism against Westernism and consumerism. These processes are analyzed in this chapter in terms of a sociological framework which embraces, somewhat eclectically, a number of theoretical perspectives.

The issue of Islamic modernization may be understood initially within the framework of Max Weber's sociology of the process of rationalization which focused on the paradoxical relationship between the process of rationalization and the problem of meaninglessness. The argument here is that Weber's sociology provides an anticipation of the current contrast between the program of modernization and the condition of postmodernism. Within this framework, Islamic fundamentalism is seen as a reaction against cultural and social differentiation and fragmentation. More specifically fundamentalism is an attempt at de-differentiation. However, it is important to avoid a sociological orientation which considers Islam in isolation from other world religions, because the major religions are necessarily involved in global processes. The emergence of universalistic standards in cultural and political life are consequently analyzed in relation to the world religions (more specifically the Abrahamic faiths.)

In order to understand the recent political and cultural history of Islamic societies, two related arguments must be considered. The first argument attempts to recognize the profound problems of having, within a world cultural system, competing world religions which claim exclusive and largely absolutist truths or values. At present, there seems little possibility of global ecumenism on a fundamentalist basis. Previous research into national forms of ecumenism has drawn attention to the profound difficulties of securing agreement between churches of the same religion claiming separate versions of truth.

The problem on a global level, when dealing with exclusive fundamentalist religious movements, is clearly more difficult and the future relations between the Abrahamic faiths in particular is uncertain. The poignancy of the relationship between the Abrahamic faiths is nowhere better illustrated than in their separate, exclusive, and largely incompatible claims to Jerusalem. The first problem then is how to contain, within a single global environment, absolutist religious positions presented by mutually conflictual religious systems. In the case of Islam, the relationship between the Household of Islam and the sphere of war gives rise to particularly profound political problems.

The second argument is concerned with the problem of relationship between the cultural, aesthetic, and stylistic pluralism of postmodernism and the fundamentalist commitment to the coherent and unified world organized around values, styles and beliefs which are held to be incontrovertibly true. The problem of meaningfulness arises from consumer culture on a global scale which makes alternative life-styles, beliefs, and attitudes appear as a set of commodities for sale on a world cultural market. However, against Weber and his followers, Islam was perfectly compatible with the modernization project involving, as it did, a high degree of secularization of traditional religious cultures, but Islam cannot deal satisfactorily with postmodernism which threatens to deconstruct religious messages into mere fairy tales and to destroy the everyday world by the challenge of cultural diversity. The problem of cultural perspectivism is an effect of the pluralization of life-worlds brought about by the spread of a diversified, global system of consumption.

The debate about contemporary fundamentalism has to see these social movements as attempts to secure political hegemony within the global political structure, while at the same time securing at the local level a degree of control over the life-world by attempting to exclude the pluralism of contemporary patterns of consumption. Modern fundamentalism is a two-pronged movement to secure control within the global system and also to maintain a local regulation of the life-world. Fundamentalism in both Islam and Christianity can therefore be analyzed as a value-system which actually promoted modernization, because modernization was an attack on magical beliefs, local culture, traditionalism, and hedonism. Fundamentalism is therefore the cultural defense of modernity against postmodernity.

Political Modernization: Max Weber's Theory of Social Change

Weber has often been interpreted very narrowly as being interested in the relationship between religion and capitalist development. More recent interpretations of Weber's sociology have, however, drawn attention to the concept of rationalization as the core theme of Weber's entire sociological concern (Brubaker 1984; Hennis 1987; Roth and Schluchter 1979). Even this theme of rationalization was merely an aspect of Weber's more general interest in the origins of modernism and modernization. Briefly, modernism is the outcome in cultural, social, and political terms of the broad process of rationalization by which the world is controlled and regulated by an ethic of world mastery involving the subordination of the self, social relations, and nature to a program of detailed control and regulation. The modernization project is the imposition of rationality (in terms of means-ends schemes) to the total environment. The history of modernization is the history of reason as the instrumental regulation of man and environment as described classically in the *Dialectic of Enlightenment* (Adorno and Horkeimer 1944).

Weber's account of modernism and modernization can be understood initially in terms of his model of social relations outlined abstractly in the introductory section of *Economy and Society* (1968). Weber distinguished first between social relations which are either open or closed to outsiders. This involves social closure to secure the monopolistic advantages of resources against unqualified intruders. Second, following the comparison (Toennies 1957) between *Gemeinschaft* and *Gesellschaft*, Weber distinguished between communal and associational relationships. Communal relations are based upon traditional or effectual forms of interaction, involving dense reciprocities between people linked together by customs and local practices. By contrast, associational relations are more impersonal, fleeting, and contractual. By combining these two dimensions, we can form an ideal type of social relations (Figure 9–1).

If we interpret Weber's typology in a dynamic and historical fashion, then we can argue that the process of European history was from social relations which were predominantly closed and communal to relations which were primarily open and associational. In terms of social stratification, this was a movement from estates, communities, and castes to classes, organized in terms of market principles (Turner 1988a). Rather like Sir Henry Maine in *Ancient Law*, Weber saw the development of modern societies as a process from status to contract. As a jurisprudential theorist (Kronman 1983), Weber saw the progress of modern societies as a transition from status arrangements involving the total personality in a set of magical and traditional bonds to a social system in which impersonal contracts of a legal character linked persons together into open associational relations. He argued that originally contracts were magical acts binding persons together through a form of fraternization, but contemporary contracts are "purposive contracts" which are important for the development of modern market places. We may note in passing that Weber's conception of the emergence of modern capitalism in these terms was not unlike that of Marx for whom the cash nexus in modern societies is the primary bond between persons (Turner 1988b).

FIGURE 9-1
Weber's Typology of Social Relations

Open	Closed	
church	village	**Communal**
market	political party	**Associational**

If we examine Weber's typology within the context of the historical development of modern societies, then it is clear that the classical sociological tradition saw this evolution from village to market, or from *Gemeinschaft* to *Gesellschaft*. In this transition to an "open society," Protestant Christianity (specifically Calvinism) provides a crucial cultural level. Of course, there were empirically many alternative historical processes whereby various combinations of social relations were maintained which are in principle incompatible with open-associational relations. The continuity of ethnicity and gender are the primary illustrations. This model of social relations has two major contributions for this analysis of Islamic fundamentalism in a global perspective.

First, while conventional theories of secularization often assume that religion and modernization stand in a contradictory relationship, Weber's study of the Protestant ethic suggests an alternative interpretation. Ascetic fundamentalism—far from being incompatible with modernity—actually pushed societies from closed-communal to open-associational relations. In this respect, Protestant denominations emerged as the religious counterpart of trading associations. However, as the consumer market threatens to break out into a new stage of fragmented postmodernism in late capitalism, fundamentalism now acts as a brake on the historical development of world capitalism. Fundamentalism appears now in a "reactionary" guise as the defender of the project of modernity against disjointed pluralism of postmodernity.

The second aspect of the argument is that Weber's model provides some clues about the possible range of images of the globe. For example, the image of the world as a global system may be presented in terms of a global supermarket (open-associational space) or as a super-church (open-communal) or as a global village (closed-communal). As the world-system moves towards modernism and then beyond into the postmodern age, fundamentalism pulls this process back towards a more traditional mode, but in particular towards the trajectory of either the global "church" or the global "party." In terms of Islamic system, fundamentalism points towards a genuinely global Household of Faith which must place some limits on membership and which must retain some element of conflict with other absolutist systems (such as Marxism).

This discussion of Islam and modernization is not concerned with the specifically economic or historical feature of these developments because the aim here is to focus on the cultural and religious implication of this transition from a society grounded in traditional and effectual relations to societies based more and more upon economic contracts of an open and impersonal or associational character. While it was the Calvinistic sects which made possible the transition from closed, communal societies to contemporary capitalist or industrial civilizations, Weber had argued that because there was no dynamic contradiction between the sacred and the profane that Buddhism, Confucianism, and Hinduism were unable to provide the social and cultural leverage for the emergence of the modern world.

Given this emphasis on Calvinism, Weber was forced to argue that the other Abrahamic faiths (Islam and Judaism) were unable to provide the historical leverage (via ethical prophecy and the critique of society and human relations) for a transition to modernity (Turner 1974; 1978; 1987). In Judaism, the inner-worldly quest for mastery was turned outward into dietary and other exclusively social practices. In Islam, the inner-worldly salvational quest was turned outward and externalized into a quest for land and military dominance. Even within Christianity, the emotional sectarian movements associated with pietism and Methodism translated the salvational problem into personal emotion. It was the stern ascetic discipline and theology of the Calvinistic sects which, through their irrational inner quest for meaning, produced an external world of discipline, vocations, and rational mastery. As we know from Weber's own work in *The Protestant Ethic and the Spirit of Capitalism*, he argued that once the treadmill of modern rationalization has been set in motion, capitalism no longer required the supportive foundations of spirituality, since modern rational systems have a logic of their own.

What were the implications of these religious and cultural changes for political doctrines and social systems? The historic evolution of the market place corresponds in an important fashion with the gradual evolution of an emphasis on the individual and in later historical epochs with an emphasis on individualism as a specific doctrine of social rights (Abercrombie, Hill, and Turner 1984.) Indeed, the liberating impact of impersonal, open, associational relations within the exchanges of the market place can be seen in terms of a transition from holistic conceptions of reality to individualistic cultures (Dumont 1983; 1986).

For Weber, the emergence of modern capitalism (or more generally the emergence of rational market places) created the conditions for the emergence of the autonomous, self-directed personality, which also had its roots in the emergence of the abstract, religious soul, linked to an abstract monotheistic God by a series of connections of rational belief and religious faith. While the God of Christianity was a personal God, the individual in modern society emerges as an abstract and general, public character. This impersonal dimension is specifically important in the political realm or the public arena, where the particularistic characteristics of individuals (such as age, sex, or race) become from a political point of view increasingly unimportant.

Following the work of T.H. Marshall, the expansion of social citizenship rights entails an expansion of the definition of the social and the social arena, with the consequence that the individual citizen constantly emerges as a more abstract, universalistic, and free agent within political space (Turner 1986). The political citizen within a modern democratic culture is no longer defined in terms of property-holding, sex, racial characteristics, or any such particularistic dimension, but rather emerges as the abstract bearer of general rights of social participation and membership.

Another way of expressing this argument is that modern social systems are dominated by the principles of egalitarian citizenship and by the quest for political and social equality (Prager 1985). This development of the abstract citizen is the political counterpart to the historical transition from *Gemeinschaft* to *Gesellschaft*; citizenship can be regarded as an index of secularization in which the City of God gives way to the modern *polis* of abstract strangers linked together by legal entitlement and abstract exchange relationships. The expansion of political citizenship in terms of this abstract framework can also be connected with the notion that the growth of a money market produces the idea of the abstract individual user of financial facilities (Simmel 1978). There is therefore a certain interpenetration of the economic development of abstract individualism and the long-term historical implications of the individualism of the Abrahamic faiths. This idea was also taken up by Talcott Parsons (1963) who noted that the contractual nature of the relationship between man and God, and the individualism of the Christian tradition created the conditions for a radical egalitarianism which liquidated the notion of religious bonds based upon ethnic particularism. The importance of Christianity for the emergence of a political community was that it undermined fundamentally the particularistic relationship of blood in favor of a community based upon a universalistic faith (Weber 1958).

The logical extension of this sociological argument is that the abstract citizen must emerge eventually as a global agent within a world political system, since the individual (within the logic of the process of rationalization) can no longer be contained within the nation-state. The paradox of the emerging, egalitarian individualism of nineteenth-century capitalism, especially in England, was that the growth of the abstract individual also followed historically the emergence of the nation-state as a closed and particularistic entity in which social membership is ultimately located in one particular language or dialect. There is, as both Marx and Weber implicitly recognized, a potential conflict between the abstract, globally located, citizen-individual and the particularistic requirements of the nation-state as the political encasement of the individual.

It is possible to link this argument about individualism and globalism to the world-system theory of Wallerstein (1974; 1980). Wallerstein has argued that globally the world has moved from a system of large-scale empires (based upon local economies) to a world, structured by one global economy but articulated through particular political systems. If we transpose this argument into the context of the world-religious systems, at least Islam and Christianity conceptualized themselves or thematized themselves as world religions, and therefore they have a particularly problematic relationship to local political systems.

In the pre-modern period, the world religious systems had little opportunity to realize themselves globally, because the systems of communication and transport were wholly underdeveloped or non-existent. Prior to the emergence of modern communication systems, the world religions operated on a largely localized basis with tenuous linkages to their cultural centers and articulated at a global level by an underdeveloped and fragile system of trading relationships (Mann 1986).

In the modern period, the possibility of achieving global religious systems has been facilitated by the emergence of modern forms of transport, communication, and integration. This produces a number of tensions and paradoxes between the abstract individual and the demands of nation-state political commitments, and between the universalism of the religious system in a competitive world cultural environment, where fundamentalist versions of the Abrahamic faiths are forced to conflict with each other over local sites, sources of recruitment, and geo-political influence.

Weber also had a negative, pessimistic, and demonic version of the modernization project which in some respects anticipated modern debates about anti-modernism and postmodernism. Following the work of Nietzsche, Weber recognized that with the death of God, the pluralization of life worlds, and the secularization of culture, we live in a world which is relativized and which forces social theorists to adopt perspectivism as their primary orientation to cultural facts. For Nietzsche, the therapeutic capacity of art and music had been undermined by the growth of cultural nihilism. In Nietzsche's epistemology, languages are merely metaphorical accounts of reality; he proceeded to de-construct the underlying metaphors of religion and science. While Nietzsche himself rejected nihilism, his philosophical views had a profoundly disturbing effect on subsequent German philosophy. Nietzsche was received as a great nihilist of culture, whereas the primary emphasis in Nietzsche's own solution lay on the re-evaluation of values. In response to the problems of secularization, Weber converted Nietzsche's philosophy into a sociology of social action and personality, which gave a primary emphasis to the ethic of responsibility and a vocation in science (Stauth and Turner 1986; 1988).

Weber's theory of rationalization provides a basis in sociological theory for an analysis of contemporary movements in culture which are either fundamentalist or neo-conservative by attempting to restore moral coherence as the basis of modern religious and social practices. On the one hand, Weber recognized a profound process of rationalization and modernization in society leading to the differentiation of religious, scientific, and moral realms and a profound secularization of values. On the other hand, Weber recognized, following Nietzsche, that the project of reason always discovers its own unreasonableness by exposing the arbitrary character of all forms of rationalization. While rationality can select appropriate means for action, it cannot provide a rational ground for ends.

Fundamentalism is a response both to modernization and to post-modernism since fundamentalism is a process of de-differentiation (Lechner 1985a, 1985b; Robertson and Chirico 1985). We might also treat these social movements of fundamentalization as forms of collective nostalgia which seek to restructure the world in terms of more simple entities and communal cultural relations (Turner 1987). In political terms, fundamentalism attempts to create a set of boundaries which will contain political pluralism and the abstract generalization of the citizen on a global scale, but in terms of some notion of community or household. In the cultural arena, fundamentalism is an attempt to impose certain boundaries on modernization, and more particularly on post-modernism. It attempts to reverse the historical process towards a hyper-secular consumerism and pluralism by providing paradoxically a traditional defense of modernity. We can consider these developments through a brief sketch of the evolution of contemporary Islam.

The Polity of the Household of Faith

In theological terms, Islam is based on an idealistic construction (or reconstruction) of the Umma (community) which Islam has never successfully institutionalized. The idealistic conception involves an integration of politico-religious authority, a terrain or household in which Islamic practice is uniformly followed, and an outward religious thrust or Jihad involving a struggle against unbelief. While Islam normatively considered itself as a universalistic faith, it is important to recognize the Arabism of Islam, since for example the Quran as an Arabic expression of divine revelation has a crucial part to play in the authoritative structure of Islamic cultures. In addition, the Prophet's lineage has been of enormous significance, and finally Islam is rooted in a holy space (Mecca and Medina) which is obviously profoundly Arabic.

This ideal community could never entirely resolve the problem of authority, especially the problems of political control through either the claims of lineage or those of elected leaders, a tension which contributed in part to the emergence of two distinct forms of Islamic faith, namely Sunni Islam and Shi'ism. More importantly, Islam was unable to impose its authority on minor or subordinate groups within the household of faith, and there developed throughout Islam a millet system which permitted internal pluralism and ethnic diversity to continue.

Finally, we should note an important variation within Islam between the ascetic traditions of literary Islam within the urban tradition and mystical Islam which flourished in Sufism, permitting the development of saintship, local cults, and hierarchical forms of practice which conflicted with, or at least stood in contradiction to, the egalitarian principles of the core tradition (Gellner 1969; 1981). The history of Islam in part revolves around these problems of local and global authority, giving rise to periodic social movements of Islamization in which the ascetic and literary codes were imposed upon localist forms of Sufism. The reform of Islam has normally assumed a recurrent pattern in which strong political leaders attempt to impose political control over the hinterland in the name of a monotheistic conception of Islam against the polytheistic tendencies of the periphery.

However, before the emergence of modern forms of communication and transportation, the imposition of unitarian control around a monotheistic culture had always been limited by certain technical-military problems and by the inability of dynastic power to secure its control through time and space (Mann 1986). While in Weberian terms the Household of Islam was patrimonial, the political structure was in fact decentralized into local, dynastic authorities which competed with the patrimonial core for authority. We can therefore conceptualize premodern Islamic politics in terms of a constant tension between patrimonial centers and local sources of political authority (Turner 1981).

There is some general agreement among historians that Islamic cities in the pre-modern period lacked feudal estates and there was no significant development in Islam of urban centers like urban communes or municipalities of Europe. Islamic imperial rule depended upon local notables who were either scholars (Ulama), or notables (A'yan), or commanders of local garrisons who provided political skills at the local level for the imposition of Islamic authority. There was a certain integration or structural symbiosis between the state, merchants, and Ulama who provided clerical services for the state bureaucracy. The achievement of local autonomy on the part of towns developed in Islam through two channels, either by the weakening of imperial control (for example, Timbuktu in West Africa), or by local rebellions (for example, Seville in Muslim Spain, or Tripoli, or Tyre) (Shoshan 1986).

It is important to understand this pre-modern structure in order to comprehend the character of modern fundamentalism as a political movement. Despite the truism that Islam requires the unity of religion and politics, in pre-modern times, that is before the emergence of European colonialism, Muslim rulers were unable to impose their political authority on religious leaders. Within these empires, the ruling elites were forced to depend on the intermediary role and functions of local notables, who claimed to be descendants of the Prophet, or were the Ashref, merchants and local garrison leaders. It is the availability in modern times of effective global communication systems which makes possible for the first time a globalization of Islam which in fact is the Islamization of cultures through the norms and practices of Islamic fundamentalism. While Islam has always claimed a universalistic status, it was, prior to the emergence of contemporary communication systems, actually unable to impose this type of uniformity and universalism. The paradox of modern systems of communication is that it makes Islam simultaneously exposed to western consumerism and provides the mechanism for the distribution of a global Islamic message. This observation is an extension of Marx's ironic judgment that the railway system and the press would explode the Asiatic mode of production in India.

From Colonization to Fundamentalism

Between Napoleon's invasion of Egypt and the end of the nineteenth century, three separate but related social and economic processes transformed the Islamic regions. First, the Ottoman empire was broken up by colonialism into relatively separate nation-states. Second, the economies of the old Islamic world were gradually incorporated into and subordinated by a world capitalist system as highly dependent units and, third, there was a significant cultural response to these changes through various religious reform movements. The development of colonialism called forth, as it were, a new local intelligentsia of clerical workers who were often western-trained and adopted western attitudes but never achieved full integration into the western system. The result was an intense ambiguity as to the relationship between secular westernization and anti-colonial nationalism (Enayat 1982; Hourani 1962). We can regard these three processes as forms of cultural and structural differentiation of the Islamic world.

One response to western colonialism was to adopt a deliberate policy of secularization which were legitimized by a return to Islamic sources. Islamic reform involved an attack on traditional and popular forms of Islam (in particular Sufism) which was associated with political decay and social stagnation. By returning to primitive Islam (defined as an ascetic and disciplined form of Islam), it was argued that Islamic societies could be modernized while also becoming more Islamic.

One has therefore a somewhat paradoxical relationship between secularization and reformism in the liberal response of Islam to westernism.

These developments were probably most explicit in the Turkish case where Kemalist reforms involved a direct confrontation with traditional populist Islamic life-styles (Shaw and Shaw 1977). As a reformist regime, the Kemalist government was deeply influenced by western ideas about, for example, education and nationalism. Educational reform (under the leadership of Ziya Gokalp) was directed in terms of Durkheim's concept of social solidarity. Secularization involved the creation of new legal systems which typically relegated Islamic holy law (the Sharia) to the personal sphere, leaving public relations under European legal codes; and, second, secularization involved the separation of religious and secular institutions of education. Third, secularization involved changes in dress and custom, such as the introduction of the Turkish Hat Law of 1925. These changes in custom involved significant changes in the relationship between men and women (Tucker 1985; Keddie and Beck 1978). Secularization involved the differentiation of Islamic culture and social structure on the model of westernization.

The central theme of modernization was however legitimized in terms of a return to classical Islam, that is the Islam of ascetic, literary monotheism. Once Islam was liberated from its folk traditions and from foreign accretions, Islam could emerge as a dynamic and progressive component of the reform of society. The return to the Quran was in practice used to bring about profound changes in Islamic life. We can regard this as the liberal age of Islam and its major spokesmen were Jamal al-Din Al-afghani, Muhammad Abduh, and Rashid Rida (Esposito 1984). These liberal reforms are often referred to collectively as the Salafiyyah movement and restate the classical dogmas of "primitive" Islam in order to bring about a political program of liberal reform.

Islam also came to play a crucial role in the development of anti-colonial nationalist movements in North Africa, India, and Indonesia. Within these ethnically diverse and culturally complex societies, Islamic symbols were important as components of nationalist integration in Morocco, Tunisia, and Indonesia (Esposito 1984; Geertz 1968). It is important to recognize, however, that in this period Islam was seen to be a foundation for Arab nationalism; consequently, there was less emphasis on Islamic unity and global Islamdom. Since Islam was one foundation of anti-colonial nationalism, some writers have detected a movement away from Islam in the post-independence period toward more secular and nationalist ideologies which attempted to modernize and legitimate separate nation-states (Smith 1974; Wolf 1971). In the 1950s and 1960s many Muslim countries adopted a program of political nationalism, democratic sovereignty, the creation of parliamentary rights, the adoption of secular legal codes, and most importantly the development of western-styled educational systems (Gellner 1981). As national ideological systems became more and more oriented towards secularism, Islam appeared to be increasingly confined to the area of personal belief and practice.

Many of these nationalist movements assumed a distinctively socialist program. In Egypt, Iraq, and Syria, the old liberal regimes were overthrown, and nationalist and socialist programs were developed under Nasserism in Egypt, and under the Baath Party in Syria and Iraq. For these regimes modernization was to be brought about by Arab socialism under the charismatic influence of Gamal Abdel Nasser (Berque 1972). Under the Baath Party, religion was often mobilized to create a populist set of slogans for social change; but there was little in the nationalist ideology to promote Islam as a global strategy.

Alongside these nationalist/secularist political movements, we can also detect important fundamentalist Islamic reactions to secularization and westernization, especially in the emergence of the Muslim Brotherhood, founded in 1928 by Hasan al-Bamma (1906–1949) (Mitchell 1969). The Muslim Brotherhood sought the unity of the Muslim community, denounced foreign intervention in Egypt, and opposed the establishment of Israel. The relationship between the Brotherhood and the Egyptian nationalist movement has always been characterized by tension and conflict, resulting eventually in the assassination of Anwar Sadat, and in recent years the Muslim Brotherhood has increased its political representation within the Egyptian political system. Despite these examples of Islamic resurgence, the 1960s were largely dominated by more secular nationalist movements in the Middle East and South East Asia.

The emergence of fundamentalism and militant Islam is a striking feature of the 1970s and 1980s with the Iranian revolution under the influence of Ayatollah Khomeini, the political emergence of the late Zia ul-Haq in Pakistan, the Muslim resistance movement in Afghanistan, the growing importance of Shi'ism in the Middle East and the development of an Islamic resurgence in Malaysia (Nagata 1984).

Islamic fundamentalism, while different in its national and local manifestation, shares a common rejection of the modernist secular period on a variety of grounds. These include the perception that modernization has failed because its secular character could not offer coherent values. In addition, modernization failed because too rapid urbanization and inadequate agricultural policies produce gross inequalities of wealth and power, leaving the peasantry often in a precarious economic situation.

In addition, there is the notion that liberalism has failed because the polities of the nationalist, Arabic, state systems did not allow genuine political expression and democracy. For example, it is suggested that Egypt, despite radical political changes, remained dominated by traditional elites who manipulated the electoral system to maintain continuing political power under the slogan of political participation.

While the western secular program was seen to be in ruins, traditional Marxism also had little to offer in the way of either ideology or successful economic programs. Marxism remained the ideology of an elite and failed to appeal to the masses through a popular discourse which mobilized traditional Islamic themes. It was also too closely associated with the USSR, atheism, and foreign domination. Fundamentalist ideology also regards the Islamic absolutism of the Saudi regime as incompatible with the genuine message of pure Islam since the Saudi government has been corrupted by western consumerism and adherence to the foreign policy objectives of western societies (Hanafi 1979). The great appeal of ideological and intellectual leaders like Ali Shariati was that he combined traditional Islamic themes with modern political and cultural critiques derived from Marxism and French philosophy (Shariati 1979). Shariati was able to translate the implicit political philosophy of classical Islam into a modern idiom.

At the ideological level, Islam has been able to fill the gap (or at least the experience of a gap) between the promises of westernization and/or Marxism and the actual reality of social change at the everyday level. Islam has an egalitarian appeal, an ascetic world-view, a dynamic conception of social change and through its history provides an alternative therefore to the western model which was imposed by colonization. Islam through its prayer meetings and other religious institutions provided an alternative political and social platform to state institutions, and therefore in Iran and elsewhere religion provided a vehicle for the expression of oppositional and critical viewpoints which governments could not silence, because religion had deep popular roots in the broader community.

Thus, although there are major differences in the various movements of religious revitalization in contemporary Islam, "they all share the experience of recent, rapid and sometimes uncontrolled urbanization and industrialization, pervasive western influence, and the spread of literacy with the burgeoning of a critical, educated class without precedent in traditional society" (Nagata 1984: 236). Under the influence of writers like Shariati, Islam was transformed into a modern doctrine of radicalism and opposition to westernization, promoting Islamic ideals of equality and change against western liberal democratic views of political and cultural participation.

Islamization under the fundamentalist umbrella therefore involves a redefinition and re-allocation of institutions and values within an Islamic state. In particular, it involves a re-organization of educational institutions to ensure that Islamic values, beliefs, and practices are inculcated in children and young adults. This involves changes to both secondary and tertiary education systems, pulling the universities away from their western orientation. In terms of economic systems, Islamization requires a greater emphasis on the traditional Islamic objectives of an equal re-distribution of income and wealth and the creation of certain welfare institutions for orphans, the needy, and the poor. In terms of legal systems, it demands the reinstitution of the Shariah as the only source of legal thinking, thereby deprivatizing Islamic regulations and excluding secular western forms of legal organization. This would also involve of course the cooptation of the Ulama and the promotion of religious scholars into the system. From our perspective, probably a more interesting development is the reintroduction of Islam into the mass media and the regulation of broadcasting and advertising by Islamic institutions and norms. In this area Islamization is distinctively anti-consumerist and therefore anti-postmodernist. The growth of a global system of communication has made possible for the majority of Muslims the ritual necessity of pilgrimage to Mecca, thereby reinforcing the concept of Islam as a global system. At the same time, precisely these institutions of global communication spread the message of consumerism and therefore Islamic leaders have been more or less compelled to utilize a global communication system to spread the message of pan-Islamic unity:

> Ironically, the technological tools of modernization have often served to reinforce traditional belief and practice as religious leaders who initially opposed modernization now use radio, T.V., and print to preach and disseminate, to educate and proselytize. The message of Islam is not simply available from a preacher at a local Mosque. Sermons and religious education from leading preachers and writers can be transmitted to every city and village (Esposito 1984: 212).

Islam is now able to self-thematize Islamic religion as a self-reflective global system of cultural identity over and against the diversity and pluralism involved in the new consumer culture (Luhmann 1984).

Islam and Consumerism

While sociologists of religion have regularly commented on the problem of meaning and meaningfulness in contemporary society, seeing the crisis of meaning as a direct consequence of the secularization of religious values, it is more appropriate to start at the level of the pluralization of life-worlds with the proliferation of consumer life-styles as the basis for the fragmentation of religious belief and values. Consumerism offers or promises a range of possible life-styles which compete with, and in many respects, contradict the uniform life-style demanded by Islamic fundamentalism. We can see the emergence of consumerism as a consequence of the evolution of capitalism as a world cultural and economic system. Within this perspective early capitalism involved the rationalization of production systems and the discipline of labor through the imposition of religious asceticism or alternatively the imposition of Taylorism. In the twentieth century a further development of capitalist culture and organization has emerged, namely the rationalization of distribution and consumption. The development of a global distribution system was based upon certain technical developments (such as efficient refrigeration) and as a consequence of the development of global systems of transport and communication, creating a mass market for travel and tourism. In the mid-century, capitalism was further developed with the rationalization of consumerism and consumption through the development of debt financing, credit systems and the improvement of mass banking, hire purchase, and other arrangements for extended consumerism. The life-style of the middle classes with its emphasis on leisure, gratification, and hedonism has now become a global normative standard, shaping the aspirations and life-styles of subordinate classes who, while they may not directly consume, consume at the level of fantasy.

In sum, the development of a global mass culture has now begun to shape and condition the life-styles of the Third World, developing societies and state socialist societies.

These developments in terms of mass culture have also made a major impact on the world of Islam, representing for Islamic religious leaders a new form of subterranean colonial penetration, a form of internal cultural invasion. Many of these cultural changes in everyday life, which are the unanticipated consequences of mass media usage, were anticipated in Lerner's *The Passing of Traditional Society* (1958).

The development of global mass consumerism can be seen as a further extension of westernization and symbolic penetration, providing a problematic mixture of localist cultures and mass universalism (Stauth and Zubaida 1987). In the case of Sadat's Open Door Policy in Egypt, critics of Sadat's regime argued that this economic policy involved not only complete capitulation to western economics but also involved the further undermining of Egyptian values or more precisely Islamic values by the spread of consumerism and western life-styles. The critical evaluation of this situation suggested that at the level of peasant life, American consumerism stood for a further erosion of traditional values.

> As the peasant sits in the evening with his family to watch the TV that his son has purchased from the fruits of his labor in Saudi Arabia the intrigues of J.R. Ewing and Sue Ellen in Dallas strip him of what is left of his legitimacy as a culture bearer in his own culture. Between programs, he is told in English that he should be drinking Schwepps or in dubbed Arabic that he should use deodorant, and that all his problems are caused by having too many children—a total package of imported ideas (Guindi 1982: 21).

Of course, the symbolic meaning and functions of consumer items are complex and unstable. For example, during the Iranian revolution against the shah the wearing of the veil by women signified opposition to the regime, adherence to Islam, and political commitment to Shi'ism. The veil however also had a practical function since it was difficult to identify women individually on the part of the secret service while they were veiled. In the aftermath of the revolution, on a global scale the veil has come to signify a general commitment to Islamic fundamentalism. However, in Egypt poor and economically deprived university students often found veiling to be the most practical solution for avoiding sexual harassment, since the veil signifies purity, but also these students are unable to buy the very expensive western clothes which the upper classes of the Egyptian society buy to demonstrate their own personal distinction. In recent years there has also developed a more fashionable upper middle class form of veil and associated dress which has become fashionable in some areas of Cairo. Again on a global perspective it is possible to refer to these strata as 'an Islamic bourgeoisie' (Abaza 1987). Even within Islamic fundamentalism, the multiplicity of the meanings of symbolic cultures can never be entirely contained.

Conclusion

Following Jameson (1984), we can associate the emergence of a postmodernist culture with the development of consumerism and postindustrialism. While Islam responded to modernization through the development of an ascetic ethic of hard work and discipline, contemporary Islam has responded to postmodernism through a fundamentalist politics of global community and through an anti-consumerist ethic of moral purity based upon classical Islamic dogma.

These processes involve an apparent paradox: the emergence of a global system of communication made a global Islam possible, while also exposing the everyday world of Islam to the complication of pluralistic consumption and the pluralization of life-worlds. While the Abrahamic faiths successfully survived modernization, there are profound problems for religious absolutism in the era of postmodernism. In epistemological terms postmodernism threatens to deconstruct all theological accounts of reality into mere fairy tales or mythical grand narratives which disguise the metaphoricality of their commentaries by claims to (a false) authorship. These threats of deconstruction emerge out of the pluralization of life-styles and life-worlds making perspectivism into a concrete institutionalized reality.

There are various solutions to postmodernism. In terms of the Weberian model (Figure 9–1) one solution to postmodernism is a nostalgic quest for holism through fundamentalist traditionalism, whereby the village is opposed to the global market place. Another solution is nationalism which involves an associational but closed relationship in which the nation-state is opposed to the egalitarian abstraction of globalist citizenship (Figure 9–2). Within this model, ecumenicalism is a market place of beliefs which is more compatible with globalism but which still attempts to retain some credibility in terms of truth by acknowledging that there may be variations on truth in the theological market place.

FIGURE 9-2
Religio-social Movements

<u>Open</u>	<u>Closed</u>	
Islamization	Traditionalism	**<u>Communal</u>**
Ecumenicalism	Nationalism	**<u>Associational</u>**
Individualism		

Islamization is an attempt to create at the global level a new *Gemeinschaft*, a new version of the traditional household which would close off the threat of postmodernism by re-establishing a communal ideology. Islamization is a political movement to combat westernization using the methods of Western culture, namely a form of Protestantism within Islam itself. Islamization equals political radicalism plus cultural antimodernism. Within this perspective, Islamic fundamentalism is a defense of modernization against postmodernism. The outlook for global ecumenicalism does not appear to be a realistic option since, for example, the Abrahamic faiths in their fundamentalist mood claim an absolute truth. The problem is that the Islamic household must view alternative households as threatening and dangerous. Islam constantly finds itself forced up against "lands of war" and it is difficult to imagine how one can have several universalistic, global, evangelical, religions within the same world political space. How can one have mutually exclusive households within the world cultural system?

There are in a sense two problems for Islam. First, there are the problems of external relations with other faiths and traditions where the traditional millet system will no longer work. Second, there are internal relations with "deviations" such as the Copts in Egypt, or the Bahai faith in Iran, or there are the complications of the Islamization of women and the conflicting interpretations, for example, of egalitarian relations between men and women.

While in this paper I have specifically been concerned with the conditions that have promoted fundamentalism in contemporary Islam, it is clear that similar pressures operating on other world religions have produced political movements to redefine secular national boundaries in religions and traditional terms. For example, in Israel the Haredin have called for the reactivation of a pre-1948 law governing changes in religious status which would enable the Rabbinate to determine the precise religious status of converts to Judaism emigrating to Israel. One consequence of such a change of political involvement of the Rabbinate would be to block off the migration of reform or conservative Jews from North America and Europe attempting to enter Israel as Israeli citizens (Friedman 1987).

In Islam, the Muslim Brotherhood aims to establish not simply an Islamic order, but an Islamic state (by force where necessary) as a political program against, not only secularism and nationalism on the part of Arabic governments, but against western intrusion and against the state of Israel. In terms of the Brothers' political philosophy, only a war against such alien forces will bring about the re-unification of the spiritual and political world within Islamic culture. Because the Abrahamic faiths share the same spiritual space, the development of global fundamentalism promises to make the Middle East increasingly unstable in political and economic terms, but on a wider global plane it is difficult to see how fundamentalist religious movements could tolerate an ecumenicalism of ideas.

References

Abazam, M. 1987. *The Changing Image of Women in Rural Egypt: Cairo Papers in Social Science*. vol. 10, Monograph 3. The American University in Cairo Press.
Abercrombie, N., S. Hill, and B.S. Turner. 1984. *Sovereign Individuals of Capitalism*. London: Allen and Unwin.
Adorno, T.W. and M. Horkheimer. 1944. *Dialectic of the Enlightenment*. New York: Social Studies Associations.
Berque, J. 1972. *Egypt, Imperialism and Revolution*. London: Faber and Faber.
Brubaker, R. 1984. *The Limits of Rationality: An Essay on the Social and Moral Thought of Max Weber*. London: Allen and Unwin.
Dumont, L. 1983. *Essais Sur l'Individualisme*. Paris: Seoul.
_____. 1986. "Collective Identities and Universalistic Ideology, the Actual Interplay." *Theory, Culture and Society* 3:25-34.
El Guindi, F. 1982. "The Killing of Sadat and After: A Current Assessment of Egypt's Islamic Movement." *Middle East Insight* 2.
Enayat, H. 1982. *Modern Islamic Political Thought*. London: Macmillan.
Esposito, J.L. 1984. *Islam and Politics*. New York: Oxford University Press.
Friedman, T.L. 1987. "How Secular Israel? Orthodox Right Poses Challenge." *International Herald Tribune* July 1.
Geertz, C. 1968. *Islam Observed: Religious Development in Morocco and Indonesia*. New Haven: Yale University Press.
Gellner, E. 1969. *Saints of the Atlas*. London: Weidenfeld and Nicolson.
_____. 1981. *Muslim Society*. Cambridge: Cambridge University Press.
Hennis, W. 1987. *Max Weber: Essays in Reconstruction*. London: Allen and Unwin.
Hourani, A. 1962. *Arabic Thought in the Liberal Age*. Oxford: Oxford University Press.
Jameson, F. 1984. "Post-Modernism or the Cultural Logic of Late Capitalism." *New Left Review* 146-93.
Keddie, N. and L. Beck (eds.). 1978. *Women in the Muslim World*. Cambridge: Harvard University Press.
Kronman, A. 1983. *Max Weber*. London: Arnold.
Lechner, F.J. 1985a. "Fundamentalism and Socio-cultural Revitalization in America: A Sociological Interpretation." *Sociological Analysis* 46:243-60.
_____. 1985b. "Modernity and Its Discontents." 157-78 in *Neofunctionalism*, edited by J. C. Alexander. Beverly Hills: Sage.
Lerner, D. 1958. *The Passing of Traditional Society*. Glencoe, Illinois: The Free Press.
Luhmann, N. 1984. "The Self Description of Society: Crisis, Fashion and Sociological Theory." *International Journal of Comparative Sociology* 25:59-72.
Mann, M. 1986. *The Sources of Social Power, Volume 1: A History of Power from the Beginning to AD 1760*. Cambridge: Cambridge University Press.
Mitchell, R. 1969. *The Society of Muslim Brothers*. New York: Oxford University Press.
Nagata, J. 1984. *The Re-Flowering of Malaysian Islam: Modern Religious Radicals and Their Roots*. Vancouver: University of British Columbia Press.
Parsons, T. 1963. "Christianity and Modern Industrial Society." 33-70 in *Sociological Theory, Values and Socio-Cultural Change: Essays in Honor of Pitirim Sorokin*, edited by E.A. Tiryakian. New York: Free Press.
Prager, J. 1985. "Totalitarian and Liberal Democracy: Two Types of Modern Political

Order." 179–210 in *Neofunctionalism*, edited by J.C. Alexander. Beverly Hills: Sage.

Robertson, R. and J. Chirico. 1985. "Humanity, Globalization and Worldwide Religious Resurgence: A Theoretical Exploration." *Sociological Analysis* 46:219–42.

Roth, G. and W. Schluchter. 1979. *Max Weber's Vision of History: Ethics and Methods.* Berkeley: University of California Press.

Shaw, S.J. and E.K. Shaw. 1977. *History of the Ottoman Empire and Modern Turkey.* Cambridge: Cambridge University Press.

Shoshan, B., 1986. "The Politics of Notables in Medieval Islam." *Asian and African Studies* 20:179–215.

Shariati, A. 1979. *On the Sociology of Islam.* Berkeley: Mizan Press.

Simmel, G. 1978. *The Philosophy of Money.* London: Routledge and Kegan Paul.

Smith, D.E. (ed.). 1974. *Religion and Political Modernization.* New Haven: Yale University Press.

Stauth, G. and B.S. Turner. 1986. "Nietzsche in Weber oder die Geburt des Modernen Genius in Professionellen Menschen." *Zeitschrift für Soziologie* 15:81–94.

_____. 1988. *Nietzsche's Dance: Resentment, Reciprocity and Resistance in Social Life.* Oxford: Basil Blackwell.

Stauth, G. and S. Zubaida (eds.). 1987. *Mass Culture, Popular Culture and Social Life in the Middle East.* Frankfurt: Campus Verlag.

Toennies, F. 1957. *Community and Association.* East Lansing, Michigan: Michigan State University Press.

Tucker, J.E. 1985. *Women in Nineteenth Century Egypt.* Cambridge: Cambridge University Press.

Turner, B.S. 1974. *Weber and Islam: A Critical Study.* London: Routledge and Kegan Paul.

_____. 1978. *Marx and the End of Orientalism.* London: Allen and Unwin.

_____. 1981. *Citizenship and Capitalism.* London: Allen and Unwin.

_____. 1988a. *Status.* Milton Keynes: Open University Press.

_____. 1988b. "Classical Sociology and Its Legacy." *The Sociological Review* 36:146–57.

Wallerstein, I. 1974. *The Modern World System 1.* New York: Academic Press.

_____. 1980. *The Modern World System 2.* New York: Academic Press.

Weber, M. 1958. *The City.* Glencoe: Free Press.

_____. 1968. *Economy and Society.* Berkeley: University of California Press.

Wolf, E. 1971. *Peasant Wars of the Twentieth Century.* London: Faber and Faber.

10

GLOBALIZATION VERSUS RELIGIOUS NATIVISM

JAPAN'S SOKA GAKKAI
IN THE WORLD ARENA

Anson Shupe

THE RECENT HISTORICAL-ECONOMIC PERSPECTIVE of world-systems theory maintains that earth's nation-states and societies are becoming integrated into a world-system of economic-political relations (e.g., Wallerstein 1974a; 1974b; 1983). More generally, the increasing importance of multinational corporations, an explosion of mass media technological capabilities, and a reliance on scarce natural resources have only accelerated a trend that was supposed to have begun with the "Great Transformation" of the Industrial Revolution in Europe. This trend can be thought of, according to one analysis, as a series of "processes by which the world becomes a single place, both with respect to recognition of a very high degree of interdependence between spheres and locales of social activity across the entire globe and to the growth of consciousness pertaining to the globe as such" (Robertson 1985:

348). Solidly grounded in a particular Marxist tradition, Wallerstein's analysis involves the view that secularization is a unilinear fact. That is, it takes for granted the demise of organized religion as a significant social force.

However, this aspect of the globalization argument is not without its critics. Robertson and Chirico (1985), for instance, see built-in limitations to this presumed non-recursive evolution that eventually set in motion dynamics to enable religion to reassert itself as an important social fact. In their view, "The globalization process itself raises religious and quasi-religious questions.... because it is increasingly concerned with matters traditionally associated with the religious domain" (239, 225). As Robertson (1985: 348) has noted in his explicitly anti-Marxist critiques, the expansion of nation-states' "spheres of operation under the guises of enhancing the quality of life" leads the polity to cross over institutional lines into religious or sacred realms. In short, governments become embodied in value conflicts that deal with what Talcott Parsons (1978: 352–443) termed *telic matters*, i.e., ultimate concerns of destiny and meaning that occur to all reflective human beings and which were originally the preserve of religions.

Thus, any secularizing effects that accompany globalization have a "ceiling." Ironically, say the theory's critics in the sociology of religion, secularization eventually turns in on itself and creates the very conditions for a resurgence of religious influence. By extension, globalization sets in motion the dynamic for a renewed religious search for ultimate meaning, values, and resacralization. At the same time, this "bringing religion back in" is not some simple linear about-face. Says Robertson (1987a: 31), "It is all too easy to fall into the temptation of arguing that the greatly increased visibility of religion across the contemporary world signals or manifests a definite reversal of processes of secularization." That assumption would be, in other words, premature.

Nevertheless, an appreciation of religion's role, especially change-oriented or prophetic religion, on the world level is now beginning after some years of neglect (e.g., Hadden and Shupe 1986), though it is not without the expected comparative and cross-cultural difficulties in conceptualization. Of particular interest for globalization theory, therefore, should be religious movements which have world-transforming or globalizing agenda. Such a phenomenon is Japan's Soka Gakkai, a lay Buddhist organization that, along with the Church of Jesus Christ of Latter-day Saints (the Mormons), ranks as one of the world's fastest-growing movements.

Japan, as Robertson (1987b) has recently suggested, constitutes an interesting laboratory for reviewing the logic of globalization. The most "westernized" and highly industrialized nation in Asia, Japan is also currently a center of religious movement activity with global pretensions and has been since the end of World War II.

Criticizing Wallersteinian world-system theory as economically deterministic, Robertson suggests that the religious factor can play a critical role in the process of globalization—or internationalization (since social science terminology is not yet consensual on this phenomenon)—and that Japan offers a number of valuable historical examples. The country's syncretistic religious infrastructure has dealt repeatedly with an "invasion" of new religions and cultural values and yet managed to successfully reconcile these.

In this essay I examine Soka Gakkai for what this Japanese movement may tell us about a religious movement with explicit global intentions and world-transforming goals. Is Soka Gakkai a bona fide candidate for a global transformative religion, or is it mere nativism and nationalism in the latter's guise? What are its potentials? What are its obstacles?

Before moving directly to that analysis, however, I first present a cursory summary of Soka Gakkai's origins in the Nichiren Shoshu variety of Mahayana Buddhism, its doctrines and goals, and its controversial history. These are all aspects affecting its globalization posture and possibilities.

Origins of Soka Gakkai

Soka Gakkai is a lay Buddhist movement, officially established in 1951 and closely affiliated with the Nichiren Shoshu sect of Mahayana Buddhism.[1] Nichiren Shoshu was founded in thirteenth-century Japan by Nichiren (1222–1282 A.D.), a charismatic mixture of patriot, saint, and prophet. Ultra-nationalistic, Nichiren became convinced after studying various forms of traditional Buddhism, that the Lotus Sutra contained the most advanced and quintessential form of the original Gautama Buddha's message. In fact, Nichiren taught that all other Buddhist schools[2] and persuasions and even other sutras were either perversions of the ultimate truth or inconsequential. He preached that merely invoking (by changing) the name of the Lotus Sutra (*Namu Myoho Renge Kyo*—"Hail to the Wonderful Truth of the Lotus Sutra") could attain salvation for the believer in the next existence and bestow temporal benefits, such as good health and material success in this life.

In this realization, Nichiren Shoshu doctrine maintains, *Nichiren Daishonin* ("the Great Holy Sage") surpassed the accomplishments of even the original Indian Buddha. "He did more than merely inherit," claims one article in an issue of *The Soka Gakkai News*:

> He revealed the ultimate Buddhist teaching, to which his two predecessors Sakyamuni, or Gautama, and the Tendai sect in which Nichiren studied had aspired yet never realized in practice. Nichiren Daishonin took as his starting point the secret, ultimate wisdom that all outstanding Buddhists since the time of Sakyamuni had acquired as part of final enlightenment, yet never had been able to expound because the time was not ripe. (*SGN* 1978)

Thus, Nichiren himself became a Buddha. Such a trend in Japanese history, that is, to turn sectarian Buddhist sect founders into divine beings or demigods on a level equal or superior to the original Buddha and create a "founder cult," has been noted by Hoshino (1987).

Nichiren also infused his interpretation of Buddhism with millennial and elitist elements. Nichiren believed that he lived in the age of *mappo*, an analog to the "last days" in which many fundamentalist and dispensationalist Christians believe themselves to exist. The doctrine of *mappo* dictated that the world would be thrust into an apocalyptic situation, the literal "End of the Dharma." This *mappo* expectation was based on the belief that times were getting worse and true faith was about to vanish from the earth until the coming of the future (Maitreya) Buddha (Ellwood 1978: 84). The world had become so hopelessly corrupt, Nichiren believed, that the path to Nirvana as originally taught by the historical Siddhartha Gautama in sixth century B.C. India was no longer possible for most persons. Thus the altruistic assistance of Bodhisattvas (advanced beings, once humans, who have sought enlightenment not only for themselves but for others) or some other superhuman agency would be necessary. This rescue Nichiren claimed to have discovered in the Lotus Sutra.

The elitism of Nichiren Shoshu derives from Nichiren's angry declarations that other Buddhist sects and denomination were plain wrong, misguided, or unnecessary in the age of *mappo*. Not all of Nichiren offshoots adopted this uncompromising sense of being the "elect." Before World War II there were only nine separate versions of Nichiren Buddhism (due to government restrictions placed on all non-Shinto religions). However, since the late 1960s, there have appeared over forty. Yet among them Nichiren Shoshu (*shu* means "sect," *sho* means "True") remains the most strident in its exclusivist claims. Nor do the other interpretations of Nichiren Buddhism regard Nichiren the man as the Buddha for the last days of *mappo* or as a Christ-like messianic figure, as does Nichiren Shosu.

Soka Gakkai (Society for the Creation of Value) is a lay Buddhist organization affiliated with Nichiren Shoshu. It began in 1937 as the more secular Soka Kyoiku Gakkai (Society for Education in the Creation of

Values). Its founder was a Tokyo elementary school principal named Tsunesaburo Makiguchi. Basically an intellectual with existential philosophical inclinations, Makiguchi later joined his interests with those of another public school teacher named Toda Josei. Josei was the organizer-manager whereas Makiguchi was the intellectual. While the Soka Kyoiku Gakkai was still young and doctrinally formative, it affiliated with the Nichiren Shoshu sect. Subsequently both Makiguchi and Toda were imprisoned (in 1942) for refusing, under government decree, to consolidate with other Nichiren groups and participate in state Shinto worship.

Makiguchi died a martyr in prison. After his own release during the Allied Occupation in 1945, Toda took charge of the fledgling movement. He shortened the official organizational name to Soka Gakkai and infused a less educational, more evangelistic Buddhist spirit into the group, transforming it into more of a proselytizing/mobilizing arm of Nichiren Shoshu.

Indeed, the militant proselytizing of Soka Gakkai—the legacy of firebrand Nichiren Daishonin—is for many Japanese the group's most pronounced (and offensive) characteristic. It is also a major reason underlying the movement's phenomenal growth, making Soka Gakkai (and indirectly its affiliate Nichiren sect) the fastest growing religious movement in Japan and probably the Far East. Many Japanese postwar new religions (*shinko shukyo*) commonly exaggerate their membership statistics for public relations purposes, and Soka Gakkai is no exception. For example, Soka Gakkai counts families, not individuals, as its member units, and a family is entered on the rolls even if only one of its members joins. Nevertheless, Ellwood (1974: 91) estimates that approximately 7,500,000 families belonged to Soka Gakkai in 1974, a figure consistent with Brett (1979: 366) citing a possible range of ten to fifteen million individual members. Over twenty years ago Soka Gakkai's president boasted that the group was making converts at the rate of twenty thousand per month, a figure that was undoubtedly hyperbole but which did convey an accurate sense of the real dynamic of growth experienced by the group.

This dynamic growth is something of an anomaly on the Japanese religious scene, not only because of vast popular indifference to religion on a daily level but also because of Soka Gakkai's marked religious enthusiasm. Furthermore, the traditional coexistence of various strains of Buddhism with the indigenous folk religion of Shinto has bred into Japanese religious culture a low-key tolerance for most religions that is the opposite of Soka Gakkai's exclusivism.

Soka Gakkai was in part responsible for many of its early public relations problems. Contrary to the religious apathy of most Japanese who generally dislike *rikutsu* (arguing) over spiritual matters, Soka Gakkai encouraged aggressive proselytization and confrontation. During the early postwar era Soka Gakkai developed a negative image on account of its members' belligerence and occasional uncouth activities. Members were often encouraged to destroy the *kamidana* (miniature household Shinto shrines) and the ancestral tablets of *butsudan* (Buddhist) altars in their families' homes (which appalled those who still felt Confucianist obligations to honor ancestors). Some zealous followers made obscene gestures, spitting and cursing as they passed Shinto shrines and Buddhist temples of other denominations. The most controversial Soka Gakkai practice was *shakubuku* (literally, "to subdue and conquer"), a technique which sometimes came down to the use of high-pressure, coercion, and brow-beating in converting and holding members.

Many of these practices have been discouraged by publicity-conscious Soka Gakkai leaders, thus helping to improve the group's reputation. At the same time the grassroots nature of Soka Gakkai, with its diverse opportunities for popular participation that are otherwise fewer in older religious groups, may be one significant factor in its growth. Given a lay movement's lack of tradition-bound proscriptions, it can innovate, particularly in the use of modern, rational, cost-effective methods for building and maintaining membership. Thus, Wilson (1985: 15–16) concludes, "the contemporary [lay] religious movement is equipped to play a more dynamic role in society than were the religious systems of the past."

Soka Gakkai: Religious Globalization or Nationalistic Revitalization Movement?

I regard major world religions, and would-be world religions, as religious globalization schemes that possess universal goals and inclusive hopes. However, the rhetoric of such groups cannot suffice as the sole criterion for judging them truly global or potentially global, for even groups as monastic, small, and generally unappealing as the International Society for Krishna Consciousness (the Hare Krishnas) "make noise" in the direction of becoming world scale. It is more than likely that many groups in various cultures use the vocabulary of religious globalization while actually serving to satisfy *revitalization* goals of valued but endangered traditions (Wallace 1966). In the case of Soka Gakkai the evidence is mixed.

The Case for Soka Gakkai as Revitalization Movement. Soka Gakkai can be located overlapping with the postwar neo-nationalist social movement industry loosely termed the *Minzokuha*, or National Soul School, that exalts a purported racial and spiritual folk unity reminiscent of German mysticism (Buruma 1987). That judgment is probably too severe, however, for Soka Gakkai is not as stridently jingoistic as many recent ultra-nationalist groups in Japan. Nevertheless, Brannen (1968: 51) considers Soka Gakkai's (and Nichiren Shoshu's) concerted focus on the founders' patriotism and the movement's national identity as critical elements. He argues that because of Buddhism's traditional relationship to political culture in Japanese history, "a revival in Buddhism in Japan is tantamount to a recovery of the national identity."

In this view Soka Gakkai can be understood as an attempt to rekindle nationalistic sentiments and erect a new moral orthodoxy to replace the Imperial state-Shinto civil religion largely eroded by the Allied Occupation after 1945 and pushed further out of national consciousness by the erosive forces of western industrialization, consumerism, and mass urbanization. Soka Gakkai venerates a particularly Japanese set of sacred persons and symbols (e.g., the Saint/Buddha Nichiren and a succession of Nichiren Shoshu high priests, the *Daimoku* chant of *Namu Myoho Renge Kyo*, Nichiren's sacred mandala called the *Gohonzon*), and so Soka Gakkai sacralizes Japanese history in a way intended to be meaningful to modern Japanese by placing them at the center of world morality and international events. The nation's post-1945 economic recovery has allowed its citizens to reclaim their sense of global importance as industrial and scientific leaders.

But this recovery has otherwise not been accompanied by an integrating moral sense of destiny. Soka Gakkai would remedy that situation, much as pre-Meiji Restoration nationalists such as Motoori Norinaga and Sato Nobuhiro envisioned Japan as the crucible within which a new international order in the nineteenth century would be created (Tsunoda, De Bary, and Keene 1958: 15–16, 70–71). In the past the linking of such visions to revolutionary fervor proved a potent dynamic in Japan's domestic and international affairs.

Says recent Soka Gakkai president Daisaku Ikeda (*SGN* 1987: 16), "The road that Japan must choose is the way of the bridge-builder, refusing to remain enclosed within a single nation or military bloc and always seeking to make connections with a global order." Despite Ikeda's reference to a global order, however, he places Japan at the heart of its dynamic much as the pre-Copernican model of the solar system located the earth at the center.

Both Norinaga and Nobuhira wrote at a critical time in Japan's pre-modern history when the Tokugawa dynasty's power was being questioned and Japan's internal strains were reconceptualized and ideologized as having global significance. This Nipponcentric view of Japan's destiny has ever since been noticed by outside scholars. For example, based on her research during World War II, anthropologist Ruth Benedict (1967: 21) remarked that, according to the Japanese view of international events,

> There was anarchy in the world as long as every nation had absolute sovereignty; it was necessary for her to fight to establish a hierarchy under Japan, of course, since she alone represented a nation truly hierarchical from top to bottom and hence understood the necessity of taking one's proper place.

Such a glorification of Japan's mission to the world, following this logic, often appeals to the dislocated citizens of that nation's industrial urban economy who suffer anomie (Rajana 1975). It frequently draws low-status, mobile persons least integrated into networks of stable interpersonal relations and provides them a dense network of primary group support, characteristics which have been found disproportionately among Soka Gakkai converts (Dator 1969: 59–105).

This ethnocentrism and class bias in membership has been observed in at least one other controversial Japanese new religion (Davis 1980). Davis (1980; 1977) views movements such as Soka Gakkai as providing adherents with a return to the traditional particularistic values of rural Japan that industrialization and urbanization have shattered. Like eighteenth-century feudal villagers who possessed their own local deities (*ujigami*) and who believed themselves to be the deities' "children" (*ujiko*), adherents of new religions like Soka Gakkai consider themselves part of the same type of insular sub-societies that clearly distinguish members from nonmembers yet (with a modern universalistic twist) provide a much easier way for outsiders to join.

Soka Gakkai also promises those who convert, sign up, and remain loyal a rewarding future. As one leader told members of the Nichiren Shoshu of America (the United States' Soka Gakkai wing): "You should feel lucky to be in NSA. It is those who feel such fortune and who work for world peace who will get the greatest benefit now and in the days to come" (quoted in Snow 1987: 168). One Soka Gakkai director spoke to a receptive crowd in the late 1960s in patently civil religious terms:

> Twenty years from now we will occupy the majority of the seats in the National Diet and establish the Nichiren Shoshu Denomination as the national religion of Japan and construct a national altar at Mt. Fuji. (Quoted in Brannen 1968: 127)

Finally, in support of a revitalization movement view, the Soka Gakkai-inspired political party *Komeito* (Clean Government Party) has emerged as Japan's third largest party and an important power broker. In 1989 it held more than twice as many seats in both the House of Representatives and the House of Councillors as the fourth-place Democratic Socialist Party. But Komeito has lived up to none of its original, radical, alternative world-transforming intentions. It has compromised, traded votes, and even planned coalignments with its stated "global" opponents, the Japan Communist Party (Shupe, 45–6). What this suggests is that the Komeito has surrendered the reality of its claims to be a genuine alternative to the partisan denizens of the murky world of Japanese political coalitions in exchange for political acceptance and respectability. In the process it has made itself a valuable bargaining ally to the status quo party, the Liberal-Democrats.

Thus, a revitalization movement view argues that global rhetoric and the majesty of world-transforming goals have been a smokescreen for the Soka Gakkai to link national spiritual revival with the realities of urban economic life. Traditional symbols and themes have been manipulated and infused with new life through an apparently international movement, but the real focus is still at the national level.

The Case for Soka Gakkai as a Genuine Globalization Movement. An alternative view of Soka Gakkai accepts at face value its global aspiration to become the world religion that will usher in a war-free millennium. There is considerable rhetoric available in Soka Gakkai speeches and publications to support this hypothesis. I use the word "millennium" deliberately since much of Soka Gakkai doctrine, infused with Nichiren Shoshu's elaboration on the mappo theme and the need for a *maitreya* (savior) Buddha to come during the "last days" of cultural decadence, resembles Christian millenarian expectations of tribulation and salvation.

On an immediate level, Soka Gakkai uses a "dispensationalist" style model to generate long-range programs of successive approximation. For instance, in 1979 the movement consummated the "Seven Bells" program (with one "bell" equivalent to seven years). This project involved internal organizational consolidation and international outreach. Events of the seventh "bell" included the voluntary retirement of the third Soka Gakkai president Daisaku Ikeda (now lifetime honorary president) and a new Articles of Association document as well as other administrative changes. The first "bell" was conceptualized as beginning when Soka Gakkai's forerunner, Soka Kyoiku Gakkai, was founded in the 1930s. The seventh "bell" was completed with the erection of Nichiren Shoshu's Sho-Hondo temple and "the building of an unshakable foundation for Soka Gakkai to continue on toward the twenty-first century and for ages to come" (*SGN* 1979). A second ambitious "Seven Bells" program of world evangelism within the context of a *"mappo perspective"* is planned to begin in the year 2001 (*SGN* 1979).

Soka Gakkai's level of discourse is decidedly global. This has been noted by virtually all social science observers, both foreign and Japanese. The bold, global goals of Soka Gakkai as a "world-transforming movement" (Bromley and Shupe 1979) are succinctly phrased in the following poem:

SONG OF A NEW AGE

Where plays the dolphin wild and free,
Resounds our leader's command.
Over the force of the seven seas,
Forth to every land.
Know our firm and steadfast faith
Makes the whole world one.
March along—Now's the time!
We have but begun.

(Quoted in Norbeck 1970: 177)

The Soka Gakkai solution to obstacles of constructing a bona fide community of nations, united ideologically by a concern for peace and mutual tolerance, is the monolithic acceptance and promulgation of Nichiren Shoshu Buddhism through world evangelism, or *kosen-rufu*. Honorary Soka Gakkai president Daisaku Ikeda (1972: 11,16,20–21, 25) once proclaimed in a speech,

> We must bear in mind the fact that our movement is a still unrealized religious revolution of a kind the world has never seen before. ...the Buddhism of Nichiren Daishonin is a Buddhism for the whole world. And we must adopt a global view and recognize our membership in the family of man as we strive to become open-hearted, international people contributing to the happiness of mankind and to the creation of a worldwide human republic in the richest sense.

Soka Gakkai leaders envision this effort as a partly spiritual revival within Japan (hence its understandable appearance to outsiders as a mere revitalization movement) and thereafter as a global outreach. Said Ikeda (1973: 10) in a speech, "we have labored without rest in an urgent program to build the platform and framework for the worldwide propagation of our faith." Ikeda, who has shepherded Soka Gakkai through much of its important postwar growth years, sees the late twentieth and twenty-first centuries as especially propitious, "a phase in which faith in the True Buddhism can spread to truly worldwide limits, a time when a truly religious movement can take place" (Ikeda 1973: 14). Ikeda views religion as the only force, moral or otherwise, that has a realistic chance of uniting the world into a single non-violent community. And that religion can only come out of Japan through Soka Gakkai.

The vehicle for this evangelism is Soka Gakkai's antinuclear peace movement. It is a peace movement that mobilizes members, particularly in its Youth Division, for internal recommitment to its pacifistic goals as well as reaches out to the international community for affirmation of good will (see, e.g., *YDSG* 1978). Over the past decade Soka Gakkai has staged an annual World Peace Youth Festival in cities such as Hiroshima, Sapporo, and Nagoya where thousands, and sometimes tens of thousands, of Japanese and international members from dozens of nations (along with invited dignitaries) attend spectacular cavalcades of lights, dancing, gymnastics, and music. A special Soka Gakkai promotional page in a *Japan Times* (10/19/86) issue described the seventh such festival:

> It opened with the choral overtures entitled "Light Up, Earth!" and "Flag-bearers of Peace," followed by the entry of overseas representatives wearing national costume, and a parade of flags representing the 159 countries of the United Nations. One of the "high technology" features at the festival was a battery-operated instrument called WMCL (wise men's crystal light), a "bundle" of 100 acrylic fibers, each one meter long, emitting five different colors. A total of 450 performers with this instrument created waves of light on the big stage while dancing to "Light Up, Earth!"

Soka Gakkai heavily promotes a special antinuclear exhibit containing photographs and artifacts from Hiroshima and Nagasaki which it has opened in such places as Beijing, New Delhi, Canada, Geneva, and New York City. The Student Division, a Soka Gakkai training ground from which it recruits top-level leaders, has repeatedly raised millions of yen for famine relief and other worthy projects. In 1986, for example, it donated 100 million yen to the United Nations for African refugees, bringing Soka Gakkai total contributions to nearly 700 million yen (*SGN* September, 1986). Meanwhile, president Daisaku Ikeda has been a virtual one-man international lobby for peace. If the articles and photographs in *The Soka Gakkai Newsletter* over a ten-year period are to be believed (and I think they have validity), Soka Gakkai ambassador Ikeda has managed to press his peace message to an enormous number of world leaders on all continents. He has personally met with the presidents and diplomats of virtually all Asian, Eastern European, South and Central American, nations as well as various officials of the United Nations. He has held consultations with scholars such as Anatol Rapaport, Arnold Toynbee, Robert Bellah, Kenneth Boulding, Linus Pauling, John Kenneth Galbraith, Margaret Mead, Victor W. Turner, the Club of Rome's Aurelio Peccei, and Bryan Wilson. He has met with Los Angeles' Mayor Tom Bradley, New York's Mayor Ed Koch, and U.S. Senators Mike Mansfield (later an ambassador to Japan) and Edward Kennedy. Ikeda even addressed a U.N. General Assembly special session on nuclear disarmament in June, 1982 and called on the UN to designate 1991–2000 as "the U.N. Education Decade for World Citizens."

Ikeda's far-flung travels have earned him various awards, such as a Peace and Friendship Trophy from the Chinese People's Countries and the Chinese-Japanese Friendship Association as well as honorary citizenship in Dade County, Florida and Fort Worth, Texas. (Fort Worth was his 45th such title.)

Much of the real *kosen-rufu* effort is carried out through the movement's international wing, Soka Gakkai International. It currently claims members in over 115 nations, though affiliate organizations usually refer to the branches as Nichiren Shosu. In 1987, for example, Nichiren Shoshu of Zambia received government approval, the second affiliate on the African continent and the thirty-third worldwide. Spain, on the other hand, witnessed the development of the seventh affiliate (following France, Italy, Sweden, the United Kingdom, the Federal Republic of Germany, and the Netherlands). The UN is understandably a key institution to influence in SGI's view. After a lengthy application process, SGI officials negotiated for the international organization to receive the status of a "non-governmental organization [NGO] with consultative status within the United Nations Economic and Social Council (ECOSOC)" from the council's NGO committee.

Nichiren Shoshu of America claimed over 200,000 members during the mid-1970s (Snow 1987: 155) and takes every opportunity to showcase its celebrity members, such as contemporary jazz musician Herbie Hancock and rock singer Tina Turner. In 1985 the sixth Nichiren Shoshu temple was constructed in New York, others existing in Honolulu, Los Angeles, Washington DC, Chicago, and San Francisco. Whereas the SGI's growth was relatively slow as long as members were predominantly the Japanese brides of U.S. servicemen, during the past two decades expansion into the more general American population has occurred. Recently Soka Gakkai's flagship educational institution, Soka University, opened a branch campus in Los Angeles (SULA). Its initial purpose is to train students from Japan in the English language. Its missionizing potential is obvious.

In short, a second view of Soka Gakkai sees it as truly global in terms of energy and resources spent as well as in rhetoric. Similar to evangelist Sun Myung Moon, who places his nation of South Korea at the center of a dispensationalist, millennial theology, Soka Gakkai doctrine puts Japan in that unique geographical and theological role. But according to this second view, Soka Gakkai's real involvement has moved into the international arena—through effective proselytizing, building, and ceaseless diplomacy, and factors making the movement more than merely a revitalization phenomenon continue to be ascendent. The movement is in no danger of collapse and may well be on its way to becoming a contender for world-religion status along with the Church of Jesus Christ of Latter-day Saints, an American group which bears strong parallels. If nothing else, Soka Gakkai has weathered the crucial challenge to any new religion: survive the first generation's challenges and secure a foothold in at least one culture.

Soka Gakkai as a Type-between-types

I have juxtaposed two views of Soka Gakkai: first, as a revitalization movement, centered more around traditional or nativistic concerns than true global outreach; and second, as a bona fide world-transforming aspirant with better resources and prospects than most. I believe the truth lies somewhere in-between. Soka Gakkai originated first in an era of prewar ultra-nationalism, then experienced a spurt of national growth during the tumultuous postwar years when national identity struck an all-time low and revitalization of sacred symbols seemed imperative for many Japanese.

Yet it is today evolving past that crude revitalization phase into a true crusade of global design. Its antinuclear war efforts are not mere window-dressing, in my opinion. They simply occupy too much of the movement's time. This does not mean that Soka Gakkai has lost its revitalization themes and appeals or that the motives of many persons who convert or remain attached to the movement are oblivious to these. Rather, the movement has retained its revitalization appeals for Japanese but also used them as a spring board to move towards international relevance. The crucial role of Soka Gakkai's peace movement is to provide that relevance. Otherwise, a revitalization of sacred Japanese themes would have little appeal to more than a small minority of non-Japanese.

The ideological linchpin in this transition, therefore, is the postwar emphasis on a nuclear weapons-free global peace. This is the master issue which has become the primary channel through which the movement can reach out to people of all nations and gain credibility. To be sure, Ikeda and his colleagues did not invent the issue. Co-founder Josei Toda had written about the danger of atomic warfare before the modern generation of leaders.

But Japan's unique status as the only nation to suffer an atomic bomb attack has given any post-Hiroshima/Nagasaki anti-nuclear movement emanating from that nation a special credibility. Soka Gakkai has pyramided the devastation caused by those horrific explosions into an internationally noticed cause and used that cause to make itself a truly global religious movement.

The critics of secular world-systems theory maintain that secularization is an inherently self-limiting process which is cyclical rather than unilinearly evolutionary. In Soka Gakkai we have the case of a modern movement that illustrates how the process of moral regeneration can work. How religion reenters the thinking about a global community will be an interactive question, and this interaction between religion and the secular is only now being conceptualized. In the case of Soka Gakkai, the process of revitalizing the sacredness of nationalistic symbols seems a necessary prerequisite to begin expanding the definition of who can be saved, who is worthy for survival, and so forth. Nationalistic fervor linked with a religion of universal scope then can inspire a powerful movement.

This process also suggests that nativism and globalism, although most easily conceptualized as opposites in a dialectic, can in reality build on one another. Globalism, particularly through mass media, rekindles and reinforces national and regional identities. It can also infuse nativistic movements seeking to assert such identities with a broader vision such that movements initially functioning to promote nativism in *the name of global causes* eventually mature beyond that single nativism and actually do pursue those larger goals, expanding their appeal. The nativism of a subculture in an emerging global community, in other words, may no longer be relegated to the rear-guard revitalization movements which anthropologists originally encountered. Indeed, effective nativistic movements of the future—whatever their ultimate aspirations—may even find it mandatory to at least speak the rhetoric of global goals in framing their appeals.

Soka Gakkai has emerged out of one the world's most industrialized countries which presumably also encounters pressures to differentiate institutions (the religious among them) in a way consistent with general secularization expectations. Yet the religion is now spreading increasingly to nations of every economic and developmental level. Capitalizing on the fear of nuclear destruction, Soka Gakkai has been able to expand undoubtedly faster than it could otherwise. The adoption of this particular powerful theme alongside a religious message of universal salvation may reflect the fortunate happenstance that can befall a particular religion at a particular time, or there may be some deeper structure of themes and events that can help explain how religion systematically reenters the globalization process. My final caveat is a truism: we need more case studies to move inductively toward empirical generalizations.

Notes

1. I deliberately omit accent marks that would ordinarily signify long vowels in Japanese words (e.g., *Soka Gakkai* or *Nichiren Shoshu*) for simplicity's sake. For speakers of Japanese the pronunciations are already known; for those unfamiliar with the language, it will not matter.
2. It is the varying practice of scholars to refer to varieties of Japanese Buddhism as schools or sects; others term them denominations with roughly the same meaning as one can speak of Western Protestant denominations. I use the term "sect" to refer to Soka Gakkai much as I would referring to Pentecostals or Jehovah's Witnesses in Christianity. I reserve the term "denomination" for larger mainline Buddhist traditions such as the "Pure Land" groups, e.g., *Jodo-Shinshu* or *Shingon* and *Zen*, much as I would use the term to refer to Presbyterianism or Methodism in Protestant Christianity.

References

Benedict, Ruth. 1967. *The Chrysanthemum and the Sword*. New York: Meridian Books.
Brannen, Noah S. 1968. *Soka Gakkai*. Richmond, VA: John Knox Press.
Brett, Cecil C. 1979. "The Komeito and Local Japanese Politics." *Asian Survey* 366–78.
Bromley, David G. and Anson D. Shupe, Jr. 1979. *"Moonies" in America: Cult, Church and Crusade*. Beverly Hills, CA: Sage.
Buruma, Ian. 1987. "A New Japanese Nationalism." *The New York Times Magazine* April 12, Section C.
_____. 1977. *Toward Modernity: Developmental Typology of Popular Religious Affiliations in Japan*. East Asia Papers #12. Ithaca, NY: Cornell University Press.
Dator, James Allen. 1969. *Soka Gakkai: Builders of the Third Civilization*. Seattle, WA: University of Washington Press.
Davis, Winston. 1980. *Dojo: Magic and Exorcism in Modern Japan*. Stanford, CA: Stanford University Press.
Dumoulin, Henrich. 1976. "Buddhism in Modern Japan." 215–76 in *Buddhism in the Modern World*, edited by Henrich Dumoulin and John C. Maraldo. New York: Macmillan.

Ellwood, Jr., Robert S. 1974. *The Eagle and the Rising Sun*. Philadelphia: The Westminster Press.
Hadden, Jeffrey K. and Anson Shupe, eds. 1986. *Prophetic Religions and Politics*. New York: Paragon House.
Hoshino, Eiki. 1987. "A Pillar of Japanese Buddhism: Founder Belief." *The Journal of Oriental Studies*, vol. 26: 78–89.
Ikeda, Daisaku. 1986. "Toward A Global Movement for a Lasting Peace." 1–15 in *Buddhism and Leadership for Peace*. Tokyo: Soka University Peace Research Institute Monograph.
_____. 1973. *The Global Unity of Mankind*. Tokyo: Soka Gakkai.
_____. 1972. *Proposal for Lasting Peace*. Tokyo: Soka Gakkai.
McFarland, H. Neill. 1967. *The Rush Hour of the Gods*. New York: Macmillan.
Nakano, Tsuyoshi. 1986. "Buddhism and Peace in Modern Japan: A Preliminary Overview." 82–97 in *Buddhism and Leadership for Peace*. Tokyo: Soka University, Peace Research Institute Monograph.
Norbeck, Edward. 1970. *Religion and Society in Modern Japan: Continuity and Change*. Houston: Tourmaline Press.
Parsons, Talcott. 1978. *Action Theory and the Human Condition*. New York: The Free Press.
Rajana, Eini Watanabe. 1975. "New Religions in Japan: An Appraisal of Two Theories." 187–97 in *Modern Japan: Aspects of History, Literature and Society*, edited by W.G. Beasley. Berkeley, CA: University of California Press,
Robertson, Roland. 1985. "The Sacred and the World System." 347–58 in *The Sacred in a Secular Age*, edited by Phillip E. Hammond. Berkeley, CA: University of California Press.
_____. 1987a. "From Secularization to Globalization." *The Journal of Oriental Studies* 26: 28–32.
_____. 1987b. "Globalization and Societal Modernization: A Note on Japan and Japanese Religions." *Sociological Analysis* 47(S): 35–42 .
_____ and Jo Ann Chirico. 1985. "Humanity, Globalization, and Worldwide Religious Resurgence: A Theoretical Explanation." *Sociological Analysis* 46(3): 219–42.
SGN. 1978. "President: Completion of 'Seven Bells.'" *The Soka Gakkai News* #74: July 15.
_____. 1979. "Completion of 'Seven Bells' Program." *The Soka Gakkai News* #92: May 15.
_____. *The Soka Gakkai News* #212: March.
Shupe, Anson. 1986. "Militancy and Accommodation in the Third Civilization: The Case of Japan's Soka Gakkai Movement." 235–53 in *Prophetic Religions and Politics*, edited by Jeffrey K. Hadden and Anson Shupe. New York: Paragon House.
Snow, David A. 1987. "Organization, Ideology, and Mobilization: The Case of Nichiren Shoshu of America." 153–72 in *The Future of New Religious Movements*, edited by David G. Bromley and Phillip E. Hammond. Macon, GA: Mercer University Press.
Tsunoda, Rysaku, Wm. Theodore DeBary, and Donald Keene, eds. 1958. *Sources of Japanese Tradition*, vol. II. New York: Columbia University Press.
Wallerstein, Immanuel. 1974a. *The Modern World System*. New York: Academic Press.
_____. 1974b. "The Rise and Future Demise of the World Capitalist System: Concepts for Comparative Analysis." *Comparative Studies in Society and History* 16: 387–415.

_____. 1983. "Crisis: The World-Economy, the Movements, and the Ideologies." 21–36 in *Crisis in the World System*, edited by Albert Bergesen. Beverly Hills, CA: Sage.
Wallace, Anthony F.C. 1966. *Religion: An Anthropological View*. New York: Random House.
_____. 1956. "Revitalization Movements." *American Anthropologist* 58: 264–81.
Wilson, Bryan. 1985. "Excerpts From a Lecture Entitled, 'The Role of Modern Religious Movements in Society.'" *The Soka Gakkai Newsletter* #202: 15–18.
YDSG (Youth Division of Soka Gakkai). 1978. *Cries for Peace: Experiences of Japanese Victims of World War II*. Tokyo: *The Japan Times*.

11

THE WHOLE WORLD IN HIS HAND?
WAYS AND MEANS OF ESTABLISHING A UNIFICATIONIST THEOCRACY

Eileen V. Barker

HISTORY IS FULL OF THE RISE AND FALL OF RELIGIOUS MOVEMENTS that have had a vision of One World, united by the One Truth. Although most of the thousand or so new religions that have become visible in the West during the past two decades would like to see global changes, few of them appear to be affecting more than a small circle of those who most immediately surround them—even when (as in the case of, for example, the Children of God or the Raelians) their avowed aim is to establish a new world order.[1]

Insofar as the movements attempt to do something about establishing their conception of the Kingdom of Heaven on earth, the majority tend to concentrate on changing people's hearts rather than on changing social structures, and the methods employed are unlikely to be of the kind that empirical investigation has shown to be particularly effective in societal, let alone global, transformations: prayer, meditation, chanting, and yoga are among the methods most commonly employed. There are, of course, exceptions, such as the Soka Gakkai (Nichiren

Buddhism), Rissho Kosei Kai, perhaps the Ananda Marga and the Brahma Kumaris, and possibly the Church of Scientology. Another major exception is the Unification Church.

To give it its full title, the Holy Spirit Association for the Unification of World Christianity (HSA-UWC) has taken upon itself the task of unifying not merely Christianity, but the whole of the world—of overcoming atheistic communism, and of setting up a global theocracy in which every child will be carefully tutored in the understanding of God that has been revealed by the Reverend Sun Myung Moon.[2]

May 1, 1954 is the date celebrated as the establishment of the HSA-UWC in Korea. At that time, it is doubtful whether any but the most faithful of Rev. Moon's followers would have believed that this small band of unknown men and women could possibly achieve more than a mild notoriety as one bunch of religious zealots among many others; very few would have thought that Sun Myung Moon would become a household name throughout the Western world within the short span of thirty years.

The Unification Church's aims are, in general terms, clear enough: to restore the Kingdom of Heaven on earth. Rev. Moon claims that God has chosen him to play a messianic role in the restoration process; he has the key to understanding God's laws—His Divine Principles—and, so long as enough people are prepared to live by these Principles, under his guidance, there could be the world-wide establishment of a God-centered community, based on the fundamental unit of the God-centered family. In this new global order, local differences will continue to exist and, it is sometimes said, different religions may flourish. It is fairly clear, however, that the different religions will be considered minor variations of the one true religion which celebrates the truth as revealed by Rev. Moon.

As with other movements that aspire to change society, it is relatively easy to gather details about the evils of the contemporary world and, thus, to learn what the new order will not look like. The Unification theocracy will have no place for atheistic communism; there will be no pornography; sexual activity will be confined to marriage; crime will have been drastically reduced, if not entirely eliminated; wars will be eradicated; exploitation, the use of people as means rather than as ends in themselves, will be a thing of the past; racial prejudice will have disappeared—and there will be no need for passports.

We have also some clues as to what the global order will be like. It will, first of all, be a global order; the Unification Church is not interested merely in setting up a self-sufficient community, or even a network of communities. God is relying on the Unificationists to restore the whole of His created world. At the individual level, children will be born without the Fallen Nature (original sin) that we have all inherited from the first parents, Adam and Eve, as a result of the Fall—which Unificationists attribute to Adam and Eve having had a sexual relationship before they were ready to be blessed in marriage by God.

It is, however, extremely difficult to get anything like a coherent response from rank-and-file members of the Unification Church when one asks them for detailed information about the social or political structure of the Kingdom for which they are working. It is, moreover, possible to detect a change over time during which Unificationists have become more prosaic in their understanding of what changes might take place, and more concerned to see that the means employed to achieve the ends bear some visible relationship to the ultimate goal.[3] This essay is, however, confined to a description and an assessment of the means—that is, to the consideration of some of the methods that have been used in the Unification Church's attempts to establish a particular kind of global order; the Kingdom of Heaven on earth.

In its kingdom-building, the Unification Church has not proceeded on one front—or even on a limited number of fronts. Although there are overlaps, it is possible to distinguish three levels at which the movement attempts to establish its new global order; that of individual members, that of the Unification Church itself, and that of the "outside" society.

At the individual level the basic idea is to change the heart (the personality and the characteristic behavior) of people so that they become loving, co-operative, full of goodness rather than sin, and, above all, centered on God and freely prepared to lead a Principled life as part of a loving 'give-and-take' relationship with Him and with their fellow human beings.

Unificationists believe that a crucially significant transformation in their lives occurs during the *Holy Wine Ceremony*, which follows the matching (engagement) ceremony when Rev. Moon selects the member's potential spouse and which precedes the actual Blessing (mass marriage) ceremony. During the Holy Wine ceremony, it is believed, the "blood lineage" of the participants is radically changed and, consequently, children born to the blessed couples inherit no Fallen Nature.[4] This is not to say that the children may not fall (as did Adam and Eve), but that they will be born with only the Original Nature with which God created the original human beings. It is believed that a world populated by such children would, in itself, result in a very different order from that which now exists.

Lest it be thought that the Unification Church is relying upon what might appear to outsiders to be little more than a supernatural or magical ritual in its attempt to create a new race of men and women, it should be pointed out that this great change is not to take place merely as the result of a single ceremony. Members are expected to have made their contribution by achieving a certain level of maturity in their spiritual development before they become eligible to marry. The preparation includes three-year periods of fundraising and of witnessing, during which the member is meant to have acquired at least three "spiritual children" to whom he or she will become a "spiritual parent" in preparation for becoming the physical parent of a "Blessed child."[5]

There are two further ways in which it is believed that the Unificationist concept of marriage can contribute to the establishment of a new global order. First, and most important, is the belief that the Kingdom of Heaven on earth will have the God-centered family as its basic unit. According to Unification theology, there is a special sense in which individuals are not born complete persons, but can become so only through a 'give and take' partnership with their spouse. It is within this God-centered unit that their children will be nurtured—away from the satanic influences of a fallen world. A second reason why Unification marriages can be thought of as contributing towards the establishment of a new global order is because a not inconsiderable number take place between people of different races.

Turning to the outside world, Rev. Moon has attempted to awaken the divine consciousness and conscience of his audience at numerous rallies around the United States and in other parts of the world, and, as already mentioned, each Unificationist is expected to spend at least three years 'witnessing' to others about the ideals of the Unification church. A further type of grassroots "outreach" that Unificationists have made to non-members is through the *Home Church* movement. The concept of the Home Church, first introduced in 1978, requires Unificationists to look after a "parish" of 360 persons living in their immediate environment through offering such services as mowing lawns for the elderly or shopping for the house-bound.[6]

It is, however, when we consider the work of Unificationists not as individuals by themselves, but, rather, as organizers of the numerous institutions that have been established under Rev. Moon's leadership, frequently co-opting non-members to prominent positions (with honorary titles, generous expenses, and honoraria), that the full range of Unification activities starts to become apparent. Space does not permit the detailing of anything but the tiniest proportion of the numerous organizations that Unification Church members have instituted in the

West during the past two decades, but mention of some of the more prominent ones might give a flavor of their scope and variety.[7]

Many of the more obviously religious organizations began at the Unification Theological Seminary in Barrytown, New York, where, from the mid-1970s, non-Unificationist scholars were invited to speak and then to organize a number of exchanges between the students and members of other faiths, the proceedings of which were subsequently published.[8] Out of these meetings grew further conferences, first local, then national, then international. *New ERA* (the New Ecumenical Research Association), founded in 1980, continues to promote conferences on a variety of subjects, including the sociology of new religious movements.[9] A related development was the *Youth Seminar on World Religions* in which a group of non-Unificationist students and scholars travelled around the world, studying the world's religions. This has recently been replaced by the more practical *Religious Youth Service* (RYS), which invites young non-Unificationists to "Come, spend your summer with us, and experience the joy of service." The project is seen in terms of establishing a new global order through practical service: in his Opening Address to the 120 young people from 33 nations who participated in the RYS program in Manila in 1986, a top-ranking Unificationist declared: "We live in a global village, and young people from all over the world...long to move in one direction, worldwide."[10]

In 1983, the *International Religious Foundation* (IRF) was incorporated "in order to bring under one umbrella the various interfaith and ecumenical activities sponsored by the Unification Church." The IRF has organized countless conferences, some with less than twenty participants, others with several hundreds of participants—theologians, ministers of religion, and various kinds of religion-related scholars. *The Parliament of World Religions*, which the IRF is planning for 1993, "seeks through its program to discern patterns of unity among the world's religions."[11]

Although anyone attending a Unification conference for the first time is unlikely to learn much about Unification theology, participants may subsequently be invited to an *Introductory Seminar on the Unification Movement* at which they will learn about the *Divine Principle* and the movement's ideals. The *Unification News* has reported such a conference under the heading "A Global Mission."[12] Non-Unificationists who have some specialist knowledge of or influence in the world and have been involved in one or other of the movement's organizations may also find themselves invited to join the *Advisory Council to the Unification Movement* (ACUMI) which was established in the mid-1980s. Members of ACUMI are expected not only to advise Unificationists on possible future developments, but also to act as an intermediate source of information about the Unification Church to the world at large.

Among other organizations that have fallen under the umbrella of the IRF are the *Sun Myung Moon Institute*, the avowed purpose of which is "to encourage scholarly study of the interaction between East and West in the past and the present," and the *International Christians for Unity and Social Action* (ICUSA) which has focused largely on inner-city poverty in the United States, in close cooperation with many of the black churches.

One of the visions of the New Age is that entertainment should be decent, clean, and wholesome, and Unification foundations for this have been laid in music, dance, and the fine arts. *The Little Angels*, a dance troupe formed in Korea in 1963, has danced at a Royal Command Performance before Queen Elizabeth II and many other dignitaries; the *Korean Folk Ballet* has delighted audiences around the world for nearly as long. The name of the *New York City Symphony* has existed for over 60 years, but it came under Unification auspices during the 1970s. The movement also promotes a number of groups such as the *Go World Brass Band*, and the *New Hope Singers International*; it has encouraged some of its artists to paint holy pictures and contribute to some of its publications; and it spent a small fortune on *Inchon*, a film about the Korean War, which included stars such as Sir Laurence Olivier in its cast.

Moving on to sport, *Striders International* (founded in 1967) has helped several hundred young blacks to attend college on athletic scholarships, more than a score of whom have gone on to compete in the Olympics. Indeed, in a number of ways, Unificationists had an exceptionally high profile during the 1988 Olympic Games in Seoul, with two of Rev. Moon's own children competing in equestrian events.

So far as education is concerned, the movement is about to open a university in Seoul where it already has The Little Angels School, to which non-Unificationists are evidently eager to send their children. Many of the movement's western leaders have obtained a master's degree in Religious Education at the Unification Theological Seminary, which was founded in 1975; some were then sponsored by the Church to proceed to Ivy League and other top American universities, where they have been awarded doctorates.

In global terms, the charitable relief work in which the Unification Church has been engaged can hardly be said even to scratch the surface of the world's poverty and other ills, but a considerable effort has been made in this direction by some Unificationists. For example, the Oakland-based *Project Volunteer* distributes food to the needy in California;

and the *International Relief Friendship Foundation* (IRFF) was founded in 1976 as "a non-profit agency whose purpose is to relieve poverty, suffering and disease"—on a global level, with global effects.[13] One of its brochures proclaims that:

> Global stability affects everyone. The hope for peace will unfold through communication of ideas, cultural exchange, and a unified effort to improve the quality of life. In all parts of the world IRFF acts as a catalyst to bring about this achievement.[14]

At the geographical level, Rev. Moon has proposed the building of an *International Highway* which will link the countries of the East and West. It is thus, he declares, that "it would eventually become possible to connect the upper and lower classes of the world with the yellow peoples serving as mediator."[15]

The venture has been defined in highly idealistic terms, with clear implications for the global order:

> The International Highway Project proposes that all the nations of the world stop pursuing their own self-interests in hostility and struggle, and that each one of them can have a new sense of value from a higher-level global view of love for humanity and that a straight highway passing through all the countries of the world be constructed so that all the people on the earth may equally enjoy freedom, peace and happiness on the basis of wealthy economic conditions supported by scientific technology, thus realizing a terrestrial paradise where all humankind is one family.[16]

Numerous publications have been produced by the Unification Church and its subsidiaries. There is internal literature;[17] there is the literature that is used for proselytizing and fundraising;[18] and there is literature which informs outsiders (and, of course, the membership) about the movement's activities.[19] More interesting in the present context are the Unification publications whose contents are not directly concerned with the Unification Church, but which do, nonetheless, aim to promote the kind of global order to which the movement aspires.

Within the field of journalism, the best known of a number of Unification newspapers in the West is *The Washington Times*, which was first published in 1982.[20] Other publications that aim to promote a Unificationist perspective at a more cultural level include the monthly magazine *The World and I* (each issue covering 700 pages of such topics as current affairs, the arts, developments in science, and special features on people, regions of the world, and recent books), *International Journal on World Peace* (published since 1984 by the Unification-inspired Professors World Peace Academy), and *Dialogue and Alliance* (started in

1987 in order "to facilitate dialogue and alliance among the religions of the world as a means of promoting world peace and harmony"). So far as the publication of books is concerned, the church-financed *Paragon House* now has well over a hundred titles on its list.

Although the editors of most Unification-sponsored publications are not themselves Unificationists, they, like others who work for Unification-associated organizations, tend to share at least some of the global goals that Rev. Moon has articulated. And, as in other areas, the Unification Church has involved professionals beyond those who work directly for one of its organizations. The *World Media Conference*(s), which have become an (almost) annual event, are attended by journalists from a wide variety of publications throughout the world; these have, on occasion, included all-expenses-paid "fact-finding" tours in places like Latin America where the battle between communist and right-wing factions is rife.

To list Unification-related financial endeavors would take several pages. Suffice it to say that the movement's interests in fishing, ginseng products, manufacturing (especially machine parts), and a host of other businesses is considerable in Japan, North America, and Korea, and by no means insignificant in Europe, Latin America, and mainland China. The movement also has valuable holdings in real estate. One might, indeed, view Unification-related businesses, were they to be regarded as a single entity, as comprising a not inconsiderable multinational corporation. No one outside the movement has been able to work out precisely where all the money in the so-called "Moon Empire" comes from or where it all goes, but there are numerous reports (some of which have been vehemently denied) of large sums being channelled to subsidize individuals and organizations that have no official contact with the Unification Church but are, nevertheless, working towards related goals—especially the eradication of communism.[21]

For a number of reasons, the Unification Church tends to be somewhat reticent about its more directly political activities. There has been a Unificationist member of the French parliament, and throughout the world Unificationists have certainly been active in their support of candidates who share some of their political opinions (especially anticommunism). But, unlike the Soka Gakkai, which is closely associated with Japan's third largest political party, *Komeito*, Unificationists have, so far, made only limited attempts to operate directly within party political processes. There is, however, absolutely no doubt that almost everything that the movement does can be seen as part of the battle against the atheistic communism that holds sway over so great a proportion of the present global order—and which was responsible for Rev. Moon's imprisonment during the Korean War.

An early example of a Unification organization directly concerned with anti-communist activities was the *Freedom Leadership Foundation* (FLF) which began in 1969 with the "primary objective...to develop the standards of leadership necessary to advance the cause of freedom in the struggle against Communism."[22] *The Professors World Peace Academy* (PWPA), which has gained a membership of several thousands of scholars, many of whom have been invited to conferences, has among its stated goals the determination "to work towards a new world order" and "to influence public opinion and public policy throughout the world."[23] More recently, *CAUSA International* has been the movement's most prominent political arm.[24] CAUSA has developed its own political ideology, called *Godism*, which is presented as the alternative ideology to Marxism.[25]

Still on the political front, but at a far more sophisticated level, there is *The Washington Institute for Values in Public Policy*. Richard Rubenstein, the Institute's President, is a widely respected scholar who, although not himself a member of the Unification Church, is one of a group of top academics who greatly admire Rev. Moon and is happy to support him in at least some of his ventures. The Institute has been responsible for a program of forums (a number of which have taken place in House and Senate office meetings on Capitol Hill) and a number of publications on various policy issues that have involved an impressive array of scholars and policy makers.

And so one could continue; but enough has, I hope, been said to indicate something of the scope and variety of fronts on which the Unification Church has been trying to change the global order. The rest of this chapter is devoted to an attempt to assess these Kingdom-building efforts.

Let us start by questioning the extent to which a radically improved character of Unification membership could, in itself, result in a new global order. One is immediately forced to make a fairly fundamental observation: the number of full-time members of the Unification Church is, and always has been, tiny. It is unlikely that there have ever been more than 15,000 fully committed members working for the movement in the West, or 50,000 world wide, at any one time (although there have been several tens of thousands who have been members and then left the movement, and there are, perhaps, several hundreds of thousands more, particularly in Japan and South Korea, who are sympathetic or in some way affiliated to the movement, although they do not work full-time for it).[26]

There are two reasons why the small numbers and the high turn-over rate are important. First, the small number of fully committed members could mean that it is unlikely that the effect of what is being done internally, at either the individual level or the group level, will make all that much of an impact. Second, the high turn-over rate suggests that, at least as yet, the movement has not found a method of convincing people that the Unification Church can do all that they want it to do or achieve all they want it to achieve. This is a serious problem for a movement that wants to establish a global order—especially insofar as it claims that once people have heard the truth and seen it in practice, they will find it so self-evidently correct that there will be no need to persuade any one of its truth. It is sometimes argued that it is particularly difficult to persuade people of Unification truths when so much of the world does not live according to the Principle—that once a critical mass has been established and sufficient example is available, the rest of the people will want to follow. The trouble with this argument is that there is, as yet, little evidence, at least so far as numbers are concerned, that the Unification Church is moving toward such a critical mass. Numbers of conversions have not shown any signs of increasing (they have, indeed, been falling) during the 1980s.

A further problem arises from the fact that a critical mass has not been reached when one examines what can happen to the crucially important God-centered family. As Unificationists do not want merely to set up small cells of Unificationism (like the Hutterites or the Amish), but to establish the Kingdom of Heaven on a global basis, the wider environment needs to be set to rights. Unificationists have frequently found themselves being sent on missions that separate husbands from wives and parents from children. It is, indeed, possible to argue that, at least up to the present stage in the restoration process, many Unification families have been less successful in establishing the ideal model than they might have been had they not been trying to establish their global order. The same kind of observation may be made about the example that Rev. Moon himself is expected to present as the Messianic ideal father, husband, and son.[27]

Although far more non-Unificationists than Unificationists have been involved in marriages between people of different races and cultures, it might be argued that those that have taken place with the Unification Church could have a globalizing effect (in the sense that they would, genetically and perhaps culturally, reduce the potency of national boundaries). It has to be admitted, however, that several of these marriages are not working—and that not infrequently the reasons that the unhappy partners give are related precisely to the fact that they are married to someone of a different race. Again, it can be argued that, given time and a critical mass, the differences that give rise to such difficulties will dissolve. Perhaps. But we might want to ask whether there is any evidence that such a critical mass is being promoted by what some Unificationists have themselves, somewhat ruefully, referred to as the mixed-Blessing policy.

Similar doubts might be raised concerning other aspects of community life within the Unification Church. For present purposes, however, it is probably sufficient to reiterate that the small numbers involved make it unlikely that Unificationism will sweep the world and establish a new global order as a result of its *internal* functioning.

The paucity of numbers also limits the efficacy of several *external* avenues that Unificationists pursue in their attempts to establish the new world order. Even if each member were to make a positive impression on every one of the 360 persons within his or her Home Church area, less than 0.3 percent of the North American population and perhaps no more than 0.1 percent of the European population would benefit from such attentions. In fact, few Unificationists have been able to develop any kind of relationship with more than a handful of people in their area, usually because they are far too busy with or concerned about other missions that seem to be of a more pressing nature.

Rev. Moon's public appearances are, by themselves, unlikely to mobilize the masses to follow his lead to the new global order. The publicity that he has received by these and other means has, of course, increased his visibility, but the normal reaction of those of his audience who have had no prior association with the Unification Church has tended to fall somewhere between mild boredom and decided hostility. Similarly, many Unificationist attempts at improving the worlds of art, entertainment, and sport, and, indeed, attempts to help people through the Home Church or the various charitable enterprises, such as food distribution or the supply of medical aid, have back-fired in so far as the media, and the movement's opponents, have interpreted these as no more than devious attempts at gaining respectability. There can be little doubt that it was not merely the artistic standard of *Inchon* that killed its reception at, or even before, its launching—it was also the "Moon-connection" that led to its ignoble failure.

In other words, while such endeavors may impress the Unification membership, and while the external opposition might result in the members being urged to greater battle, many become discouraged, and several ventures have failed merely because the Unification Church is publicly defined as "a bad thing," even (perhaps especially) when it does things that its critics would applaud were they performed by others. Indeed, throughout its history, the movement has repeatedly been rebuffed and its organizations branded as dangerous or sinister 'fronts.'

To take but one further example, this time from the field of economics, there was a small flurry of excitement in the British press in 1986 as the result of headlines reporting "Top Thatcher aides linked to Moonie cult."[28] This mini-scandal concerned a Unification free-market organization called the *Global Economic Action Group* which had held a number of international conferences on economic and political matters.

What about the unification of the world's religions? Those who have attended a "Global Congress of the World's Religions," a "God Conference" or some other Unification-sponsored ecumenical or inter-faith meetings, have frequently recorded their gratitude for the opportunity to talk to people with different beliefs and to learn something of their religious practices.[29] The conferences have, however, been a cause for division when non-attenders have attacked those who do attend Unification conferences as indulging in disreputable, dangerous or, possibly, evil, practices. This is, furthermore, not infrequently a posture adopted by people who claim an interest in fostering, on a global scale, an understanding and dialogue between people of other faiths. Some non-Unification conferences that have been and are being planned for such purposes have made a point of declaring that Unification personnel are specifically excluded from the proceedings.

How far the Highway Project will progress is, at this stage, impossible to say, but, with a reported allocation of $43,000,000 and a considerable amount of preparatory investigation (both geological and political) already under way, it is not inconceivable that at least part of the project could be completed.[30] More questionable for the skeptic is whether such a highway would result in the utopian image spelled out by Moon and his followers. No doubt, increasingly facilitated mobility between countries would have some effect on the global order, but with the increase in air (and space) travel and telecommunications, it is not immediately obvious that facilitated ground transport is either necessary or sufficient for the envisaged goal of world peace and harmony. It might even, in some areas, be counter-productive.

Turning to politics, the mobilization of Unification resources at times of elections or campaigns in North America or Europe cannot be said to add up to as much as that whipped up by many another religion-political lobby. Although Unification participation on such occasions may make some difference, the lobbying efforts of Catholics, Methodists, Jews, and Episcopalians—even secular humanists—would seem to be capable of making a far greater difference. In assessing the effect of CAUSA, it might be remarked that while the Unification Church has been relatively successful in gathering together an impressive number of people who share an anti-communist stance, it is not so obvious that these people, many of whom are decidedly strange bed-fellows, are happy with the Godism alternative; many have, in fact, expressed strong feelings of revulsion toward it. There can be little doubt that Unificationists have had considerably more success in gathering together those who are against certain aspects of the current world order than they have had in bonding such people to faith in the alternative global order that the movement would like to establish.

If one returns to the movement's theology to see what it is that the Unificationists themselves believe will happen with respect to communism and the establishment of the godly global order, one can find the following statement:

> At the consummation of human history, both the heavenly side and the satanic side have come to operate on the world-wide level. Thus, the two worlds of democracy and Communism coexist. But after the third world struggle, these two worlds will be united. Seen from God's dispensation, the Third World War will inevitably take place. However, there are two ways for that war to be fought.
>
> First, the satanic world could be subjugated by a wholly internal fight through ideology. God does not desire judgement or destruction (Ezek. 33:14–16), but salvation. Thus he desires Satan to submit ideologically, and with the least amount of external sacrifice. If this fails, the satanic side will inevitably attack the heavenly side. The heavenly side must then defeat the satanic side by force.[31]

Given this belief, one might expect that the Unification Church would make every effort to persuade communists of the error of their ways. This has certainly been attempted indirectly, but it is interesting, and informative, that the practical move toward a direct, institutionalized exchange of ideas between the two "worlds" was not initiated from the top of the movement, but at a comparatively low level. A New Era *Christian-Marxist Dialogue* was planned as the result of a discussion at a conference between a non-Unificationist scholar who was already "into" Christian-Marxist dialogue and a couple of Unificationists working with New Era. It was not until after all the arrangements had been made that those with ultimate authority in the IRF were informed. A report of the meeting (which included a number of Marxist scholars from Eastern Europe) appeared in an internal Unification magazine, *Today's World*,[32] and was greeted with some surprise, even shock, by the more conservative members of the movement. The western Unificationists who were responsible for organizing the dialogue were mightily relieved (one expressed considerable astonishment) when it was learned that Rev. Moon had not only approved, but even agreed to there being at least two further such meetings.

The point of this story is that, although it is uncommon for western Unificationists to do something quite so radical without approval from the Korean leadership, it does, in some way, epitomize the procedure that Rev. Moon has and still does adopt in his overall leadership of the restoration process. It is probably true to say that most of his "visions" are the result of someone else's suggestion—either a Unificationist's or, not infrequently, of one of the movement's paid advisors or outside sympathizers. What he does is not only to encourage people to have ideas, but also to provide the means (or at least allow for the possibility) to try these ideas out in practice. This has resulted in a considerable number of mistakes and some minor disasters for the movement. Some projects scarcely get off the ground; others prosper for a short time and are then dropped, yet others go from strength to strength. Competition is rife within the movement to get access to the resources (money, personnel, and, above all, his blessing) needed for the various proposals.

This well-nigh survival-of-the-fittest, trial-and-error strategy is costly; but it can be argued, and I would be prepared to argue, that it is one of the main reasons for both the successes and the failures of Unification efforts to establish a new global order. The important point to make is that many of the projects are little more than enabling stages in the wider, more global, process, and it is well-nigh impossible for either rank-and-file Unificationists or outsiders (and even, perhaps, for Unification leaders) to know just what the outcome of any short-term venture will be—let alone what the next stage might be.[33]

A final twist to this particular story illustrates the Unificationist procedure (or lack thereof) as it occurs in its widely diverse and often uncoordinated functioning. While New ERA organized its second Christian-Marxist Dialogue in Austria to start on 12 August 1987, *CARP*, the student wing of the Unification Church, has organized its 4th Convention of World Students in Berlin for August 4–8.[34] During the CARP Convention, "provocative rallies [were held] on the border... [with] 40 students managing to penetrate GDR territory at Checkpoint Charlie before being repulsed."[35] One consequence of this confrontation between the "heavenly" and "satanic" sides was that East German participants did not turn up for the Dialogue in Austria. The incident may also have explained the last-minute cancellations of the Marxist scholars who were expected to come from Russia and Poland.[36] This example of the right hand not knowing what the left hand was doing and a show of confrontational defiance interfering with a show of willingness to exchange and to try to understand opposing views is unlikely to surprise many familiar with the internal operations of the Unification Church.

How then might one assess the aspirations and achievements of a movement like the Unification Church in its attempts to establish a new global order? The short answer is, of course, that one cannot—not with any hope of accurate prediction. One can, nonetheless, make a few observations. First, it would seem clear that, in terms of absolute and relative numbers of members, the movement is extremely unlikely to achieve any significant global changes either through transformation in the lives of the individual members, or by creating a new model movement that could provide an example which the other inhabitants of the globe would rush to follow.

When I first started to study the Unification Church, I was interested in the way in which the internal organizational structure, with Rev. Moon as its apex, functioned so that the membership might be mobilized to implement the global changes demanded by its theology. After several years of study, however, it became apparent that although this vertical organization was certainly interesting, the external, horizontal organization that the movement was institutionalizing had become increasingly crucial to an understanding of the movement's potential and actual influence.

In other words, Rev. Moon's most telling achievement lies not in the changes that he has wrought in the lives of Unificationists, momentous though these be for some of the individuals concerned; nor does it lie in the hierarchial organization of the movement itself. It lies, rather, in the networks that he and his followers have organized throughout those structures and cultures that lie beyond the boundaries of the Unification Church.

It is not a contradiction, but possibly the key to what success the Unification enterprise enjoys, that Rev. Moon is eager to use non-Unificationists members to further his goals, even when some of them have publicly denounced (at least part of) his ideological position. Not all those who contribute to the movement's global aspirations are aware of the role they play. Some quite explicitly exploit the resources of the movement to further their own, not always complementary, goals.

It is possible to conceive of several concentric circles consisting of people upon whom the Unification movement may call. At the outer right there are people who have made some minimal commitment to what is probably a single-issue position. This they may have done through, for example, the PWPA collecting the signatures of tens of thousands of scholars throughout the world. Most of these people will serve "the cause" merely by contributing to the number of people that the Unificationists can claim to have signed the requisite piece of paper; the more prominent among them may also provide a name that can be mentioned in connection with the movement's enterprises. Coming slightly further towards the center, there are those members of the Advisory Council for the Unification Movement International (ACUMI) who are prepared to speak to others about the Unification Church, its beliefs and practices. Then (with some overlap of personnel) there are those who agree to organize conferences or, moving even further towards the center, who receive retainers or are employed by one of the movement's enterprises.

Much of the usefulness of these people lies in the very fact that they are not Unificationists—if they are academics, they know and are trusted by other academics who can be approached to attend an academic conference and who may, in turn, be drawn further into the network; if they are journalists, they bring their professionalism and an air of respectability to the Unification newspapers. This is particularly important in the case of *The Washington Times* which, although it, like other Unification publications, is produced at considerable financial loss, has succeeded in gaining itself something of a reputation in political circles. Unificationists have boasted that it is one of the four papers that President Bush reads on a regular basis. Whether or not this is true, it is undoubtedly the case that many anti-communists admire the paper's reporting and its political stance, and, conversely, that it has been attacked in virulent terms by both liberals and the left.[37] How much influence the paper has in indirectly furthering Unification goals is, of course, impossible to assess. It is also impossible to assess the influence of the numerous networks that have been set up by non-Unificationists who have been brought together from different disciplines and different continents by a Unificationist conference and who, because they have a common interest, have started projects that are completely independent of the Unification Church, but are, nonetheless, contributing to one or other of its ideological aims.

Despite the fact that nearly all Unification enterprises have been regarded with suspicion and hostility, most of its Kingdom-building has been relatively open to the investigator's inspection. One can, however, hear persistent whispers, from Unificationists and non-Unificationists alike, of less public negotiations and networking—particularly so far as the flow of money and political intelligence is concerned. There are few areas of the world in which the movement's anti-communist activities do not take place at some level. Much of this activity would seem to be concentrated in the Far East and in Latin America, but many Unification-watchers are convinced that the movement also has fingers in certain political pies in the United States. How far the movement is successful in exploiting its contacts and how far the movement is being exploited by its contacts, and to what extent the Unification Church and its contacts share the same goals is, as intimated earlier, unknown to all but a few—it may even be unknown to anyone.

In a democratic society, power lies neither in the barrel of a gun, nor, except as an ultimate non-violent sanction, does it lie with the ballot box. Each individual does not count as an equal vote in the politics of power and global transformation, but Rev. Moon does not make any such assumption. His genius, such as it is, must lie in the extent to which he has managed to establish an entree to corridors of world power. Impressive as Unification networking is, it is probably only through the movement's having the ear of those who already hold key positions in the "outside" world that it could hope to affect significantly the social life of the planet at a global level. To have the ear of, let us say, a Colonel who himself has the ear of the White House and the Pentagon is, in practical terms, worth many hundreds, perhaps even several million, followers. So long, that is, as the Colonel is not incapacitatingly disgraced and so long as those whose ear he has remain in power.

But, to extend the metaphor, the corridors of power in a pluralistic democracy comprise a veritable maze, seething with Kingdom-builders, Kingdom-wreckers and Kingdom-preservers of many a hue. No one has sight of the complete map, let alone the population that tip-toe, stride, or sit along these corridors. Explorations can be made, and Rev. Moon and his movement have penetrated far further than most would have guessed conceivable. But there are others, many others, in the corridors.

To conclude, there can be no question but that the Unification Church has accomplished much, and is likely to accomplish much more. How valuable Unification achievements are must be left to others to decide. As with those who wish to establish the Kingdom, it is easier to attempt a description of what will not happen, at least in the relatively short term, then what will happen. My personal assessment (and perhaps the assessment is in part a reflection of my lack of belief in Unification theology) is that those who hope for and expect a Unification theocracy to be established within their life-time (or that of their grandchildren) are doomed to disappointment.

Since this paper was first written, the Unification movement has, true to form, instituted many further changes and continues to introduce new organizations, to contact new people and to spread its network of influence. Members of the movement tell me that the Unification Church is now the largest Christian denomination in Japan and that we can expect it to be the main guiding force in Korea by the mid-1990s.

And, of course, it can be pointed out quite correctly that movements that have historically fashioned much of the present global order started from small beginnings with the ideas of men who had no more than a few followers during their life-time. Christianity and Marxism are but two of the more obvious examples.

But while Sun Myung Moon and his Unification Church may have achieved enough to allow me to understand why some of his followers believe (and some of his strongest opponents fear) he will succeed in his global aspirations, an assessment of the achievements, within the context of contemporary society with its multifarious opposing forces, leaves me unconvinced that he (or any other messiah) can realistically expect to celebrate the third millennium by holding anything like the whole world in his hand.

Acknowledgments

I would like to thank the Nuffield Foundation for a grant that helped me to collect data from which this paper draws.

Notes

1. For a description of the variety of ways in which a wide range of contemporary new religious movements view the political order and what they propose to do about it, see Barker (1987).
2. See, *inter alia*, Eu (1983); "Master Speaks"; and "Reverend Sun Myung Moon Speaks on...." I have described the history and the theology of the Unification Church in more detail in Barker (1984).
3. See Barker (1987) Part VI for a typology of different types of Kingdom-Builders.
4. See Grace (1985) Chapter 5 for a discussion of the variety of meanings attributed to the Holy Wine Ceremony within the movement itself.
5. In practice, the period of three years for each of these "missions" tends to be negotiable for some, but not all, of the members.
6. The concept of Home Church has also been used to describe members who neither live in Unification Centers nor work full-time for the movement.
7. In this paper, when I refer to Unification-associated organizations, my interest is *sociological* and should not be taken as implying any particular legal or political association. For example, I have no quarrel with the statement "The World Media Conference is not sponsored or funded by the Unification Church. It is, however, a product of the vision and inspiration of Reverend Moon" (*Unification News*, October 1986).
8. See, for example, Quebedeux and Sawatsky (1979); Quebedeaux (1982); Tsirpanlis (1981).
9. A series of books were published as a result of these (and the other conferences)

with eminent scholars such as Bryan Wilson, Joseph Fichter, and Rodney Stark as their editors.
10. "Youth's Responsibility in Our Global Village," *Unification News*, August 1986, 7.
11. International Religious Foundation Inc. Brochure, n.d. 13.
12. *Unification News* April 1987, 10–11.
13. *Frontiers in Development*, Newsletter of the International Relief Friendship Foundation, Spring 1985, 4.
14. IRFF leaflet, 1983.
15. Moon, Sun Myung (1982), 16.
16. Kajikura (n.d.), 1.
17. For example: *Today's World*; *The Blessing Quarterly*; and Sun Myung Moon's speeches to his followers.
18. E.g. *One World*; *New Tomorrow*.
19. E.g. *Unification News*; *Unification Newsletter*; or, at the more specific level, the *International Religious Foundation Newsletter*; or *The Academician*, published by the Unification-associated Professors World Peace Academy of Japan.
20. Other daily papers published by Unificationist associates include *Sekai Nippo* (launched in Japan in 1975), the *News World* (launched in 1976 and changed to the *New York City Tribune* in 1983), and, for the New York Hispanic community, *Noticias del Mundo* appeared in 1980. In 1989, *Segye Ilbo* appeared on the streets in Seoul. Sun Myung Moon has also been associated with the setting up of the *Middle East Times* (in 1982) and a news service, *News World Communications*.
21. See, for example, *The Washington Post* 16 & 17 September 1984; *Le Monde Diplomatique* February 1985; *The Guardian* 3 March 1985; *Greater Phoenix Jewish News* 1 April 1987; *U.S. News & World Report*, 27 March 1989.
22. *Ideology and Foreign Policy: An Interview with Neil Albert Salonen*, FLF Foreign Policy Study Series, Washington D.C., n.d.
23. PWPA brochure, n.d. 4.
24. CAUSA originally was said to be an acronym for the *Confederation of the Association for the Unification of the Societies of the Americas*, and it focused primarily on combating communism in Latin America. More recently, however, it has expanded its activities to the other continents and the name CAUSA is explained solely through its Spanish meaning as Cause, CAUSA standing for the First Cause of the universe, God.
25. See *CAUSA Lecture Manual*, CAUSA Institute, New York, 1985; and *Introduction to the CAUSA Worldview*, CAUSA Institute, New York, 1985.
26. Although it is true that about 18,000 couples had been "Blessed" by October 1988, many of these marriages (estimates have ranged from 12–15 percent) broke up before they were consummated or before the birth of children. Indeed, some of the persons involved have been counted twice as they have been blessed a second time after an initial failure.
27. I have discussed this dilemma for Unificationists in some detail in Barker (1983), 35–52.
28. *The Sunday Times*, 6 July 1986.
29. For a serious debate by sociologists of religion on the question of attending Unification conferences, see *Sociological Analysis*, volume 44/3, Fall 1983.
30. See "A Report on the International Highway Project," *Today's World*, March 1987, 43–4.

31. Kwak, Chung Hwan, (1980) 197–8.
32. January 1987, 38–9. See also the publicly available *Unification News*, March 1987, 5.
33. The kind of process that is being described might be elaborated further from the perspective of probability theory; see Bartholemew (1984) It could also be analyzed in terms of the characteristics of a charismatic leadership.
34. CARP is an acronym for the *Collegiate Association for the Research of Principles* and is currently the chief Unification organization concerned with "witnessing" (recruitment) in the West. It produces its own journal, the *World Student Times*, which describes itself as "your international campus paper," and contains some vehement attacks on communism—see, for example, the issue of 18 November 1983 which contains a number of highly critical news items about communism in Latin America and a long article entitled "Why a Christian can't be a Communist" (8), as well as the promise of CARP as a "Creative Alternative to Marxism" and a plea for "Global Patriotism" (4).
35. *The Independent*, 11 August 1987.
36. There were, nonetheless, Marxist participants from other countries, including the People's Republic of China, Bulgaria, Yugoslavia—and the United States.
37. It is, however, noteworthy that an article in the *Guardian* of 13 March 1989, declared, without rancor, that the paper neither could nor should be lightly dismissed.

References

Barker, Eileen. 1983. "Doing Love: Tensions in the Ideal Family." In Gene G. James (ed.), *The Family and the Unification Church*. New York: Rose of Sharon Press.
———. 1984. *The Making of a Moonie: Brainwashing or Choice?* Oxford and New York: Blackwell.
———. 1987. *New Religious Movements and Political Orders*. Centre for the Study of Religion and Society Pamphlet Library No. 15, University of Kent.
Bartholemew, David. 1984. *New Religious Movements and Political Orders*. Centre for the Study of Religion and Society Pamphlet Library No. 15, University of Kent.
Bartholemew, David. 1984. *The God of Chance*. London: SCM Press.
Eu, Hyo Won. 1982. *Divine Principle*. Washington DC: HSA-UWC, 1982.
Grace, James H. 1985. *Sex and Marriage in the Unification Movement: A Sociological Study*. New York and Toronto: Edwin Mellen Press.
Kajikura, G. (n.d.) "A Prospectus" in Brochure of The International Highway Construction Corporation, J-150 Tokyo, Japan.
Kwak, Chung Hwan. 1980. *Outline of the Principle: Level 4*. New York: Holy Spirit Association for the Unification of World Christianity.
Moon, Sun Myung. 1982. "Founder's Address." In *The Search for Absolute Values and the Creation of the New World*, volume I, Proceedings of the Tenth ICUS, November 1981, Seoul, Korea. New York: ICF Press.
Quebedeaux, Richard and Rodney Sawatsky (eds.). 1979. *Evangelical-Unification Dialogue*. New York: Rose of Sharon Press.
Quebedeaux, Richard (ed.). 1982. *Lifestyle: Conversations with Members of the Unification Church*. New York: Rose of Sharon Press.
Tsirpanlis, C. (ed.). 1981. *Orthodox-Unification Dialogue*. New York: Rose of Sharon Press.

12

THE GLOBALIZATION OF AMERICAN TELEVANGELISM

Jeffrey K. Hadden

In the Beginning

"IN THE BEGINNING GOD CREATED THE HEAVEN AND THE EARTH" (Gen. 1:1). Thus begins the sacred texts of Christendom. In the nineteenth century there was another beginning; the beginning of the electronic communication revolution. To evangelical Christians who take seriously Christ's commandment to go into all the world and preach the gospel to every creature (Mark 16:15), this revolution is not just one among many significant scientific advances in the nineteenth and early twentieth century. Rather, it is perhaps the paramount event in history since God sent his Son to offer atonement for human sin. The ability to transmit the voice and the visual image of the preacher has, for the first time, made it possible to reach all humankind with the Gospel message.

It is not accidental that evangelical Christians should single out electronic communication as a development of such importance. While the fundamental rudiments of electronic communication were unfolding in the United States, England, and Italy, a millenarian movement of profound importance was unfolding in England and the U.S. Inspired by John Nelson Darby, dispensational pre-millennialism postulated a new eschatology which forecasted the immanent return of Christ. But

Christ's return was necessarily contingent upon fulfillment of his commandment to preach the gospel to all the world.

In this context, the confluence of belief that the end of history was near and the creation of broadcast technologies took on a special significance. For those who became involved in religious broadcasting, this medium was early recognized as the instrument God had provided to made possible the fulfillment of Christ's Great Commission.[1]

To the secular mind, the perspective is baffling and even preposterous. The electronic communication revolution which has brought us radio and television was merely the logical culmination of hundreds of experimental successes and failures which unfolded during the nineteenth and early twentieth centuries. In secular histories of broadcasting one finds virtually no mention of religion or religious broadcasting.[2] But those evangelical Christians who have so effectively harnessed the airwaves for the purpose of propagating the Gospel know a different history. For them, the unfolding of the mysteries that gave birth to radio and television had profound providential guidance.

If the hard-nosed secular cynic sees the evangelical "creation [of broadcasting] story" as utter nonsense, one who listens attentively and with an open mind will soon understand why some evangelicals attribute so much significance to the development of broadcast technology as well as why they are so deeply committed to mastering the use of this technology. An examination of the development of electronic communications from their perspective presents to unbelievers an almost unnerving sense of the intertwining, indeed seeming inseparability, of the milestones of broadcasting and acts of faith. To believers, this history provides a confirmation of God's providential hand. Let me briefly recount a few central milestones in their creation story.

- If it was Samuel F.B. Morse's diligence that led to the installation in 1844 of the first successful telegraphic line connecting Washington and Baltimore, Morse himself seemed clearly to have experienced a sense of awe, even sacredness in what he was doing. This is evidenced by the choice of his first transmission: "WHAT HATH GOD WROUGHT!" (Head 1972: 108)
- Radio, as we now know it, began in 1896 with Guglielmo Marconi's discovery of wireless communication, but the first successful voice transmission occurred a decade later when a Canadian engineer, Reginald Fessenden, beamed a signal from the coast of Massachusetts to ships at sea. The date was December 24, 1906, Christmas Eve. The content of this first transmission was a religious service which included a violin solo (Gounod's "O Holy

Night"), readings from the gospel of Luke, and the singing of a sacred song (Handel's "Largo").

Religious broadcasters, to the person, agree with broadcast historian J. Harold Ellens that "[i]t is not without significance that the first voice broadcast was a Christian religious celebration" (1974: 16). Given the rapid expansion and experimentation with wireless transmission, any number of persons might have been the first to transmit a human voice. But God chose this time, the eve of the birth of Christ, and this man, a devout Christian who understood the significance of his act to foretell the most significant development of the twentieth century. Of all the developments in the history of broadcasting this is the most central in the creation story. But there are other developments which may be seen as signs of God's Providential engagement.

- Radio station KDKA in Pittsburgh became the first commercially licensed station to transmit programs for the general public. Their programming commenced on November 2, 1920 with the reporting of the Harding-Cox presidential election returns. Two months later on Sunday evening, January 2, 1921, KDKA claimed the first remote broadcast and the first broadcast of a church service. It was also an ecumenical service of sorts. To be as unobtrusive as possible, the two engineers, one Roman Catholic, the other Jewish, decked themselves in robes and sat with the choir at the Calvary Episcopal Church located some ten miles from the transmitting studio (Armstrong 1979: 19, 20).
- Marconi, who left Italy for England when he was unable to drum up interest in his experiments, returned to his native land to provide technical assistance in the construction of Vatican Radio, an instrument created for the purpose of communicating with Catholics around the globe. The task was accomplished in 1931. It was Marconi, the "father of radio," who introduced the Holy Father to the world in the inauguration of the first global network (Browne 1982: 306).[3]
- Before Franklin Roosevelt's radio "fireside chats" to a depression-stricken nation, or Adolph Hitler's use of radio to arouse Nazism in Germany, or Winston Churchill's use of the BBC to calm Londoners during the *blitzkrieg*, Father Charles E. Coughlin, a Roman Catholic priest from Detroit, was the first person to attract a large and loyal radio following.[4] Many evangelical Christians then and now, would not want to associate themselves with either Coughlin's religious or political messages. But the unequivocal lesson of Father Coughlin's tenure as a broadcaster is that he

demonstrated how a charismatic figure can utilize the airwaves to mobilize the masses.

From a modest beginning in October, 1926 on station WJR in Detroit, Father Coughlin rapidly broadened his base and in 1930 commenced broadcasting nationally on CBS. By 1932 his audience had reportedly reached forty-five million weekly.[5] By 1934 Coughlin's mail was reported to have "exceeded that of every other human being" and *Fortune magazine* heralded Coughlin as "the biggest thing that every happened to radio" (Ellens 1974: 57).

Perhaps even more revealing of his popularity in America was a survey conducted by a Philadelphia radio station. When listeners were asked if they would prefer Father Coughlin or the New York Philharmonic on Sunday afternoons, Coughlin was the choice by an amazing 187,000 votes to 12,000 for the Philharmonic (Barnouw 1968: 46)!

Much of Coughlin's popularity can be attributed to his appeal to the working classes and underprivileged during the depression years. But in spite of his enormous popularity, Coughlin did not succeed in molding his loyal radio audience into a social movement army.[6] What he demonstrated, however, was the potential for a fiery charismatic orator to move the masses.

- The development of the technological capability to transmit video images did not lag far behind audio transmission. The British Broadcasting Corporation began operating a limited television service in 1936, and RCA excited visitors to the 1939 World's Fair in New York City with the exhibition of a television system. But World War II displaced parts and personnel in this emerging industry (Bogart 1972: 8). It didn't take long after the war, however, before the development of television took off, much like the explosion of radio in the early 1920s.

When television became available to the masses, religion was again on center stage. Roman Catholic Bishop Fulton Sheen was the first superstar of television. The television industry generally attributes this acclaim to comedian Milton Berle; but when Sheen and Berle were aired head to head the bishop pulled the larger audience. Sheen's combination of a simple inspirational message punctuated with humor, his flowing crimson robe, the "angels" who erased his blackboard, and the close-up camera shots capturing the twinkle in his eyes, made him the top figure in all of television until a church superior, alleged to be jealous of Sheen's success, forced him to give up his telecast.

After the formative years, and the prominent role played by Roman Catholics in the milestone events cited above, the Catholic Church has not been a major player in the development of the burgeoning religious broadcasting industry in the U.S. Given that Roman Catholics constitute the single largest religious body in the U.S., they are conspicuous by their absence. But the absence of Catholics is no more conspicuous than that of all the major Protestant denominations. Of the ten largest religious bodies in the U.S. only the Southern Baptists have a significant presence in media. And the Southern Baptists, of course, are a conservative evangelical body.

The religious airwaves in America are dominated by those conservative evangelicals who, from the beginning, envisioned broadcast technology to be God's way of making possible the fulfillment of the Great Commission. But it was not always this way. For the first quarter of a century of broadcasting, evangelical broadcasters fought a losing struggle to keep a foothold in broadcasting. Their adversaries were not only the secular broadcasters who didn't particularly want to deal with them, but also liberal Protestant broadcasters who were in competition with them. Liberal Protestant periodicals were quick to label the emotional style and fund-raising techniques of evangelicals as "religious hucksterism." Only gradually did the balance of power shift to the evangelicals.

From the Margin to Domination

From the time the networks began to form in the mid-1920s, evangelical broadcasters had a progressively difficult time getting on the air. By the mid-1940s they had become firmly convinced that the networks and the liberal Protestant traditions were actively engaged in a conspiracy to keep them off the air. In 1944 evangelicals created the National Religious Broadcasters as a step toward redressing their grievance.

The first official act of this newly created trade organization was to retain a Washington-based communications attorney. Second, they created a code of ethics which placed distance between themselves and certain broadcasters which the liberal church traditions had explicitly label "radio racketeers." Third, they petitioned the networks to reconsider their policies. And, fourth, they lobbied the Federal Communications Commission for help in ameliorating the unequal distribution of air time. One of the most important policy decision they made, commencing in 1956, was to hold their annual meetings in Washington. It didn't take long before they began to learn their way around political circles in the nation's capitol. Their annual Congressional Breakfasts brings scores of dignitaries from Capitol Hill, and the annual Federal

Communications Commission Luncheon usually finds most of the Commissioners at the head table.

The most important breakthrough for evangelicals came in 1960 when the FCC handed down a ruling which erased a long standing distinction between free (sustaining) air time and commercially sponsored programming. Prior to this ruling, radio and television stations had been reluctant to sell air time, and the free time they allocated went largely to more "mainline" or "establishment" religious traditions.

The Communications Act of 1934 gave the FCC the authority to license individual stations, which amounted to a monopoly of a scarce commodity. There was a tacit understanding that those who were granted the monopoly owed the community an unspecified amount of "public service" broadcasting. The significance of the FCC ruling was that stations could now sell air time and also receive "public interest credit." Evangelicals rushed in and bought up all the available air time and the liberal Protestant and Catholic traditions, which had received air time free as part of the "public service" arrangement, found themselves unwilling or unable to pay for air time. As a result, they were mostly squeezed from the air. The technological advancements of the 1970s and 1980s have all worked to enhance the advantage gained by the evangelicals in the 1960s. Communication satellites and the expansion of the number of channels available for transmission created the opportunity for broadcasting entrepreneurs to create religious networks. The invention of the video tape made it possible for many more would-be broadcasters to inexpensively get in on the action. The availability of the religious networks provided an outlet for the distribution of programs. And the expansion of cable during the 1980s has significantly enhanced the opportunities for religious networks to deliver their programs to households across the country.

Religious broadcasting in the U.S. now exists on a vastly larger scale than in any other nation. In fact, it exists on a scale beyond the recognition of most Americans. Furthermore, it is presently experiencing a period of enormous growth.

In 1985, *The Directory of Religious Broadcasting* reported a total of 1,043 religious radio stations and 96 religious television stations in the U.S. The 1989 Directory shows these figures increasing to 1,485 and 336 respectively. This represents a 42 percent growth in radio and a 265 percent growth in television stations. The power of these stations ranges from very low to large enough to blanket major markets. The most recent *Directory* reports a total of 648 organizations producing religious radio programs and 476 organizations producing religious television programs. For both radio and television production, this represents a little better than a 25 percent growth in a half a decade. Furthermore, the number of organizations producing radio and television programs for distribution outside the U.S. has grown in this same time frame from 211 to 301, an increase of 43 percent.

One important explanation for this phenomenal growth is the fact that several relatively new evangelical schools have created departments or schools which offer degrees in radio and television broadcasting. CBN University, Liberty University, Jimmy Swaggart Bible College, and Oral Roberts University are a few of the more visible schools. In colleges and universities of the proselytizing traditions, the broadcast curriculum is very popular. Thus, in addition to the traditional practice of producing graduates who go out and start new churches, these broadcast-oriented schools are now producing a generation of graduates who are going out and raising the money to start radio and television stations.

How much future growth this burgeoning industry might sustain is difficult to estimate. At the present time there is very little commercial sponsorship for either religious radio or TV. If religious broadcasters are able to make a breakthrough in commercial sponsorship (advertising) then growth could likely be sustained for perhaps decades. Without a commercial breakthrough it seems fairly clear that growth will necessarily taper off for lack of financial resources.

In addition to its sheer size, religious broadcasting in the U.S. has three defining characteristics. First, as noted above, broadcasting is dominated by conservative evangelical traditions. Of the seventy-five or so syndicated television broadcasters, the large majority can be classified as either fundamentalist or Pentecostal. A similar preponderance of conservative traditions is found in syndicated radio. And the vast majority of religious radio and television stations are owned by religious conservatives.

Second, there is very little denominational sponsorship of religious broadcasting. While some individual broadcasters belong to denominations, they operate their radio/television ministries outside any authority structure of denominations. Many of the broadcasters pastor churches, but they have independently incorporated their broadcast ministries as autonomous *parachurch* structures, answerable only to boards they have hand selected.

Third, the vast majority of religious broadcasting is quasi-commercial. In television, broadcasters purchase the time to air their programs from local stations. Unlike normal commercial broadcasting, where advertisers purchase time, most religious broadcasters use a proportion of their air time to solicit contribution from audiences. Others offer premiums, like books, jewelry, records, and cassette tapes in exchange for a donation of a specified amount. Over the years the amount of sustaining (free) time offered by local stations and networks has diminished to less than five percent of all religious broadcast time. Most religious broadcasting on radio is aired over non-profit religious stations. Both the stations and the syndicated broadcasters whom they air seek contributions from the audience or offer items for sale.

The question might still remain: Why can't the "mainline" religious traditions get in on the action?[7] There are several reasons. First, as should be implicit from the discussion above, religious broadcasting has found its niche within the broader context of the free-enterprise system. Evangelicals have a product to sell. The product is Jesus Christ and his gift of salvation to those who will accept. Evangelicals are energetic and enthusiastic proselytizers. They are not ashamed of the Gospel, nor are they ashamed to ask others to contribute financially to their work. Both on and off the air, they are unrelenting in their pleas for money to support their ministries.

Notwithstanding the expressed intent to evangelize among the unsaved, the natural constituency for evangelical broadcasters are believers. As a group, evangelical believers tend to be more deeply involved in experiencing and practicing their religion. The advent of religious broadcasting provided yet another way, not an alternative for them to involve themselves in their faith. Furthermore, evangelicals have a tradition of generous giving.

All of this adds up to a success formula for evangelicals that the mainline Protestant and Catholic traditions cannot match. To begin with, the liberal church traditions have rather more reserved notions of evangelism, witness, and Christ's commandment to spread the Good News. They tend to believe that Christian witness is exhibited in the character and quality of one's life. The very thought of confronting one's neighbor or fellow worker to ask if he or she is saved is, to put it mildly, rather tacky if not downright abhorrent. In a word heavy-handed proselytization is not a part of the mainline Protestant and Catholic traditions. Furthermore, most of them consider both the on and off air fund-raising appeals of evangelicals to be down right tasteless.

So, where are they to raise the funds to support radio and television ministries? No denomination has sufficient discretionary budget to support the high cost of national television. A national television program could only be financed with a very large philanthropic gift, or a fund-raising campaign.

Instructive of the latter is the case of the United Methodist Church, the third largest religious body (behind Roman Catholics and Southern

Baptists) in the U.S. In the early part of this decade the Methodists launched a $25 million fund-raising campaign. Their plan was to purchase a major metropolitan area television station and with the profits from this station develop and pay for the distribution of religious programming. The campaign was a dismal failure. In the end, they had a difficult time paying back the $1 million they borrowed for the campaign (Lyles 1982: 685).

There are many reasons why the Methodist effort failed and why other denominations would not likely have much success with a capital campaign. Denominational bureaucracies are cumbersome structures for the creation of new initiatives, especially when the initiative requires a significant capital outlay. Resources are scarce and people have different priorities. Even if a denomination could agree on a strategy that everyone could get behind, they would still face the problem of deciding who, among the many worthy preachers in the denomination, would be the featured speaker.

The mainline Protestant and Catholic traditions simply don't have the organizational structure or fiscal resources to successfully compete with the evangelical broadcasters. The entrepreneurial model, free from the constraints of church bureaucracy, is simply a more efficient means for developing a television ministry.

In the battle for access to the airwaves, representatives of mainline Protestant traditions have substantially been reduced to protesting the FCC policies that have effectively squeezed them off the air and criticizing the evangelical broadcasters.

So what is the future of evangelical religious broadcasters in the U.S.? On the one hand we have seen the evidence of sustained growth in both radio and television. On the other hand loom the televangelism scandals of 1987 and 1988. Clearly the sexual and financial scandals in the Jim Bakker and Jimmy Swaggart ministries did tarnish the public image of all broadcasters. But not all ministries were hurt, and some that immediately felt the shock waves recovered fairly quickly. The financial and audience losses of some of the majors provided the opportunity for other broadcasters to attract new listeners and viewers.

There is no question that religious broadcasting in America is now going through a major shake up and period of transition. In the end, I think religious broadcasting will be strengthened rather than weakened by the scandals.

There are some interest groups in the U.S. who would like to get the religious broadcasters off the air altogether. The scandals provided them the opportunity to promote this perspective. It is very unlikely, however, that this will happen. The First Amendment of the U.S.

Constitution which grants free exercise and free establishment of religion, serves as a powerful protection against Congressional legislation or Federal Communications Commission regulations which would treat religious broadcasters differently from other broadcasters. As long as the U.S. pursues a policy of maximizing access to the air waves, religious broadcasters will not be excluded.

As religious broadcasting struggles in the U.S. to overcome the negative effects of the scandals, I think we can expect to see renewed efforts at developing international broadcasting. The final section of this paper examines the role of America in international broadcasting in the past and explores the prospects for an expansionist role in the future.

The Global Quest

The *World Radio TV Handbook* recently identified 27 international religious broadcasting organizations (Frost 1985). Of these, four may be identified as major organizations: Far East Broadcasting Association (FEBA), Far East Broadcasting Company (FEBC), Heralding Christ Jesus' Blessing (HCJB), and Trans World Radio (TWR). Three of the "Big Four" were founded and are operated by Americans. The fourth, FEBA, is a British organization. In addition, as noted above, there are more than 300 American agencies producing programming for foreign transmission. Much of this material is broadcast over one of the three major networks.

The first international evangelical radio station was HCJ8, and they went on the air from Quito, Ecuador on Christmas Day of 1931. Vatican Radio had commenced broadcasting in February of that same year.[8] In the beginning, they broadcast two hours daily on shortwave radio in Spanish from a converted sheep shed. From this location high in the Andes mountains their signal could be picked up in much of South America.

The expansion of international broadcasting was a latent and unanticipated consequence of World War II. Surplus equipment offered the foundation of a global radio ministry as abandoned war radio transmitter stations were resurrected as international outposts for missionary transmissions.

Robert Bowman, who established the Far East Broadcasting Company in Manila in 1948, and Paul Freed, who founded Trans World Radio in Morocco, in 1954, were the most successful of the religious broadcasting entrepreneurs.

Bowman's objective, from the beginning, was to reach Chinese with the Gospel message. With voluntary contributions FEBC soon had transmitters spread across several Far East islands beamed toward China. Within a few years FEBC was broadcasting in 36 languages and dialects to both mainland China and parts of Asia. Bowman has retained a strong interest in Asia, and in reaching persons in nations where missionary activity is prohibited, but his operations have become global. In 1987, FEBC operated 32 international broadcasting stations with transmitters in five nations. They had a broadcast schedule of 300 program hours daily in over 100 languages and dialects. Their 1987 operations budget was $10.9 million.

Freed used a Nazi propaganda transmitter base in Tangier, Morocco to launch Trans World Radio's global ministry. From this strategic location TWR could reach people in Europe, North Africa, the Middle East, and behind the Iron Curtain. In 1956, just two years after its launch date, TWR was broadcasting in 20 languages and reaching 40 nations via two 10,000 watt transmitters. In 1987 TWR had transmitters in seven locations with a total transmission power of 4.4 million watts. Programs were broadcast in more than 75 languages. TWR has a staff of 700 and in 1987 their operations budget was $18 million.

HCJB has retained its location in the Andes mountains as its headquarters and focal point for transnational broadcast operations. In addition, they have developed a multi media presence in Ecuador which includes AM/FM radio and television. Over the years HCJB has expanded their operations so that by 1985 they had personnel in 22 countries. This staff seeks to develop programing that is appropriate and sensitive to the diverse cultural regions where they broadcast. In addition to covering South and Central America and the Caribbean, their signals are beamed into the South Pacific and, in the evenings, to Eastern Europe. Their total operating budget for 1987 was $9.7 million, representing a growth of 13.8 percent over 1986.

International electronic evangelization has three significant foci or targets. The first thrust of religious broadcasting activity is aimed at what I would call forbidden territories. This includes the communist nations of Eastern Europe, the USSR, and China and virtually all of the 40 nations in which the majority of the population is Muslim. A considerable proportion of the resources of international broadcasting has been expended in developing transnational radio signals which can reach those peoples of the earth whose governments do not permit religious broadcasting, or in the case of Islamic nations, prohibit Christian broadcasting.

A second focus of broadcasting activity has been aimed at non-Christian nations of the Third World. The non-Muslim nations of Africa, especially nations with large proportions of tribal religious traditions, have long been a favorite target of broadcasters and missionaries. In the Far East, broadcasting can claim some role in the rapid growth of Christianity in Korea and is likely to play an increasing role in the immediate future.

The third target involves evangelical missionaries and broadcasters engaging in head on competition with Roman Catholicism. This effort is substantially, although not exclusively, located in Central American and South America. In Brazil and throughout Central America Pentecostals have experienced very significant growth. Broadcasting seems to have played an important role in this growth.

The combined efforts of transnational religious broadcasters is quite impressive. Robert Fortner, an authority on international broadcasting, estimates that the three major transnational broadcasters alone produce approximately 20,000 hours of programing each week in over 125 languages. This makes them "the largest single international radio users, broadcasting more hours per week in more languages than any other transnational service," according to Fortner (1988: 1). The 1983 *Annual Report and Handbook* of the BBC reported that the total external broadcasting services from the ten largest national exporters was 9,459 hours (in Head 1985: 343). If Fortner's figures are reliable, the religious broadcasters far exceed all other transnational broadcasters. Even if these figures represent a substantial overestimation of broadcast hours, it is still evident that we are looking at a significant world-wide presence.[9]

The sheer volume of broadcasting tells us nothing about the size of the audiences they are reaching or their effectiveness in communicating their messages to their audiences. Audience research is not a highly developed science, but existing research suggests that transnational broadcasters typically do not draw large audiences. Still, one can reasonably conclude that if transnational broadcasting were totally ineffective some countries, particularly the Soviet Union, would not spend large sums of money to jam the signals.

Compared to other major transnational broadcasters like the BBC, Radio Moscow, and the Voice of America, existing audience research suggests that the religious broadcasters do not fare particularly well. The religious broadcasters, however, are skeptical of audience studies and prefer to rely on their mail as an indirect indicator of audience penetration. No broadcaster systematically publishes figures on mail volume, and the wide range of figures which periodically appear in their publications gives cause to question the accuracy of at least some the numbers reported.

Once major broadcaster recently published a brochure in which they claimed to have reached a milestone of 500,000 letters in 1978, but no where in their literature could I find an update for total mail volume. Perhaps a more reliable figure comes from a broadcaster claiming the receipt of 91,000 letters in 1988 from 127 countries (Goerzen 1989: 14). More frequently, one finds figures for specific programs.

An interesting datum was recently reported by the Far East Broadcasting Company. Transmitting to all 11 time zones in the Soviet Union, FEBC claims that "glasnost" has had a dramatic impact on their mail from the USSR. Prior to "glasnost," FEBC was receiving approximately a dozen letters a month. This meager response began to change significantly in 1988 and, by March 1989, the mail room received 1,623 from the USSR (Hague 1989: 10).

Just as it is difficult to assess the accuracy of the claims about mail volume, we have no way of estimating what mail volume might indicate in terms of audience size. It does seems reasonable, however, to assume that the proportion of listeners who write has to be a very small ratio of the total listening audience.

All of this leaves us with the unsatisfactory, but unavoidable, conclusion that we don't really know what kind of impact the transnational religious broadcasters are having. There is undeniably a global presence. Those who are engaging in this broadcast activity are receiving sufficient positive reinforcement to encourage them not only to continue, but to expand their broadcasting activities. But just how much collective impact they are having is unknown and probably unknowable by measures that would satisfy the criteria of social science inquiry.

My own assessment is that they are likely having a greater impact than their critics would acknowledge, but they are probably significantly less effective than their own propaganda claims.

I began this inquiry by noting that rhetorical zeal for reaching all the world with the Gospel before the Second Coming of Christ has undergirded evangelical interest in broadcasting from the beginning of radio. Even casual listening to American broadcasters will reveal that this rhetoric continues unabated today. But if we apply the standard of resource allocation, it quickly becomes evident that the rhetoric is not matched with resources.

In 1987 the three giant international religious broadcasters had a combined budget of $38.6 million. By comparison, the three largest U.S. television broadcasters had combined budgets in excess of $400 million. The total budget for domestic radio and television broadcasting in the U.S. most certainly exceeded one million dollars in 1987. It is very doubtful that the total U.S. sponsored transnational broadcasting reached one-tenth of that sum.

Most of the American televangelists have some involvement in international broadcasting, but their actual outlays for transnational broadcasting tends to be small. The Christian Broadcasting Network, which probably has the most extensive engagement in foreign broadcasting, spent $8.1 million (4.6 percent) of its 1987 budget for this purpose.[10] Compared to U.S. expenditures for religious broadcasting, thus, the international effort is meager. If the effectiveness of international religious broadcasting to date is unclear, I think it quite likely that both the volume and effectiveness of this activity will increase significantly for the balance of this century and well into the next. It is unlikely that any nation will ever experience the sheer volume of religious broadcasting that we have in the U.S. At the same time, it seems quite probable that in many countries the character of culture and politics will, in some measure, be shaped by religious broadcasting. This will not happen merely by an increased volume of broadcasting, but by significant enhancement and sophistication in the delivery and content of the broadcasters' messages.

I would cite two important reasons to expect a significant thrust in global broadcasting activities during the final decade of the twentieth century. First, there has been a veritable explosion of enthusiasm for reaching the whole world with the Gospel by the year 2000. David Barrett, editor of the celebrated *World Christian Encyclopedia*, has identified 230 separate plans for evangelizing the world by 2000! Most of these evangelism efforts involve the utilization of broadcasting and/or other instruments of electronic communication, e.g., films, video cassettes, and audio cassettes. Furthermore, there is evidence to indicate that many of these programs are cooperating with other efforts, sharing resources, avoiding duplicated efforts, etc. Some of the major transnational broadcasters have entered formal agreements in order to try and maximize their impact (Frazee 1989: 12).

A second factor which bodes well for increasing efforts in international broadcasting is the tremendous advances in broadcasting technology over the past couple of decades. Increasingly sophisticated delivery systems, including direct broadcast satellites which have sufficient power to be received by small antennas, reduce the cost of getting messages almost anywhere. And the rapidly declining cost of audio and video cassette opens a world of programming opportunities.

An attempt to develop a detailed analysis of how the emerging technologies will be adapted to the interests of international religious broadcasters would be premature at this point. Nor can we precisely specify how the broadcasters will become more sophisticated in the delivery of their messages. But some general perimeters are evident. In considerable measure, these perimeters are discernable from the lessons learned by U.S. broadcasters.

The most important lesson of American radio and television is that broadcasters are learning how to discern their audiences and deliver a message to them. The big news in radio broadcasting during the past decade-and-a-half has been the recognition of market segmentation. Taking advantage of both the FM and the AM bans, highly segmented broadcasting has emerged to meet the needs of many highly diverse interest groups.

The explosion of community Christian radio stations reflects a recognition of, and a taking advantage of, this market segmentation. The local community station provides an outlet for local religious news and broadcasts as well as an expansion of opportunities for syndicated programming.

Religious television broadcasters too have come to recognize the need to target broadcasts to their natural constituencies. This was a lesson that didn't come easy. From the advent of video tape and the subsequent rapid expansion of program syndication, until the mid-1980s, American televangelists operated on the principle that "more is better." The major broadcasters got their programs in virtually every market in the country and, in the major markets, they bought multiple time slots. Gradually they came to recognize that audience size and revenues were not simply a function of saturation, but that time slots were very important and that some markets were much better than others.

During the 1970s, the emergence of satellites provided a technology for a much more efficient delivery system. Pat Robertson, recognizing this, created the Christian Broadcasting System. He was followed by Jim Bakker (PTL Inspirational Network) and Paul Crouch (Trinity Broadcasting System). During the 1980s, the rapid expansion of cable systems in the U.S. provided the means for receiving religious broadcasts without the high costs of buying time for syndicated telecasts in every market. Systematic research conducted by CBN revealed that satellite to cable was a much more economical and efficient delivery system.[11]

From the beginning, the transnational religious broadcasters have had an abiding commitment to reaching those who have not heard the Gospel message. Some critics would say that they have had an obsession with reaching those in the forbidden zones, e.g., those in communist and Muslim nations. With the benefit of hindsight, it is evident that a good bit of their broadcasting was based on the assumption that if they could penetrate into zones where missionaries could not preach, that God would miraculously use their culturally naive words to reach the hearts of those who had no background for comprehending the Christian message. And like their counterparts in the U.S., they operated on the assumption that more is better. They have built more powerful transmitters, broadcast more hours, and translated into an ever greater number of languages on the assumption that all of these efforts would reap dividends of saved souls according to a formula that only God almighty understood.

It is unlikely that the major transnationals are going to significantly abandon these assumptions or their preoccupation with reaching the multitudes in communist and Muslim nations. But what we can expect, as a new generation of leadership takes over these organizations and new organizations become significant players, is a more sophisticated and subtle approach. We can expect to see programming that meets specific cultural needs of the audiences they are seeking to reach. And, in direct proportion to their ability to meet indigenous needs, they will have an opportunity to introduce Gospel messages. And they will learn to do so in ways that are sensitive to the cultural traditions of their specific audiences.[12]

The new generation of international religious broadcasters will be much more adept at asking hard-nosed market questions. What is the evidence that we are reaching the audiences we want to reach? How many are we reaching? Are we effectively communicating? What is the evidence of results?

This new pragmatism will lead broadcasters to invest their resources where they can see that they are getting results. As the pragmatists consider the results of their efforts, they will eschew spending money to get their programs on the high-powered transmitters of TWR, HCJB, and FEBC. Emphasis, rather, will be on segmenting markets where they can more readily assess the impact of their work. This will likely lead to an emphasis on broadcasting in counties that are open to missionaries. The success of Pentecostals in Central America is a good illustration of how missionaries and broadcasters have worked together with indigenous Christians with considerable success (Poloma 1981; Smith 1988).

Three broad strategies for broadcast evangelism can be identified. The first is the transnational strategy. A significant proportion of the international effort to date can be so characterized. American broadcasters working in varying degrees with indigenous people have sought to beam broadcasts into nations without the authorization of local officials.

A second strategy is to create syndicated programming which is adapted for broadcasting within specific nations. This may involve (1) merely translating programs into local languages, (2) adapting programming, or (3) creating programming for specific nations and cultures.

All three of these methods of syndication have been used with some effectiveness in Central America (Smith 1988). In a four-nation survey conducted in Central America before the revelation of Jimmy Swaggart's involvement with a prostitute in New Orleans, Dennis Smith found that Swaggart had a phenomenal name recognition of 73 percent. Among non-Catholics, the recognition was 84 percent (Smith 1988: 77). Several other radio and television evangelists had name recognitions above the fifty percent level, testifying to the power of broadcasting to capture public consciousness.[13]

In a pragmatic marketplace, success will attract more vendors. Pentecostals have clearly had some success in many countries throughout Central and South America. Hence, others are certain to follow. The fact that a single language opens most of the continent will be another incentive attracting more broadcasters.

The third strategy for developing international impact is to work with indigenous leadership. Successful indigenous evangelists, wherever they are located, can be expected to try and expand their ministries by radio and/or television. The new pragmatists will recognize the value of providing technical and financial support.

Over the next decade, the rush to evangelize the world by the year 2000 is likely to lead some of the newcomers to international broadcasting to repeat the worst mistakes that were earlier made by the now maturing transnational broadcasters. Zealotry and cultural insensitivity will have made Christian broadcasters very unpopular in some regions where broadcasting and missionary activity is today at least tolerated. But there will also be successes.

The religious broadcasters of the early twenty-first century will learn from both the excesses and the successes of the late twentieth century. Beyond the borders of the United States there are two very significant developments emerging that have relevance for global religious broadcasting. The first is occurring in Western Europe and other democratic nations; the second is a Third-World phenomenon.

If the BBC has long represented a paragon of responsible and culturally enlightened broadcasting, admired and emulated by other nations of the free world, it has also had a stultifying impact on popular culture. It has now been three decades since pirate stations began broadcasting from the North Sea. Today, most informed persons would agree that the pirates did much to stimulate the broadening of the range of broadcasting options in Europe (Head 1985: 112–16). Most of Europe has taken steps toward expanding broadcasting opportunities in a manner that has some similarity to the American commercial model.

The second development in broadcasting can be succinctly characterized as the battle over the New World Information Order (NWIO) principle. NWIO is a declaration of communications sovereignty by Third World nations against the developed nations. The declaration maintains that the free flow doctrine of communication, which is embraced by the United Nations Declaration of Freedom of Information in 1946, is not really free flow, but a one-way stream of cultural indoctrination.

Military colonialism, according to the NWIO advocates, has been replaced by a neocolonialism in which the communication flow is the foundation for economic and cultural dominance (Head 1985: 378–394). Much of the West, but especially the United States, sees the case as overstated and, further, that it results in an unholy alliance between Third World countries and totalitarian regimes.

Both of these developments have implications for the future of international evangelical broadcasting. Some scholars feel that the opening up of commercial broadcasting options in Europe will, sooner or later, result in the transfer of the already limited religious broadcasting to the commercial stations. There, under the laws of the free market, religious broadcasting will die for lack of interest. This analysis could be correct insofar as it goes, but it ignores the fact that evangelicals were among the major advertisers on the pirate stations (Head 1985: 114; Harris 1970: 55).

There are two potential lessons here. First, if religious broadcasting were to effectively disappear from Europe, it could well invite a return of the pirates. This time the pirates would be evangelicals committed to the proposition that God's law and purposes stand above the laws of men. Assuming the broadcast pirates were Americans, it could create international diplomatic riffs. But potentially more important, the fact that the broadcasting had been declared illegal could help stimulate the development of an evangelical movement in Europe.

The second implication emerges in the context of the growing sophistication and increasing inexpensive broadcast technologies. In a sense, transnational broadcasting is a form of pirate broadcasting. At least it is so viewed by nations that do not welcome the invaders. Domestic pirating is usually associated with revolutionary activity, such as Fidel Castro's illegal broadcasts from the mountains in western Cuba. But, in fact, domestic pirating is more common than is generally recognized. It occurs in many forms, including what might be called "electronic graffiti" (Head 1985: 112). The potential for domestic pirating is much greater that anything we have seen to date.

It seems quite unlikely that any nation could stop the flow of audio and video cassettes across its borders. Further, Direct-Broadcast Satellites are popping up all over the world. In short, the prospects of keeping materials out of a country are virtually impossible. And light-weight mobile equipment could be very difficult to track. While it is no doubt far-fetched to predict that the Third World will become infested with evangelical broadcast pirates, it is not unreasonable to imagine that there will be some instances. And, further, it is possible that these bandits could have a significant political impact in some regions if not entire countries.

The more probable route for evangelical broadcasters to make significant inroads in the Third World is by holding out attractive contracts to the leaders of resource poor nations. The leadership of the Third World is not uniformly committed to the NWIO philosophy. But even some who are find themselves, nevertheless, short of both money and technological know-how to develop broadcasting.

Some evangelical broadcasters will be in a position to offer the broadcasting equipment along with the manpower to install and run both radio and television stations in exchange for the right to produce some limited amount of religious broadcasting. And some Third World leaders are likely to find the exchange sufficiently attractive that they will discount the prospect of the evangelicals making any significant proselytizing inroads in their country. And as HCJB has done with the government of Ecuador, the broadcasters may be willing to make agreements to avoiding broadcasting that would be critical of the government. Further, Third World nation leaders will likely assume that they can evict broadcasters if they become troublesome.

Conclusion

From the very beginning of radio transmission, evangelicals have viewed broadcasting as having a unique place in their escatology. The transmission of the human voice, and then visual images, is a special gift which God has provided to permit the completion of the Great Commandment to preach the Gospel to all the world.

During the twentieth century, this theology has interfaced with ever-expanding broadcast technologies in a free market economy to produce a religious broadcasting empire that is quite unlike anything else in the world. In this paper I have attempted to explain how this has happened as a requisite to examining the potential for religious global conquest via the airwaves.

Religious broadcasters already represent the largest single component of transnational broadcasting. While there is reason to question how effective they have been, I have tried to indicate how they might well become more effective in the future. I hope I have presented sufficient evidence and reasoned speculation to encourage others to join in developing a better understanding of the evangelical Christians' efforts to utilize the airwaves to spread the Gospel.

Finally, but not parenthetically, future inquiry should also explore the role of broadcasting in both the growth of Islam and its radicalization in some sectors. Broadcast content in Muslim countries is strongly influenced by the Islamic faith. Saudi Arabia has developed a powerful transnational broadcast capability. The potential for Muslims to use the airwaves to proselytize may be equal or even greater than the evangelical Christians.

Notes

1. It is highly significant to note that religious broadcasting in the United States is dominated by those who are committed to a premillennial theology. The postmillennial traditions, principally liberal Protestantism, have simply not found broadcasting to be so central to their mission. Their concern, to be theologically consistent, is to be about the business of building of God's kingdom on earth in advance of Christ's return. While radio and television can be useful for this purpose, they must be used with care and are not necessarily essential. At the very least, broadcasting does not have as high a priority.
2. See, for example, Eric Barnouw's highly respected three volume history of broadcasting in the United States (1966; 1968; 1970).
3. Whether Vatican Radio was the first international radio station boils down to a matter of semantics. In 1927 Holland commenced broadcasting beamed at Dutch citizens beyond their borders. Germany in 1929 and France in 1931 followed suit. In none of these instances is the intent international but, rather, to reach citizens or expatriots abroad (Browne 1982: 48-9). In 1974 Radio Moscow claimed first use of radio for the transmission of "foreign" languages (1923) and propaganda in a dispute with Romania (1926). These claims may or may not be legitimate but, if legitimate, the transmissions appear to have been short-lived (Browne 1982: 57). Vatican Radio, thus, appears to be the first transnational network.
4. Adolph Hitler's skills in utilizing radio to arouse public emotion is well known. His rise to power, however, involved little use of radio. Regular radio broadcasting began in the German Reich in late 1923, but the broadcasting format was substantially entertainment. News and public affairs broadcasting was limited and tightly controlled (Hoffman-Riem 1988: 91). Hence, it was not until after the National Socialists seized power in 1933 that Hitler was able to begin using radio as an instrument for movement propaganda.
5. The audience estimate of 45 million appears fairly consistently in a number of

resources. I have not been able, however, to locate a primary source or an explanation of how this estimate was reached. This estimate, like the claims of television broadcasters before 1980, is likely an exaggerated figure. The total population of the U.S. in 1930 was 123 million, and there were approximately 75 million adults. To have achieved an audience of 45 million would have constituted approximately 36 percent of the total U.S. population. While it is generally believed that radio audiences were higher in the early years of broadcasting, it seems unlikely that Coughlin would have achieved such a large following. Still, there can be no doubt regarding his extraordinary popularity.

6. There are many explanations for why Coughlin did not succeed in transforming his radio audience into a significant social or political movement. Part of the reason, at least, rests with the fact that Coughlin's positions were erratic and inconsistent, and he lacked specific programs to address the problems he identified. Coughlin biographer Charles Tull described the priest as "a frustrated, disgruntled demagogue lashing out at the world around him" (1965: 246). Continued Tull, "to catalogue him left, right, or center is impossible; the man is simply too erratic to be so neatly classified as a particular species of political animal" (1965: 246).

7. In the fall of 1988 an interfaith coalition of "mainline" churches launched a cable-TV network called VISN (Vision Interfaith Satellite Network). The idea for the network was claimed to be in the planning stages for several years. However, the collapse of PTL provided momentum for the effort when Tele-Communications Inc., one of the larger cable-TV companies in the U.S. and a carrier of PTL, offered to loan an estimated $5 million for start-up costs (Associated Press 1988). By the summer of 1989 VISN was broadcasting 18 hours a day with at least 22 religious bodies cooperating. At this writing, the organization continues to face serious financial difficulties. The leadership is publicly optimistic, but the prospects of this network getting through the initial period of high start-up costs are difficult, at best.

8. From the onset, Vatican Radio was viewed as an instrument for the Pope to communicate with Catholics. It has never been conceived as an instrument for change in the Church or reaching out to communicate with non-Catholics. Over the years there has been little news or discussion of the vital debates occurring in the church. Donald Browne wrote recently that "[m]ost listeners would find to this day that much of the station's programming is uninteresting and/or incomprehensible to any but theologians" (1982: 307).

9. Fortner does not detail how he derives this figure. Resources I have from these three broadcasters report a total number of broadcast hours which exceeds the 20,000 hours per week Fortner reports. Hence, he is not merely relying on the broadcasters' figures.

10. Before the scandals and subsequent financial crisis, the Jimmy Swaggart Ministries appeared to have been expending considerable resources for international broadcasting. Some ministries clearly have used international broadcasting as a come-on to encourage donations. Jim Bakker (PTL) repeatedly made claims of significant international broadcasting projects in order to raise funds. Charles Shepard (1989) documents that these claims were substantially a sham. When Bakker did make good on promises to assist others with international broadcasting, it was usually because he had his back to the wall and was forced to make good on public promises.

11. CBN initially had a broadcast schedule consisting exclusively of religious programming. PTL and CBN followed with the same format and, indeed, carried many of the same programs. CBN then shifted its broadcast format to family- oriented programming, limiting religious broadcasts to its flagship program, "The 700 Club," and a few additional hours of religious broadcasting. Advertising time is now sold on the non-religious programs and these revenues provide significant resources for other CBN activities, including CBN University. Heritage USA and PTL Inspirational Network declared bankruptcy in 1987 and in 1989 it was purchased by a Canadian businessman. As of this writing, the number of cable systems carrying PTL Inspirational Network has shrunk dramatically; and it is unlikely that the network will survive. Largely unnoticed by the American press, Paul Crouch has quietly developed CBN into a network of considerable strength. In addition to being carried over many cable systems, CBN owns over 100 television stations, including 12 full-power UHF stations. In early 1989, the net worth of CBN was estimated at $500 million (Pinsky 1989). Crouch, thus, has become the major broadcaster of religious programming in the U.S. In addition, there are a number of smaller religious broadcasting networks. And, most of the major broadcasters are still using syndication for delivery. Syndicated broadcasting will continue into the indefinite future, but it seems clear that satellite transmission to cable systems is clearly the most efficient method to reach the religious marketplace.
12. Critics of transnational evangelical broadcasters cite many examples of cultural insensitivity. Fortner (1988), for example, relays a story which illustrates how the Gospel message may be completely misunderstood. Among the Zanaki of the Lake Victoria region, it is common practice for a thief to knock on the door of the hut they aspire to burglarize. If they hear no noise they proceed with their mission, but if they can detect movement inside the hut, they make a quick exit. In contrast, an honest man will call out the name of the person he wants to see. An insensitive missionary or broadcaster who quoted Christ "Behold, I stand at the door and knock" (Rev. 3:20), would be telling his Zanki audience that Christ is a thief (Fortner 1988: 9–10).
13. Smith (1988) does not provide sufficient methodological detail for us to have confidence in the statistical representatives of his sample in the four countries surveyed (Costa Rica, Honduras, Guatemala, and El Salvador). Still, it seems clear that Smith, who is not very sympathetic to the broadcasters, was not intentionally sampling so as to exaggerate the broadcasters impact.

References

Armstrong, Ben. 1979. *The Electric Church*. Nashville: Thomas Nelson Publishers.
———, (ed.). 1985. *The Directory of Religious Broadcasting: 1985*. Morristown, NJ: National Religious Broadcasters.
———, (ed.). 1989. *The Directory of Religious Broadcasting: 1989*. Morristown, NJ: National Religious Broadcasters.
Associated Press. 1988. "Religious Network To Begin." *Charlotte Observer* (March 12).
Barnouw, Eric. 1966. *A Tower in Babel*. A History of Broadcasting in the United States, vol. I. New York: Oxford University Press.

_____. 1968. *The Golden Web*. A History of Broadcasting in the United States, vol. II. New York: Oxford University Press.
_____. 1970. *The Image Empire*. A History of Broadcasting in the United States, vol. III. New York: Oxford University Press.
Barrett, David B., ed. 1982. *World Christian Encyclopedia*. New York: Oxford University Press.
Bogart, Leo. 1972. *The Age of Television*. Third edition. New York: Frederick Ungar Publishing.
Browne, Donald R. 1982. *International Radio Broadcasting*. New York: Praeger Publishers.
Comstock, George. 1980. *Television in America*. Beverly Hills, CA: Sage Publications.
Ellens, J. Harold. 1974. *Models of Religious Broadcasting*. Grand Rapids, MI: Eerdmans Publishing Co.
Fortner, Robert S. 1988. "Cross-Cultural Aspects of Evangelical Broadcasting: Prospects and Difficulties." Unpublished paper presented at a conference entitled "Evangelicals, the Mass Media, and American Culture." Billy Graham Center, Wheaton College. (September 28–October 1).
Frazee, Ron. 1989. "Can All of Africa Hear by the Year 2000?" *Religious Broadcasting* (June), 12–13, 32.
Frost, J.M. (ed.). 1985. *World Radio and TV Handbook*. New York: Billboard Publications.
Goerzen, Harold. 1989. "HCJB's International Call-In Programs Catch Hold." *Religious Broadcasting* (June), 14, 32.
Hague, Barbara. 1989. "'Glasnost' Opens Doors for Bibles to Enter the USSR." *Religious Broadcasting* (June), 10, 32.
Harris, Paul. 1970. *When Pirates Ruled the Waves*. London: Impulse Books.
Head, Sydney. 1985. *World Broadcasting Systems*. Belmont, CA: Wadsworth Publishing Co.
Hoffman-Riem, Wolfgang. 1988. "Federal Republic of Germany." In *International Handbook of Broadcasting Systems*, Phillip T. Rosen (ed). New York: Greenwood Press, 91–103.
Lee, Phillip (ed.). 1983. *Communication for All*. Maryknoll, NY: Orbis Books (US distributors).
Lyles, Jean Caffey. 1982. "TV Ministry: Back to the Drawing Board." *Christian Ministry* (June 9–16), 685–86.
McPhail, Thomas L. 1987. *Electronic Colonialism: The Future of International Broadcasting and Communications*. 2nd ed. Beverly Hills, CA: Sage.
Merril, J.C. (ed.). 1983. *Global Journalism: A Survey of the World's Mass Media*. New York: Longman.
Nordenstreng, K. 1984. *The Mass Media Declaration of UNESCO*. Norwood, NJ: Ablex.
Pinsky, Mark I. 1989. "Satellites Spread the Scriptures." *Los Angeles Times* (January 26).
Poloma, Margaret M. 1986. "Pentecostals and Politics in North and Central America." In Jeffrey K. Hadden and Anson Shupe (eds.), *Prophetic Religions and Politics. Religion and the Political Order*, vol. I, 329–352. New York: Paragon.
Shepard, Charles E. 1989. *Forgiven: The Rise and Fall of Jim Bakker and the PTL Ministry*. New York: Atlantic Monthly Press.
Smith, Dennis A. 1988. "The Impact of Religious Programming in the Electronic Media

on the Active Christian Population in Central America." *Latin American Pastoral Issues* XV/1 (July) 67–84.

Sterling, Christopher H. 1984. *Electronic Media: A Guide to Trends in Broadcasting and Newer Technologies 1920–1983*. New York: Praeger.

Tull, Charles J. 1965. *Father Coughlin and The New Deal*. Syracuse, NY: Syracuse University Press.

13

RADICAL DEMOCRATIZATION AND RADICAL MONOTHEISM

MANNHEIM AND NIEBUHR ON GLOBAL ORDER

Lonnie D. Kliever

THE QUEST FOR GLOBAL ORDER RAISES A PRIOR QUESTION about the nature of any sociocultural order, be it regional, national, or international. Must a society finally present itself both as a form of political organization and as a kind of ideological faith? The contemporary discussion is sharply divided over this question. Most commentators, following the "classical" philosophers and social scientists, insist that every enduring society rests on some over-arching set of constitutive values, whether those values are extramurally grounded or intramurally defined (Luckmann 1971). More recently, some interpreters argue that the modern world is producing new forms of society which are free of all such over-arching principles of integration and legitimation (Touraine 1977).

While recognizing that the verdict is still out on the question of substantive versus instrumental order, this paper assesses that global, no less than local, order must be political and philosophical. Human beings are bound together by structures and by symbols. Social structures without shared symbolic meanings can only be sustained by coercive force. Symbolic meanings without concrete social embodiments can only be maintained in private fantasy. There can be no enduring global order without global political structures and global philosophical ideals. How these two components are related to one another is not unlike the age-old riddle of psychosomatic relations. As in the case of mind-body relations, commentators will disagree over whether the relations between the political and the philosophical are those of interactionism, parallelism, or epiphenomenalism. But whatever dogma is finally espoused, the interpreter of global order must show how the political and the philosophical are related in the world of historical and social experience.

This paper will explore the movement toward global order embodied in a great congeries of cultural and religious movements which Karl Mannheim calls "radical democratization" and H. Richard Niebuhr denominates "radical monotheism." These rather cumbersome phrases are chosen in preference to the more common terms of "democracy" and "theism" for good reason. The word "democracy" is usually associated with those principles and arrangements of government committed to human equality and freedom. The word "theism" is usually identified with those religious traditions and movements centered in a personal and sovereign God. But these popular concepts are too closely tied to specific political systems and religious traditions to reveal their underlying and inherent movement toward global order. Here the term "radical democratization" refers to a multi-centered and self-revising social order that pervades the whole of world culture. The term "radical monotheism" points to a transcendent principle of value and obligation that embraces the whole of finite being. In each instance, the term "radical" points to a structure of reality or to a projection of ideality lying beyond their embodiment in actual political and social, economic, and educational institutions. As such, these twin movements of human order are both within and beyond human history.

Radical Democratization

As Karl Mannheim has brilliantly argued, the "democratization" of politics is but one expression of a wider on-going process in the culture at large (Mannheim 1956). Indeed, the democratization of the political order could not have begun apart from these wider cultural transformations. Mannheim makes his case anecdotally by showing how democratic ideals are supplanting aristocratic ideals. In an aristocratic culture, the elites are elevated above the masses, but the process of democratization narrows down this distance in all areas of cultural life.

In manners, the hereditary superiority of the upper classes and the genteel professions has given way to egalitarian relationships and bureaucratic labor. Democratic sociology accepts the dignity of ordinary persons and everyday work. In speech, the elevated language of cultured wisdom and human wisdom has given way to vernacular discourse and common sense. Democratic linguistics affirms the virtue of candid talk and free discussion. In education, the authoritarian relationship between teacher and pupil has given way to the collaborative pursuit of the truth. Democratic pedagogy assumes the plasticity of all minds and the availability of all knowledge. In reflection, dogmatic appeals to private channels of knowledge have given way to public methods of articulation and verification. Democratic philosophy stresses the unlimited accessibility and communicability of all truth. In art, the classical conventions of monumental art have given way to the intimate realism of perspectival style and easel painting. Democratic aesthetics celebrates the single beauty of everyday activities and commonplace objects. In religion, the sacral mystique of an incontestable priesthood and a magic liturgy has given way to lay involvement and private piety. Democratic theology shrinks the distance between the individual believer and the central symbols and rituals of the faith.

The transformations which Mannheim identifies foreshadow a radical negation of aristocratic distance throughout the modern world. This "dedistantiation" opens the way for individuals to find ever-widening opportunities for influencing all aspects of personal and social life. The sheer number of individuals actively participating in cultural life, both as its creators and its recipients, has become increasingly extensive and intensive. The growth of autonomous individualism has become the pervasive principle of the whole of Western culture. This historical trend has not only provoked profound changes within established societies but has also opened the door to the emergence of a global culture. The rise of individualism, most evident thus far in the Western world, invites an axial shift from "tribal brotherhood to universal otherhood" where the kinship of all individual others is affirmed (Nelson 1969). But this expansion of individual autonomy also presents the greatest danger for Western culture. An individualism which is devoid of concrete social affiliations and responsibilities is the breeding ground for all totalitarian movements. Indeed, Mannheim believed that we have more to fear from *anomie* than from tyranny. Thus, Mannheim devoted his entire intellectual life to locating the grounds for responsible individualism within a changing world (Loader 1985; cf. Kettler 1984; Woldring 1986).

Mannheim's search carried him through three distinctive phases of intellectual development, each phase corresponding roughly to the three very different cultural contexts of his life and work (Loader 1985). During the first period of development, covering his Hungarian and early German years as a student, Mannheim worked toward a new philosophical synthesis of culture which reached culmination in his essay "Historicism" (1952). Here Mannheim addressed the modern breakdown of organic culture through a historicist uncovering of a new philosophical center emerging out of a new life situation.

The middle period of Mannheim's development, spanning his German years as a professor, represented a shift from a philosophical to a political synthesis of culture. He broke with the monadic historicist's quest for comprehending the totality and unity of history in favor of a more problematic and pluralistic view of sociocultural order as seen in *Ideology and Utopia* (1936). But this collection of essays was both an unmasking of the utopian pretensions of every ideology and an affirmation of the partial truth of rival ideologies. His highly original "sociology of knowledge" provided the organon for reconciling competing and conflicting values and aspirations through a "relational" mode of thinking which accepts the multidimensionality of human meaning.

The final period of Mannheim's development began with his forced emigration to England. The Nazi rise to power in Germany convinced him that he had underestimated the irrationality of partisan ideologies and had overestimated the influence of a free-floating intelligentsia. In the English context, he returned to his earlier conviction that consensus values are indispensable for a democratic society. But such a democratic consensus is an historical achievement rather than a universal endowment. The virtues of democracy are perpetuated by the twin processes of "education in democracy" and "planning for democracy," which Mannheim spelled out in *Diagnosis of Our Time* (1944) and *Freedom, Power, and Democratic Planning* (1950). Only in this final phase of development did Mannheim work out a clear and consistent vision of what he calls "radical democratization" which balances consensus values and individual spontaneity in a continuously changing world (Mannheim 1956: 240).

Radical Democratization as Dynamic Order. Though more movement than institution, radical democratization does rest on certain fundamental structural principles, both in the narrow sphere of politics as well as in the broad context of culture. According to Mannheim, there are three such principles. The first fundamental principle of democratization is the equality of all persons (Mannheim 1956: 176–177, 180–188). In pre-democratic societies, social authority was linked to the idea of the inherent superiority of the person, family, or party wielding authority. Kingship is the most obvious example of inherent superiority, but we see the same stratification in notions of magic charisma, inherent genius, social caste, racial privilege, or divine election. But democratic societies deny all such essential vertical distances between the leaders and the led. Thus, for example, democratized politics extends the sharing of governmental power to all because it is convinced of the essential equality of all human beings.

Of course, the process of democratization has by no means eliminated all the vertical divisions of higher and lower orders in today's world. Nor does the principle of equality of all human beings imply a mechanical leveling of all quantitative differences within modern society. The point is not that all persons possess equal abilities and endowments, nor even that they all deserve equal recognitions and rewards. But all embody the same value of humanness as such. The democratic principle of equality need not prevent some people from becoming superior to others under the conditions of competition. It only demands that the competition be fair as well as free—that no person, class, or caste be given greater opportunity and higher status by the accident of birth alone.

The second fundamental principle of democratization is the autonomy of each person (Mannheim 1956: 177–179, 188–199). In pre-democratic societies, social order is regulated and enforced strictly from above. Most individuals were simply denied an autonomous life of their own. The family, the guild, the state, and the church are all authoritarian regions which rule by divine right or hereditary privilege. Exacting obedience from the masses is usually no problem since these absolute rulers can count on the docility of the common man. But democratized societies extend to the many the freedom to challenge leaders, to question traditions and to change institutions. In democracies, social consensus is fashioned from below out of discussion and compromise rather than being imposed from above by entitlement and force.

Once again, in today's world the process of democratization falls far short of mobilizing the vital energies of all individuals in shaping the common will. Moreover, the principle of autonomy does not mean that every individual can constantly make full use of his or her right to influence public decisions. Orderly social life would be impossible if each individual constantly influenced every public decision. Every democratic society must somehow find ways to limit the exercise of individual freedom. But the healthy democracy finds ways to ensure that these renunciations of individual freedom are essentially voluntary in nature. Thus, for example, representative democracies limit individual freedom by vesting power in the hands of an elected elite, but individuals and groups are still able to make their aspirations and grievances known through their elected representatives and the electoral process.

The third fundamental principle of democratization is the openness of ruling elites (Mannheim 1956: 179–180, 200–229). Democracies no less than other ways of ordering social life are led by elites. Democratization does not do away with all differences between elites and masses. To be sure, there is a leveling of the distance between the two in democratized cultures, but even in political democracies there must still be small groups who explore new cultural possibilities, shape public policy, and manage daily affairs. Social order in all but the smallest groups is unthinkable without the inspiration and leadership of elites. But democratization does bring about a new mode of elite selection and elite sensibility. In pre-democratic societies, elites are formed and maintained by hereditary privilege, feudal monopoly, divine right, or military prowess. Such aristocratic elites rigorously maintain a qualitative distance between themselves and the masses, even when they are disposed to champion the cause or heed the needs of the masses. Aristocratic elites remains resolutely closed to the masses both with respect to membership and accountability. By contrast, democratic elites are open to the masses in a double sense—numbers of democratic elites in some way rise out of the masses and are in some way answerable to the masses.

Democratic elites are chosen from the masses they represent. Of course, there are different ways that democratic elites are selected and maintained in today's world. As Mannheim explains, people may rise into elite positions of social and especially political leadership by three different routes—bureaucratic advancement, unregulated competition, or class pressures. Most democratic societies maintain their stability and continuity through managerial bureaucracies, which provide new leadership through a systematic pattern of bureaucratic advancement. But democratic leadership, particularly in the area of politics, may also arise out of popular competition. Still others are advanced to positions of democratic leadership through membership in some political party or militant minority. The most important thing in democratic-elite selection is not the particular manner of choice so much as the breadth of the basis of selection. A system is truly democratic only if elite recruitment is not limited to some closed group within the larger society.

Democratic elites are also answerable to the masses they serve. The members of the elite are accountable to the masses in the obvious sense that there are mechanisms for their removal or replacement if they do not handle the leadership entrusted to them in an adequate way. But members of democratic elites are answerable to the masses in a more profound way. The elite is responsible for transmitting its new insights and sharing its highest achievements with the masses. This responsibility may lead to the broadening of the elite by including more people from more diverse backgrounds in places of leadership and privilege.

But such broadening only proves successful when it represents a "leveling-up" of the masses rather than a mere "leveling-down" of the elite. Herein is the most distinctive feature of democratic elites—they reduce the distance between themselves and the masses by drawing the masses higher and higher toward their own standard of life. The truly democratic elite seeks to cultivate among the masses the specialized knowledge, cultured taste and refined skills required for full access to the highest levels of achievement and leadership within the society. Ideally, democratic elites are self-neutralizing groups bent on sharing with others what they themselves have achieved.

Radical Democratization as Chronic Disorder. In light of its three fundamental principles of order, we can see how easily democratization can fall into chronic forms of disorder that paralyze individual freedom and equality. The very strength of democracy can prove to be its own undoing. Indeed, there is within the process of democratization itself a recurrent ambiguity or instability growing out of the inherent tension between the ideals of universal equality and individual autonomy (Mannheim 1956: 226). As noted above, the equality of every person is an affirmation of value, rather than an estimate of ability or a calculus of achievement. In a democratized society, there may still be great inequalities of individual ability and achievement. The divergent interests and aspirations born of empirical differences between individuals can create severe problems for the democratic society precisely because these differing individuals are also granted the autonomous right to assert themselves within the political process. The principle of equality thus comes into conflict with the principle of autonomy, a contradiction which can never be resolved as long as individual needs and ideals are radically divergent. Of course, the democratic elites bear the responsibility for neutralizing such chaotic conflicts and competition through short-term manipulation and long-term education of the masses. But as the elites themselves becomes more representative of a fragmented society, the same potential for chaotic conflict and competition is carried into the very heart of the social order.

Faced with this unresolved antinomy between its own fundamental principles, democratization as an ongoing process often swings precariously between two aberrant forms of democratic social order—totalitarian and massification (Mannheim 1956: 171–173, 195–205). Mannheim points out that, far from being the antithesis of democracy, totalitarianism, even in the extreme form of dictatorship, represents one of the ways a democratic society may try to overcome the governing elite's failure to achieve a workable consensus. Indeed, modern totalitarians are made possible by the fluidity of leadership and the precariousness of order within democracies, particularly in their early stages of formation or following some massive breakdown of social order such as economic collapse or military defeat. In the early stages of the democratization of a given society, the reins of power may pass to a military junta or revolutionary cadre totally unprepared for orchestrating the free play of political and social forces within the society as a whole. Democratization may then be short-circuited in favor of a totalitarian phase. Even if the political process passes into the halls of an experienced elite, their leadership is often taxed beyond capacity by new groups not yet familiar with political realities who use their universal suffrage to embark on wildly utopian schemes or dangerously partisan pursuits. Burdened by such demands, even dictatorship may seem like an acceptable way to discipline the mass and to restore order. Democracies that cannot mobilize or neutralize the divergent interests within their own society are always threatened by the rise of totalitarian elites who will take drastic measures to regain control of a society in shambles.

The other ever-present danger to an immature democracy is what Mannheim calls massification—the achievement of social solidarity through the radical homogenization of culture. As we have seen, democratization is a process of social and cultural "de-distantiation." In a true democracy, the individual finds an ever-widening scope for influencing political, economic, and cultural life. But a curious inversion of individual influence can occur if this process is carried to the extreme. As the distance between the typical individual and the social and cultural elites becomes less, the everyday perspective of the typical individual becomes more dominant. As the pre-democratic gradations between high and low, aristocrat and commoner, sacred and secular are leveled, social and cultural experience becomes ever more homogeneous. In a field of experience where every single thing carries equal weight, none retains a special dignity or distinctive character. If no object or person is respected above any other, the value of the individual disappears in the mass. Under these circumstances, some kind of "re-distantiation" is required to save the individual from disappearing in the masses.

Here then are the twin nemeses of the process of democratization, born of the unresolvable conflict between the fundamental principles of democracy itself. The failure to achieve a consensus based on reasonable compromise because individual autonomy runs unchecked may lead to totalitarianism as the tragic price for restoring order. The individual then counts for nothing and universal equality is lost. The opposite peril is equally daunting. The failure to avoid a consensus based on homogeneity because universal equality reigns supreme may lead to massification as the tragic price for maintaining order. Here, once again, the individual counts for nothing and individual autonomy is lost. In other words, each of these aberrant forms of democracy cancels out one or the other of the fundamental principles of democratization, thus undercutting the freedom and the dignity of the individual.

Is there no way to avoid these twin perils? Can the developing democratic society avoid the expediency of totalitarianism and the excesses of massification? Is the fully democratic society impossible to achieve by the very nature of its inherent principles? These questions suggest that the process of democratization must finally draw on resources beyond its own fundamental principles in order to maintain the delicate balance between individual autonomy and universal equality. Democratic societies are not self-regulating mechanisms which automatically balance out competing interests and conflicting procedures. To be sure, enduring democracies have built up a system, of checks and balances, which place limits on partisan power and levy penalties for social disruption. An elaborate system of procedural values, bureaucratic structures, and technical mechanics encourages and enforces socially responsible behavior.

But these impersonal patterns of order are never fully effective or persuasive. These rational procedures operate only so long as the majority of people operate and cooperate within them. Democratic societies no less than their aristocratic predecessors depend upon the renunciation of power by the masses, with the one momentous difference that in democracies this individual renunciation of power is voluntary and conditional. In democratized societies, individuals will delegate power to their ruling elites only so long as those elites skillfully maintain order and maximize justice. Thus, democratic societies are finally held together by a moral bond of public responsibility and disinterested goodwill. Though housed in rational structures, the process of democratization rests upon moral foundations.

Mannheim located the moral foundations of English culture in what he called "paradigmatic Christianity" (Mannheim 1944: 109–178). Despite his own Jewish heritage, he became closely identified with a group of British intellectuals, including the likes of T.S. Eliot and John

Middleton Murry, who were dedicated to the survival of Christian culture. Mannheim was convinced that a Christianity stripped of its doctrinal rigidity and otherworldly piety could play an important role in shaping the communal consensus necessary for the survival of democratic society. Only those groups which are bound together by the deeper values of conscience traditionally developed in religion can justify the sacrifices and withstand the crises of the democratic process itself. Like other religions, Christianity consists of certain "paradigmatic experiences" which join individuals together in communal groups. Indeed, Mannheim saw the very values of a viable democracy—brotherly love, fair play, community spirit, creative tolerance, and mutual cooperation—embedded in the paradigmatic "archetypes" of historic Christianity. Little wonder that he looked to liberal Christianity for the character formation, consistent conduct, and cooperative existence required of a social order that maximizes spontaneous freedom while maintaining enduring order. In that religion he saw a trans-societal perspective which joins both the masses and the elite in common concern.

Mannheim's late turn to religion as an ally in his quest for a viable democracy that balances individualism and regimentation is fully understandable. Whence will come that civic consciousness, that public responsibility and disinterested goodwill which every democratic system of checks and balances requires, without some kind of religious supports and sanctions? Will individuals surrender their own private power and interests for the sake of the public order and good without the threat of this-worldly punishments and other-worldly compensations? What other than shared religious beliefs and practices can unify the complex interests and diverse groups within a democratic society, to say nothing of a democratic world?

But asking these questions points to even deeper questions. How can religion be a unifying factor and force when religion itself is so deeply divided and divisive? The only place where specific religious traditions seem to have retained something of their social binding power are in those societies which have barely begun the democratizing process or where a state church holds a monopoly over religious traditions. Religious pluralism and religious privation are among the main distinguishing features of all democratized societies. Of course, distinctive religious traditions persist as historically identifiable and socially organized communities within democratized societies, but these religious groups are no less segmented and rationalized than other interest groups in these social orders. Indeed, they are even more segmented and less rationalized than many other differentiated groups or institutions because of the high degree of privatized religious meaning among their constituencies. Religious groups are prevented from pursuing clearcut moral objectives in the wider society or from imposing moral discipline upon their membership because of their own internal moral diversity and fluidity. Religious organizations in democratized societies survive by supplying rather than by defining what their members want and need (Kliever 1981: 187-195).

Needless to say, the diversity and divisiveness of religion is magnified many times over when we cross the familiar boundaries of nationality and language, to say nothing of culture and civilization. On the one hand, even the most refined classificatory schemes do not capture the myriad ways of being religious among the peoples of earth. On the other hand, even these most simplified generalizations about Eastern and Western religions leave us with unreconcilable images of the human and the divine. As things stand, religion seems to hold no promise for even bringing democratized societies together, much less for fashioning a democratized world.

This pessimistic conclusion seems unavoidable so long as we think in terms of one particular religion providing the foundations for a global order. The thousand-year experiment of Christendom led to increasing disorder rather than enduring order. Attempts have been made in the recent past to rebuild the ideal of Christendom on broader ideas and values. The late nineteenth and early twentieth centuries saw the recasting of the medieval ideal of the "absolute religion" in a variety of *Kultur* philosophies and theologies. But these encompassing worldviews were either bent to nationalistic purposes or bypassed by critical reflection (cf. Dietrich 1986). Such utopian visions of a world order and global religion were shattered by the events of contemporary history and rejected by the fashions of contemporary thought.

Clearly another approach to religion and global order is required. Religious pluralism and religious privatism have progressed too far to hope for the establishment of a single world religion. Moreover, the dangers of a fanaticism that declares one's own religion the "absolute religion" are too evident in past and present history even to want to move in this direction. If a religious base for global order can be found, it must allow for a plurality of religious confessions and a diversity of religious institutions. The religious values and ideas that bind groups and nations together cannot be the property of one religious group or tradition. There can be no global order apart from the emergence of such religiously "neutral" states. In such situations, no single religious institution would be given special standing in the state nor would any single religious tradition be seen as the indispensable religious element in culture.

But can such a "religion beyond the religions" be found? Arguments to the contrary notwithstanding, our modern sense of the historicity of all values and ideas closes the door to intuitive apperception or transcendental deductions of a core of religious convictions which are the innate heritage and common possession of all humankind. Religious values and ideas are given in history even if their object and origin lie beyond history. But is there a religion in history that transcends its own history? In one sense, every enduring religion exhibits if not admits some tension between its essence and its manifestations. Yet such transformations are not radical in the proper sense of that word since they do not reach the root metaphors and meanings of the religion. When all is said and done, can there be a religion that pursues the fuller truth about itself and the universe in and through but always above and beyond its own highest revelations and noblest achievements?

Radical Monotheism

H. Richard Niebuhr has brilliantly argued that biblical monotheism, rightly understood, is such a religion (Niebuhr 1960; cf. Kliever 1977: 63–112). Niebuhr insists that biblical monotheism is a radical monotheism because it affirms both the radical sovereignty of God and the radical historicity of humankind. God's transcendence and humankind's dependence are inseparable correlates of one another. As such, Niebuhr rejects both the committed dogmatist's claim of one absolute authority and the consistent skeptic's denial of any reliable authority within human history. Against skeptic and dogmatist alike, Niebuhr affirms the relative within the Absolute and the Absolute beyond the relative. In other words, Niebuhr's radical monotheism contains a permanent critical and constructive principle of personality foundation and world construction which implicitly if not explicitly envisions and requires a global order.

Radical Monotheism as Regulative Ideal. For Niebuhr, radical monotheism is not a collection of religious beliefs but a form of human faith (Niebuhr 1960a: 24–37; cf. Kliever 1977: 85–112). He speaks of "human" faith in order to draw attention to the fact that some form of faith is always given with human life. As long as persons live, they live by trusting in and being loyal to something that makes their lives worth living. More precisely, Niebuhr defines faith as a triadic structure of trust-loyalty relationships. Human selves are bound together by relationships born of trust in and loyalty to one another. But these reciprocal relationships between selves always depend upon some shared cause which gives value to each person and demands loyalty of each person. All three tests of faith (the self, the other, and the cause) are involved in all expressions of faith, but the determinative factor is the cause. This "terminal" of the triad of faith determines the moral shape and social scope of the relationships within the triad. As such, these shared causes function as centers of value, since they establish life's value and determine life's duty. Put in religious terms, human life in all of its reflective, affective, and active expressions is religiously grounded because all persons live by faith in some "god."

This god is seldom the God of radical monotheism. Indeed, the preferred gods of human choice are the gods of social "henotheism" or the gods of self-serving "polytheism." For henotheistic faith, some social unit (such as family, race, nation, church, civilization, even humanity) fulfills the function of god by conferring the group's prestige and imposing the group's duties on its members. Polytheistic faith derives a sense of personal worth from many centers of concern (such as health, fame, wealth, pleasure) and accordingly calculates its obligations toward those who share and supply these varied interests. Against all these finite gods that divide the human community and the human personality into fractured and fracturing parts stands the Infinite God of radical monotheism. For radical monotheism faith's value-center is neither some closed society nor some tangible good. Rather, the faith of radical monotheism is centered in the principle of all being and value—in the One beyond the many in whom the many are one (Niebuhr 1960a: 33). Radical monotheism dethrones all absolute beings short of the Principle of Being itself. At the same time, radical monotheism embraces all relative beings within the Principle of Value itself. In Niebuhr's terms, the two great mottos of radical monotheistic faith are: "Thou shalt have no other gods before me!" and "Whatever is, is good."

Niebuhr sees this contrast between the three forms of human faith as a permanent struggle rather than as a temporal sequence (Niebuhr 1960b: 250). Human communities and human beings do not progress from a polytheistic, through a henotheistic, to a monotheistic form of faith in some grand process of religious maturation or evolution. Rather, the faith of radical monotheism stands in perpetual conflict with its polytheistic and henotheistic rivals. Indeed, the faith of radical monotheism is a call to metanoia—the reformation and transformation of historical life which does not come to an end in this life or this time. This "permanent revolution" is a continuous process of breaking down and building up a "commonwealth of being and value" that is not identical with any of the communities of this world.

As such, the faith of radical monotheism is the regulative ideal (whether implicit or explicit) beneath and behind every program for radically unifying consciousness and culture. Anything less than exclusive trust in God as the principle of being, all-inclusive loyalty toward others within the realm of being, falls short of building universal community. Niebuhr further clarifies the substance and scope of this regulative ideal by distinguishing radical faith from mixed forms of faith which are usually thought to be universal but which fall short of the comprehensiveness of radical monotheism. Humanism certainly represents a positive move toward universal faith assurance and faith loyalty.

But the human community does not exhaust God's realm of being and value. Vitalism encompasses a wider domain of trust-loyalty relationships than humanism's preoccupation with human life and meaning. But limiting being and worth to the community of living things relieves faith of any concern for all that which is no longer alive or that was never alive. Even Naturalism which includes the inorganic in the circle of being and value falls short of a truly radical faith by ruling out other provinces of being and value, perhaps ideal or perhaps real, that transcend the natural order. All such ways of faith, each arising as a protest against narrower circles of being and value, can be seen as critical and constructive movements in the direction of radical monotheism. Yet they fall short of truly radical expression. Each excludes some realm of being from the sphere of value (Niebuhr 1960a: 35–37).

Radical Monotheism as Cultural Movement. Faith, for Niebuhr, whether in its negative forms as henotheism and polytheism or in its positive form as radical monotheism, cannot be reduced to mystical intuitions or verbalized beliefs. Faith is a structure of relationships that brings human beings together in communities of trust and loyalty. Faith is a process of development that binds human beings together in communities of trust and hope. Faith is always embodied in personal history and social institutions (Niebuhr 1960a: 38–48). Indeed, every cultural system is finally an expression of one or another of the typical forms of faith. A given culture's politics and economics, sciences, and arts are no less an expression of faith than its religions. Religious systems focus directly on personal and social relations to divine powers. But such systems of doctrine and ritual, of polity and piety, by no means constitute the whole of faith. Faith is always embodied in total life—in public institutions as well as private intuitions, in corporate endeavors as well as individual activities, in secular pursuits as well as sacred experiences.

Niebuhr illustrates the way in which radical faith is embodied both negatively and positively in Western politics and Western religion (Niebuhr 1960a: 64–77; Niebuhr 1961: 20–71). Modern nations no less than ancient empires present perfectly clear examples of political manifestations of henotheistic faith (Niebuhr 1960a: 68–72). Ancient political communities in which magistracy and priesthood, church and state, society and god were identified seem no less guilty of regarding the political community itself as the source of ultimate value and the object of ultimate loyalty than their modern counterparts where *vox populi* is *vox deus*. Moreover, democratic and republican states no less than fascist and communist governments regularly arrogate ultimate beatitude and sovereignty to themselves.

But such "nationalistic" faith is forever challenged and qualified by monotheistic faith. This ferment of monotheistic conviction is especially clear in developed democracies where freedom, equality, and justice all point beyond the political order to their larger ground and goal (Niebuhr 1961: 59–71). Government of the people, for the people and by the people seems possible only where the governed and the governing are answerable to a kind of "universal government" that both limits and legitimizes the power of the state as well as the power of the citizenry. To be sure, that "universal government" is more a possibility than an actuality, more a hope than a datum. But to the extent that democratic principles remain operative, they reflect (though only partially and ambiguously) a trust and a loyalty that transcends national trust and loyalty.

The "organized" Western religions of Judaism and Christianity, which are officially monotheistic, are no less involved in the struggle with henotheistic and polytheistic forms of faith than are other expressions of culture (Niebuhr 1960a: 49–63). If we look at these organized religions as they present themselves in their present-day practices and beliefs, as well as in their historical development and institutions, it is difficult to regard them as representative of a universal community of being and value. Rather, these religious movements are riddled by factionalism and partisanship. Their histories are marked by continuous struggle between social henotheism and radical monotheism. Setting aside all internal divisions and differences, Israel's identity as a "chosen people under God's Law" and Christianity's identity as a "believing community under Christ's Lordship" are constantly drawn toward henotheistic definition. Throughout their separate histories, Judaism has tended to become a closed culture while Christianity has tended to become a closed religion. Yet the pressure toward universality is always there in their shared symbol and sense of God as the world's Creator, Judge, and Redeemer. As such, though divided and divisive, these organized religions point beyond themselves to the "Radical One" by which all religions are tested and transformed, including their own.

As noted above, Niebuhr sees the struggle of faith as continuous. Every area of personal and social life including religion, even for those persons and groups whose institutions and rites are officially monotheistic, is a conflict of radical monotheism with its henotheistic and polytheistic rivals. Radical faith is refracted in only broken and partial ways in faith's typical cultural expression. But precisely this theocentric critique of all human claims to finality and completeness is what makes radical monotheism a permanent critical and constructive principle for unifying human consciousness and culture. As such, radical monotheism both evokes and energizes the drive toward global order by at once facilitating and undermining attachment to a particular society. If radical monotheism is true, then the whole sweep of nature and history must be understood and experienced as a single epic. The entire universe—animate and inanimate, natural and historical, individual and collective, even living and dead, must be entered into as the one family of the Father God, the one kingdom of the Sovereign God.

Though analyzed separately by thinkers from very different disciplines with very different philosophies, Mannheim's radical democratization and Niebuhr's radical monotheism are complementary ways of viewing the quest for global order. Radical monotheism is not only religion but presents itself also as political action. Radical democratization appears not only as a form of political organization but as a kind of faith. Indeed, radical democratization extended beyond particular societal expressions is radical monotheism in its secular form; and radical monotheism extended beyond its particular historical embodiments is radical democratization in its sacral tide. Radical democratization includes those settled social habits and modes of thought that tend to prevent the absolute control of individual citizens and minority groups. Radical monotheism undergirds those transcendent ideals of freedom and equality that tend to facilitate the ultimate unification of persons and parties. Of course, these dynamic forces of movement and countermovement are far from complete and consistent realizations in today's world. But taken seriously and taken together, these twin principles of radical individuation and radical iconoclasm may provide the foundations for a workable and durable global order.

References

Dietrich, Wendell S. 1986. *Cohen and Troeltsch: Ethical Monotheism and Theory of Culture*. Atlanta: Scholars Press.
Kettler, David, Volker Meja, and Nico Stehr. 1984. *Karl Mannheim: The Development of His Thought*. Chichester: Ellis Horwood Limited.
Kliever, Lonnie D. 1977. *H. Richard Niebuhr*. Waco: Word Books.
———. 1981. *The Shattered Spectrum: A Survey of Contemporary Theology*. Atlanta: John Knox Press.
Loader, Colin. 1985. *The Intellectual Development of Karl Mannheim: Culture, Politics and Planning*. Cambridge: Cambridge University Press.
Luckmann, Thomas. 1971. *The Invisible Religion*. New York: Macmillan Press.
Mannheim, Karl. 1936. *Ideology and Utopia: An Introduction to the Sociology of Knowledge*. London: Routledge & Kegan Paul Ltd.
———. 1944. *Diagnosis of Our Time*. New York: Oxford University Press.
———. 1950. *Freedom, Power, and Democratic Planning*. New York: Oxford University Press.
———. 1952 [1924]. "Historicism." 84–133 in *Essays on the Sociology of Knowledge*, edited by Paul Kecskemiti. New York: Oxford University Press.
———. 1956 [1933]. "The Democratization of Culture." 171–246 in *Essays on the Sociology of Culture*, edited by Ernest Manheim and Paul Kecskemiti. London: Routledge & Kegan Paul Ltd.
Nelson, Benjamin. 1969. *The Idea of Usury*. Chicago: University of Chicago Press.
Niebuhr, H. Richard. 1960a. *Radical Monotheism and Western Culture*. New York: Harper and Brothers.
———. 1960b. "Reformation: Continuing Imperative." *Christian Century* 77: 248–251.
———. 1961. "The Protestant Movement and Democracy in the United States." 20–71 in *The Shaping of American Religion*, edited by James Ward Smith and R. Leland Jamison. Princeton: Princeton University Press.
Touraine, Alain. 1977. *The Self-Production of Society*. Chicago: University of Chicago Press.
Woldring, Henk E.S. 1986. *Karl Mannheim: The Development of His Thought*. New York: St. Martin's Press.

14
RELIGION, LAW, AND GLOBAL ORDER
Frank J. Lechner

GLOBAL ORDER EXISTS AND IS THEREFORE POSSIBLE. But how is it possible? That is the question. To answer it we have to be more precise about what we mean by global order. Of course we don't want it to refer to absence of conflict, to a smoothly functioning social organism. If the sociological tradition has accomplished anything it is to have found a way of thinking about order without religious or romantic blinders. By order sociologists generally refer simply to a structured set of relationships between actors or institutions whose actions are supposed to be governed by some minimal shared norms and beliefs. Thus global order exists if a number of significant actors across the globe engage in regular interaction and hold a cultural conception of "globality" when they share a sense that they belong to and participate in one global cultural arena. If they define global order as real, the construct is real in its consequences.

But the existence of such a construct is not enough from a sociological point of view. Global order is more than a globally plausible world view; the content of the global cultural system must acquire social form.

Thus if we are to study global order as sociologists and answer the question how it is possible, we must search for globally institutionalized modes of communication and association, of competition and conflict which involve interaction on an unprecedented scale and are guided by normative principles of unprecedented scope.

In spite of pioneering work by some sociologists (e.g. Nettl and Robertson 1968; Robertson and Chirico 1985), a solid generally accepted body of good theory on global matters is still sorely lacking. Yet we know the answers that won't work. On the one hand utilitarian accounts (Bergesen 1980) according to which global order is the natural result of interaction between independent self-interested parties are not sufficient. All the old criticisms of utilitarian approaches to order apply. But so do criticisms of idealist accounts which in this case are more likely to be accepted by religious scholars and activists and present global order as the natural realization of sacred principles which guide all human action. They are equally misleading. Global order cannot be "explained" as the mere realization of some ultimate values. In the sociological tradition, the concern with institutionalization prevented such inadequate "solutions" to the problem of order. I suggest that the problem of institutionalization of global forms of thought and action needs to be at the heart of world system analysis as well.

The current global order, such as it is, is not the only possible one. It is one possible world among many. So the more specific problem is: how is this global order possible? We arrived at this condition via a specific path, an historical process of globalization that has produced a peculiar world system of societies. What we need, therefore, is not only a theory of institutionalization, but also a theory of "possible worlds," one that can also provide a coherent description of the world "system" we now have. The peculiarities of this currently realized world order are such, in fact, that the orderliness of the system is often underestimated, so that many actors on the global scene keep searching for a more real, more satisfying global order. There is a pattern to those searches as well; but this can only be fully understood on the basis of an adequate sociological account of the historically, objectively possible global order that has emerged in the late twentieth century.

In the context of this volume it is important to note that the really existing global order is not in any obvious sense a religious one. Of course this does not imply that religion is therefore irrelevant for world system analysis. Structurally, some of the world religions clearly function as global institutions. From a cultural point of view religion remains at the core of at least some civilization complexes, as one element among others in world culture. Historically, "religion" is certainly part of the causal chain of globalization; in the West, to state just the obvious, a religious world system preceded the later political economic one. From a practical point of view, interpretations of, and reactions against, globalization are in many cases religiously inspired. But just as coherent institutions, high levels of religious belief, or the presence of "revivals," do not constitute a reversal of secularization in individual societies, so the global significance of religion(s) does not affect the essential secularity of the world system itself. This is in fact a religious problem. The world is worldly, all too worldly by religious standards (whether innerworldly or otherworldly), and I suggest that it cannot be otherwise. There is no return possible from global *Gesellschaft*; any specifically and exclusively religious search for a more meaningful global order is self-defeating. But to say this is only a starting point. Secularization, whether global or societal, makes religion interesting. What was taken for granted, at least ideal-typically speaking, becomes problematic and open to critical examination; and this is the essential task for the sociology of religion.

In this chapter I take a very indirect approach to the theme of religion and global order by shifting attention from religion to law. One important reason is that, in world system studies, law has been sadly neglected. This is surprising, since law is surely a crucial component of almost any social order. The theoretical neglect of law needs to be remedied. Second, focusing on religion runs the risk of thinking about global order mainly in terms of values, of ideas. If we want to avoid idealist accounts of global order, it makes sense to focus on law as the quintessential institutionalized normative order. This brings us closer to the general and historical questions of global order.

Moreover, since institutionalization is the primary sociological concern, the contribution of religion to social order is likely to take place via law; any institutionalization of religious views of global order will require legal specification in any case. Finally, the field of international law in particular constitutes perhaps the longest continuing intellectual quest for global order, but one that has received very little attention in sociological world system studies. The changing relationships between "religion" and "global order" are in fact partly reflected in the history of international law which had its roots in the European society of Christian nations but gradually became a distinctly secular intellectual and practical endeavor. In short, it is a tradition with interesting links to religious beliefs and one that needs to be mobilized for sociological purposes. This chapter is a modest attempt to do just that.

International Law and the Study of Global Order

Conventional world system analysis in sociology has largely ignored law. Wallerstein (1974; 1980) pays even less attention to law than to religion. This is somewhat surprising since expanding exchange relations are the core of the Wallersteinian world system; these exchanges require rules and assumptions that are shared by all participants which, in the early modern period, were part of a growing body of international commercial law. Of course it is possible to argue, with some difficulty, that in the formative period of the Wallersteinian world system transnational law was only rudimentary and not very important. What counts here is the simple lack of argument.

The (problematic) Wallersteinian thesis that core status was more likely to be achieved by strong states also requires some attention to legal mechanisms used to extend internal control by centralizing states. Only Meyer and Boli Bennett (1980), in their study of national constitutions, are a partial exception to the common neglect of law; but for them law simply becomes one component of a "world polity." Yet international law, in theory and practice, is significant for the study of global order. There are several, essentially historical, reasons why any sensible form of world system analysis, and thus any future "history of global order," ought to incorporate a study of international law. Not only can the development of international law be treated as an "indicator" of changes in other dimensions of the world system, it has contributed to the normative structuring of exchange, domination, and conflict in the global arena; in addition, it is the intellectual tradition in which emerging conceptions of global order were reflexively examined and in which potential global values gradually crystallized.

First, international law is obviously itself part of global order insofar as it defines the relevant actors and regulates their interaction. Traditionally, the focus was on the regulation of political conflict between states and on the regulation of economic transactions between public and private parties. By analogy with normative order within societies we can say that international law provided for many centuries and even before the official "start" of the Wallersteinian world system, the pre-conflictual elements in international conflict and the pre-contractual elements in trans-societal contracts.

In the twentieth century a vast expansion took place, so that we now have more than 500 international organizations and more than 20,000 treaties and conventions. International commercial law has become an intricate, autonomous legal order on a transnational scale, developed over many centuries by participants in a truly transnational community

(Berman 1982: 2, 7). A fully universal international society with global rules and institutions, again a long time in the making, is a twentieth-century product (Bull 1984). The process of globalization after World War II is reflected in the more diverse subjects of international law (with the focus less strictly on states) as well as in qualitative changes (e.g. the new emphasis on human rights) (cf. Cassese 1986: ch. 4; Onuf 1982: 7). Most importantly, there is a body of fundamental principles that governs international relations, ranging from the sovereign equality of states to respect for human rights (Cassese 1986: ch. 6), elaborated or applied by a functioning set of distinctly global institutions including the General Assembly of the U.N. and the World Court.

Second, international law is in part a tradition of systematic reflection about global order. For Grotius, this order was essentially the *magna communitas humani generis*. Many subsequent authors did not make similar assumptions about the society of states, and instead focused on sovereign states as such and relations between them. More generally, the tradition centered around the old problem whether international law is really law, and whether there really exists an international (legal) order. In an arena of independent, self-interested actors without any central authority or general sanctioning procedures, no fully legal order appeared to be possible.

The problem, in other words, was analogous to the problem of social order as treated by Parsons, with the dilemmas produced by positivist and realist doctrines playing the role of Parsons's utilitarian dilemma. A full examination of these issues must wait for another context. Beyond specific theories of order legal reflection on the problem of global order also involved various "visions of world order" (Stone 1984).

For example, world order has been viewed as an emerging legal order moving toward humanity-wide criteria of right and wrong (Jenks), as centered around policy-oriented world power processes (McDougal), or as the functional legal ordering of planetary humanity realizing fundamental human claims (Falk). While each of these visions is inadequate, as Stone points out, they are interesting as manifestations of different, potentially influential approaches to world order. In spite of specific deficiencies, what is important is that there is a tradition of reflection about global order. Social order generally is not simply a synchronic, structural arrangement of components but also has a diachronic dimension; the existence of a tradition, however conflict-ridden, of global thought and practice is therefore crucial to answer the question about the possibility of global order. As Alasdair MacIntyre (1988) has noted, institutions in part consist of arguments about how they ought to operate. The tradition of argument about the proper form of global order is thus crucial in the study of the latter's institutionalization.

Third, international law is also an important arena of conflict. Competing views of the world are brought into play, and conflicting interests are asserted. Resolving disputes is the "stuff" of international law as it is of municipal law. Traditionally, many of these disputes centered on the interpretation of the *jus ad bellum* and the *jus in bello*. While the actual constraining influence of international law in this area has always been problematic, it laid down at least some legitimate ways in which violence could be used in international conflict.

Today, conflicts concerning international law range from the problem of distributive justice (focusing on the possible creation of a New International Economic Order), to the rights and duties of states to the exploitation of "global" resources (especially in the Law of the Sea), and to the meaning of human rights and "mankind." If our focus is on the institutionalization of global order, it is not sufficient simply to think of conflict as power struggles between independent actors. Conflict, as the tradition of legal thought makes clear, is itself subject to the governance of norms. Of course this is not to say that such regulation is always smooth and easy. Quite the contrary. But clearly the institutionalization of a global order gives rise to multiple conflicts, and we cannot explain these without incorporating the legal framework into our analysis.

Fourth, the world system did not emerge on the scene in a sudden burst. Its institutionalization took time and went through various stages. In a loose sense international law can be used as an indicator of phases in this process of major changes in the world system. For example, as Bull (1977: 27ff.) argues, in the still essentially Christian international society of the sixteenth and seventeenth centuries, natural law was primary; rules of coexistence were based on the assumption of the existence of a universal society. Yet, as we know, this Christian society had itself become fragmented. After the Reformation Protestants began to challenge the previously dominant Catholic view of global order; international law itself became practically important precisely in dealing with the aftermath of the Wars of Religion.

To generalize rather drastically, in the following centuries, with the rise of a European international society, positive law took precedence; and sovereignty was recognized as a dominant principle. Although Europeans no longer thought of global order in specifically Christian terms, a new exclusive standard of "civilization" became the criterion for inclusion of new members in the state system and interstate relations in the nineteenth and early twentieth century (Gong 1984). Recent modifications in international law reflect new political and economic relationships after World War II in the new world international society.

Most generally, then, it is possible in principle to link developments in international law to the expansion of capitalism and of the nation state system, as well as to the process of secularization. However, its historical global significance actually precedes the advent of modernity since some of its basic elements emerged out of inter-civilizational encounters before the eleventh century, and are thus not strictly Christian in origin (Ago 1977).

Finally, international law is important as a value. If we are interested in institutionalization, we have to ask: institutionalization of what? In the global arena, part of the answer has to be: the idea of law-as-value. The very attempt to identify law, as distinguished from "morality" or "religion," as a crucial component of global order betrays a Western bias in thinking about order. The idea of legal order has special religious significance in the Western tradition. Law has come to be treated as sacred; and to some extent this view has been globalized as well, although it is by no means universally accepted (Bozeman 1971). Global worldview analysis, to adopt a term from Ninian Smart (1987), thus involves analysis of different interpretations and meanings of law and legal principles around the globe. Precisely the extent to which law as a Western-derived value will remain plausible in world culture is problematic. If by religious conflict we mean conflict centering on what human beings hold to be of transcendent importance, then at least from a Western point of view, conflicts about (international) law acquire religious connotations.

International Law and Globalization

Globalization is the process by which a new social order comes about on a global scale, bringing culturally distinct communities into interaction with each other. It is the process of the institutionalization of a global (social and cultural) order. The term was coined by Robertson, who has produced a plausible and coherent perspective on the process. The point of this section is to suggest that some aspects of international law can significantly enhance current work on globalization. While the previous section emphasized historical arguments, here the focus is on theoretical proposals for the analysis of global order as such.

One important thesis in globalization theory is that national societies and individual selves are being "relativized" in the context of a world system of societies and the category of mankind (Robertson and Chirico 1985). If such "relativization" is to be more than a description of cultural developments involving elites concerned about the position and identity of their societies in the world system, we should find it expressed in rules governing global interaction and in global institutions. In other words, we should find that the new global categories and their relationships are institutionally specified, at the very least in the form of norms governing the constitution of and relationships between societies, as well as norms governing the use of the category of humanity in concrete contexts. It is therefore interesting to note that precisely the four components mentioned above, as well as the relationships between them, constitute the main concerns of international law as well, although the latter also focuses on what might be called global mediating structures, such as international organizations. Of course some of the primary principles have to do with the nature of sovereign states and the proper relations between them. Increasingly, attention is also paid to the rights of individuals in relation to states, as well as to the rights of individuals as human beings. In part through international law, a clearer conception of a world system of societies developed, and the notion of humankind is increasingly treated in natural law-like fashion as a fundamental principle from which rights and duties can be derived. Simply put, then, global order as presented by globalization theory is made possible by the normative regulation of the main components of the global situation in relation to each other (which of course leads to the further, perhaps equally thorny, problem how such normative regulation in turn is possible).[1]

We can go at least one step further. In the modern world system, as globalization theory suggests, societies are formed in part under the impact of a global normative model for social organization. Societal organization must be globally legitimated and must satisfy certain global standards (Meyer 1980). By analogy with Durkheim's account of social order in a differentiated society on the basis of the cult of the individual, we can say that a world system of societies is made possible by the cult of the nation state, or "institutionalized societalism" (Lechner 1989). A particular form of society has become an ultimate, sacred symbol, and an institutionalized set of global norms. "Society," more than a self-sufficient political entity with specific self-interests and more than a moral community to which members can become subjectively attached, has become a global fact. As an ultimate symbol with global institutional backing, societalism provides normative anchorage for all particular societies as the legitimate actors on the global scene which are expected to pursue their self-interest almost irrespective of their internal functioning.

For this argument to hold, we should find more than the symbolic trappings of societalism but rather some specific form of "global, institutional backing." The point here is that this is indeed present in the form of law. When Meyer (1980: 117) speaks of the external "rules defining the nation-state system as legitimate," rules which define the structural form of the nation-state as the most highly legitimated, or which define the purposes to which it is to be devoted and legitimate its control over territory, population, and the means of violence, these are, concretely, the rules of public international law. Thus an "institutional" analysis of global order has to rely in part on the tradition and substance of international law.[2]

A third link between international law and globalization has to do with possible interpretations of or reactions against globalization. Like any process of institutionalization, it is hardly the mechanical implementation of a blueprint. The sociological task is to chart the fundamental ways in which the main thrust of the process is challenged and the alternative conceptions of global order that may influence the process. If we take the Robertson-Chirico (1985) scheme as a starting point, then each of the four structural components of the emerging world system can logically become a basis for such a reaction or for alternative conceptions of global order, and each can be chosen, for example, by anti-systemic movements, in Wallerstein's sense, as the corner stone of (an alternative) global order (Robertson 1991). Now if the process of global institutionalization is real and the thesis concerning alternative conceptions of order plausible, then we should find such alternative, critical approaches to global order reflected in international law as well.

Indeed, the four possible responses to global order to be derived from the Robertson-Chirico scheme are closely parallelled by different approaches to world order in the tradition of international law (cf. Bull 1977: 24ff., following Martin Wight; Onuf 1979). Hobbesian realism of course focuses on societies as independent self-interested entities, engaged in a war of all against all, constrained only by considerations of prudence and expediency; order becomes at best a fragile balance of power, in which the interests of individuals or humanity as a whole are of secondary importance. Kantian universalism, at least in an extreme form, focuses on the transnational bonds between human beings who, on the basis of their common humanity, are assumed to have the same fundamental rights and interests, which will be realized in the emerging cosmopolitan society; the operations of societies and relations between them are supposed to be governed by more universal norms producing a truly international community. Lockean individualism (not mentioned by Bull but a logical fourth possibility; cf. Onuf 1979) focuses on individuals (perhaps also certain organized collectivities) as the ultimately real actors on the global scene, who may have diverse interests which can be realized either by private or by social contracts in a global institutional setting; given rational and peaceful interaction between individuals, order in the actions and relations of states emerges as an aggregate outcome.

Grotian internationalism views world order as a society of states or an international society, in which states are the primary actors but are necessarily related to other states on the basis of common rules and institutions; there are limits to sovereignty; the interests of individuals or mankind are of secondary importance. Bull argues that the Grotian model, in various versions, has been the dominant one in doctrine and practice. Cassese (1986: 31-2) adds that it usually existed in combination with the Hobbesian model, and that new developments in international law (for example in the area of human rights) may be patterned more on the Kantian model.[3] The implications for the Grotian order, as well as the tensions with Hobbesian realism and Lockean individualism, remain to be studied. Onuf (1979) makes clear that there is no scholarly consensus on the "right" view of global (legal) order. While this may be problematic for international lawyers, this lack of consensus is only to be expected from a sociological point of view. The very conflicts manifested by the scholarly debates reflect tensions built into the normative structure of a global order in the process of institutionalization.

Religion and Law in the World System

After the historical and theoretical arguments of the previous sections, this section focuses on an important, but neglected, substantive problem in the institutionalization of global order namely: How does religion affect the role of law in the quest for global order? Even though it is clear to many scholars that in most civilizations there is a very close relationship between law and religion, there are surprisingly few scholarly treatments of this relationship. Berman (1984) and Bozeman (1971) are exceptions. Sociologists have long recognized the importance of religious traditions for the analysis of institutionalization. The meaning and practical significance of religions may differ, but such traditions are an obvious source of values to be institutionalized of conceptions about the proper structuring of institutions. Where essential values are in conflict, where conceptions of the sacred differ, institutionalization becomes more problematic. Clearly, in the current global condition of religious pluralism this issue is of great practical significance. Specifically, then, if different actors on the global scene hold different sets of ultimate beliefs, how can a global order be created by legal means?[4]

In general it is clear that patterns of ultimate belief and conceptions of transcendent reality are closely tied to views of societal ordering. Subjecting human conduct to the governance of norms, backed by authoritative sanctions, to paraphrase Lon Fuller, normally involves the most important symbolic resources of a society; visions of transcendent order usually need to be specified in quasi-legal terms to become accepted and routinized; the symbolic boundaries between sacred and profane (however difficult it may be to apply that distinction across all civilizations) are usually matched by specific mechanisms defining the boundaries of a community, including full members and excluding all others.

But, as Bozeman shows, beyond such basic connections there is in fact great variability in the law-religion relationship. In the West, law as a relatively abstract code of concepts and as a principle of societal organization founded in the final analysis on the person as the basic legal concept, symbolizes major value-orientations. It implies shared values, effective social control, and faith in the future. In Islam, however, Shari'a remains the principle source of legislation; it is essentially religious law, the practical rules of religion; but in principle the law tolerates social diversity and leaves mechanisms of institutionalization in the community relatively vague.

In African traditions, law is essentially identified with custom, and as such not differentiated from either ethics or communal practices. In India, Hindu law originates in religion and myth; action is governed by dharma, persons are not regarded as citizens carrying rights and the introduction of a Western legal system in spite of its practical dominance, remains implausible within the civilizational framework.

With respect to the problem of global order such differences have at least two major implications according to Bozeman. First, international law is the Western conception of law globalized. The differentiation between law, on the one hand, and policy or morality, on the other; the distinction between war and peace; the coexistence of independent, territorially delimited states; and the assumption that governments, representing states, can undertake voluntary and binding obligations in their relations all are principles that are "distinctly Occidental in origin," highly implausible from a civilizational point of view and by no means universally accepted (Bozeman 1971: 180ff.).

In the West, law, nature, and religion were set apart; only in the West was the individual emancipated from the collectivity as an autonomous person and as a citizen—"the only view of the human being that allows for meaningful universalization"; only in the West were discovery, risk, and reform themselves part of the dominant tradition; conceptions of "humanity" and "world order" could emerge only in the West, not in Oriental Empires (Bozeman 1984: 390, 394).

In short, in spite of mutual borrowing, civilizational frameworks remain fundamentally incommensurable and in particular there cannot be a basis for organizing the relations between different kinds or conceptions of law. "We do not have a globally meaningful system because the world society consists today, as it did before the nineteenth century, of a plurality of diverse political systems, each an outgrowth of culture specific concepts" (Bozeman 1984: 404). Thus Bozeman proposes a strong thesis: fundamental cultural differences prevent the institutionalization of a legally grounded global order. This calls into question the very possibility of an international legal order and of the institutionalization of global order more generally.

But Bozeman proves too much. For one thing it can be shown that in spite of local and regional differences, significant as they are, there is in fact a set of transnational rules and relationships that are by and large accepted by the main participants on the global scene. To be sure, even common rules may be interpreted very differently by many of these parties; but social and cultural conflict now takes place in one common framework, Western in origin but not in operation, as is shown by authors with rather different orientations (Cassese 1986; Jenks 1967; Schwarzenberger 1976). The impact of incommensurable local value patterns is itself variable and mitigated by a pattern of global secularization. The state, an entity in trouble according to Bozeman, maintains a rather vigorous presence in the global arena. International law, rather than simply serving the cause of political rhetoric and tactics, also represents a set of global understandings about global problems; what is more, the notion that global order does fundamentally involve such a legal dimension has itself been globalized, and at least some presuppositions for interaction between states remain operative.

Beyond the institutional and cultural reality of international law the history of its development also provides crucial counter evidence. As Gong (1984) has demonstrated, the inclusion of new nation states as full members of international society (most notably Japan) involved conformity to a standard of civilization imposed by the major powers. The record shows that in spite of cultural differences it was possible for several new actors on the global scene to make the required internal legal reforms and to operate externally according to international standards. With the decline of the old exclusive standard of civilization, the Western-derived content of international norms and the burden of change on new global actors have only diminished. Finally, to complete the refutation of Bozeman's thesis, incompatible values simply do not prevent similarity of interests, allegiance to universal principles, interaction on non-local terms, and a gradual increase of mutual understanding (Dore 1984).

According to Bozeman, just as international order is an empty shell, "mutual understanding" is a vain hope (1971: 18, 29), since the interpenetration of many modes of thought has made understanding the "other" in his authenticity more difficult in the twentieth century. In particular, the general devaluation of Western conceptions in the global-borrowing process makes understanding by means of a Western cognitive apparatus increasingly difficult. This is the second implication of legal cultural diversity for global order. Universal understanding, like universal (legal) order, is a matter of Western wishful thinking. Or, to put it very differently, Western cognitive universalism is undermined by traditions that remain genuinely inaccessible; and Western moral universalism is undermined by traditions that practically reject most Western values. Actual empirical relativism undermines the trans-societal rule of law and tends to reduce relationships to power relationships, a position with which international law scholars of the realist persuasion would sympathize.

In this respect the predicament of religious and legal traditions is quite similar. With Western history now centered in world history, the identity of the traditions, legal and religious, is put to the test; precisely when the actual historical consciousness and the belief in a providential history declines, the global challenge is to provide an historical reconstruction of what this tradition means (cf. Berman 1988).

But this challenge is not limited to the West, for, as Robertson has argued, globalization produces pressure for societal and civilizational self-identification. Yet Bozeman may be right in one sense, namely insofar as the assumption of mutual understandability and of the adequacy of rational means of *Verstehen* were part of the Western tradition itself; similarly, the explicit rejection of universalism and the absence of a plausible providential conception of world order may be more problematic from a Western point of view. In the West, maintaining social order traditionally has been tied not so much to the existence of "common values" but to an ongoing tradition (cf. Berman 1983). The coexistence of incommensurable civilizational complexes and the rejection of the possibility of one, overarching, purposeful tradition undermines the very notion of tradition; if the assumptions are correct the very possibility of "global order" would have to be questioned as well. This would solve the "problem of global order," in a clear but negative fashion. Having challenged Bozeman's assumptions I suggest that sociologists studying the institutionalization of global order are unlikely to be satisfied with this "solution." Not only do the requirements of complete mutual understanding and a fully shared tradition imply a rather too restrictive view of order, from a plausible historical point of view the emergence of a new tradition, one constituted in part by the interaction of preexisting traditions, is an objective possibility. The development of international law itself suggests that this possibility is now being realized.

Paradoxes of Globalization

Globalization, to repeat, is the process by which a new social order comes about on a global scale, bringing culturally distinct communities into interaction with each other. Since this process involves a shift in the level of social organization and an integration of distinct elements into one system, it is likely to be subject to various tensions and conflicts. These can take the form of anti-systemic movements or of efforts at reform by elites. They are also reflected in several "paradoxes of globalization," which I will briefly describe in a speculative vein.

First, globalization is universalization. The components of Western social order have become universal; Western modes of thought have become universal; Western universalism has become universal. But globalization is also particularization. In the global order societies must identify themselves; traditions must be reconstructed in permanent civilizational encounters; universal principles must be locally interpreted and applied. The need to be different has been universalized; the meaning of universalism has been particularized. Particularist attachments are universally legitimated; universal principles are given particular forms. The problem of constructing particular collective identities is now a universal one; universal tools of social organization support very distinct structures. Particularism has become universalized, universalism particularized (cf. Robertson 1987). This is the paradox of universalization.

Second, in the process of globalization societies have become institutionalized as global facts. As organizations, they operate in secular terms; in their relations, they follow secular rules; hardly any religious tradition attributes transcendent significance to worldly societies in their present form. Yet secular *Gesellschaft* also has become ultimately valuable, the object of profound loyalties, the context for any meaningful social existence, and around the world a matter of life and death. Society is sacred, if not divine. By the standards of most religious traditions, institutionalized societalism amounts to idolatry. But this means that life within a society also has become a challenge for traditional religion. Let us call this the paradox of societalization.

Third, global order though obviously influenced at least indirectly by Western religious beliefs is a secular order. International law is not grounded in divinely inspired principles; political and economic transactions occasionally call for divine sanction but their thrust is overwhelmingly innerworldly; no one religious tradition can provide a satisfactory account of the meaning of world order. Yet precisely because global order is an institutionalized normative order it is plausible that there emerges some search for an "ultimate" foundation, for some transcendent reality beyond this world in relation to which the latter could be more clearly defined (Dumont 1980). More simply put, insofar as secularization generally leads to the production of sects (deviant within a tradition where the latter still holds) or cults (outside a tradition) according to Stark and Bainbridge (1985) we can expect this to work at the highest level as well. Not only will we find various global "sects," deviating from standard world order as represented for example in international law, but after the cult of the individual and the cult of society we may also expect the arrival of the cult(s) of the globe. This can be called the paradox of secularization.

Fourth, globalization shatters the glass of civilizations, to paraphrase Al Ghazzali. Once shattered, these cannot be put back together as such; but the shattering may also produce a strong pressure to do so. Globalization produces a genuinely pluralistic world order; but precisely such pluralism may stimulate pressure toward a more coherent, more satisfying monism. World order is highly differentiated, at many levels; precisely such differentiation can produce a reactive, if not reactionary, thrust toward unification. But in principle pluralism and differentiation cannot be undone. In particular, a specifically religious quest for a more "solid" global order is doomed to fail. Such a quest must proceed, if it is not to be imposed by force, by means of discourse on the basis of "soft" proofs, satisfying shared rather than distinctive epistemological standards, since the ultimate incommensurability of civilizational logic cannot be overcome.

The maximum possible "unification" is what Smart (1987) has called soft non-relativism. This position assumes that there are some common elements in different traditions, claims that some form of "open" society is best, and robs participants in various traditions of the "right to be legitimately certain" (Smart 1987). Presumably, this requires a combination of global tolerance and critical exchanges, of active participation in particular communities as well as a sense of belonging to a larger whole. This is conceivable, especially for Western liberals who have not lost all hope. However, it is not a satisfactory outcome to any religious quest for global order. Such a quest remains a necessarily paradoxical process.

Fifth, globalization theory and world system analysis are sociological accounts of global order. They purport to give a general and universally valid account of the rise of this new human figuration. But sociology is itself a "localized" enterprise; in spite of its world-wide diffusion as a tradition the discipline remains tied to the assumptions of a particular civilization. Perhaps the paradox of sociology is that it operates as if there is an Archimedean point from which to give a general account of globalization, only to show that no Archimedean point exists any longer; and no universal history is possible.

One response to this is what may be called sociological fundamentalism: the claim that sociology does after all provide the one true story, the ultimately valid perspective. But then sociological analysis, in an effort meaningfully to interpret human experience, itself becomes a religious quest for global order. Unfortunately, any effort to construct a sociological Key to all Global Mythologies is self-defeating. The best we can do is to adopt, by analogy with Smart's ethical position, a cognitive soft non-relativism. Thus no account of globalization can legitimately claim certainty or completeness; all such accounts can be criticized. In all rational views of global order there will be some common elements; insofar as accounts produced from different corners of the globe vary, something may be learned from the differences. No elaborate institutional presuppositions are needed, except a general commitment to the open society, a globally realized cultural pluralism in decentralized, differentiated structures with inclusive membership and the maximum possible participation in discourse about global order. Thinking, and trying to show sociologically, that such a global open society is a possible world order, may well be an act of faith.

Notes

1. This is only to suggest that certain expectations derived from globalization theory are satisfied and that a process of global institutionalization is taking place. It is not to suggest that the notion of an "international legal order" is unproblematic; it obviously is not (Onuf 1979).
2. Gong's (1984) study of the use of the standard of "civilization" in the nineteenth and early twentieth centuries provides important support for an institutional analysis of global order by showing how, in a crucial period of European expansion, there was a set of global norms that aspiring new participants in international society had to satisfy in order to qualify as legitimate, full-fledged members.
3. In Parsonian terms, this may be viewed as value generalization in an increasingly differentiated and culturally diverse, but institutionally integrated, world system.
4. Note that both the Spanish tradition in international law focusing on the legitimacy of Spanish expansion and conquest in the Americas and the early modern thinkers on international law, following the Wars of Religion, also had to deal with the creation of a new global order by legal means in spite of clear differences in ultimate beliefs (cf. J. Muldoon, Chapter 5, this volume).

References

Ago, Roberto. 1978. "Pluralism and the Origins of the International Community." *The Italian Yearbook of International Law*, vol. III. Naples: Editoriale Scientifica.

Bergesen, Albert. 1980. "From Utilitarianism to Globology." Ch. 1 in *Studies of the Modern World System*, edited by A. Bergesen. New York: Academic Press.

Berman, Harold J. 1982. "The Law of International Commercial Transactions." In *International Business Transactions*, Part III, edited by W. S. Surrey and D. Wallace.

———. 1983. *Law and Revolution: The Formation of the Western Legal Tradition*. Cambridge: Harvard University Press.

———. 1984. *The Interaction Between Law and Religion*. Nashville: Abingdon Press.

———. 1988. "Toward an Integrative Jurisprudence: Politics, Morality, History." *California Law Review* 76: 779-801.

Boli-Bennett, John. 1980. "Global Integration and the Universal Increase of State Dominance, 1910-1970." Ch. 5 in *Studies of the Modern World System*, edited by A. Bergesen. New York: Academic Press.

Bozeman, Adda. 1971. *The Future of Law in a Multicultural World*. Princeton: Princeton University Press.

———. 1984. "The International Order in a Multicultural World." Ch. 26 in *The Expansion of International Society*, edited by H. Bull and A. Watson. Oxford: Clarendon Press.

Bull, Hedley. 1966. "The Grotian Conception of International Society." Ch. 3 in *Diplomatic Investigations*, edited by H. Butterfield and M. Wight. London: George Allen & Unwin.

———. 1977. *The Anarchical Society: A Study of Order in World Politics*. New York: Columbia University Press.

_____. 1984. "The Emergence of a Universal International Society." Ch. 8 in *The Expansion of International Society*, edited by H. Bull and A. Watson. Oxford: Clarendon Press.
Cassese, Antonio. 1986. *International Law in a Divided World*. Oxford: Clarendon Press.
Dore, Ronald. 1984. "Unity and Diversity in Contemporary World Culture." Ch. 27 in *The Expansion of International Society*, edited by H. Bull and A. Watson. Oxford: Clarendon Press.
Dumont, Louis. 1980. "On Value." 207–41 in *Proceedings of the British Academy*. Oxford: Oxford University Press.
Gong, Gerrit W. 1984. *The Standard of 'Civilization' in International Society*. Oxford: Clarendon Press.
Jenks, Wilfred C. 1967. *Law in the World Community*. London: Longmans.
Lechner, Frank J. 1989. "Cultural Aspects of the Modern World-System." 11–28 in *Religious Politics in Global and Comparative Perspective*, edited by William Swatos, Jr. Westport: Greenwood Press.
MacIntyre, Alasdair. 1988. *Whose Justice? Which Rationality?* South Bend: University of Notre Dame Press.
Meyer, John W. 1980. "The World Polity and the Authority of the Nation-State." Ch. 6 in *Studies of the Modern World System*, edited by A. Bergesen. New York: Academic Press.
Nettl, J.P. and Roland Robertson. 1968. *International Systems and the Modernization of Societies*. New York: Basic Books.
Onuf, Nicholas G. 1979. "International Legal Order as an Idea." *American Journal of International Law* 73: 246–66.
_____. 1982. "Global Law Making and Legal Thought." Ch. 1 in *Law-Making in the Global Community*, edited by N.G. Onuf. Durham: Carolina Academic Press.
Robertson, Roland. 1987. "Globalization Theory and Civilization Analysis," *Comparative Civilizations Review* 17: 20–30.
_____. 1991. "Globality, Global Culture, and Images of World Order." In *Social Change and Modernity*, edited by Hans Haferkamp and Neil Smelser. Berkeley: University of California Press.
Robertson, Roland and JoAnn Chirico. 1985. "Humanity, Globalization and Worldwide Religious Resurgence: A Theoretical Exploration." *Sociological Analysis* 46(3): 219–42.
Schwarzenberger, Georg. 1976. *The Dynamics of International Law*. Abingdon: Professional Books.
Smart, Ninian. 1987. *Religion and the Western Mind*. Albany: State University of New York Press.
Stark, Rodney and William Sims Bainbridge. 1985. *The Future of Religion: Secularization, Revival, and Cult Formation*. Berkeley: University of California Press.
Stone, Julius. 1984. *Visions of World Order*. Baltimore: The Johns Hopkins University Press.
Wallerstein, Immanuel. 1974. *The Modern World System*. New York: Academic Press.
_____. 1980. *The Modern World System II*. New York: Academic Press.

15

GLOBALIZATION, MODERNIZATION, AND POSTMODERNIZATION

THE AMBIGUOUS POSITION OF RELIGION

Roland Robertson

> Humanity is simply another word for the totality of human societies, for the ongoing process of the figuration which all the various survival units form with each other.... In former days the term humanity often served as a symbol of a far-fetched ideal beyond the reach of social science inquiries. It is far-fetched no longer. Nor is it an ideal. At a time when all the different tribes, all states of the world, are drawn together more closely, humanity increasingly represents a purely factual frame of reference of sociological inquiries into past no less than present phases of social development. (Elias 1987: 244)

> Social systems are societies if they include all operations that, for them, have the quality of communication. Societies are encompassing systems.... Historically, societies may be said to expand because of increasing communication potential; currently, in fact, only one society exists, the world society that includes all meaningful communication and excludes everything else. (Luhmann 1987: 114)

My first concern in this brief discussion is to express as succinctly as possible the main ingredients of what is becoming known as globalization theory, with particular reference to the significance of religion. Since my own formulations in the sphere of globalization theory have often centered upon consideration of religion—although they did not actually start with the latter as an empirical focus—this is not simply an exercise in the application of a theory or an analytical point of view. Rather, it is an attempt to sketch the relevance of religion to any general project of theorizing about globalization. My second, closely related concern is to consider religion in the context of what some now call the post-modern condition; in particular the status of religion as a *genre* of expression, communication, legitimation, and consumption in the contemporary world.

Globalization

In one sense what I and others call globalization theory preceded and has very little to do with what has become known as world-system(s) theory, but in another sense it has been pursued as an alternative to the latter. Since, however, I have no wish in the present context to trace the history of the globalization-theoretic research program I can only pause briefly to indicate in the most skeletal terms the major differences between world-system(s) theory and globalization theory. Indeed this would not be necessary at all were it not for the fact—at least, I see it as a fact—that the world-system(s) perspective, as it has crystallized in the social sciences since the mid-1970s, is at a very general level widely shared beyond the confines of particular sets of sociologists, political scientists, economists, and other professional academicians. Indeed the emphasis upon the globally compressing aspects and effects of the congealing of the world economy has become a cliché of public discourse across the world. (That is not, of course, to say that the theory and ideology—as opposed to the diffuse empirical claims—of world-system(s) theory are widely shared.) In other words, economic interdependence and interpenetration at the global level constitute the most commonly and explicitly specified ingredient and dynamic of globalization.

On the other hand, I have been insisting that that is but one aspect of one dimension of the overall process of globalization. Specifically, the economic factor is only one of the facets of the making of the modern international system, which itself (the process of global internationalization) is, in turn, but one of a number of dimensions of globalization. Even more specifically, I have argued—for reasons which cannot be explicated here—that the process of global *internationalization* (the expansion and consolidation of the international system) has to be set conceptually and empirically alongside processes of global *societalization* (the global generalization of a particular conception of the modern form of society); global *individualization* (the global generalization of a conception of the modern person); and global *humanization* (the global diffusion of a conception of a homogenous, but gender-distinguished, humankind). I regard each of these four major dimensions of globalization as relatively autonomous but also as highly interdependent. In other words, they are related on the basis of autonomy-within-reciprocity; although empirical relationships between and among them have varied and continue to vary in intensity and directional flow.

Thus with the general concept of globalization I summarize the terms in which the world as a whole becomes what I have heretofore called a "single place." I originally selected the latter term in order to avoid encouraging my listeners or readers into believing that I was promoting an image of a harmonious, integrated world. I was even more concerned to avoid giving the impression that globalization is necessarily progressive in the sense of the world as a whole becoming a better place. Unfortunately, in spite of much insistence on my part my careful choice of words has not always led to successful communication. So let me repeat yet again that to speak of the world becoming a single place (with four major processual components: societies, individuals, the international system of societies, and humankind) does not in and of itself say anything about global unification in any idealistic respect.

In one sense the concept of a globalized world is analytically neutral on that issue—although I should say that there is a kind of pretheoretical commitment on my part to the idea that any sociocultural entity must manifest variety in order to perpetuate itself (Robertson 1987b). Thus the idea of a homogenized world—along the lines of Durkheim's conception of mechanical solidarity—is not merely unattractive; it is lacking in sensibility even as a theoretical idea and most definitely it is unrealistic. In any case the fact that I include societalization and individualization as dimensions of globalization itself indicates—or at least, is intended to indicate—that particularism and localism go hand in hand, so to say, with universalism and cosmopolitanism.[1]

Globalization itself produces variety—more accurately, it encourages heterogeneity-within-homogeneity, or difference-within-identity. Put another way, globalization involves, in the most general terms, the universalization of particularism and the particularization of universalism. Civilizational, societal, ethnic, communal and individual lifestyle differences are exacerbated—indeed, produced—in the globalization process; while, on the other hand, globalization involves the crystallization and concretization of the world as a whole—sociologically and geographically.

This, I insist, is how we must as relatively detached observers consider the contemporary world as a whole. Now that does not mean to say that universalism or cosmopolitanism cannot appear—for example, from the point of view of a Christian fundamentalist in Tennessee or Alabama—as the respective opposites of a preferred particularism or localism, for in those and other areas of the contemporary world the claim that "one worldism" is literally an evil has been advanced. But the very fact that the universalism-particularism and cosmopolitanism-localism themes are invoked across the world in which we now live ought to require us in our roles of observers to say that they are indeed global phenomena and to wonder seriously as to why and how this mode of thinking has taken hold so extensively.

However, it should be added very quickly that to claim that such themes have been globally generalized is not by any means to overlook the fact that ideas expressing relationships between in-groups and out-groups, parts and wholes, relativism and universalism, and so on, have been central themes in the long histories of civilizations and religions. Indeed, systematic comparative-historical analysis of the theory and practice of what might generically be called inclusion and exclusion must be a pivotal feature of research into the phenomenon of globalization. The only truly critical difference between such historical research and analysis of the contemporary globalization process arises from the fact that the world as a whole is now concretely "one place." And religious organizations and movements increasingly respond to that phenomenon of what I call globality (Robertson 1991). (However, emphasis on the contemporary concreteness of the contemporary world as a whole should not create the impression that one can indicate a particular date before which the world was not truly a whole in a sociological sense.)

Before, however, talking in more detail about such matters I want to return more directly to the notion of the world as a single place—with which I originally meant to describe a situation in which the whole world is a constraining as well as an enabling setting for what sociologists have traditionally thought of as intrasocietal or intracivilizational affairs. I consciously resisted, in opting for the concept of "a single place," Luhmann's adamantly expressed claim that the only "real" society in the modern world is world society. I must now confess that I find it difficult to resist the general force of Luhmann's argument, although I do not think that he has provided reasons, nuances, and caveats sufficient to convince on a large scale. So let me make Luhmann's point in my own way.

The notion of a society is in a distinctively periodized sense a modern phenomenon. If we follow Polanyi's (1957) argument we see that as that term has been used by social scientists it is approximately two hundred years old and refers to a politically and territorially organized entity in which social interactions occur and are emphatically bounded. Another way of looking at the issue would be to regard Rousseau's ideas concerning the requirements of societality as an historical indicator of "the rise of society." In any event, it is no accident of the history of ideas that the sociological sense of society took firm hold in the 1890s under Toennies' influence as a way of demarcating the past of Western "societies" (i.e., "communities") from the kind of social formation which had crystallized in Europe and America by the end of the nineteenth century (i.e., the emergent mixture of individualistic volunteerism and state domination characteristic of the national vehicles in which we now live). For it was in roughly that same period of the late nineteenth and early twentieth centuries that the concept of "civilization" as a standard which societal members of "international society" has to conform to was crystallized among European nations and then imposed outside Europe (Gong 1984)—and that the idea that a society ought to have a cohesive collective identity was spread widely across the world, extending from the Americas in the West to Japan in the East (Gluck 1985: 37–41). Such developments were, I suggest, echoed in the emphasis placed upon national-cultural homogeneity in Max Weber's and upon civil-religious societal identity in Durkheim's writings.

The point I am trying to make, then, is that much of the thinking about societies in the late nineteenth and early twentieth centuries was developed in reference to a global context, that it was the constraints and perception of the latter which shaped the notion that societies had to be nationally particularistic with fully incorporated individuals and groups. Thus in sociological terms Weber's concern with the problem of the Germanic status of Poles, Jews, and Catholics and Durkheim's interest in the enhancement of institutions which would link the individual to (French) society were but intellectual refractions of a generalized interest in producing national-societal identity within the context of both increasingly global ideas concerning what a viable society should "look like" and a sense that societal viability in an increasingly interdependent world was possible only by promoting or consolidating societal solidarity and membership. In a nutshell, modern nationalism and citizenship have all along been partly global phenomena—not only in the obvious sense of widespreadness but, much more important, because they arose in large part in response to globally diffused expectations.

Such considerations suggest that we have to be very careful to avoid overemphasis upon purely intrasocietal or even intracivilizational accounts of many sociocultural trends. Elias and Luhmann—although their respective accounts are different in substance—both neglect the degree to which globally diffused ideas about "society" have been crucial. The concept of civilization, conceived by Elias in processual terms, was a critical ingredient of international discourse—as a standard for societies—in the critical take-off period of modern globalization. Thus the civilizing process has not been so unplanned as Elias implies.

At the same time against Luhmann it has to be said that the contemporary significance of societies cannot be easily diminished in spite of his cogency as far as the force of processes of functional differentiation are concerned.[2] According to Luhmann the dominant form of differentiation (and hence, in a special sense, of social organization) in the normally recognized societal pattern has been internally structured social stratification; while the contemporary dominant form is functional differentiation—the latter extending beyond societal containers in such a way as to make it virtually impossible for any given society to operate only in terms of its own "information." The only "true" society is thus world society because no society can or does stand on its own in terms of the information (in the broadest sense of that word) which it and its members need or utilize. While the thrust of Luhmann's insight is, as I have said, persuasive there is no direct consideration in Luhmann's writing on "world society" of the factors which have made the general fate of the national society problematic.

My own argument is that the problem of "world society" has developed in interpenetrating tandem with "the problem of societies." Thus I now think, with some continuing reservations, that it is appropriate to think realistically and conceptually in terms of a world society, so long as we retain the concept of national society and fully acknowledge that world society is a qualitatively new societal type, one which is indeed a single place in a very important sense. For world society is, in part, the earth and its thematization enhances the symbolic-geographical significance of societies and civilizational traditions (Wagstaff 1987).

Religion, Modernity, and Societality

It is no accident that the rise of society was accompanied by the notion that religion was to be regarded as separate from the systemic domains of politics and economy. Thus through the nineteenth century the idea of the private, relatively sequestered status of religion was cultivated and widely diffused. If one has to pinpoint a period when that development took off in earnest it would, of course, be the late 1780s and early

1790s—when in France and the newly born U.S.A. the claim that religion (in the specific sense of its being supernaturally revealed, socially organized, and politically significant) is at least potentially destructive of society made considerable impact. Of course, there were great differences between the French and the American declarations in that regard; but that does not seriously qualify the general thesis that after the early 1890s the separation of "church and state" rapidly gained ground—and in effect laid the basis for the development of the idea at the end of the nineteenth century that religion could and should be studied as an isolable sphere of sociocultural life.

I am thus proposing that there is an apparently paradoxical relationship between modernity and religion. "Religion" is a category and a problem of modernity, a motif which was produced in the circumstance of modernity "in order to" show what modernity was leaving behind. On the other hand, positive subscription to the idea of religion has largely constituted, in varying degrees, a critique of modernity itself. In those terms we would regard the religious studies "movement" as having developed in opposition to *Gesellschaft* and the sociology of religion as a discipline torn between the modernist attempt to thematize the peripherality of religion (religion as a dependent variable) and the anti-modernist effort to give religion a privileged status, usually as a supplier of meaning. Hence the obsession with the problematic of secularization in the sociology of religion; for the latter has two parents who are not very compatible: the modernity which issued from the Enlightenment and envisaged a world without religion and the anti-modernity which has not been able to embrace the idea of a world without religion. The concern with secularization is an expression of the offspring's dilemma.

Thus while societalization has been regarded as the primary enemy of religion (Wilson 1982) it can, I think, be shown that it is globally institutionalized societalism (Lechner 1987) which has actually installed religion as a global category. Following the French and the American revolutions the place of religion in "duly constituted" societies became a widespread problem. A number of the newly independent societies of Latin America tried in various ways during the nineteenth century to promote a secular state alongside a sequestered sphere of religion; while by the end of that period the principle of the freedom of religion had been spread eastwards from Europe—indeed as far as Japan.

At the same time the insistence upon societies having identities considerably blurred the issue of what was to count as religion. Thus in Meiji Japan the national polity (*kokutai*) was embellished with an allegedly dereligionized form of national Shinto, largely in order to conform to Western expectations concerning the sequestered status and freedom of religion. (State Shinto was declared to be a moral rather than a religious institution.) Later in Kemalist Turkey a secular state was adamantly promoted—and yet Durkeiheimian ideas concerning the need for societies to have some kind of civil religion were very influential. And so on—into the period of the post-1945 beginnings of the Third World, marked by India's political elite wrestling with the alien problem of defining religion in order to establish a secular state. Thus the supposedly integrating—or, at least, identifying—functions of religion continued to be taken seriously but "real religion" was considered to be an impediment to the secularization which, it was thought, was a desideratum of societalization.

Religion, Postmodernism, and Globality

The depoliticization of religion has been a central myth of the project of societal modernization (Robertson 1989). The contemporary repoliticization of religion thus indicates something important. My suggestion is that the process of repoliticization is a manifestation of a new phase in the long-term globalization process—involving massive processes of relativization of societal traditions and of citizenly involvement of individuals in nationally constituted societies. Parsons (1971) argued that a hallmark of the making of the modern world system of societies was the emphasis upon the self-sufficiency of the national society—a standard which above all involved the requirement that the "overwhelming majority" of the society's members not be "radically 'alienated'" (Parsons 1971: 9). At the same time he noted that as the system of societies crystallized on a global, as opposed to a European-Atlantic, basis the problem of "the intersocietal institutionalization of a new value system...becomes crucial" (Parsons 1971: 121). The global generalization of the idea of (self-sufficient) societality has now, I suggest, entered a new phase in which the emphasis is upon liberation of both societies and individuals—that constituting a new paradox, insofar as deepening of the idea of societal self-sufficiency is clearly not compatible in the long run with generalization of the idea that individuals should be freed from heavy limitations on their conceptions of citizenly involvement.

The new problem is, in a nutshell, the degree and form of participation in global society (Robertson 1987b). Whereas the first major modern phase of globalization involved the near-global generalization of conceptions of functionally self-sufficient societies, including individual membership thereof, the phase which we are now rapidly entering centers upon that of societal and individual location in a broader context of humankind (as well as the system of societies)—an extension of the notion of self-sufficiency to deeper, "primordial" concerns and an extrapolation of the emphasis upon individual choice. (At the same time the problem of national culture has acquired a new form, for whereas in the nineteenth century the idea was developed and widely diffused that societies should have integrating common cultures it now seems to be the case that the globally diffused conception of the modern state [Meyer 1980] necessitates a common "cultural literacy" [Gellner 1983].)[3]

The consequences for religion are that, given its thematization as a sociocultural category, it now appears as both a mode of collective identity—as a relatively independent resource for the legitimation of collective action—and as a form of consumption at the level of individuals. Religion has been made globally available as a source of collective identity declarations—most notably in Islamic fundamentalism and liberation theology—as well as something to be consumed or spent by individuals.

It is along such lines that, I believe, some light can be cast upon the relationship between globalization and postmodernization (in the sense of the trends noted by postmodernists and analysts of alleged postmodernism). One of the central motifs of postmodernist theory is, of course, the claim that "grand narratives" are no longer viable—that we live increasingly in a situation in which it is unrealistic and implausible to think that there are long-term directional trends and universalistically historical projects in human life. That argument has been directed particularly at the so-called Enlightenment project, which I have been talking about in terms of societalization and modernization.

However, although it has not been entirely neglected, there has been insufficient attention in this regard to the fact that just as modernity was in its origins a European-Atlantic phenomenon so too is postmodernism—at least as a "theory"—a primarily Western (particularly French) point of view. We have not pressed hard enough the idea that postmodernism as an intellectual standpoint is a response to a globalization process which relativizes the West. A West which is no longer "in control of itself" and the future of the world responds to that circumstance by the production of ideas which deny any grand narratives. Similarly the relativization of Western modernity encourages the view that modernity is dead.

However, it is clear that grand narratives are not dying in Latin America or Asia, and, indeed, their (religious) vitality is probably in part a response to a precarious state of the grand narrative in the West (most particularly in Western Europe). On a global scale we are, I suggest, witnessing the rise of a generalized constraint on societies and civilizations to produce their own unique accounts of their places in world history. Religion is obviously playing a crucial role in this—outside most of Europe. At the same time, however, religion appears to have become simply a lifestyle option in quite a few areas of the world.4 Therein lies the paradox of religion in the globalized and partly postmodernized world.

Notes

1. This is not to say that universalism equals cosmopolitanism or that particularism equals localism. (One, but only one, of the reasons for not making the first equation is that "cosmopolitanism" has become part of the language of contemporary advertising.)
2. See, however, Luhmann (1984).
3. What would seem to distinguish this emphasis upon cultural literacy from nineteenth century ideas about educating the working class is that the former involves much greater concern with knowledge of one's own culture—at least that is the way in which Hirsch (1987) has recently applied Gellner's ideas prescriptively to the U.S.A. The expectation that societies should have common cultures and identities is a theme which should be inserted in the dominant ideology debate (Abercrombie *et al.* 1980).
4. Whether one could now speak seriously of societies choosing global-participatory "lifestyles" is a point worth pursuing. Related to such a consideration is the increasing probability of individuals self-consciously opting for closed, fundamentalist lifestyles. Is that modern or postmodern?

References

Abercrombie, Nicholas, Stephen Hill, and Bryan S. Turner. 1980. *The Dominant Ideology Thesis*. London: Allen and Unwin.
Elias, Norbert. 1982. *State Formation and Civilization*. Oxford: Blackwell.
_____. 1987. "The Retreat of Sociologists into the Present." *Theory, Culture and Society* 4 (2–3): 223–48.
Featherstone, Mike. 1989. "Towards a Sociology of Postmodern Culture." (Mimeo).
Gellner, Ernest. 1983. *Nations and Nationalism*. Ithaca: Cornell University Press.
Gong, Gerrit W. 1984. *The Standard of 'Civilization' in International Society*. Oxford: Clarendon Press.
Gluck, Carol. 1985. *Japan's Modern Myths*. Princeton: Princeton University Press.
Hirsch, E.D., Jr. 1987. *Cultural Literacy: What Every American Needs to Know*. Boston: Houghton Mifflin.
Jameson, Frederic. 1986. "Third-World Literature in the Era of Multinational Capitalism." *Social Text* 15 (Fall): 65–88.
Lechner, Frank. 1987. "Modernity and Its Procontents: Societal Solidarity in Comparative Perspective." Paper presented at American Sociological Association and Association for the Sociology of Religion annual meetings. (Mimeo).

Luhmann, Niklas. 1984. "The Self Description of Society: Crisis, Fashion and Sociological Theory." *International Journal of Comparative Sociology* 25: 59–72.

Luhmann, Niklas. 1987. "The Evolutionary Differentiation Between Society and Interaction." 112–31 in Jeffrey C. Alexander *et al.* (eds.), *The Micro-Macro Link*. Berkeley: University of California Press.

Meyer, John W. 1980. "The World Polity and the Authority of the Nation-State." 77–137 in Albert Bergesen (ed.), *Studies of the Modern World System*. New York: Academic Press.

Parsons, Talcott. 1971. *The System of Modern Societies*. Englewood Cliffs: Prentice Hall.

Polanyi, Karl. 1957. *The Great Transformation*. Boston: Beacon.

Robertson, Roland. 1987a. "Globalization and Societal Modernization: A Note on Japan and Japanese Religion." *Sociological Analysis* 47 (S): 35–42.

_____. 1987b. "Globalization Theory and Civilization Analysis." *Comparative Civilizations Review* 17.

_____. 1989. "Globalization, Politics, and Religion." In James Beckford and Thomas Luckmann (eds.), *The Changing Face of Religion*. London: Sage.

_____. 1991. "Globality, Global Culture and Images of World Order." Hans Haferkamp and Neil Smelser (eds.), *Social Change and Modernity*. Berkeley: University of California Press.

Turner, Bryan S. 1986. *Citizenship and Capitalism*. London: Allen and Unwin.

Wagstaff, J.M. (ed.). 1976. *Landscape and Culture*. Oxford: Blackwell.

Wilson, Bryan. 1982. *Religion in Sociological Perspective*. New York: Oxford University Press.

Contributors

Eileen V. Barker, Senior Lecturer, Department of Sociology, London School of Economics, London, England.

Mike Featherstone, Reader, Department of Administrative and Social Studies, Teesside Polytechnic, Middlesbrough, Cleveland, England.

William R. Garrett, Professor, Department of Sociology, St. Michael's College, Colchester, Vermont.

Jeffrey K. Hadden, Professor, Department of Sociology, University of Virginia, Charlottesville, Virginia.

Stanley Johannesen, Assistant Professor, Department of History, University of Waterloo, Waterloo, Ontario, Canada.

Lonnie D. Kliever, Professor, Department of Religious Studies, Southern Methodist University, Dallas, Texas.

Frank J. Lechner, Associate Professor, Department of Sociology, Emory University, Atlanta, Georgia.

Theodore E. Long, Dean, Arts and Sciences, Merrimack College, North Andover, Massachusetts.

James M. Muldoon, Professor, Department of History, Rutgers University, Camden, New Jersey.

Roland Robertson, Professor, Departments of Sociology and Religious Studies, University of Pittsburgh, Pittsburgh, Pennsylvania.

Anson Shupe, Professor, Department of Anthropology/Sociology, Indiana-Purdue University, Fort Wayne, Indiana.

John H. Simpson, Professor, Department of Sociology, University of Toronto, Mississauga, Ontario, Canada.

James F. Strange, Professor, Department of Religious Studies, University of South Florida, Tampa, Florida.

Bryan S. Turner, Professor, Department of Sociology, University of Essex, Colchester, Essex, England.

Glenn E. Yocum, Professor, Department of Religion, Whittier College, Whittier, California.

List of Tables

Table 2–1	Dimensions of Universalism and Particularism in Hebrew Religion	28
Map 6–1	The Minaksi Temple	90
Map 6–2	Madurai: old city center	92
Map 6–3	The Atmanatacuvami Temple	101
Figure 9–1	Weber's Typology of Social Relations	164
Figure 9–2	Religio-social Movements	178

Index

A

aborigines 71
abortion 83
Abraham 22
    God of 24
Abrahamic faiths 162, 165, 178, 179
    fundamentalist versions of 168
    individualism of 167
    monotheisms 88
absolute
    authority 256
    religion 12
absolutes 12
absolutist
    truths or values 162
academics 149, 152, 216
activism
    inner-worldly 58
Adam 203
Advisory Council to the Unification Movement (ACUMI) 205, 216
aesthetic
    experiences 151
    value sphere
        elevation of 135
Aestheticism 140
Aeterni Patris 81
Agni 93
    turtham 107
Al-afghani, Jamal al-Din 172
Alagarkoil 95-98
Alakar-Visnu 95-98, 111
al-Bamma, Hasan 173
Alexander VI, Pope
Al Ghazzali 277
alienation 122
American
    Catholics 83
    civic religion 146
    Declaration of Independence 59
    holiness denominations 126
    televangelism xxi
    televangelists 235

(and) international broadcasting 234
Amish 210
amman temple 89
Anabaptism 52
Ananda Marga 202
ancestors
    Confucianist
        obligations to honor 188
Anglican Church 52
anjali mudra 110
anomie 190, 248
anthropology 155
Apologie for the Oath of Allegiance 75
apostates 78
Aquinas, Thomas 68, 72, 81
    work of 83
Arab socialism 173
architectonics 93, 98
Ardra Darsanan festival 102, 105, 108, 110
argument
    (and) global order 267
aristocratic culture 247
Art 151
    (the) body as 150
    development of autonomous 135
    occupations
        respectability of 153
artist(s) 141, 149, 152
    (as) hero 136, 140
artistic
    avant-garde 151
    modernism 151
arupa (formless) 102
aruvam 102
ascetic
    fundamentalism 165
asceticism 48, 113
Ashref 171
association 264
associational relations 164
    open 165
atheism 174

Athenagoras 42
atman 113
Atamanatar 102, 104, 108, 109
    Atamanatcuvami 102
    divine guru 102, 105
    temple of 100-101
Atmanatcuvami
    temple of 88, 99, 101 (map)
atonement 42, 221
Atupa Ganapati 103
Austrian Hapsburgs 81
authority 9
    problem of 169
autocracies xii
autonomy-within-reciprocity 283
Avadayarkoil 88, 99 passim
A'yan (notables) 170
Ayatollah Khomeini 173
Azusa Street mission 126

B

Baath Party 173
Backus, Isaac 56
Bahai faith 179
Bakker, Jim 229, 235, 241n
balances of power
    levelling out of 139
    shift in 142
Baptism 128
Baptist(s) 47, 49, 57
Baudelaire 149
belief(s) 134, 140
    changes in 142
    disregard for formal 145
    problem of 141
    systems
        attraction of 145
    vacuum in 143
    valuation of 141
believers
    individual integrity of 55
belligerence ix
beneficence ix
Berg, Daniel 122
Berger, Peter 134
Bethelship Norwegian Methodist
    Church 123
Bhiksatana 107

biblical monotheism 256
Bill of Rights 59
Blessing (mass marriages) 203
"blood lineage" 203
Bodhisattavas (advanced beings) 186
body
    aesthetics of 150
    beautiful 138
    (as) "temple" of the Holy Ghost
        128
Book of Revelation 57
Brahma 91, 94
    Kumaris 202
Brahmin(s) 91, 93, 100
    priests 89
    (and) Saivas
        separation between 110
brahmotsava-s 95, 102
British
    Broadcasting Corporation (BBC)
        224, 232, 237
    mercantilism 112
broadcast
    curriculum in colleges and
        universities 227
    evangelism
        strategies 236
    pirates 238
    technology 222
broadcasting
    (and the) eschatology of
        evangelicals 239
    (and) evangelical competition 232
    (and) growth of Christianity in
        Korea 232
    history of 223
    (and) market segmentation 235
    power to capture consciousness 237
    technology 234
    (and) Third World 231
Brownist 57
Buddha 186
Buddhism 165, 186
    relationship to political culture 189
    various strains of 187
business-Christian ethic 138
butsudan (Buddhist) 188

INDEX

C

cable 226
Calvin 52, 61n, 130
    (and) legitimate revolution 53
    (and) sacramental theology 129
Calvinism 48, 53, 54, 164, 165
    transformational ethic of 53
Calvinist(s)
    awakening 129
    orthodox 54
    religiosity 53
    sects
        (and) industrial civilizations 165
    symbol system 53
    thought 52
Canaan 23, 24, 26
Candikesvara 96, 104
Cankam poems 88
cannibalism 84
canon law 74
    revolution in x
capital
    entrepreneurial organization of 51
capitalism 4, 166
    emergence of x, 164
    expansion of 269
    innovative instruments of 49
    profane goods of 146
    (as) social system 51
    spread of 2, 6
    take off of 48
    transition of feudalism to 3
capitalist expansion 51
Carnegie Endowment for International Peace 82
carnivalesque
    liminal 156
    transgressions of 151
CARP 214
castes
    "impure" 90
Catholic(s)
    Church
        teachings of 78
    communions 48
    (and) infidel
        relations between 74, 78
    -Protestant
        clashes 53
        relations 74-76
    social and political thought
        developments in 82
    thought
        (and) contemporary values 83
Catholicism
    hegemony of 54
    Tridentine 54
CAUSA 209
    effect of 212
CBN University 227
celestial and sanctified beings
    physical presences of 130
censure 76
chanting 201
chants 147
chaos theorists xvii
character
    shifting from the virtues of 139
charisma 124, 147, 249
    (as) belonging to function 128
charismatic gifts 127
Charlemagne 121
Charles I of Castile (also known as Charles V, Holy Roman Emperor) 72
Cheng Ho xvii
child marriage 82
Children of God 201
Cholas 99
chosen people 22, 29
Christ (see also Jesus) 68
    body of 129
    coming of 72
    jurisdiction of 67
    return of 221
    second coming of 58, 233
    universal nature of (his) message 65
Christendom 255
    sacred texts of 221
Christian
    Broadcasting Network (CBN) 234, 235, 242n
    Broadcasting system 235
    Europe 66
    Global Order 65, 71
Christian
    -infidel
        relations 65, 76
    -Jewish
        relations 81
    law 67
    -*Marxist Dialogue* 213

missionaries 73
    opposition to 80
    (and) non-Christian
        relations between 81
pantheon 126
piety
    nature of 120
radio stations
    explosion of 235
society 66, 67
tradition
    individualism of 167
Christianity xii, 21, 35 passim, 65, 72, 218
    basic ideas of earliest 42
    (and) henotheistic definition 259
    organized 54
    paradigmatic "archetypes" of 254
christianization 129
Church
    (of) Jesus Christ of Latter-Day Saints (Mormons) 184, 195
    (of) Scientology 202
    (as) sole agency of salvation 53
    spiritual responsibilities of 71
    (and) State
        conflict between 65
        relations 52
        separation 287
    -type unity
        disintegration of 54
cirappu (honors) 104
circumcision 22
Cistercian development 61n
cities
    multilingual and multinational 37
    (of) moral order 112
citizenship
    (as an) index of secularization 167
"Cittirai festival" 94-98
City of God 167
civa 109
civam (essence) 107
Civananapotam 105
civil
    ethic 129
    religion 288
    rights 32, 58
civilization
    concept of 285, 286
    "standard of" 268

claims to finality
    theocentric critique of 260
Classics of International Law 82
cleanliness restrictions 22
Cluniac order 61
coercion 80, 188
coexistence
    rules of 268
collective
    decision-making 128
    memory
        deprivation of 124
    representations 145
colonial systems 5
colonialism 170
Columbus, Christopher 68, 70, 83, 84
command structure
    flexibility in 153
commodification 146
commodity(ies)
    production of 8
    use of 146
common humanity 147
Commonwealth 10
communal
    ideology 178
    memory
        sanctification of 124
    relations 163
        closed 165
communication(s) 264
    Act (1934) 226
    global order of xix
communis opinio 68
communism 202, 213
    eradication of 208
    struggle against 209
communist
    revolution xix
communitas
    creation of a ritual 146
community
    liturgical element of 127
competition ix, 249, 264
    (and) democratic elites 250, 252
compromise ix
conflict 165, 264
    (and) international law 268
    social and cultural 274
Confucianism 165

congregational purity 52
conquest
    legitimacy of 70, 71
    traditional arguments about 72
conscience
    sensitized by the Holy Ghost 128
consciousness
    stream of 3
consumer culture xxi, 137 passim, 162
    (and) ethic 143
    imagery of 138
    (as) universal culture 154
consumerism 137, 147, 175, 176, 189
consumption ethic 138, 142
contracts 164, 165
contractualism 22
conversion(s) 23, 73, 210
    adult 22
    cost of 79
Coppe 57
Copts 179
core
    (and) periphery processes 5
corruption 26
cosmic order 88
    images of 141
    renewal 97
cosmopolitanism xvi, xx, 29, 283, 284
cosmos
    creation of 93
    (as) organism 93
    sacred 91
Coughlin, Charles E. 223, 224, 241n
counter culture 152
Counter Reformation 48
    Catholicism 54
covenant 21, 22, 26, 29
    ark of 24
    break of 23
    (with) Israel 27
    limits imposed by 30
    (with) monotheistic god 20
    threatened 25, 26
Cromwell's New Model Army 56
Crouch, Paul 235, 242n
cujus regio, ejus religio 53, 77
cult 277
cultural
    capital
        accumulating 141

de-classification 136, 155
development xvii
disorder 136, 148 passim
    images of 156
dominance 148
heritage xvii
identity xii
cultural
    indoctrination 238
    insensitivity 242n
    integration 112
    myth of 143
    meaning 144
    methodology 155
    modernism 144
        deleterious effects of 145
    nihilism 168
    order 136
    perspectivism 162
    pluralism 278
    Revolution xix
    stagnation xvii
    traditions 60
culture 152
    de-monopolization and
        de-classification of 137
    (of) diversity and heterogeneity 151
    homogenization of 252
    Islamization of 171
    movement towards postmodern 135
    (and) social integration 144
    sociology of 133
    synthesis of 248
cuvami temple 89

D

Dadaism 140
Daimoku 189
daivaka 91
daksina 101
Daksinamurti 108
dancing 147
Darby, John Nelson 221
darsan 97, 103, 104, 107, 108
Das Kapital xvii
David, reign of 24, 26

Day of Atonement 40
Defence of the Catholic and Apostolic Faith, A 75
Defensor Pacis 76
deity(ies) 89, 90, 93, 97,
    image of 113
democracy xviii, xix, 5, 174
democratic
    aesthetics 247
    egalitarianism 26
    linguistics 247
    pedagogy 247
    philosophy 247
    sociology 247
    theology 247
democratization 139, 250, 252
    (and) chronic disorder 251
    first fundamental principle of 249
    moral foundations of 253
    nemeses of 253
destiny
    ultimate concerns of 184
detente ix
development
    model of 6
developmentalism 6
    American model of 10
devotee
    (and) object of devotion
        psychological and moral distance between 126
devotion 126, 127
    (as) principle of loyalty and bonding 125
devotional attitude 125
dharma 88, 94, 110, 273
dharmic society 93
Dialetic of Enlightenment 163
Dialogue and Alliance 207
dictatorship 252
Didache 41
differentiation 286
Diggers 47, 57
diparadhana (waving of lamps) 109
Direct-Broadcast Satellites 239
Directory of Religious Broadcasting, The 226
discordance ix
disenchantment 146
dissent 125
distribution 29
disunity 55
divine
    consciousness 204
    election 249
    pedigree 94
    power 113
    Principles 202
    right 249
    teacher 110
doctrine
    (of) second experience 126
dominance
    struggle for 148
dominant ideology debate 290
dominium 68
Dominus mundi (lord of the world) 72
drsan 98
due process 56
Durkheim 133, 145-147
    (and his) account of social order 270
    (and) civil-religious society 285
    (and his) conception of mechanical solidarity 283
    (and) social solidarity 172
dynastic power
    inability to secure control 170

E

ecclesiastical order 52
ecclesiology 119
economic
    development xvii
    sanctions xix
Economy and Society 163
ecumenicalism
    (of) ideas 179
ecumenism 162
education 152, 172
Edwards, Jonathan 58
egalitarian
    citizenship 166
    individualism 167
    principles 170
    relationships 247
egalitarianism
    conditions for radical 167

INDEX

Egypt
    (and) traditional elites 174
elect nation 22
electoral process 50
electronic
    communication 221, 222
    evangelization
        (and) forbidden territories 231
elites 170, 250-251, 253
    reform efforts by 276
    struggle between 146
Elizabeth I, Queen 74
embodiment
    crisis of 128
emotional
    regression 153
    solidarity 147
empire 3, 10
empirical relativism 275
emulation 139
English Civil War xxi, 48
Enlightenment x, xii, xiv, 287
    philosophy 56, 60
    project 289
    reflection
        mistaken vestige of 61
equality
    (and) autonomy 251
    (in the) eyes of God 26
    (of) persons 249
    political and social 166
equalization 139
eroticism 135, 136
eschatological urgency 120
eschatology 119, 221
eschaton 57
established intellectuals
    de-monopolization of power of 155
ethical
    (and) legal principles
        development 20
ethics 127
ethnic
    diversity 169
ethnicity 120
    continuity of 164
    rise of x
ethnocentrism 190
European culture
    secularization experience of xiv

evangelical(s) 225
    Christians 222, 223
    success formula 228
evangelization
    lay 120
evangelizing
    (the) world
        plans for 234
Eve 203
exchange processes 15
exclusivity and privilege
    breakdown of 142
existential predicament 141

F

faith 257-259
    struggle of 260
Fallen Nature (original sin) 203
Falwell, Jerry 60
familist 57
    God-centered 202, 204
Far East Broadcasting Association
    (FEBA) 230, 231, 233, 236
fashion 139, 140
Federal Communications Commission
    225, 230
Fessenden, Reginald 222
Fifth Monarchy Men 57
fin de millennium 137, 149
First Amendment 229
force
    use of 79
formulation
    (of) belief
        religious authority in 54
fragmentation 136
fraternization 164
Free
    Church tradition 51, 54
    labor 51
Freed, Paul 230, 231
Freedom
    (of) assembly 55
    (of) conscience
        unalienable right to 55
    Leadership Foundation (FLF) 209
    (of the) press 14, 56
    (of) speech 14, 56

French Declaration of the Rights of Man and Citizens 59
fundamentalism(s) 1, 12, 163
    (as) brake on capitalism 165
    character of 170
    (and) militant Islam
        emergence of 173
    (as) response to modernization and post-modernism 169
    rise of 129
    (as a) value system 163
fundamentalist
    ideology 174
fundamentalization
    (as) forms of collective nostalgia 169

G

Ganesa 96, 103
garbhaqrha (or garbhagrha) 89, 102, 113
Gautama 186
    message of 185
Gemeinschaft 178
Gemeinschaft and Gessellschaft 3, 12, 13, 163, 164
    historical transition of 167
    tension between 11
gender
    continuity of 164
General Assembly of U.N. and World Court 267
genius 249
German historicism 143
Gessellschaft 3, 265, 276, 287
Global
    circumstance
        perception of 155
    Congress of the World's Religions 212
    Economic Action Group 212
    ecumenism 162
    order
        contribution of Catholic thought to 82
        Christian theory of 67
        consumerism, postmodernism and 154
        creation by legal means 279
        development of pluralistic 83
        establishment of 204
        Hindu quest for 88
        institutional analysis of 271, 279n
        institutionalization of 268, 272, 274, 275
        liberal theory of 82
        normative structure of 272
Global
    order
        political and philosophical 246
        quest for 260, 278
        shifts in 148
        significance of religion in xxi
        sociological accounts of 278
        theory of 67, 68, 74
        (and) ultimate values 264
        Unification efforts to establish 214
    relations
        theory of 72
    society
        degree of participation in 288
    theocracy 202
    tolerance 277
    system xi
globalism x, 196
globality 284
globalization 11, 13, 276
    causal chain of 265
    conversation 2, 3
    (and) economic interdependence 282
    historical process of 264
    logic of 184
    paradoxes of 276
    (and) postmodernism 289
    process(es) of ix, xi, xii, xiii, xiv, xx, 137, 267, 282
        relation of religion to xv, xxi, 185
    relevance of religion to 282
    research
        contributions of Stanford School to 2
    theories of xiv, 3, 4, 10, 279n
    universalizing tendencies of xx
Glorious Revolution 58-59
Glossolalia 122
Go World Brass Band 206
God (and gods) 22, 36, 49, 91, 107
    absolutist messages of 30
    conference 212

death of 168
direct relation to 49
embodiment of 89
grant from 56
(of) history 27
images of 90
incarnate 109
kingdom of 53
laws of 202
love of 26
marriage by 203
mobile 24
monotheistic 166
one family of the Father 260
personal of Christianity 166
personal and sovereign 246
God (and gods)
power of
  faith in 29
(and his) promise 21-23
Providential
  engagement of 223
  hand of 222
(of) radical monotheism 257
radical sovereignty of 256
relationship with his people 27
single 24
symbol of 113
-teacher 107
transcendence of 256
ultimate 25
understanding of 202
vision of 91
goddess 99, 100, 102, 103, 111
  shrine 109
Godism 209, 213
Gohonzon 189
Gokalp, Ziya 172
Golden Lotus Tank 89, 97
goporakumara 104
gopuram-s 90, 95, 99
gopuras (gates) 113
Gopuravelavan 104
Gospel 79
  message 221
  preachers of 80
  preaching of 73
  utilizing airwaves to spread the 240
government 67
governmental power

sharing of 249
grand narrative 289
Great
  Commandment 239
  Commission 222
  Transformation 183
Greco-roman culture xxi, 41
Greek culture 36
Grotius, Hugo 69, 82, 267
group(s)
  identity 120
  status and power structure of 142
Guptas 112
guru-priest-god 109
guruship 110

H

Habermas 135
Haredin 179
Hebrew(s) 22
  community 31
  religion 20
hedonism 137, 138
hegemony 6
  (in) maintenance of world order 12
henotheism 257-259
Heralding Christ Jesus' Blessing (HCJB)
  230, 231, 236, 239
hereditary privilege 249
heresy 77
heretics 68, 76
heterogeneity-within-homogeneity 283
Hillell 36
Hindu(s) 88
  data 87
  dharmic order 91
  ideology and ritual 111
  norm 113
  polarity 88
  tradition 8
Hinduism 165
historical
  experience
    periodization of xi
  options x
Historicism 248
historicity 20, 27, 30
  agents of 27

historiography
    neo-Marxist 49
history
    end of 150, 222
    interpretation of xix
Holiness 127
    doctrines
        problems with 126
    (and) Methodist Congregations 122
holism
    nostalgic quest for 178
Holy
    Ghost xxi, 119 passim
        Baptism 122, 126, 127
        (as) carrier of spiritual grace 130
        indwelling of 128
        infilling of after Salvation 126
        power of 126, 127
        (as) principle of the holy 126
        visitation of 127
    Land 67
    Roman Emperor 66, 75
    Spirit
        Association for the Unification of World Christianity (HSA-UWC) 202
        gifts of 128
        Wine Ceremony 203
Home Church 204, 211
Host
    presence of Christ in 130
Household of Faith 165
    patrimonial 170
    polity of 169 passim
Household of Islam
    (and the) sphere of war 162
human
    cultures
        plurality of 88
    nature 153
    rights 48, 59, 147, 267
        meaning of 268
        tradition 59, 60
    sacrifice 82, 84
humanism 258
humanity 281
    conceptions of 274
    generalized notion of 6
humanization 283
humankind
    historicity of 256
    (as) fundamental principle 270
    gender-distinguished 283
    societal and individual location in 288
humanness
    (and) equality 249
Hutterites 210

I

icon(s) 94, 102
iconoclasm
    radical 260
iconographic themes 103
ideational perspectives ix
identity
    differentiated xvi
    formation 139
Ideology(ies) 138, 213
    (of) charisma 141
    irrationality of partisan 248
    partial truth of 248
    (and) Utopia 248
idolatry 25, 80
idols
    destruction of 80
Ikeda, Daisaku 189, 191-194, 196
image(s) 125, 136, 146, 156
    devotion to 128
    (of the) globe 165
    (of the) other
        prevalence of 155
    overload of 154
    overproduction of 135
imitation 139
immanent development xi
Imperial edict (1436) xvii
incarnations 98
Inchon 206, 211
inclusion and exclusion
    (as) pivotal in globalization research 284
income and wealth
    re-distribution of 175
independents 58
individual
    choice 289
    conscience 52
    cult of 270

INDEX 307

dignity 52
"enfranchisement" of 49, 55
freedom
    limiting the exercise of 249, 250
    (and) nation-state 167
    rights
        inviolability of 56
    salvation 52
individualism 47 passim, 166
    development of abstract 167
    growth of autonomous 247
    legitimation of 51
    Lockean 271, 272
    responsible 248
individualization 283
individuation
    radical 260
Indra 93, 97
Industrial revolution xvii, 183
industrialization 87
    processes of 134
inequality(ies) 8, 26
infidel(s) 67, 72, 79, 80
    property and political rights
        legitimacy of 71
    rights of 73
    ruler 81
    societies
        Christian intervention in 73
        problem of co-existence with 83
information
    circulating between fields 150
    overload of 154, 155
    primacy of 148-149
inheritance 42
initiation 102, 105, 109
    formal 110
    ritual enactment of 107
inner religious life
    cultivation of 54
Innocent III, Pope 66, 67
Innocent IV, Pope 67-69, 72
institution(s)
    (and) exchange processes 16
institutional
    bases
        erosion of 134
    Church
        (as) *depositum fide* 52
institutionalization 264, 269
integration and legitimation

    overarching principles of 245
intellectual(s) 141, 149, 152
    (as) interpreter 156
internal order 77
International
    *Christians for Unity and Social
        Action* (ICUSA) 206
    electronic evangelization 231
    Highway 207
    Journal on World Peace 207
    law xxi, 68, 74, 265 passim
        origins of 82
        Spanish thinking on 69
    order 76
        Catholic theory of 74
        without the pope 77
    relations 77
    Relief Friendship Foundation
        (IRFF) 207
    Religious Foundation (IRF) 205
    Society for Krishna Consciousness
        (Hare Krishnas) 188
internationalism
    Grotian 272
internationalization 282
Introductory Seminar on the Unification
    Movement 205
invasion 81
inversions 144
Iranian
    revolution 173
irantar kalattal 107
Isaiah
    (and his) vision of the world at
        peace 22
Islam
    (and) anti-colonial nationalist
        movements 172
    Arabism of 169
    ascetic tradition of literary 170
    ascetic worldview of 174
    (and) authority 170
    egalitarian appeal of 174
    exposed to Western consumerism
        171
    (as) foundation for Arab
        nationalism 172
    globalization of 171
    liberal age of 172
    (and) modernization 162, 165
    monotheistic conception of 170

mystical 170
   (and) postmodernism 162
   reform of 170
   religious revitalization in 174
Islam
   response to westernism 171
   role of broadcasting in growth of 240
   (and the) salvational quest 165
Islamdom 172
Islamic
   civilization 14
   cultures 161, 172
   fundamentalism 161, 164, 171, 173, 176, 177
      (and) collective identity 289
   holy law 172
   globalism
      politics and culture in xxi
   imperial rule 170
   modernization 161
   state
      re-allocation of institutions in 175
Islamization 178
   (of) women 179
Israel
   (as) chosen people 259
Israelite
   community
      exclusiveness of 25
   political kingdom 26

J

Jains 94
James I 75-77
Japan
   (as) hierarchical nation 190
Japanese Buddhism 197
Jefferson 59
Jeremiah 24
Jesus (Christ) 36, 37, 43n, 120
   (as) product to sell 228
Jewish culture 36
Jihad 169
Jimmy Swaggart
   Bible College 227
   Ministries 241n
jnanamudra 110

jnanic-sannyasic 104
jnani-s (strivers after wisdom) 103
Jodo-Shinshu 197n
John of Leyden 57
Josei, Toda 187, 196
Josephus 37, 39
Judaic tradition 19
Judaism 20, 21, 23, 27, 51
   converts to 179
   post-biblical 36
   (and the) quest for mastery 165
   religious tradition of 49
   (and the) struggle with other faiths 259
Judaism
   universalistic 30
Jugendstil 140
jus ad bellum 268
jus gentium (or ius gentium) 73, 74, 80
jus in bello 268
just war 66, 67, 81
   declaration of 79
   theory of 70
   thought of 69
justice 20, 26, 30
   distributive 268
   economic 26
   (in) Israel
      breakdown of 26
   moral or legal 26
   political 26
   religious 26
   (as) standard of ethics and polity 26
   theory of 60
Justin Martyr 42

K

Kalayana Mantapam 89, 97
Kallar 96, 98
   caste 95
Kaminada (Shinto shrines) 188
Karitikkai days 101
Karuppanacuvami 95
   devotees of 96
Kavacam 102, 105
Kemalist reforms 172
Khomeini 14

Kingdom
  (of) God 57
    transcendental image of 53
  (of) Heaven 201-204, 210
    social and political structure of 203
  (of) the world 53
kingship 249
knowledge 113, 142
  availability of 247
  class 152
  paradigms of 151
  parotic and nomadic 150
  practical uses of 141
  significance of practical 141
  sociology of 248
Kokutai (national policy) 287
"*Kollektivarbeit*" 48
Komeito (Clean Government Party) 191, 208
Korean Folk Ballet 206
kosen-rufu (world evangelism)
  (of) Soka Gakkai 192, 194
Koyil 88
  nakar 111
Kstriyas 93
Kultur pessimismus 145
kumara 96
kuruntu tree 104-106, 108, 109
Kutalalakar temple 91

L

Laksmi Pujas 111
latitudinarian Deism 55
law 20, 25
  (in) African traditions 273
  Hindu 273
  knowledge of 26
  (of) nature 82
  (and) policy or morality 273
  positive 268
  -religion
    relationship 272-273
  (of the) Sea 268
  (-as)-value 269
leadership 250, 251
Leo XIII 81
Levellers 47, 55-59
  human rights commitments of xxi

liberalism 173
Liberation Theology 57
  (and) collective identity 289
Liberty
  (of) conscience 47, 55
  University 227
life
  aesthetic justification of 141, 153
  aestheticization of 136, 151, 153
  anesthetization of 135
  -meaning
    sense of 151
  stylization of 135, 136, 138, 140
lifestyle
  cultivation of 138
  transformation 139
lineage
  (of the) Prophet 169
lingam 102, 104, 105, 108
Literati xvii
Little Angels, The 206
  School 206
liturgical
  community 122
  practice 124
localism xvi, xx, 112, 283, 284
Locke 55, 59
Lockean political theory
  Whig version of 59
Lord
  Alakar 95, 96
  Kutalakar 98
  (of the) Self 113
Lords of the Eight Directions 97
loss of referent(s) 138, 151
Lotus Sutra 185, 186
Lukan Church 120, 121, 127
Luther 52, 53
  (and) doctrine of two kingdoms 53
  (and his) separation from the
    Roman communion 52
Lutheran(s) 54, 121
  Reformation 121
Lutheranism 48, 53, 54, 124

M

Maci 96
Madurai 88, 92 (map), 93, 94 passim

INDEX

Nayaks 112
Magikuchi, Tsunesaburo 187
Magna Carta 74
magna communitas humani generis 267
Mahayana Buddhism 185
Maitreya (see also Buddha) 186, 191
management
    less authoritarian modes of 153
mandala 89, 91, 93, 97, 98
    (of) Nichiren 189
Manikkavacakar 102, 104, 106, 107
    initiation of 105, 108
manikkavackar peruman 111
Manikkavakar 102
Mannheim, Karl xxi, 245 passim
mantapam-s 99, 105
mantra(s) 94, 105
    power of 109
manusa 91
mappo (last days) 186, 192
Marconi, Guglielmo 222, 223
market 152
    forces 51
    place
        associational relations within 166
    profitability 4
    system 5
marriage 202
    Unification concept of 204
Marsilius of Padua 76
Marx
    (and the) cash nexus 164
    (and the) citizen-individual 167
Marxism xvii, 165, 209, 218
    (as) ideology of elite 174
Marxist
    economics 184
    reductionism 15
Mary (see also Virgin)
    honor of 126
mass
    commodity markets 51
    consumption 137, 139, 144, 147
massification 252, 253
matha 100
matching (engagement) 203
Mauryas 112
May Fourth Movement (1919) xvii, xix
meaning

    creation or emergence of 134
    crisis of 3, 134, 175
meaninglessness
    problem of 161
    quest for 166
Mecca and Medina 169
Mede 57
media surveillance xix
medieval Christianity
    Calvin's war on 130
meditation 201
Mennonites 52
messiah 27, 218
metanoia 257
Methodism 166
Methodist spiritual discipline 129
Mihaksi-Sundaresvarar 98
millenarian(s) 52
    Utopian vision of 57
    utopianism 58
millennial
    order 58
    thought 57, 60
millennialism 60
    Anglo-American 57
millennium 58
millet system 169, 170
Milton 55
Minaksi 88 passim
Minakshi-Sundaresvara 88, 89
Minashi temple 90 (map), 93 passim
Ming dynasty xvii
Minusius Felix 42
Minzokuha (National Soul School) 189
miracles 120
missionary
    goals
        use of force for 70
    zeal 120
mixed marriages
    Ezra's separation of 23
mode of perception
    aestheticization of 151
    capitalist 4
modern societies
    development of 164
modernism 163
    culture of 143
    literary and artistic 149
    (in the) United States 144

INDEX

modernity xiv, 6-8, 143, 146, 269
    changes in 142
    problem of 141
    transcendence of 135
    western
        universalizability of 137
modernization 13, 130, 173
    history of 163
    process of 161
moksa 88, 110
monadic MTV 154
monastic
    Catholicism 51
    order(s) 50, 61n
monism 277
monotheism(s) 20, 24, 26, 28, 88
    (and) democracy xxi
    "pure" 25
monotheistic traditions
    tendency of 111
Moon, Sun Myung 195, 202, 204, 212, 214, 218
    "Empire" 208
    genius of 217
    (and) global goals 208
    (and) Messianic ideal 210
    (and) structure of Unification Church 215
More, Richard 57
Morse, Samuel F. B. 222
Mosaic law 67
    establishment of 22
    formation of 25
Moses 24, 31
Moslem(s) 66, 68
Muensterites 57
Mughals 112
mulastanam 89
multinational corporations 183
mundra-s 109
Murakan (or Murukan) 95-97, 101, 104
    shrines 109
Muslim Brotherhood 173
    (and the) establishment of an Islamic state 179
    potential to use airwaves 240
    resistance movement 173
myths 113
    capacity of 15, 16

N

Nakak kings 91
naksatras 91
name civaya (obeisance to Siva) 109
nana (wisdom) 107, 109
Nandi 107
Nasser, Gamal Abdel 173
Nasserism 173
Natana Sabha (or Nirutta Sabha) 103
Nataraja 107
    shrines 109
    temple 102, 103
nation 129
national
    culture 145, 289
    kingdoms 66
    Religious Broadcasters 225
nationalism 172, 178, 185
    anti-colonial 171
    (and) citizenship 285
    coming of age of x
nationalist
    ideology 173
    fervor
        (and) religion 196
nation-state(s) ix, x, xix, 1, 3, 7, 171, 183
    (and) civilizational complexes
        power balances between 137
    cult of 270
    emergence of 167
    expansion of 184, 269
    formal similarity of 9
    (as) legitimate system 8, 271
    shifts in the balance of power between 148
    system of 5
nativism 185, 196
natural
    law 67, 72, 73, 74, 84, 268
    reason 80
    right(s) 56, 71, 80
naturalism 258
nature
    sacredness of 147
    subordination of 163
Nayak(s) 99, 100, 112
    rule 88
Nehru dynasty 112
neocolonialism

(and) cultural dominance 238
neo-confucianism xvii
neo-Protestantism 49
New
    ERA (New Ecumenical Research Association) 205
    Hope Singers International 206
    International Economic Order 268
New
    order
        signs of 149
    world
        Information Order (NWIO) 238, 239
        order 201
        (as) part of European consciousness 83
        possession of 69
        Spanish domination of 73
    York City Symphony 206
Newton 57
Nichiren
    Buddhism 186, 201-202
    Daishonin (the Great Holy Sage) 185-187, 192
    Soshu 185 passim
        Buddhism 192
        Denomination 190
        elitism of 186
Niebuhr, H. Richard xxi, 245 passim
Nietzsche
    (and) epistemology 168
nihilism 154
Nipponcentric view 190
Nirvana
    path to 186
Nobuhiro, Sata 189, 190
non
    -human species
        sacredness of 147
    -image
        mystery of 102
    -relativism 277
    -Shinto religions
        government restrictions on 186
Norinaga, Motoori 189, 190
norms
    institutionalization of 10
Norwegian
    historiography 121
    states
        sanctification of 122

O

oath 75, 77
obligation 129
official church
    elitism and rationalism of 125
Olav, Saint 121, 122
"one worldism" 284
oneness 14
Open Door Policy
    (of) Sadat 176
"open society"
    transition to 164
Oral Roberts University 227
order
    (and) balance of power 271
    creation through religious symbols 99
    natural law basis of 83
    spatial-ritual 99
ordination 128
organized religion
    demise of 184
Original Nature 203
Orthodox Lutheran thought 52
orthodoxy 125
"other"
    (as) alien
        loss of the sense of 155
otherness
    celebration of 136, 144
    openness to 155
Ottoman empire 171
otuvar-s (chanters) 103, 109, 110

P

pagan
    practices 121
    rites 80
paganism 138
pagus 150
palliyarai (bed chamber) 103
pancaksara mantra 109
Pandyan(s) 99, 100, 108
    dynasty 89, 94
    king(s) 88, 105, 106
Pankuni 96
papacy x, 66

INDEX

Papal
    Bulls 70
    intervention 80
    leadership 66
    power 72
        defenders of 75
    spiritual jurisdiction 72
Paragon House 208
Parliament of World Religions 205
particularism xvi, xviii, xx, 27, 30, 31, 33, 283, 284
    meanings of 28
    overgrowth of 21
    universalization 276
particularistic mode xvii
part/whole issues xviii
Parvati 107
Patanjali 103
pattapisekam 97
Paul, St. 41
    (and) universalization of Christianity 43n
Peace
    (of) Augsburg (1555) 53
    (of) Westphalia 77
Pentecostal(s) 123
    broadcasters 227
    (in) Central America 236
    movement(s) 129
        appeal among Norwegians 124
        canonical episode for 126
        critical survey of 128
        revival of 130
    piety 127
    revival 119
        in Norway 121
Pentecostalism 119, 120
    classical 26
    (as) final mass-movement phase of Calvinist movement 129
perfectionism
    assisted by the Holy host 126
    Wesleyan 126
person
    autonomy of 249
    sacredness of 147
personal regeneration 49
personality 139
perumai (reputation) 107
Pethrus, Lewi 122
pietism 53, 121, 166

pietists 54
piety 125, 128
    (of) experience of holiness 129
    (of) Holy Ghost
        (as) mimesis of Church in Acts 129
    shifting from devotion to witnessing 127
pisaca 91
pitam (altar) 102, 104, 106, 108
pitha 102
Pius V, Pope 74
    bull of 75
Pius IX, Pope 81
planet
    social organization of xx
Plantation Agreement (1640) 56
pluralism 136, 169, 277
    conflict of 14
    disjointed 165
    empirical xx
Polanyi 285
political
    citizen 166
    citizenship
        expansion of 167
    community
        importance for the emergence of 167
    hegemony 162
    power 68
politics
    "democratization" of
polyculturalism 148
polyculturist perspective 155
polygamy 82
polytheism 257, 258
polytheistic tendencies 170
pope 76
    coercive power of 76
    subordination to 75
    (as) temporal head of mankind 72
    (as) universal judge 80
    (and) "universal rights of the church" 79
population growth 87
postmillennial theories 58
postmodern
    age xiv, 60, 165
    culture 148
    world xiv, 61

postmodernism xxi, 135 passim, 161, 162, 289
postmodernité 149
postmodernity
    135 passim, 165
postmodernization 135
potam (foundation) 107, 108
power 9, 68, 120
    balances 141
        shift of 155
    equal distribution of 26
    experience of 127
pradaksina (circumambulation) 97, 109
prakaram-s 89, 91, 100, 102 passim, 114n
pranayama(yogi breath control) 109
prasadam 109
prayer 201
premillennial thought 58
pre-millennialism 221
Presbyterians 58
price competition 4
priesthood of believers 49
priests 30
primeval man
    sacrificial dismemberment of 93
Problemstellung xx
production
    for exchange 5
Professors World Peace Academy (PWPA) 209
progress 87
    norms of 10
Project Volunteer 206
promised land 20, 21, 23, 24, 29
    limits imposed by 30
prophecy 30
Prophet(s)
    classical 26
    Israelite 21, 30
    (as) mediums for God 31
    traditional high view of 14
prophetic
    leadership 88
    religion 184
proselytization 23
Protectorate 58
Protestant(s) 47, 48
    dilemma
        heart of 55

ethic 48, 51, 60
    challenged 49
Ethic and the Spirit of Capitalism, The 48
(as) heretics 74
individualism 56
piety 119
Reformation 59
Protestantism 48-50, 55, 112
    Achilles heel of 54
    change introduced by 52
    (and) cultural elite 144
    (and the) Lukan Church 120
    sectarian 53
    significance of 51
providential history
    belief in 275
PTL Inspirational Network 235
public order
    place of religion in 78
Pudukkottai 100
    Stupatis 112
puja (ritual homage) 108, 110
purification 113
Puritan
    -capitalist connection 49
    dissenters 54
    heritage 138
Puritanism 52, 130
purusa 91, 93
pustaka hasta 110
Putney and Whitehall debates 56

Q

Quaker 49
qopuram 103
Quran
    (as) Arabic expression of divine revelation 169
    return to the 172

R

Rabbinate 179
racial privilege 249
radical
    democratization 245 passim

INDEX

Radio
    HCJ8
    first evangelical station 230
    Moscow 232
Raelians 201
rahasyam (mystery) 102, 108, 111
Raj 112
rajagopuram 103
Ramarayar mantapam 98
Ramnad
    rajas of 100, 112
Ranters 57
rationalists 52
rationalization 11, 51, 134, 146, 176
    arbitrary character of 169
Raveda 93
Reagan, President 83
Real presence
    Calvin's rejection of 129
realism
    Hobbesian 271, 272
reality
    aesthetic hallucination of 135
    languages as metaphorical account
        of 168
    transcendent 273, 277
    transformation into images 151
    unity of 107
reason
    project of 169
rebellion 81
redemption 42
Reformation x, 47 passim, 78, 81, 121, 129
    (and) Christian society 268
    ideology 50
    radical wing of xxi
regionalism 112
Regnans in excelsi 74
relationship(s)
    abstract exchange 167
    (between) man and God
        contractual nature of 167
    power 275
    trust-loyalty
        triadic structure of 256
relativization
    (of) national societies and selves 269

monotheism 245 passim
    (as) political action 260
    processes of 12, 288
relectio 71
religion(s)
    anchorage of society in 141
    (and) consumer culture 135
    (in) consumer market place 134
    decline of 134
    depoliticization and
        repoliticization of 288
    (as) differentiated institution 13
    dissipation of 134
    free establishment of 230
    freedom of 288
        principle of 287
    global significance of 265
    (as) lifestyle option 290
    (as a) mode of collective identity 289
    (as) modernity 287
    (and) modernization 164
    (as) normative direction xv
    paradox of 290
    (as) personal devotion 78
    (and) politics
        unity of 170
    relationship with other institutions 15
    replacement by art 143
    (and) society 287
    sociology of 2, 3, 133, 161, 184, 287
    (as) supplier of meaning 287
    wars of 53
religiosity
    (of) events 154
religious
    absolutism
        problems of 178
    broadcast time 228
    broadcasters
        impact of 233
    broadcasting
        denominational sponsorship of 227
        first thrust of 231
        politics and culture 234
        (in the) US 226, 227, 229, 240n
    decline xiv
    ideas
        (and) secular cultural forms 61
        utopian aspect of 60

networks 226
pluralism 254, 272
radio or TV
    commercial sponsorship for 227
    revival 141
    stations
        non-profit 228
    television
        broadcasters 235
        programs 226
    tolerance 55
    toleration 60
Religious Youth Service (RYS) 205
Renaissance 51
renunciation 100, 110
Rerum Novarum 81
resacralization 184
responsibility
    ethic of 168
Restoration 58
resurrection 42
revival 126
revivalism 121
revivalist and Pietist tradition 130
revolution
    theory of 61
Rhode Island
    colony of 52
Rida, Rashid 172
right
    (of) missionaries
        to preach freely 78
    (to) preach and to hear 79
    (to) travel freely 73, 74, 80
rikutsu (arguing) 188
Rissho kosei kai 202
ritual(s) 145, 146, 147
    activity 87
    consecration 89
    gestures 147
    homage 89
    process 99
Robertson, Pat 235
role performance
    flexibility in 153
Roman
    culture 36, 41, 42
    empire 41, 50, 66
        Christianization of 72
        peak of 72
        urbanization of 37
        imperial domination 72
        law 72
romantic movement 152
Rousseau 56
    -Marxian alternative 60
    (and) society 285
royal patronage 42
rudraska 108
rule
    (of) law 129
    (of) "saints" 58
ruling elites
    openness of 250
Rushdie affair 14

S

sabbath 22
sabha-s (halls) 103
sacrality 112
sacrament 128
sacred 137 passim
    conception of 272
    end of the 154
    geography 87
    geometry 93
    persons and sacralized territory
        rejection of the link between 130
    /profane
        conflict between 146
        distinctions 146
        space 127
        symbolic boundaries between 273
        trivializing of 146
sacrifice 42
Sadat, Anwar
    assassination of 173
saints 125, 129
Saiva
    gods and saints 107
    temples 88, 96, 101, 102, 104
Sakyamuni 186
Salafiyyah movement 172
salvation 57, 185
    means of 52
    revivalist doctrine of 126
    this-worldly 135
samadhi 100
    nakar 111

INDEX

sanctification 126
sanctifying patron
    (and) sanctified territory 126
sanctity
    transference of 128
sannyasic symbolism 103
sannyasi-s (renouncers) 103
Satan 213
Satanic Verses, The 14
Saudi regime
    Islamic absolutism of 174
schism 77
schismatic(s) 68, 76
    Greeks 66
science xviii
sectarian
    movements 54
    worldview 119
secular xii
    culture
        onslaught of 49
    frame of reference x
    nationalism 124
    state
        (and) India 288
secularization xii, xiv, 3, 146, 171, 184, 265
    notion of 3
    paradox of 277
    process of 269
    (and the) production of sects 277
    (and) reformism 171
    (and the) sociology of religion 287
    theory(ies) 2, 164
self 126, 128
    concepts of 57
    control 153
    (in) direct communion with God 52
    emancipated from corporate church structures 49
    -expression 138
    government
        right of all men to 74
    journey into 113
    nature and dignity of 51
    restraint 154
    sacrifice 113
    -society relations 52
    subordination of the 163

transformation 139
sensation
    aesthetic of 150
sense of reality
    loss of 151
"separated brethren" 59
separation thesis 20, 31
Serapis 36, 40, 43n
Sermon on the Mount 36
Seven Bells program 191, 192
sexual
    activity 202
    relationship of Adam and Eve 203
shakubuku 188
Sharia (or Shariah. See also Islamic holy law) 175, 273
Shariati, Ali 174
Sheen, Fulton 224
Shi'ism 169, 173, 177
Shingon 197n
shinko shukyo 187
Shinto 287
    moral institution 288
    religion 189
    worship 187
sho (True) 186
Sho-Hondo-temple
    erection of 191
shu (sect) 186
Siddhartha Gautama 186
sign(s) 136, 146
    overload of 154, 155
    overproduction of 138
    profusion of 135
sin(s) 76, 203
    retribution for 24
sinlessness
    condition of 126
    doctrine of 126
Siva 89, 91, 94, 99 passim
    dance of 103
    different manifestations of 102
    (as) guru 105
    (and his) spouse
        relationship between 103
sivalingam 89
Siva-Sundaresvara 94
Sivayoganaki 103
Skanda 96
social

bond
   crisis in effectiveness of 134
   caste 249
   consensus 249
   differentiation 134
   disintegration 154
   groupings x
   life
      cultural dimension of 133
      symbolic and sacred dimension of 154
   obligations
      freedom from 138
   organization 67
   stratifications(s) 164, 286
   structures xi
   systems 281
   transformation xii
   values
      conflict between 146
societal solidarity
   (and) membership 285
societalism 270
   (and) idolatry 276
societalization 283, 288
   (as) institutionalized societalism 287
society(ies)
   (and) collective identity 285
   differentiation and pluralization of xiii
   higher integrated notion of 136
   (and) individuals
      liberation of 288
   moral basis of 82
   notion of 285
   transformation of 113
sociological fundamentalism 278
sociology 278
Soka Gakkai (Society for the Creation of Value) xxi
183 passim, 201, 208
   exclusivism of 187
   (as) Globalization Movement 191
   (and) patriotism 189
   (and) peace movement 195
   (as) Revitalization Movement 189, 195
Soka Kyoiku Gakkai (Society for Education in the Creation of Value) 186, 187, 191

sola fide
   Lutheran-Calvinistic notions of 49
solidarity 29, 147
Somaskanda 96
"son of God" 42
Southern Baptists
   (and) media 225
sovereignty 110
   (as a) dominant principle 268
   limits to 272
space and time
   universalizing and sacralizing 112
Spanish
   Armada 75
   Hapsburgs 81
   scholasticism
      Golden Age of 69
spirit
   gifts of 127
spiritual
   crisis 141
   leadership 66
   mission 71
spiritualist sects 52
Standing Order Churches 58
state 52
   formation
      cultural dimension of 146
   power 259
   (as) secular institution 56
   sovereign equality of 267
Sthala vrksa 90, 104
sthalapurana 93, 94
stratification 249
Striders International 206
structures of thought
   "absoluteness" of xi
Suàrez, Francisco 69, 74-83
Subrahmanya 96
Sudras 93
Sufism 170, 171
sumptuary
   ethics 119
   laws
      transcendence of 139
Sun Myung Moon Institute 206
Sundaresvara 88 passim
Sundaresvara-Siva 96
Sunni Islam 169
supernatural beings 129

INDEX

supremacy
    papal claims to 75
Sutapas 97
sutras 185
suttee 82
suvarnakkauvalai 102
svayambhu linqam 89
Swaggart, Jimmy 229, 237
Syllabus of Errors 81
symbolic
    classifications 146
    goods
        transmission, circulation and reception of 148
    hierarchies 136, 152
        de-construction of 155
    inversions 144
    production 137, 138, 143
    repertoires 144
symbolism
    ascetic and liberation-oriented 111
symbols 146
syndicated
    broadcasting 242n
    programming 236
    radio
        conservative traditions in 227

T

Talvallan shrines 109
Tamil
    culture
        center of 88
        hagiography 109
    Nadu 90, 99
    Saiva saints 109, 110
tapa 113
Taylorism 176
technology xii, 5
    (and the) Great Commission 225
    rational 51
televangelism scandals 229
television ministry
    (and the) entrepreneurial model 229
telic matters 184
Temple
    life
        practices of 25

    (and) sacred topography 113
territoriality
    conception of 129
territory 120
Thatcherism 153
thinking
    relational mode of 248
Third world
    (and) evangelical broadcast pirates 239
    nation-states of 6
    (and) totalitarian regimes
        unholy alliance between 238
Thirty Years War 81
Thiruvavaduthurai 110
    Adheenam 100
Thomist revival 82
Thomistic tradition 83
time
    fragmentation of 151
Tirumala Nayak 95, 96, 98
Tirupparankunram 97
Tirupperunturai Villakam (holy utterances) 102, 103
Tiruvacakam 106, 107, 110
Tiruvatavurar Puranam 105, 106
Tiruvilaiyatal Puranam 94, 105
Today's World 213
Tokugawa dynasty 190
tolerance 37, 52
toleration
    absolute 82
    principle of 55
totalitarian movements
    breeding ground for 247
totalitarianism 252, 253
tradition(s) 147
    notion undermined 275
    revitalization 188
traditionalism xii, 9, 11
Trans World Radio (TWR) 230, 231, 236
transcendence
    non-positive 148
transcendent 31
    awareness and liberation 111
transcendental self 113
transformation within 113
transgressions 144
transnational
    religious broadcasters

(and the) forbidden zones 235
Trinity Broadcasting System 235
True Buddhism 193
truth 113, 210
   (as) revealed by Rev. Moon 202
Turkish Hat Law 172
tyranny 248

U

ujigami 190
ujiko 190
Ulama (scholars) 170, 175
ultimate
   beliefs
      different sets of 272
   meaning xvii, 134
Umma community
   idealistic construction of 169
unbelievers
   conversion and coercion of 78
Unification
   businesses
      (as) multinational corporation 208
   Church 202 passim
      membership 209
   movement xxi
   theocracy 202, 217
   Theological Seminary 205, 206
   theology 60, 204, 205
Unificationism 211
   cells of 210
Unificationists 203
   work of 204
United Methodist Church 228
United Nations Declaration of Freedom of Information 238
unity
   accommodated xvi
   (of the) Church
      fragmentation of 59
Universal
   ascetic lord 110
   Declaration of Human Rights 59
   government 259
   history
      philosophy xi
   knowledge 156
   order(s) xv

   Hindu sense of 112
   models of xxi, 112
   polycentric 87
   participation xix
universalism xvi, xvii, xx, 59, 60, 283, 284, 290n
   cosmopolitan 28
   definition of 35
   Hebrew experience with 32
   Kantian 271
   legal 25
   moral 25, 29
   morality of 32
   Old Testament 19 passim
   organizational dimensions of 29
   (and) particularism 20, 276
   political 36
universalism
   prophetic 31
   prophetic mediation of 30
   rejection of 275
   spatial and temporal dimensions of 28
   Western cognitive and moral 275
universalization
   (of) Western modes 276
universe
   creation of an ordered 98
   within
      ritual ordering of 113
upadesa 105
upatacam (or upatecam) 105, 109, 110
upatecakkatci 107, 109, 110
urbanization 134
urimai (customary rights) 107
utsavamurti 96, 101, 104, 109
Uyirkku Uyir (soul of the soul) 102

V

Vaisyas 93
Valladolid conference (1550) 70
value
   affirmation of 251
   conflict(s) 184, 272
   consensus 248
   creation 10
   higher center of 53
   historicity of 256
   means of defining 9

re-evaluation of 168
shared 273
varna-s 93
vastumandala 91, 96
vastuprursamandala 91
Vatican Radio 223, 230, 240n, 241n
Vedic
   gods 91
   sacrifice
      ideology of 91
Verstehen 275
Veyihuvanta Vinayakar 103
vibhuti (sacred ash) 109
videotape
   invention of 226
vigraha (immovable image) 105
Vinayakar (see also Ganesa) 96, 104, 109
Virabhadra 109
Virgin Mary 128
   devotee of 125
Vision Interfaith Satellite Network (VISN) 241n
visions 125
Visnu 91, 94, 95, 97, 98
visual experience 126
vitalism 258
Vitoria, Francisco de 69-73, 78-80, 82, 83
vocation 49
Voice of America 232
Vyaghrapada 103
vyakhyanamudra 110

W

Wars of Religion 268
Washington
   Institute for Values in Public Policy 209
   Times, The 207, 216
wealth
   corrupting piety 57
   equal distribution of 26
   inequalities of 7, 173
Weber, Max 133-135, 142
   (and the) citizen-individual 167
   (and) dynamic contradiction 165
   (and the) emergence of capitalism 166
   (and the) Enlightenment x

   (and) high culture 144
   (and) modernization 168
   (and) monotheism 24
   (and) national-cultural homogeneity 285
   norms and action 11
   (and) order 3
   (and) problems of secularization 168
   (and) Protestant Ethic 51, 60, 164-165
   (and) rationalization 49, 163, 168
   (and the) Reformation 48
   (and) sociology of culture 133
   (and) sociology of rationalization 161
   (and his) theory of social change 163
   (and the) transition to capitalism 50
   (and his) typology of social relations 164
   (and) universalism 19, 20, 32
   (and) universalizing prophets 31
Weberian
   alternative 61
   model 178
Western modernity
   relativization of 289
Whigs 56
Williams, Roger 55-60
wireless transmission 223
wisdom
   realization of 110
   search for hidden 113
World
   brought into the realm of sanctity 129
   Christian Encyclopedia 234
   (as) coextensive with the Holy Ghost 128
   (as) continuous of desires of the self 130
World
   creating a stable 111
   discontinuities in the 4
   dissolving of territorial character of 130
   economic order
      power of United States over 154
   economy
      congealing of 282
   elites 10

-empires 4
empirical unity and disunity of 4
fragmented view of 151
(as) function of perception 128
(and) I 207
ideational oneness of 4
integrated into international capitalist system 50
law 82
localized in selves 128
lord of the 72
Media Conference(s) 208
(as) medium in and through the self 130
mythological unity of 3
order
   absence of ideology of 130
   conceptions of 274
   intellectual basis for concept of 82
   meaning of 277
   providential conception of 275
   (as the) reign of anti-Christ 119
   utopian visions of 255
pluralistic nature of 82
plurality of 16
polity 9
Radio TV Handbook 230
religions 4, 264
   ordering of 130
renovation of 53
renunciation 88
(as) single space 283, 284
singularity of 6
society 284
   (and the) problem of societies 286
(as) substance rather than place 129
system
   approach 2
   pathos of 10
   take-off x
   theory of 282
   Wallerstein's theory of 4
/transforming action
   ideological justification to 58
   withdrawal from 65
worldview(s) 255
   rationalization and differentiation of 135
work
   attitudes toward xiii

Y

Yahweh 25, 31
   "cult" 19
yoga 201
Yogambika (mother of yoga) 103, 109, 111
Yoganayaki 103
Youth Seminar on World Religions 205

Z

Zen 197
Zeus 36, 40
Zia ul-Haq 173